SHARING BREATH

SHARING BREATH

Embodied Learning *and* Decolonization

edited by Sheila Batacharya *and* Yuk-Lin Renita Wong

AU PRESS

Copyright © 2018 Sheila Batacharya and Yuk-Lin Renita Wong
Published by AU Press, Athabasca University
1200, 10011 – 109 Street, Edmonton, AB T5J 3S8

ISBN 978-1-77199-191-9 (pbk.)   9-781-77199-192-6 (PDF)   978-1-77199-193-3 (epub)
doi: 10.15215/aupress/9781771991919.01

Chapter 1, by Roxana Ng, originally appeared in *Valences of Interdisciplinarity:
Theory, Practice, Pedagogy*, edited by Raphael Foshay, 343–65 (Edmonton: Athabasca
University Press, 2011). It is reprinted here with minor revisions.

Cover image: Still from Lisa Myers, *Through Surface Tension* (2013)
Cover design by Martyn Schmoll
Interior design by Sergiy Kozakov
Printed and bound in Canada

Library and Archives Canada Cataloguing in Publication

    Sharing breath : embodied learning and decolonization / edited by Sheila
Batacharya and Yuk-Lin Renita Wong.

(Cultural dialectics)
Includes bibliographical references and index.
Issued in print and electronic formats.

    1. Critical pedagogy. I. Batacharya, Sheila, 1969-, editor II. Wong, Yuk-Lin
Renita, 1962-, editor III. Series: Cultural dialectics

LC196.S53 2018   370.11'5   C2017-902956-8
                                                      C2017-902957-6

This book has been published with the help of a grant from the Federation for the
Humanities and Social Sciences, through the Awards to Scholarly Publications
Program, using funds provided by the Social Sciences and Humanities Research
Council of Canada.

We acknowledge the financial support of the Government of Canada through the
Canada Book Fund (CBF) for our publishing activities and the assistance provided
by the Government of Alberta through the Alberta Media Fund.

Canadä
                  Government

Contents

Acknowledgements

We are indebted beyond measure to the contributors to this collection. Thank you for sharing your important scholarship and for your patience with the editorial process. We deeply value your work and have truly enjoyed our collaboration throughout this project. A special thanks to Lisa Myers for her beautiful artwork that graces the cover of the book.

Athabasca University Press has provided tremendous support for this book project. We are sincerely grateful to Pamela Holway, senior editor, who championed the collection from the start and who took time to give each chapter of the book the benefits of her editorial expertise and scholarly training. Her constructively critical attention resulted in significant improvements to the collection as a whole. We also thank Joyce Hildebrand for her reflective engagement with the text during the copyediting process. Our heartfelt thanks as well to Megan Hall and Karyn Wisselink for their collaborative approach to creating the cover design and promoting the book. We were thrilled to receive an Awards to Scholarly Publications Program (ASPP) grant for this book, and we thank the Federation for the Humanities and Social Sciences for their support.

Sheila. Renita, I am grateful for your scholarly expertise, administrative finesse, and deep commitment to our project. Your wise guidance throughout Roxana's illness and death, and then your support during my pregnancy the following year, made it possible for me to continue this work. Thank you for our many conversations about lived experience and being present with body, breath, emotions, and spirit with respect to writing, loss, babies, animals, photography, walks, and, academic work. Editing this collection with you has been an honour and a pleasure.

I studied with exceptional OISE/UT scholars at a time when critical race, anticolonial, and decolonizing scholarship faced particular forms of institutional opposition, many of which persist and continue to be resisted.

I am indebted to my teachers Roxana Ng, George J. Sefa Dei, and Sherene Razack and to my peers who have made invaluable contributions to critical scholarship: I write with you all in mind and do my best to keep up!

My gratitude to Roxana is multifold. She was a challenging and supportive doctoral supervisor and a trusted mentor. She was also a delightful person with whom to collaborate on a book project, and I'm sure that she would be as overjoyed as I am now that it has come to fruition. I remember the two of us sitting in Roxana's backyard, working together on the book and laughing when she suddenly exclaimed, "This is fun!" Working with Roxana *was* fun: she approached her scholarly and community work with meticulous concentration as well as enthusiasm and curiosity. I miss her dearly.

Soraya, thank you for writing and phone tea.

Prasad, Soumil, and Rushil: love and thanks every day.

Renita. My deep gratitude goes to Roxana Ng for her support, mentorship, and friendship throughout my doctoral years and subsequent academic career. Her move to reclaim Traditional Chinese Medicine (TCM), a system of knowledge from her (and my own) cultural roots, affirmed my way of being and of knowing, which likewise insists on the fundamental integration of the body-heart-mind-spirit. Her courage in bringing TCM from the margins into the academy and placing it at the centre of her teaching and scholarship inspired me to push the boundaries of critical scholarship as I pursued my research into mindfulness as a decolonizing embodied pedagogy rooted in Buddhist onto-epistemology.

Sheila, my heartfelt thanks to you for inviting me to join this book project following Roxana's untimely passing. Your thorough knowledge of the literature on embodiment and your vigorous engagement with Indigenous scholarship have brought my own work in these areas to a new level. At every stage of this project, your insightful input always moved the book toward greater depth and complexity, while your thoughtful idea of gathering the contributors together in conversation made the process of editing this book a concrete experience of embodiment in relations.

A lotus bow and hugs to my dharma-sister, Marisela Gomez, for our sharing in heart and spirit over the years about our mindfulness practice in social justice work. Thank you for your clear observation in your reading of my chapter in this book. My gratitude and love to Mino and Mudita, my feline family, for their calming companionship and for showing me the power of being grounded in the body and the grace of life in unison with nature, a state from which we humans have grown distant and to which we must return.

SHARING BREATH

Introduction

This volume considers embodiment and embodied learning in relationship to pedagogical and decolonization theories and practices. Writing from a variety of experiential standpoints, the contributors participate in an ongoing critique of Western liberal education and colonialism by investigating how to develop and use embodied and decolonizing ways of learning and teaching. Contemporary theories of embodiment and embodied learning foreground the relationship between sentient and social lived experience—how we experience ourselves and the world around us in terms of material and discursive aspects of mind-body-spirit and social relations of power. Attention to the material aspects of pedagogy and decolonization coincides with a key concern in embodiment scholarship: that is, the importance of addressing more than solely discursive approaches to experience and knowledge production. Just as knowing and learning involves more than cognitive thinking (Ng 2012), and decolonization requires more than theorizing (Tuck and Yang 2012), the contributors to this collection address the symbiotic relationship between discursive-material and sentient-social observation, meaning making, and action.

Among social and cultural theorists, the body has been a topic of interest for several decades, a trend somewhat inaugurated in the West by Michel Foucault's *Discipline and Punish* (1977). The first edition of Bryan Turner's *The Body and Society* appeared in 1984, and the following decade saw the publication of studies such as Drew Leder's *The Absent Body* (1990), Susan Bordo's *Unbearable Weight,* Judith Butler's *Bodies That Matter,* and Chris Shilling's *The Body and Social Theory* (all three published in 1993), and Elizabeth Grosz's *Volatile Bodies* (1994). Writing in the preface to the second edition of *The Body and Social Theory,* Shilling (2003, viii) was able to declare that "the body has moved to the very centre of academic analysis," serving as "an important stimulus for interdisciplinary work."

While, in keeping with their interdisciplinary character, academic investigations of embodiment spanned a wide array of perspectives. However, the emphasis in these studies tended to fall on the body as signifier—on the social construction of the body through discourse and the representation of the body in word and image. Attention was also given to the body as an object capable of manipulation, whether through medical procedures and other technological interventions or as a vehicle for the expression of a particular self-identity. Visible in at least some of this scholarship, however, was an emerging focus on embodiment itself—on our experience of our bodies and the ways in which that experience influences our relationship to the surrounding world. Examples include Simon Williams and Gillian Bendelow's *The Lived Body* (1998), and John Tambornino's *The Corporeal Turn* (2002), as well as collections edited by Maxine Sheets-Johnstone (1992) and by Thomas Csordas (1994). All the same, the dominant influence of the discursive turn prompted Karen Barad to complain, in 2003, that "language has been granted too much power"—that even materiality itself had been transformed into "a matter of language or some other form of cultural representation" (2003, 801).

The purpose of this volume is to address embodiment and embodied learning as an important counter-hegemonic aspect of critical pedagogical and decolonization theory and practice. Authors in this collection ask: How are lived experiences shaped by social relations of power? Studies of embodiment address many of the same social and cultural issues raised in poststructural and postmodern theorizing. However, this collection also challenges the ways in which the sentient, material body was, for the most part, dismissed in the linguistic turn. At the same time, this collection questions theories of embodied learning, such as those grounded in the concept of transformative learning or in holistic approaches to education, as sometimes ambiguous when it comes to examining both socially constructed and materially embodied experience in terms of power relations. Even as they write the body back into learning, such theories are apt to write out the social and political forces that impinge both on individual perception and on the ideological frameworks that at once structure and are reinforced by normative approaches to education.

The contributors to the collection understand embodied learning as a process of becoming attuned to sentient-social experience—that is, of learning to be aware of, and responsive to, our lived experience as jointly constituted through sentient and social relations. In so doing, they theorize bodies as knowledgeable in ways that are not solely cognitive, and furthermore, how cognition itself is affected by other aspects of perception. While recognizing the value of discursive analyses that question existing power constellations and encourage the inculcating of critical consciousness among students, the essays in this collection also point to the profound divisions that such analytic approaches can reproduce: the separation of the mind-intellect from the body-spirit, as well as the isolation of discourse from material realities. In other words, this collection addresses the body-mind-spirit in pedagogical and decolonization projects from critical discursive and materialist perspectives.

Inevitably, of course, this volume is a contribution to discourse. Although the essays in it challenge conventional understandings of knowledge construction and emphasize practice, the book itself is a printed text and is thus limited to describing material contexts and actions. With respect to decolonization, this limitation must be acknowledged. Eve Tuck and Wayne Yang (2012) caution against the substitution of abstract, discursive readings of the term *decolonization* for its concrete meaning: the repatriation of land and life. In acknowledging the Huron-Wendat and Petun First Nations, the Seneca, and the Mississaugas of the New Credit First Nations we identify the Indigenous and settler relationship in territories, now called Toronto, in which we write, work, and live our lives.[1] This recognition of land theft, while important, is discursive and thus remains limited. Indeed, our determination, as non-Indigenous inhabitants of the northern part of Turtle Island, to respect treaty relationships and acknowledge settler responsibility for the historical appropriation of Indigenous land is inescapably compromised, given that, in Canada, land can evidently be stolen and not returned provided you admit to wrongdoing, say you're sorry, speak solemnly about the

---

1 See the acknowledgement at "Research Guides: The Indigenous History of Tkaronto," *University of Toronto Libraries*, https://guides.library.utoronto.ca/Toronto (last updated 10 August 2018).

need for reconciliation, and continue to make promises that, in fact, have never materialized. Settlers are, as Christi Belcourt (2013) aptly puts it, in a stolen truck that has yet to be returned, with damages paid.

As a discursive move, the acknowledgement of the historical and legal relationship between Indigenous and settler peoples may hold the potential for material effects. Yet material inequities are obviously not remedied by discourse alone. Acknowledging Indigenous territory is a beginning, not an end. Nor, of course, is it possible for a book to do the material work of decolonization. The contributors to this collection respond to the reality of colonialism in a variety of specific ways, but all use their gifts as researchers and writers in an attempt to resist and disrupt what Tuck and Wang (2012, 9) identify as "settler moves to innocence" and what Sherene Razack (2015, 210) calls the "fantasy of settler civility." To the extent that dominant educational frameworks are complicit in settler colonialism, they, too, demand disruption.

In summary, this volume pursues embodied and decolonizing ways of teaching, learning and knowing in academic contexts. It presents challenges to Western educational frameworks and colonialism from within and beyond academic settings by way of addressing the symbiotic relationship between the discursive and material; investigating embodiment and embodied learning as a practice of sentient-social attunement; and highlighting embodiment and embodied learning in pedagogical and decolonization processes. What sets this collection apart from the bulk of embodiment scholarship is that embodiment and embodied learning are addressed with attention to decolonization, discursive and material social relations of power, and lived experiences of mind, body and spirit.

Embodied Learning: The Work of Roxana Ng

Over the past several decades, Canadian scholars working from feminist antiracist and Indigenous feminist perspectives have made important contributions to research on embodiment, not only in relation to the representation of the body but also from the standpoint of lived experience and social relations of power. The work of these scholars—published, for example, in collections edited by Himani Bannerji (1993) and by Enakshi Dua and Angela Robertson (1999), as well as, more recently, in *States of Race* (Razack, Smith, and Thobani 2010)—collectively constitutes a critical

intervention into universalist assumptions and liberal individualist frameworks, one that has exposed dominant and subordinate social positioning,
population surveillance and regulation, and the history of Canada as a colonial settler state engaged in a white supremacist project of nation building.
One of the early contributors in this critical undertaking was the late Roxana
Ng, whose work has been a central source of inspiration for the present
collection.

A forerunner in antiracist feminist scholarship and activism in the 1980s
and 1990s, Ng is recognized for her early work on immigrant women and
on the sexism and racism embedded in the Canadian state (see Ng 1988,
1990, 1992, 1993a, 1993b; Ng and Estable 1987; Ng and Ramirez 1981; Ng,
Walker, and Muller 1990). But Ng was also among the first to develop an
embodied pedagogy that aims to disrupt the Eurocentric ontological and
epistemological assumptions that undergird knowledge construction in the
academy (see Ng 1993c, 1998, 2000a, 2000b, 2004, 2005, 2011; Ng, Staton,
and Scane 1995). Ng began this work in the early 1990s, at a time when
relatively few scholars explicitly linked embodied or holistic teaching and
learning to issues of inequity and colonization.

Ng was the first woman of colour hired to the faculty at the Ontario
Institute of Studies in Education (OISE), where she began teaching in 1988.
As she later recalled, once she arrived at OISE, she became "the lightning
rod for everything having to do with the politics of racism, anti-racism,
sexism and feminism in the institution," owing in part to her innovative
approaches in the classroom. "What was most painful," she observed, "was
that the attacks did not only come from the conservative elements of the
institution, but from faculty and students who claimed to be feminist and
anti-racist." In reflecting on her academic life, while also dealing with illness,
Ng went through a period of contemplation that led her to ask: "How is it
that the oppressor and oppressed co-participate in the acts of oppression?"
She became, she said, "acutely aware of the inadequacy of feminism and
anti-racism, in fact any kind of progressive, ideology and politic, that takes
up issues only intellectually without attention to emotion, body and spirit"
(2004, 2). This insight led her to explore new ways to integrate embodied
experience into her pedagogical practice.

In the late 1980s and early 1990s, Ng "(re)discovered" traditional Chinese
medicine (TCM) and qigong. In the British colony of Hong Kong, where

she grew up, TCM and qigong were known as "folk medicine" and, similar to other colonized territories, Western medicine held a privileged status over Indigenous healing systems. Practicing TCM and qigong significantly improved her health, and she became increasingly conscious of "the colonizing effects of Eurocentric, male-stream thoughts," as well as the extent to which these thoughts had contributed to the bifurcation of her own consciousness (2000a, 178). "Studying TCM," she wrote, "made me more fully appreciate the disembodiment of scientific knowledge and how feminist and postcolonial scholarship participate in the privileging of the mind over the body. TCM's philosophy of the unity of mind and body allowed me to explore ways of re-embodying the knower as subject in scholarly pursuit" (179). Ng's experiences with TCM and qigong marked the beginning of her work on embodied pedagogy and decolonization.

Ng became interested in how we know and make sense of the world. Like other embodiment scholars trained in historical materialism, she began to integrate her understanding of the material world with a focus on embodied experience and on how our interpretation of the knowledge that comes to us through our bodies shapes our actions—our way of being in the world. With respect to the practice of teaching, she commented:

> My major interest is to disrupt the body/mind binary and to explore what a pedagogy of integrating body-spirit in critical education may look like and what it may be capable of in interrogating and challenging dominant forms of knowledge, including critical knowledges. I want to encourage self and collective reflections, not only through discourse, but more crucially through an exploration of how experience, in this case, bodily experience, participates in enabling, limiting, and mediating the production of knowledge—what I call the inside-out approach. (1998, 3)

Ng thus positioned the body at the forefront of knowledge construction— and, she centred this in her investigation of decolonization.

In seeking to integrate the body into learning, Ng was concerned in part with the way in which oppression is housed in our bodies. In *Black Skin, White Masks,* Frantz Fanon (1967) draws our attention to territorial and political colonization as well as the colonization of our psyches. To this, Ng insists on the place of the body in processes of colonization and decolonization. As she observes in "Decolonizing Teaching and Learning Through Embodied Learning" (reprinted as chapter 1 in this volume), "relationships of power are never enacted *merely* in the form of intellectual encounters": they also have embodied consequences. "Most intellectual encounters," she writes, "entail a confrontation of bodies, which are differently inscribed. Power plays are both enacted and absorbed by people physically, as they assert or challenge authority, and the marks of such confrontations are stored in the body" (2011, 346). As she had earlier put it, "although we have learned to think critically, dominant ways of being are so normalized that we are 'programmed' to act in ways that reproduce and sustain oppression" (2004, 3). Though there had been attempts to bring the body in social theory and cultural theory, most of the writings focus on how the body is represented and what is being done to the body in postmodernity, which Ng called the "outside-in approach" (Ng 1998). Rather than limit her investigation to discourse, Ng urged us to dive into the visceral experience of our bodies as a source of knowing. This approach can be threatening not only to the colonizer but also to the colonized. The internal legacies of colonization—the histories of pain and oppression, as well as the guilt-ridden memories of the perpetration of injustice—have been stored up in the body, and the process of recovering and releasing them can be overwhelming and can often take a tremendous toll despite the potential benefits of remedy and repair.

In insisting on moving from the inside out, Ng also reclaimed a system of knowledge from her own cultural roots—TCM, as well as the related physical and meditative practice of qigong—the epistemological and ontological foundations of which differ from those of the Eurocentric world view. She brought this system of knowledge from the margins to the academy, placing it at the centre of her teaching on embodied learning, health, and healing. In so doing, she issued a fundamental challenge to the Eurocentric construction of knowledge so integral to the Western academy. Similar to other contributors to this collection, who draw from knowledge systems that not only contrast with Western knowledges but contest their hegemonic dominance, Ng asserted the integrity, coherence, and validity of TCM and qigong, while at the same time acknowledging their imbrication in relationships of power in periods prior to colonization, as well as exploring the impact of colonialism on these knowledges and their practice. Ng did not privilege TCM and qigong over other systems of knowledge. For her, the decision to position them at the centre of her pedagogy was based on teaching what she knew. In addition, her focus on a unified system of knowledge, such as TCM, was a declaration of resistance to a "boutique approach" (Ng 2000, 177) that can be found in much New Age knowledge production that aims to conflate non-Western knowledges in the pursuit of commercialization, enabled through cultural appropriations of traditional and Indigenous knowledges.

Embodiment Scholarship

As Lisa Blackman (2008, 8) points out, the challenge of "thinking through the body" is inevitably concerned with the problem of separation—not only that between mind and body but also with a host of related dualisms. People who are marginalized and oppressed have sometimes reacted to their objectification and inferiorization by deconstructing discourses that relegate them to the "body" side of the mind/body divide, together with its various permutations such as rational/irrational, modern/primitive, cultural/natural, and social/biological. However, while the "relocation of the body to the culture side of the nature/culture dualism" (Bordo 1993, 34) has produced important disruptions of sexist and racist discourse, it has also served to *de*nature the body, placing the material, lived body on the subordinate side of another divide, that between discourse and matter. In their introduction to *Material Feminisms*, Stacy Alaimo and Susan Hekman (2008a, 6) rightly call attention to the need for "a new way of understanding the relationship between discourse and matter that does not privilege the former to the exclusion of the latter."

This challenge echoes one of the key concerns in Roxana Ng's work, namely, how the socially constructed body—the body as constituted through discourse, or what Ng called the "outside-in" view of the body—intertwines with an "inside-out" experience of our bodies as more than merely a creation of discourse. Foregrounding the material body does not imply that concerns surrounding the body as discursive construct have been dismissed. Rather, as do the contributors to this collection, relatively recent work on embodiment (see, for example, the essays in Alaimo and Hekman 2008b; Alexander and Knowles 2005; and Shilling 2007) integrates the two perspectives, seeking to demonstrate how sentient experience and social relations are inextricably bound up with each other, as well as in the complexities of knowledge production.

In relation to pedagogy, embodiment has been a topic of interest not only among educators but also in social work and Indigenous studies—fields that share a concern with concrete action, be it counselling, community building, or political activism. In the field of education, collections edited by John Jack Miller and Yoshiharu Nakagawa (2002) and by John P. Miller (2005) challenge mind-body dualisms through pedagogical approaches termed transformative learning and holistic learning, while Roxana Ng's work on embodied learning challenged the field to address both socially constructed and materially embodied experiences in terms of power relations. In social work, Narda Razack (2002) and many others (Gates 2011; Mensinga 2011; Peile 1998; Tangenberg and Kemp 2002; Wong 2004, 2013, 2014) examine how classroom teaching and experiential learning are embodied and mediated through race, gender, class, and sexual orientation. In Indigenous studies, numerous scholars (see, for example, Battiste 2000; Battiste and Henderson 2000; Dei, Hall, and Rosenberg 2000; Graveline 1998; Lattas 1993; Monture-Angus 1995, 1999; Oyĕwùmí 1997; Sunseri 2011; Simpson 2011) have critiqued the fracturing of knowledge that results from Western dualisms, which mistakenly assign science, spirituality, medicine, the natural environment, animal life, storytelling, social relationships, and so on to separate compartments. For these scholars, and others, embodiment is necessarily both discursive and material: the two are inextricable.

Especially among feminist scholars, many writing from a critical antiracist standpoint, embodiment has similarly been understood as a phenomenon co-constituted through physical, mental, emotional, spiritual, and social experience. Some have focused attention on bodies as the site of both physical health and emotional and spiritual well-being (see, for example, Davis 2007; Dua et al. 1994; Harding 2005; White 1994). Some, such as Jacqui Alexander (2005), Ruth Frankenberg (2004), and Traci West (1999), explicitly stress the transformative potential of spirituality and the sacred. Yet others have worked to develop anti-oppressive pedagogies that seek to heal the mind-body split by incorporating soul and emotion into education (see hooks 1993; Nadeau and Young 2006; Ng 2000a, 2000b, 2005, 2011; Orr 2002, 2005; Piran 2001; Rice and Russell 1995a, 1995b). And yet the study of embodiment still hovers on the margins of mainstream academic knowledge production, including critical scholarship.

This tendency to hold embodiment scholarship at arm's length is itself reflective of Eurocentric bias. In the West, the "rational turn" (commonly known as the Enlightenment) entailed the rejection of spiritual knowledge and practice. As Jacqui Alexander (2005, 15) observes, "There is a tacit understanding that no self-respecting postmodernist would want to align herself (at least in public) with a category such as the spiritual, which appears so fixed, so unchanging, so redolent of tradition." Our system of education teaches us to hold those who talk in terms of spirituality in pity if not explicit disdain, while inculcating what Susan Bordo (1993, 40) described as "masculinist, Eurocentric norms of 'professional' behavior and accomplishment." Rather than recoil from spirituality, however, we could instead, as Alexander (2005, 15) suggests, "engage the Sacred as an ever-changing yet permanent condition of the universe, and not as an embarrassingly unfortunate by-product of tradition in which women are disproportionately caught."

Clearly, focusing our attention on embodiment does not necessarily imply a conversion to some form of spiritual belief, nor do embodied approaches to learning seek to encourage narcissistic self-absorption, of the sort often associated with New Age spirituality. Rather, the focus falls on the knowledge gained through critical reflection on our experience of embodiment, in an effort to understand how our perceptions and the meanings we attach to them reflect the position we occupy within social relations of power. Meditative practices, of the sort found in many spiritual traditions, broaden our range of perceptions, opening us up to what might be called an epistemology of the body—that is, to sources of information that are not mediated exclusively by our intellect. In this way, embodied approaches to learning offer "a means for knowledge construction that does not negate the materiality of our being" (Ng 2000a, 186–87). When our intellect operates within a Eurocentric positivist paradigm, it will instruct us to reject perceptions that cannot be aligned with rational frameworks of explanation. Yet, in repudiating portions of our experience as essentially irrelevant to knowledge, we cooperate in perpetuating dominant configurations of power.

Bodies are not ahistorical. Immersion in sentient experience grounds our consciousness in a specific time and place, serving to remind us that "thought processes are inevitably historically and spatially specific" and hence open to change (Ng 2011, 354). As Ann Mathew and her colleagues (2008, 61) observe, "there is an intimate and necessary relationship between individual change and social change. . . . Without self-reflection and self-interrogation, we run the risk of reproducing conditioned patterns of behaviour and social arrangements." Embodied approaches to learning necessitate engagement with the material foundations of our experience and encourage us to engage critically with our own consciousness—to examine our perceptions and our reactions to them and thus begin to unsettle responses conditioned by colonial frameworks.

Embodiment and Decolonization

In 2005, in an article titled "Decolonizing Antiracism," Bonita Lawrence and Enakshi Dua offered a compelling critique of antiracist and postcolonial theory for its tendency either to ignore the continuing colonization of Indigenous peoples in North America entirely or else to situate Indigenous struggles for decolonization within a liberal-pluralist framework, as one social justice pursuit among many. But, as Lawrence and Dua recognize, fundamental to decolonization is the restoration of sovereignty and territory. "To speak of Indigenous nationhood," they write, "is to speak of land as Indigenous, in ways that are neither rhetorical nor metaphorical" (2005, 124). By failing to confront the ongoing occupation of land and the denial of Indigenous sovereignty, they argue, antiracist and postcolonial theorizing participates in the perpetuation of colonial power.

In the wake of the Truth and Reconciliation Commission and its ninety-four calls to action (2015), such critiques might too easily be dismissed as no longer relevant. Much like Duncan Campbell Scott, nearly a century ago, settler Canadians would like to be "rid of the Indian problem," and one senses the hope that, at long last, adequate reparations have been made.[2] But the decolonization struggles of Indigenous people in Canada

2 In 1920, during testimony to a special parliamentary committee of the House of Commons convened in connection with proposed revisions to the Indian Act, Scott—the deputy superintendent of general of the Department of Indian Affairs— stated: "I want to get rid of the Indian problem." As he subsequently explained, "Our objective is to continue until there is not a single Indian in Canada that has not been absorbed into the body politic and there is no Indian question, and no Indian

require more than a discursive admission that the country's continued complicity in colonialism is the primary source of political, social, economic and cultural injustice. As Lawrence and Dua (2005, 123) point out, settler states are "founded on, and maintained through, policies of direct extermination, displacement, or assimilation." For several centuries now, the oppression of Indigenous peoples has remained central to relations of power in Canada, including racial, religious, gender and sexual hierarchies. While this fact is now more widely acknowledged than it once was, calling for action is not equivalent to taking action.

In the words of Chandra Mohanty (2003, 7), decolonization is "a historical and collective process" that "involves profound transformations of self, community, and governance structures" and "can only be engaged through active withdrawal of consent and resistance to structures of psychic and social domination." Decolonization seeks the final eradication of colonial power—the overthrow of relations of power understood to be "not simply foreign or alien, but rather as imposed and dominating" (Dei and Asgharzadeh 2001, 300). Although decolonization is an explicitly anti-imperial and anticolonial project (Duara 2004, 2), it is not purely oppositional. Decolonization includes revitalization, resurgence, creativity, and Indigenous knowledge production that together decentre colonialism as a determining and all-encompassing force (Simpson 2011; Sunseri 2011).

In "Decolonization Is Not a Metaphor," Eve Tuck and Wayne Yang (2012) take aim at the recent trend, especially within the discourse of education, toward the appropriation of the term *decolonization* to refer to any struggle against oppression. This discursive theft, they argue—this "too-easy adoption of decolonizing discourse" (3)—effaces the material truth of colonization, namely, the ongoing dispossession and displacement of Indigenous peoples and the refusal to acknowledge Indigenous sovereignty. As they explain, the transformation of decolonization into a metaphor, as "an approximation of other experiences of oppression," collaborates in what Tuck and Yang call "settler moves to innocence," tactics designed to perpetuate existing social relations while allowing settlers to relieve themselves of guilt over historical injustices and deny their

---

Department." His remarks have been quoted many times. The original testimony is in Library and Archives Canada, RG 10, vol. 6810, file 470-2-3, vol. 7, pp. 55 (L-3) and 63 (N-3).

complicity in present-day colonial relations. "When metaphor invades decolonization," they write, "it kills the very possibility of decolonization: it recenters whiteness, it resettles theory, it extends innocence to the settler, it entertains a settler future" (2012, 3).

In *Red Skin, White Masks,* Glen Coulthard (2014, 25) reminds us of Fanon's insight into the psychological dimensions of colonization: "In situations where colonial rule does not depend solely on the exercise of state violence, its reproduction instead rests on the ability to entice Indigenous peoples to *identify,* either implicitly or explicitly, with the profoundly *asymmetrical* and *nonreciprocal* forms of recognition either imposed on or granted to them by the settler state and society." Building on this insight, Coulthard exposes another discursive move, namely, the shift of colonial power relations in Canada "from a more or less unconcealed structure of domination to a form of colonial governance that works through the medium of state recognition and accommodation" (25). Yet, despite the emergence of this "seemingly more conciliatory set of discourses and institutional practices," he argues, "the relationship between Indigenous peoples and the state has remained *colonial* to its foundation" (6). Coulthard rejects the fiction that colonial power will be undone through a discursive politics of recognition that aims at reconciliation while ignoring the continued occupation of Indigenous land by settlers and the ongoing denial of Indigenous rights to self-determination.

Like Coulthard, Tuck and Yang insist that discourse cannot substitute for material processes of decolonization that seek to overturn colonial relations of power in specific and concrete form. These scholars recognize, in other words, that *doing* decolonization, as opposed to simply thinking it or talking about it, requires actions that will be deeply and necessarily uncomfortable for settlers. As Tuck and Wang (2012, 35) make very clear, decolonization is not concerned with questions about what the result will "look like" for the settler: "Decolonization is not accountable to settlers, or settler futurity." They argue for an "ethics of incommensurability, which guides moves that unsettle innocence," in place of the "aims of reconciliation, which motivate settler moves to innocence" (35). The repatriation of land and the restoration of Indigenous political, economic, and cultural sovereignty are the indispensable material goals of decolonization, for which no words can substitute.

Relations of power are at once discursive and material. No discussion of decolonization can therefore proceed without directly confronting the impact of colonization on the body—the ways in which colonial relations of power have shaped not only the discursive construction of a hierarchy of bodies but also the lived experience of embodiment. Tuck and Yang (2012, 19–20) note that, in their appropriation of decolonization as a metaphor for the pursuit of social justice more generally, educators have been encouraged by progressive philosophies of education that derive in particular from Paulo Freire's *Pedagogy of the Oppressed* (1970). As they point out, in contrast to Fanon, who "always positioned the work of liberation in the particularities of colonization" (2012, 20), Freire "situates the work of liberation in the minds of the oppressed" (19), thereby reducing "internal colonization" to "mental colonization." This, in turn, leads to the conclusion that if the mind is decolonized, "the rest will follow" (20). In this respect, the distinction between mental experience (that is, thought) and internal experience is significant. Citing comments made by Audre Lorde, Tuck and Yang note that "freedom is a possibility that is not just mentally generated; it is particular and felt" (20). It is, in other words, a matter as much of sensation and emotion as of thought. Decolonizing the body, we would argue, is not a metaphor: it is a material entry point to the dislodging of colonial power, which has been imprinted not merely on minds but on the body-spirit that is inseparable from the lands we are dependent on for life.

As noted earlier, embodied learning is a mental process as well as a body-spirit one. In insisting that the body is a site of knowledge, embodied approaches to learning also demand that we reflect on that knowledge—that, in addition to becoming aware of sentient experience, we interrogate it, particularly from the standpoint of social relations of power. This process can, of course, help us to become more sensitive to oppression of all sorts. In relation to decolonization, however, the objective is not merely to expand the scope of our conscience but to allow us to critically examine how colonization emerges in our emotions and our felt relationship to our bodies. As Lorde (1984, 38) famously stated, "I feel, therefore I can be free." Decolonization is not some sort of abstract freedom from oppression but a liberation specifically from the material consequences of colonial configurations of power, consequences that are, in some measure, present in our bodies.

Author Conversations

This collection is in many ways an excursion into disruption. By exploring the possibilities that arise when connections among embodiment, pedagogy, and decolonization are not simply identified but critically engaged, it both complicates and enriches histories of knowledge production. A number of themes weave through the chapters, some of which cluster around Indigenous knowledges: the decolonizing potential of reclaiming Indigenous epistemologies and ways of being that connect the individual to the relational collective and to the land; decolonization as a process that does not simply stand in opposition to Western colonization but that also promotes healing and the restoration of inner wholeness; and the pursuit of critical dialogues among Indigenous knowledges drawn from a variety of traditions. In addition, the collection explores the relationship between embodied writing and decolonizing knowledge production; the ethics of undoing or unsettling privileged subjectivities; and the implications of the intertwinement of colonialism with capitalism.

Roxana Ng was involved in this volume at its inception, as one of its editors. Not long after initial submissions were reviewed, she was diagnosed with an aggressive form of cancer that, in January 2013, took her life. Her death was a grave loss. In recognition of the formative influence of her ideas, we open the collection with her essay "Decolonizing Teaching and Learning Through Embodied Learning: Toward an Integrated Approach," which first appeared in a volume titled *Valences of Interdisciplinarity* (Foshay 2011), published not long before her death. In it, Ng develops what she calls an "integrative critical embodied pedagogy," bringing together key concerns and observations from her long and distinguished career as a researcher and teacher. As she explains, over the course of that career, she came to view embodied learning "as a form of decolonizing pedagogy." For Ng, the process of decolonization entails integration: it requires that we free ourselves from sources of separation. Decolonization, she writes, "dissolves the boundaries between self and collectivity, between the individual and the system," while it also asks how "we, as individuals living within and being part of collectivities, reproduce and sustain systems of oppression." In her essay, we find the interrelated themes of embodiment, pedagogy, and decolonization that are the focus of this collection.

Much as Ng reclaimed Indigenous knowledges of her own heritage in her teaching, in "Embodying Indigenous Resurgence," Alannah Young Leon and Denise Nadeau draw on the epistemological insights embedded in the Indigenous teaching of "all my relations" to develop an embodied pedagogy centred on rebuilding relationships, a process vital to Indigenous resurgence. "In retraining our senses to remember how we are related to the rest of creation," they write, "we provide both an intervention that seeks to decolonize the body's sense of disconnection and an entry point into the principle of *nindinawemagnidog*—all our relations." Young Leon and Nadeau move the discussion of embodiment and decolonization beyond the individual integration of mind, spirit, and body to highlight the collective unity of mind, spirit, and land as it exists in relation to the Canadian settler state. Cautioning against settler forms of "spiritual bypass"—that is, appropriating Indigenous spiritual practices as a way to avoid acknowledging one's complicity in dispossession—they insist that doing embodied work requires engagement with the reality of one's historical and psychological relationship to colonialism.

Three other chapters, by Devi Mucina, Sheila Batacharya, and Yuk-Lin Renita Wong, also address decolonization as a process that, through the reclaiming of Indigenous knowledges, methodologies, and/or practices, connects the individual to the relational collective. In "The Journey to You, Baba," Mucina illustrates the pedagogical power of African oral narrative. As he tells his story about how colonialism has fragmented his family, he reveals the impact of colonization on other African families as well. By centring his decolonizing dialogue with his family within a relational framework grounded in Ubuntu philosophy, he fuses the political and the personal and invites his readers to share his embodied journey into the geopolitical and social landscape of race, colonialism, sexism, and politics.

In "Resistance and Remedy Through Embodied Learning," Batacharya investigates the practice of yoga as a counterhegemonic healing strategy through which young South Asian women are able to explore their cultural identity and contest racism, colonialism, and cultural essentialism. Her discussions with participants in a series of yoga workshops reveal the potential of Indigenous knowledges and practices to serve as both individual *and* collective forms of resistance and to ameliorate the painful consequences of violence and oppression. Similarly, in "Please Call Me by My True Names,"

Wong explores the use of Buddhist practices of mindfulness to engage students in embodied critical reflection. She observes how students began to recognize their interbeing with all things when they were grounded in the physicality of their own bodies through mindfulness. This deep inward seeing not only helped the students to reclaim who they were in their particular history of relations with the world but also imbued them with energy, enabling them to turn outward and act in the world from the centre of their being, anchored in a relational consciousness.

In developing an integrative critical embodied pedagogy, Ng emphasizes that traditional Chinese medicine and qigong should not be placed in opposition to Western knowledges, as an alternative or an antithesis. This theme of moving beyond oppositional theorizing—which merely creates yet another dualism—runs through several other chapters in the book, notably those by authors who draw on Indigenous knowledge systems. Young Leon and Nadeau observe, for example, that the focus of "all my relations" pedagogy on the well-being of land, community, and future generations is intended to move us "out of a deconstructive agenda into a constructive one." Wong likewise identifies the need for knowledges and pedagogies that do not rest on oppositional frameworks. As she points out, discursive-analytical investigations of power encourage a binary framing of the oppressive and the anti-oppressive, a framing that in turn implies the opposition of "bad" to "good." Such dualistic conceptions, she argues, "allow those who self-identify as anti-oppressive (and morally 'good') or as the oppressed to claim innocence and to avoid examining their own implication in oppression along the multiple axes of power." Moreover, rather than fostering a sense of the interrelatedness of being, such as Wong's students gained through the practice of mindfulness, oppositional thinking promotes the hardening of boundaries between self-constructed identities and, in so doing, ultimately undermines healing.

Related themes surface in Temitope Adefarakan's "Integrating Mind, Body, and Spirit Through the Yoruba Concept of *Ori*," which explores pedagogical practices founded on Indigenous African cosmology. Adefarakan introduces the Yoruba concept of *ori*—literally "head," but also "destiny" or "purpose"—as a multilayered element of the Yoruba "worldsense," a term coined by Oyèrónké Oyĕwùmí (1997) to describe a way of grasping the world that does not privilege sight. In the creation of *ori*, spirit and matter merge: the one cannot exist without the other, nor can an individual exist except in relation to the collective. We cannot align ourselves with our *ori*, thereby embracing our destiny, unless we recognize our fundamental interconnection to all other human beings. Especially, though not exclusively, for African students who have grown up in diaspora, conceptualizing oneself in terms of *ori*, as the fusion of body and spirit, offers an empowering complement to Western pedagogical approaches.

Besides arguing for Indigenous knowledges and practices as counter-hegemonic healing strategies, the chapters by Batacharya and by Candace Brunette-Debassige create a contrapuntal conversation about the Western appropriation of Indigenous knowledge systems, specifically yoga. As Batacharya notes, young South Asian women who are seeking to recover from the damages inflicted by racism and colonialism are highly critical and selective in their choices surrounding the learning and practice of yoga. This caution arises partly in light of New Age appropriations of yoga, but it also reflects the fact that yoga may be associated with a variety of hegemonic, and deeply hierarchical, discourses—orthodox religious, nationalistic, patriarchal.

In "From Subjugation to Embodied Self-in-Relation," Brunette-Debassige, a Cree embodied learning educator who teaches yoga, explains how she negotiates the ethics of engagement with a tradition not her own while at the same time integrating yoga into the process of healing from colonization. In settler colonial Canada, she notes, Indigenous peoples were taught the habit of self-restraint—taught to ignore what their bodies were telling them and to resist the impulse to speak out. In her own experience of healing, Brunette-Debassige learned through the practice of yoga to overcome the internal fragmentation that she had inherited. But, as an Indigenous woman who is also a yoga instructor, she tells us, "I felt the responsibility to reflect critically upon my teaching in relation to the history and globalization of yogic knowledge(s)." In teaching yoga to Indigenous students, Brunette-Debassige seeks to challenge "the kinesthetic reality of colonization" through processes of embodied learning.

Drawing on her background in theatre, Brunette-Debassige also illuminates the decolonizing power of an embodied approach to performance writing. Such writing strengthens her inner voice, as it allows her to explore her place in the world and then to share her story through breath and body.

In "Poetry: Learning Through Embodied Language," Sheila Stewart likewise takes up the theme of embodied writing and its potential for decolonizing Eurocentric ways of knowing and being. As she points out, "poetry is poised in the moment between the sentient and the social, a moment of dialogue." Poetry demands to be spoken and heard: it demands to be embodied. In its rhythms and cadences, it evokes the visceral and emotional, while its fragmentary, imagistic quality, its insistence on pushing language beyond its ordinary limitations, allows poet to access "fluid thinking-feeling states and embrace embodied forms of learning and being." Reflecting on Tuck and Yang's examination of decolonization in relationship to land, Stewart further suggests that poetic writing "can be a way to *dwell* in the complex space of connections and disconnections among body, word, and place, where learning, integration, and healing are possible."

Two other authors—Susan Ferguson and Wendy Peters—also focus on embodied forms of writing. Ferguson's chapter, "Embodied Writing and the Social Production of Pain," explores the possibilities of embodied writing for social research and its implications for decolonizing knowledge production about and of the body. Despite considerable interest in issues of subjectivity and embodiment in fields such as sociology, education, and women's studies, theories of embodiment tend to reproduce dominant understandings of the relationship of the body to knowledge production, through writing practices that (re)produce disembodied relations to text. Beginning with the understanding that writing is a key, but contested, site of knowledge production in Western society, Ferguson treats writing as a social and bodily practice. Using an examination of the social production of bodily pain to illustrate her approach, she brings together disability studies, feminist autobiography, and phenomenologically informed interpretive sociology to develop an understanding of embodied writing as a pedagogical practice, one that can support a project of decolonizing knowledge production through the recognition of embodied difference and the cultivation of alternative ways of knowing.

In "Patient Stories: Renarrating Illness and Valuing the Rejected Body," Peters also interrogates Western constructions of the body and their affective, social, and material consequences. In 1997, Peters was diagnosed with a pituitary tumour, and during the period of her illness and subsequent recovery from surgery, she kept a journal. In her chapter, she returns to the journal to engage in a self-reflexive meditation on her experience. As she critically revisits her illness narrative, Peters recognizes how Eurocentric epistemologies and normative discourses informed both her conceptualization of and her reactions to her illness. In particular, she explores her previously unquestioned assumptions surrounding the ideal of bodily normalcy—the "expectation of perpetual good health" and its implications for identity, friendship, and broader social interactions. In revealing her complicity in an internalized sense of dominance founded on the possession of a "normal" body, Peters elucidates some of the ways in which privileged subjectivities are constituted within and through the marginalization of rejected bodies—bodies perceived as flawed and, hence, as threatening.

The theme of privileged subjectivities figures centrally in two other chapters, those by Carla Rice and by Randell Nixon and Katie MacDonald. In "Volatile Bodies and Vulnerable Researchers," Rice examines the Western construction of the "normal" body specifically in relation to disability, body size, and gender variance, with the goal of exploring ethical issues that arise when one is conducting research with groups positioned as anomalous. As a methodological approach, Rice argues, critical self-reflexivity requires that the researcher be willing to become vulnerable. "Being a vulnerable researcher," she writes, "means being present and honest with ourselves throughout our projects—namely, with our contradictory, uncomplimentary, or difficult thoughts and emotions, including our fears and desires and implicatedness in others' suffering." It asks us to participate in the experience of weakness and lack of power—a condition associated in our culture with the socially excluded, the differently abled, and the culturally and politically oppressed. At the same time, vulnerability directs researchers "to attend to the partiality and cultural specificity of their knowledge claims." In other words, it unsettles the privileged subject. In this way, the willingness to assume a position of vulnerability assists in the project of decolonizing hegemonic ways of knowing and disrupting established hierarchies of privilege and power.

In their chapter, Nixon and MacDonald turn a decolonizing lens on another construction of vulnerability, one that reinforces a colonial and imperialist definition of the Western subject as "the bearer of knowledge and truth" on whom responsibility now falls to intervene in moral wrongs committed by the formerly colonized. "Being Moved to Action: Micropolitics,

Affect, and Embodied Understanding" explores the affective power of a video, *Kony 2012*, that formed the centrepiece of a campaign by a US-based charitable organization, Invisible Children, dedicated to spurring public outrage about the actions of Joseph Kony, leader of a guerrilla group called the Lord's Resistance Army that was active in several countries in central Africa at the time. Inspired by a combination of Christian fundamentalism and Acholi nationalism, Kony and his followers were suspected of abducting children to serve as fighters. As Nixon and MacDonald point out, far from evoking a sense of dis-ease that might prompt them to learn more about the context of the situation, the *Kony 2012* video left viewers feeling "benevolent and satisfied," content with the knowledge of how they could do their part to put a stop to Kony's activities. In no way did it require viewers to engage with the history and ongoing expressions and ramifications of colonialism or to consider their own complicity in these processes; rather, the video demanded "a seemingly intuitive action that made thinking about or reflecting upon this action counterintuitive or potentially unethical." Using *Kony 2012* as an illustration, Nixon and MacDonald explore the ethical politics of "being undone"—the experience of feeling "that *who I am* and the patterns of thinking and feeling I use to navigate the world are troubled and shaken." Acknowledging the power of emotional responses, they call for an embodied pedagogy of affect that unsettles, rather than strengthens, existing structures of inequality and helps us to recognize the ways in which we sanction and support racism, imperialism, and the assumption of Western moral superiority, all in the service of global capitalism.

Two other contributors—Stephanie Moynagh and Jamie Magnusson—also consider the intertwining of colonialism and capitalism, specifically in relation to the embodied experience of poverty and social class. As Moynagh observes in "Class and Embodiment: Making Space for Complex Capacity," in the settler state of Canada (and indeed throughout the Global North), "the production of poverty through capitalism would not survive without the theft and exploitation of Indigenous lands." The class oppression essential to capitalism is thus closely bound up with social and material inequities inherent in colonial relations of power, inequities profoundly visible in the poverty with which Indigenous peoples still live. Understanding that class is a culture, with its own ways of knowing, Moynagh explores the relationship between class identity and somatic knowledge. In particular, she argues that embodied experiences, emotional as well as physical, that are rooted in poverty-class cultures generate their own knowledges—knowledges routinely devalued within white, colonial, capitalist, and heteropatriarchal systems of education. She calls for embodied and inclusive approaches to teaching that make space for nondominant and potentially counterhegemonic ways of knowing and that, in so doing, "honour survival" while at the same time seeking transformative change.

Jamie Magnusson's chapter, "Fighting Out: Fractious Bodies and Rebel Streets," extends the theme of somatic knowledge and class oppression beyond the boundaries of individual experience to consider the place of embodied learning in solidarity building. Magnusson takes as her example "Fighting Out," a program in downtown Toronto that offers classes in qigong and civil self-defence for sex workers and LGBTQ2 populations and that, unlike most self-defence classes, encourages collective, grassroots action against state violence. Fighting Out also participates in the tradition of taking back the streets—in this case, by reclaiming urban space from processes of enclosure, privatization, and commodification. Basing her conclusions on an analysis of monopoly-finance capital, the real-estate-driven production of safe, gentrified spaces within urban landscapes, and the emergence of fractious bodies criminalized and incarcerated by the "territorializing state"—bodies that include those of queers, sex workers, poor women, and Indigenous people—Magnusson argues that the collective practice of civil self-defence can be an effective political strategy for building social movements that aim to transform the social relations, grounded in colonial histories and capitalist imperialism, that organize political violence.

Bodies exist within historically conditioned relations of power that determine the material conditions of life specific to a given time and place. Embodied learning thus requires an engagement not only with the fundamental materiality of our being but also with the social hierarchies and discursive constructions that both express and seek to perpetuate existing relations of power. Despite the recent development of a discourse of reconciliation, in Canada these relations of power remain grounded in colonialism, an ideology inherited by white settlers from their British forebears and imposed upon the colonized. If an embodied pedagogy is to contribute to decolonization, it must therefore encourage us to confront our lived experience of the material conditions produced by these colonial relations of power, including the ongoing dispossession of Indigenous peoples from their land.

In addition, an embodied pedagogy must help us to reflect critically on our lived experience and on how to develop ways of examining our perceptions as a way to challenge colonial relations of power. Given that dominant frameworks of education are founded on these relations of power, they do not promote such reflection. Rather, by presenting dominant, intellect-based epistemologies as the only reliable source of information about the world and, in so doing, tacitly disparaging other ways of knowing, they seek to normalize existing inequities. By shifting the emphasis to the sentient-social experience of our bodies as situated within a particular set of historically constituted circumstances, and that our perceptions can be enriched through attunement to our sentient-social embodiment, the contributors to this collection seek to revalue other modes of knowledge production, as well as to challenge colonial configurations of power.

In some way, all of the chapters in this collection defy conventional expectations regarding academic discourse. This is something that we, as editors, celebrate. In addition to illustrating the authors' diverse epistemological groundings, such variation renders concrete our desire to create space for nondominant approaches to knowledge building. Decolonization will not happen if we insist on the safe and familiar. As Roxana Ng once wrote,

> Understanding oppression and doing antiracist work is by definition unsafe and uncomfortable, because both involve a serious (and frequently threatening) effort to interrogate our privilege as well as our powerlessness. To speak of safety and comfort is to speak from a position of privilege, relative though it may be. For those who have existed too long on the margins, life has never been safe or comfortable. (1993c, 201)

In one way or another, the contributors to this volume interrogate their positions of privilege: they write their bodies, their emotions, and their vulnerabilities into their texts. They, and we, insist that our body-mind-spirit and our historical and geopolitical situation are materially and discursively intertwined and that both are inseparable from knowledge production and thus from the activities of teaching and learning. This "teaching against the grain," as Roxana Ng explains, "involves struggles with our colleagues and our students, as well as within ourselves" (1993, 201). It is a challenge that we embrace.

References

Ahmed, Sara. 2004. *The Cultural Politics of Emotion*. New York: Routledge.

Alaimo, Stacy, and Susan Hekman. 2008a. "Introduction: Emerging Models of Materiality in Feminist Theory." In Alaimo and Hekman 2008b, 1–19.

Alaimo, Stacy, and Susan Hekman, eds. 2008b. *Material Feminisms*. Bloomington: Indiana University Press.

Alexander, M. Jacqui. 2005. *Pedagogies of Crossing: Meditations on Feminism, Sexual Politics, Memory, and the Sacred*. Durham, NC: Duke University Press.

Alexander, Claire, and Caroline Knowles, eds. 2005. *Making Race Matter: Bodies, Space and Identity*. New York: Palgrave Macmillan.

Anzaldúa, Gloria. 1990. "Haciendo Caras, Una Entrada." In *Making Face, Making Soul / Haciendo Caras: Creative and Critical Perspectives by Feminists of Color*, edited by Gloria Anzaldúa, xv–xxviii. San Francisco: Aunt Lute Foundation Books.

Bannerji, Himani, ed. 1993. *Returning the Gaze: Essays on Racism, Feminism and Politics*. Toronto: Sister Vision Press.

Barad, Karen. 2003. "Posthumanist Performativity: Toward an Understanding of How Matter Comes to Matter." *Signs* 28 (3): 801–31.

Battiste, Marie, ed. 2000. *Reclaiming Indigenous Voice and Vision*. Vancouver: University of British Columbia Press.

Battiste, Marie, and James (Sákéj) Youngblood Henderson. 2000. *Protecting Indigenous Knowledge and Heritage: A Global Challenge*. Saskatoon: Purich Publishing.

Belcourt, Christi. 2013. "Red Man Laughing: The Christi Belcourt Interview." *Red Man Laughing* podcast, 9 September. http://www.redmanlaughing.com/listen/2013/9/s3-ep1-christi-belcourt.

Blackman, Lisa. 2008. *The Body: The Key Concepts*. New York: Berg.

Bordo, Susan. 1993. *Unbearable Weight: Feminism, Western Culture, and the Body*. Berkeley, CA: University of California Press.

Butler, Judith. 1993. *Bodies That Matter: On the Discursive Limits of "Sex."* New York: Routledge.

Calliste, Agnes, and George J. Sefa Dei, eds. 2000. *Anti-racist Feminism: Critical Race and Gender Studies*. Halifax: Fernwood Publishing.

Coulthard, Glen Sean. 2014. *Red Skin, White Masks: Rejecting the Colonial Politics of Recognition*. Minneapolis: University of Minnesota Press.

Csordas, Thomas J., ed. 1994. *Embodiment and Experience: The Existential Ground of Culture and Self*. Cambridge: Cambridge University Press.

Davis, Kathy. 2007. "Reclaiming Women's Bodies: Colonialist Trope or Critical Epistemology?" In Shilling 2007, 50–64.

Dei, George J. Sefa, and Alireza Asgharzadeh. 2001. "The Power of Social Theory: The Anti-colonial Discursive Framework." *Journal of Educational Thought* 35(3): 297–323.

Dei, George J. Sefa, Budd L. Hall, and Dorothy Goldin Rosenberg, eds. 2000. *Indigenous Knowledges in Global Contexts: Multiple Readings of Our World*. Toronto: University of Toronto Press.

Dua, Enakshi, and Angela Robertson, eds. 1999. *Scratching the Surface: Canadian Anti-racist Feminist Thought*. Toronto: Women's Press.

Dua, Enakshi, Maureen FitzGerald, Linda Gardner, Darien Taylor, and Lisa Wyndels, eds. 1994. *On Women Healthsharing*. Toronto: Women's Press.

Duara, Prasenjit. 2004. *Decolonization: Perspectives from Now and Then*. London: Routledge.

Fanon, Frantz. 1967. *Black Skin, White Masks*. Translated by Charles Lam Markmann. New York: Grove Press. Originally published as *Peau noire, masques blancs* (1952).

Foshay, Raphael, ed. 2011. *Valences of Interdisciplinarity: Theory, Practice, Pedagogy*. Edmonton: Athabasca University Press.

Foucault, Michel. 1977. *Discipline and Punish: The Birth of the Prison*. Translated by Alan Sheridan. London: Allen Lane. Originally published as *Surveiller et punir: naissance de la prison* (1975).

Frankenberg, Ruth. 2004. *Living Spirit, Living Practice: Poetics, Politics, Epistemology*. Durham, NC: Duke University Press.

Friedman, Lenore, and Susan Moon, eds. 1997. *Being Bodies: Buddhist Women on the Paradox of Embodiment*. Boston: Shambhala.

Freire, Paulo. 1970. *Pedagogy of the Oppressed*. Translated by Myra Bergman Ramos. New York: Herder and Herder. Originally published as *Pedagogia do oprimido* (1968).

Gates, Trevor G. 2011. "Coming Out in the Social Work Classroom: Reclaiming Wholeness and Finding the Teacher Within." *Social Work Education* 30(1): 70–82.

Graveline, Fyre Jean. 1998. *Circle Works: Transforming Eurocentric Consciousness*. Halifax: Fernwood Press.

Grosz, Elizabeth. 1994. *Volatile Bodies: Toward a Corporeal Feminism.* Bloomington: Indiana University Press.

Harding, G. Sophie, ed. 2005. *Surviving in the Hour of Darkness: The Health and Wellness of Women of Colour and Indigenous Women.* Calgary: University of Calgary Press.

hooks, bell. 1993. *Sisters of the Yam: Black Women and Self-Recovery.* Toronto: Between the Lines.

Lattas, Andrew. 1993. "Essentialism, Memory and Resistance: Aboriginality and the Politics of Authenticity." *Oceania* 63: 2–67.

Lawrence, Bonita, and Enakshi Dua. 2005. "Decolonizing Antiracism." *Social Justice* 32(4): 120–43.

Leder, Drew. 1990. *The Absent Body.* Chicago: University of Chicago Press.

Lorde, Audre. 1984. *Sister Outsider: Essays and Speeches.* Freedom, CA: Crossing Press.

———. 1994. "Living with Cancer." In White 1994, 27–37. Seattle: Seal Press.

Mani, Lata. 2001. *Interleaves.* Koramangala, India: Lata Mani.

Mathew, Ann, Roxana Ng, Mary Patton, Lesia Waschuk, and Joanne Wong. 2008. "Learning, Difference, Embodiment: Personal and Collective Transformations." *New Horizons in Education* 56 (1): 45–63.

Mensinga, Jo. 2011. "The Feeling of Being a Social Worker: Including Yoga as Embodied Practice in Social Work Education." *Social Work Education* 30(6): 650–62.

Merleau-Ponty, Maurice. 2004. *The Phenomenology of Perception.* Translated by Colin Smith. New York: Routledge. Originally published as *Phénoménologie de la perception* (1945).

Miller, John Jack, and Yoshiharu Nakagawa, eds. 2002. *Nurturing Our Wholeness: Perspectives on Spirituality in Education.* Routland, VT: Foundation for Educational Renewal.

Miller, John P., ed. 2005. *Holistic Learning and Spirituality in Education: Breaking New Ground.* New York: State University of New York Press.

Mohanty, Chandra Talpade. 2003. *Feminism Without Borders: Decolonizing Theory, Practicing Solidarity.* Durham, NC: Duke University Press.

Monture-Angus, Patricia. 1995. *Thunder in My Soul: A Mohawk Woman Speaks.* Halifax: Fernwood Publishing.

———. 1999. *Journeying Forward: Dreaming First Nations Independence.* Halifax: Fernwood Publishing.

Murphy, Jacqueline Shea. 2007. *The People Have Never Stopped Dancing: Native American Modern Dance Histories.* Minneapolis: University of Minnesota Press.

Nadeau, Denise, and Alannah Young. 2006. "Educating Bodies for Self-determination: A Decolonizing Strategy." *Canadian Journal of Native Education* 29(1): 87–148.

Ng, Roxana. 1988. *The Politics of Community Services: Immigrant Women, Class and State.* Toronto: Garamond Press.

———. 1990. "Immigrant Women: The Construction of a Labour Market Category." *Canadian Journal of Women and the Law* 4(1): 96–112.

———. 1992. "Managing Female Immigration: A Case of Institutional Sexism and Racism." *Canadian Woman Studies* 12(3): 20–23.

———. 1993a. "Sexism, Racism, Canadian Nationalism." In *Returning the Gaze: Essays on Racism, Feminism and Politics,* edited by Himani Bannerji, 162–96. Toronto: Sister Vision Press.

———. 1993b. "Racism, Sexism, and Nation Building in Canada." In *Race, Identity, and Representation in Education,* edited by Cameron McCarthy and Warren Crichlow, 50–59. New York and London: Routledge.

———. 1993c. "'A Woman Out of Control': Deconstructing Sexism and Racism in the University." *Canadian Journal of Education* 18(3): 189–205.

———. 1998. "Is Embodied Teaching and Learning Critical Pedagogy? Some Remarks on Teaching Health and the Body from an Eastern Perspective." Paper presented at the annual meeting of the American Educational Research Association, 13–17 April, San Diego, California.

———. 2000a. "Revisioning the Body/Mind from an Eastern Perspective: Comments on Experience, Embodiment and Pedagogy. In *Women's Bodies / Women's Lives: Health, Well-Being and Body Image,* edited by Baukji Miedema, Janet Mary Stoppard, and Vivenne Anderson, 175–93. Toronto: Sumach Press.

———. 2000b. "Toward an Embodied Pedagogy: Exploring Health and the Body Through Chinese Medicine." In *Indigenous Knowledges in Global Contexts: Multiple Readings of Our World,* edited by George J. Sefa Dei, Budd L. Hall, and Dorothy Goldin Rosenberg, 168–83. Toronto: University of Toronto Press.

———. 2004. "Embodied Pedagogy: New Forms of Learning." Workshop given at the Department of Sociology, Umea University, Umea, Sweden, 5 May, and presentation at Gavle University College, Gavle, Sweden, 10 May.

———. 2005. "'Embodied Learning and Qi Gong': Integrating the Body in Graduate Education." In *Within and Beyond Borders: Critical Multicultural Counselling in Practice,* edited by Olga Oulanova, Issac Stein, Aanchal Rai, Maya Hammer, and Patricia A. Poulin, n.p. Centre for Diversity in Counselling and Psychotherapy, Ontario Institute for Studies in Education, University of Toronto. https://www.oise.utoronto.ca/cdcp/UserFiles/File/Publications/within_and_beyond_borders.pdf.

———. 2011. "Decolonizing Teaching and Learning Through Embodied Learning: Toward an Integrated Approach." In Foshay 2011, 343–65.

Ng, Roxana, and Alma Estable. 1987. "Immigrant Women in the Labor Force: An Overview of Present Knowledge and Research Gaps." *Resources for Feminist Research* 16 (1): 29–33.

Ng, Roxana, and Judith Ramirez. 1981. *Immigrant Housewives in Canada*. Toronto: Immigrant Women's Centre.

Ng, Roxana, Pat Staton, and Joyce Scane, eds. 1995. *Anti-racism, Feminism, and Critical Approaches to Education*. Westport, CT: Greenwood.

Ng, Roxana, Gillian Walker, and Jacob Muller, eds. 1990. *Community Organization and the Canadian State*. Toronto: Garamond Press.

Orr, Deborah. 2002. "The Uses of Mindfulness in Anti-oppressive Pedagogies: Philosophy and Praxis." *Canadian Journal of Education* 27 (4): 477–90.

———. 2005. "Minding the Soul in Education: Conceptualizing and Teaching the Whole Person." In *Holistic Learning and Spirituality in Education: Breaking New Ground*, edited by John P. Miller, Selia Karsten, Diana Denton, Deborah Orr, and Isabella Colalillo Kates, 87–100. New York: State University New York Press.

Oyěwùmí, Oyèrónké. 1997. *The Invention of Women: Making Sense of Western Gender Discourses*. Minneapolis: University of Minnesota Press.

Peile, Colin. 1998. "Emotional and Embodied Knowledge: Implications for Critical Practice." *Journal of Sociology and Social Welfare* 39: 39–59.

Piran, Niva. 2001. "Re-inhabiting the Body from the Inside Out: Girls Transform Their School Environment." In *From Subjects to Subjectivities: A Handbook of Interpretive and Participatory Methods*, edited by Deborah L. Tolman and Mary Brydon-Miller, 218–38. New York: New York University Press.

Razack, Narda. 2002. *Transforming the Field: Critical Antiracist and Anti-oppressive Perspectives for the Human Services Practicum*. Halifax: Fernwood Publishing.

Razack, Sherene. 2015. *Dying from Improvement: Inquests and Inquiries into Indigenous Deaths in Custody*. Toronto: University of Toronto Press.

Razack, Sherene, Malinda Smith, and Sunera Thobani, eds. 2010. *States of Race: Critical Race Feminism for the 21st Century*. Toronto: Between the Lines.

Rice, Carla, and Vanessa Russell. 1995a. "EmBodying Equity: Putting Body and Soul into Equity Education. Part I: How Oppression Is Embodied." *Our Schools / Our Selves* (September): 14–36.

———. 1995b. "EmBodying Equity: Putting Body and Soul into Equity Education. Part II: Strategies for Change." *Our Schools / Our Selves* (December): 32–54.

Sheets-Johnstone, Maxine, ed. 1992. *Giving the Body Its Due*. New York: State University of New York Press.

Shilling, Chris. 1993. *The Body and Social Theory*. London: Sage.

Shilling, Chris, ed. 2007. *Embodying Sociology: Retrospect, Progress, and Prospects.* Special issue, *Sociological Revew* 55 (suppl. 1). Malden, MA: Blackwell Publishing.

Simpson, Leanne. 2011. *Dancing on Our Turtle's Back: Stories of Nishnaabeg Re-creation, Resurgence, and a New Emergence.* Winnepeg: Arbeiter Ring Press.

Sunseri, Lina. 2011. *Being Again of One Mind: Oneida Women and the Struggle for Decolonization.* Vancouver: University of British Columbia Press.

Tambornino, John. 2002. *The Corporeal Turn: Passion, Necessity, Politics.* Lanham, MD: Rowman and Littlefield.

Tangenberg, Kathleen M., and Susan Kemp. 2002. "Embodied Practice: Claiming the Body's Experience, Agency, and Knowledge for Social Work." *Social Work* 47(1): 9–18.

Truth and Reconciliation Commission of Canada. 2015. *Calls to Action.* Winnipeg: Truth and Reconciliation Commission of Canada. http://www.trc.ca/websites/trcinstitution/File/2015/Findings/Calls_to_Action_English2.pdf.

Tuck, Eve, and K. Wayne Yang. 2012. "Decolonization Is Not a Metaphor." *Decolonization: Indigeneity, Education and Society* 1: 1–40. http://decolonization.org/index.php/des/issue/archive.

Turner, Bryan S. 2008. *The Body and Society: Explorations in Social Theory.* 3rd ed. London: Sage.

West, Traci C. 1999. *Wounds of the Spirit: Black Women, Violence, and Resistance Ethics.* New York: New York University Press.

White, Evelyn C., ed. 1994. *The Black Women's Health Book: Speaking for Ourselves.* Seattle: Seal Press.

Williams, Simon J., and Gillian Bendelow. 1998. *The Lived Body: Sociological Themes, Embodied Issues.* London: Routledge.

Wong, Yuk-Lin Renita. 2004. "Knowing Through Discomfort: A Mindfulness-Based Critical Social Work Pedagogy." *Critical Social Work* 5(1). http://www1.uwindsor.ca/criticalsocialwork/knowing-through-discomfort-a-mindfulness-based-critical-social-work-pedagogy.

———. 2013. "Returning to Silence, Connecting to Wholeness: Contemplative Pedagogy for Critical Social Work Education." *Journal of Religion and Spirituality in Social Work* 32(3): 269–85.

———. 2014. "Radical Acceptance: Mindfulness and Critical Reflection in Social Work Education." In *Mindfulness and Acceptance in Social Work: Evidence-Based Interventions and Emerging Applications,* edited by Matthew S. Boone, 125–43. Oakland, CA: New Harbinger.

1 Decolonizing Teaching and Learning Through Embodied Learning

Toward an Integrated Approach

Roxana Ng

This essay is, first and foremost, about teaching and learning. It is both a critique of current modes of teaching that do not treat the learner as an embodied subject and an exploration of a more holistic pedagogical endeavour that explicitly acknowledges the interconnectedness of mind, body, emotion, and spirit in the construction and pursuit of knowledge. To explore this interconnection, I argue, we need to disturb the existing boundaries of educational discourse and turn to and incorporate other epistemological and philosophical traditions. But the present essay also forms part of a volume on interdisciplinary studies. Thus, in beginning, I pose the questions: What are the boundaries of interdisciplinary studies, and can an integrative approach to pedagogy be considered interdisciplinary? I invite the reader to keep these questions in mind, and I will return to them in closing.

The Argument for an Embodied Pedagogy

As I have argued elsewhere (for example, Ng 1998, 2005), contemporary Western liberal and critical education is built on a profound division: the privileging of the mind-intellect over the body-spirit.[1] By and large, educa-

---

1 By critical education I mean critical pedagogy, feminist pedagogy, and antiracist education, in Canada, and critical, emancipatory, or revolutionary multicultural

tors, including critical educators, have focused their educational efforts on developing students' intellect and capacity for critical reasoning. The body is relevant only as a vessel that houses the brain, which is regarded as the organ responsible for the mind-intellect. Although some have attempted to rescue the body and restore its agency, both in social theory (see, for example, Shilling 1993; Turner 1991) and in cultural theory (McLaren 1995, for example), most of these writings focus on how the body is represented and instrumentalized in postmodernity (what I call the outside-in approach). This attempt to incorporate the body into social and cultural theories, however, does not include the spirit, which is relegated to the domain of religion. The spirit "belongs" to theology and religious studies, not to other disciplines; this indicates the depth to which our thinking is circumscribed by existing disciplinary boundaries. Much of critical teaching is implicated in the mind-intellect versus body-spirit divide.

When I talk about the spirit, which I call the body-spirit, I do not mean "spiritual" in the common, Western, religious sense. I use this hyphenated term to indicate that we cannot talk about body, mind, and spirit (which includes our emotion and psyche) as if they were separate entities. I am aware that this topic has provided both Western and Eastern philosophical traditions with a long history of intellectual and theoretical debates too complicated to discuss here. In contrast to the other contributions in this volume, I am invoking an understanding, based in Chinese medical theory, that treats the mind, spirit or soul, and body as completely interrelated. Thus, nothing can happen in one sphere without having an effect on the others. I came to the realization of this inextricable connectedness during my doctoral studies. The pains, discomfort, and other persistent, though not serious, ailments I experienced during this intense period of intellectual concentration not only reminded me of the body's inevitable presence in our every endeavour; it also awakened me to the fact that if we ignore its presence, there can be consequences. However, it wasn't until I began teaching that a drastic shift in my consciousness occurred, informed by my experience as a minority in the professoriate. This, in turn, led to my

---

education, in the United States (see McCarthy 1995). Although the two have different roots and traditions, they do share a common goal: to expose existing inequalities and instill critical consciousness in students.

subsequent journey toward discovering and incorporating the connection between body, mind, and spirit in my teaching and praxis.

It is not easy to be a minority, a woman, and an immigrant living in a society that upholds white male supremacy. As a nation colonized by Europeans, notably the English and the French, we live with the legacy of colonialism in Canada, which began with the subordination of Aboriginal peoples. This subordination is extended to other groups that are seen to be different—physically, linguistically, culturally, ideologically—and hence inferior. As we move up in the power hierarchy, this inferiorization of the "other" becomes much more entrenched and difficult to disrupt. As part of the institutional structure created historically to preserve the privilege of certain classes of men, the academy is no exception to the entrenchment of white male privilege, values, and knowledge based on men's experience of the world. The fact that women and racial minorities have made inroads into this bastion of patriarchal power does not mean that they are now fully accepted within the academy. Indeed, there is a burgeoning literature that exposes the barriers that minorities encounter in the university, be they teachers or students, *both* because their presence challenges the once homogeneous makeup of the university *and* because they challenge the process of knowledge production based on white, male assumptions (see, for example, de Castell and Bryson 1997; Roman and Eyre 1997).

The exercise and maintenance of power takes multiple and complicated forms. Elsewhere (Ng 1993, 1995), I have identified three major power axes in the university: that between the classroom and the larger academic institution, that between the teacher and the students, and that among the students. Thus, although a faculty member has formal authority as a representative of the university, this authority can be challenged by students in the classroom. For example, a minority woman faculty member may be challenged more often than her (white) male colleagues simply because she is relatively powerless in the larger society. Faculty members whose teaching does not conform to the expected conventions in terms of content and style are likewise apt to be challenged more often. Sexism, racism, a sense of class privilege, and other such biased attitudes are operative in interactions among students as well.

What is important to point out is that relationships of power are never enacted *merely* in the form of intellectual encounters. Most intellectual encounters entail a confrontation of bodies, which are differently inscribed. Power plays are both enacted and absorbed by people physically, as they assert or challenge authority, and the marks of such confrontations are stored in the body. Each time I stand in front of a classroom, I embody the historical sexualization and racialization of an Asian female, who is thought to be docile, subservient, and sexually compliant, even as my class privilege, formal authority, and academic qualifications ameliorate some of the effects of this stereotype. My presence is a moment in the crystallization of the historical and contemporary contestation of ideas and practices that are constantly changing. That is, my physical presence in the academy in turn challenges the sexist and racist construction of the archetype of an Asian female.[2] It is indeed the encounter of bodies, not only of intellect, that gives dynamism to the process of teaching and learning. As we engage in critical teaching and bring our activism to the university and to our classrooms, this dynamism is what excites us. At the same time, going against the grain can make us physically ill (Ng 1998).

Yet, despite feminist scholarship's insistence that "the personal is political," we have no language to speak of how we embody our political and intellectual struggles. We wage these struggles in our professional and public lives, but when we get sick, we see and treat our illness as a personal and private problem that is not to be openly discussed. This bifurcation points to how fundamentally we have been influenced by Cartesian thinking, which posits a separation between the body and the mind (Bordo 1987, esp. chap. 5), and by the privileging of mental over manual labour (Marx and Engels 1970). It goes beyond compartmentalizing our lives into two spheres, the public/professional and the private/personal; it also extends beyond a simple theory-practice split and the contradiction between what we think and how we act. It has to do with the more fundamental way in which ruling ideas have become taken-for-granted practices, and it affects how we are—our *being*—in the world. These practices are *embodied*; they have become habitual ways in which we conduct our business and, more importantly, our*selves*.

---

2 I am using the term *archetype* here simply to refer to the fact that it is out of an archetype that stereotypes are developed. It is not to be confused with the way in which the term is used in Jungian psychoanalysis, where it refers to primordial, inherited, innate, and a priori modes of perception (Hyde and McGuinness 1992).

The opportunity for me to integrate my personal explorations of health and illness and my teaching, and thereby develop a mode of teaching that honours both the mind and body-spirit, came in 1991. I took over a colleague's course, "Health, Illness, and Knowledge of the Body: Education and Self-Learning Processes," when he moved into another field of study. (My experience developing this course was documented in Ng [2000].) Since that time, I have experimented with different ways of (a) insisting that embodiment be an essential part of my classroom encounters with students and (b) remaining truthful to the traditions of critical education central to my training and writing. The method of teaching, which I will describe later, has gone through numerous iterations and name changes, from "Health and Illness" to "Integrative Approach to Equity." The present iteration is reflected in the title of this essay—an integrative critical embodied pedagogy, or embodied learning, for short. I incorporate embodied learning into most of my teaching at a graduate program of education, with different degrees of success and popularity. Notably, starting in 2001, I developed a course called "Embodied Learning and Qi Gong" that places embodied learning front and centre. Central to embodied learning are two interconnected elements: I insist that physical *and* contemplative activities are part not only of the course content but also of the students' everyday life. Qigong, a meditative and breathing practice that originated in ancient China as early as five thousand years ago, is the primary tool I use to promote the interconnection of the body, mind, and spirit.

Disrupting the Body-Mind Binary Through Qigong

Simply translated, qigong is a generic term for any exercises that involve the breath—the art of cultivating *qi*, with *qi* in this context referring to the breath. It is one of the healing and martial arts. According to scholars of qigong, this form of exercise was developed by people of an agrarian society who watched and mimicked the movements of animals in relation to cycles of planting and harvesting, life and death. It was practiced originally as a form of therapeutic dance to cure rheumatism and ward off other symptoms of excess Damp Evil in the flood-prone Yellow River basin (Reid 1994, chap. 13). It has been known by many different names throughout Chinese history. In fact, the term *qigong* is fairly recent. According to Ken Cohen, a scholar and practitioner of qigong, while the term was first mentioned in Taoist (or

Daoist) texts during the Ming Dynasty (1368–1644), it was not used in its present specialized sense until the twentieth century (Cohen 1997, chap. 2).[3] While there are many forms of qigong, developed and guarded by families who practiced Chinese healing arts, most are based on Taoist principles and theory similar to those of Chinese medicine.

Chinese medical theory, or TCM (traditional Chinese medicine), is based on the central Taoist principle of the unity of opposites—yin and yang. According to Chinese creation myths, the universe was an undifferentiated whole in the beginning. Out of this emerged yin-yang: the world in its infinite forms. In both Taoism and TCM, yin-yang is a symbolic representation of universal process (including health, in the case of TCM), and it portrays a changing rather than a static process (Kaptchuk 2000, chap. 1). The important thing to understand is that the two opposite states are not mutually exclusive or independent of each other. They are mutually dependent, and they change into each other. Therefore, extreme yang becomes yin, and vice versa. The theory of yin and yang has been mistakenly represented in the West as a dualist philosophy. Chinese medical scholars such as Kaptchuk, however, argue that it is a form of dialectic that is both similar to and different from Hegelian dialectics (see Kaptchuk 2000, 174–76).

Health is considered to be the balance of yin-yang aspects of the body, and disease is the imbalance between these aspects. This is a form of dialectical thinking radically different from the causal linear thinking and logic of allopathy and positivist science. The body in TCM is understood to be in a state of dynamic interaction of yin and yang; it is constantly changing and fluctuating. On the basis of this fundamental understanding of the nature of yin-yang and health as balance, TCM views illness not so much in terms of discrete diseases as in terms of disharmony. Thus, TCM outlines eight guiding principles for determining these patterns of disharmony. According to Beinfield and Korngold (1991), the eight principles are four sets of polar categories that distinguish between and interpret the data gathered by examination: yin-yang, cold-heat, deficiency-excess, and

---

3 Daoism, or Taoism, is one of the oldest and most prominent Chinese philosophies. The way in which the term is spelled depends on the system of romanization. The older spelling, Taoism, is still in use, although the pinyin spelling, Daoism, is the one preferred by the People's Republic of China. Similarly, "qigong" is the pinyin spelling; the older one is "chikung."

interior-exterior. Again, these are not mutually exclusive but can coexist in a person.

A major difference between biomedicine and TCM theory is the way in which the body is conceptualized. The Chinese view of the body does not correspond to that of Western anatomy. For example, Chinese medical theory does not have the concept of a nervous system, yet it can treat neurological disorders. It does not speak of an endocrine system, yet it is capable of correcting what allopathy calls endocrine disorders. Although TCM language makes reference to what the West recognizes as organs such as lungs, liver, stomach, and so on, these are not conceptualized as discrete physical structures and entities located in specific areas within the body. Rather, the term *organ* is used to identify specific *functions*. Furthermore, TCM does not make a distinction between physical functions and the emotional and spiritual dimensions governed by the "organ" in question. It describes an organ not only in terms of its physiological processes and functions but also in terms of its orb—its sphere of influence (Kaptchuk 2000; Beinfield and Korngold 1991).

For example, in TCM, the Spleen is the primary organ of digestion.[4] It extracts the nutrients from food digested by the stomach and transforms them into what will become *qi* and Blood. The Spleen is thus responsible for making Blood, whereas the Liver is responsible for storing and spreading Blood. As such, the Spleen is responsible for transformation, transmutation, and transportation, and these functions apply to physical as well as mental and emotional processes. At the somatic level, "weakness" in the Spleen means that food cannot be transformed properly into nutrients that nourish the body. At the emotional and psychospiritual level, a weak Spleen diminishes our awareness of possibilities and our ability to transform possibilities into appropriate courses of action, which leads to worry and confusion. Ultimately, it affects our trustworthiness and dependability (Kaptchuk 2000, 59–66).

The body, then, is conceptualized not so much in terms of distinct parts and components as in terms of energy flow (*qi*). *Qi*, a fundamental concept in TCM and Chinese thinking, is frequently translated as "energy" or "vital

---

4 Following the convention of scholars of Chinese medicine, I am capitalizing terms such as "Spleen" and "Blood" when they are used in the Chinese way, to distinguish them from Western usages.

energy," but in fact, it has no precise conceptual correspondence in the West. *Qi* is what animates life. Thus, while there is *qi*, there is life; when there is no *qi*, life ceases. It is both material and immaterial. *Qi* is present in the universe in the air we breathe and in the breaths we take. It is the quality we share with all things, thus connecting the macrocosm with the microcosm. *Qi* circulates in the body along lines of energy flow called meridians or organ networks. Another way of conceptualizing disease is to say that it arises when *qi* is not flowing smoothly. This leads to blockage and stagnation, which, if persistent, will lead to disease (that is, pathological changes in the body). Thus, an important part of the healing process is to unblock and facilitate the free flow of *qi*. Different therapies (massage, acupuncture, and herbology) are aimed at promoting the smooth flow of *qi* and rebalancing disharmony.

Together with these notions of health and the body, the Chinese have developed exercise forms called qigong, aimed at optimizing health and balance. These are exercises or movements designed to regulate the breath, the mind, and the body simultaneously. Daniel Reid (1994, 175) identifies four basic applications of qigong: health, longevity, martial power, and spiritual enlightenment. There are literally thousands of forms of qigong, from sitting postures similar to what the West recognizes as postures conducive to meditation to tai ji juan, which, at its most advanced, is a form of martial art aimed at honing the body, mind, and spirit to respond to external attack without the use of force. Practitioners of qigong believe that by disciplining, activating, and regulating the normally automatic, involuntary way of breathing, they are able to regulate and alter other functions of the body such as heartbeat, blood flow, and other physical and emotional functions. Thus, qigong is not *simply* a physical exercise. Nancy Zi (1986, 3), a professional vocalist who uses qigong to enhance her operatic singing, puts it concisely: "The practice of *chi kung* . . . encompasses the ancient Chinese understanding of disciplined breathing as a means of acquiring total control over body and mind. It gives us physiological and psychological balance and the balance of *yin* and *yang*." Qigong is thus based on the same principles as TCM; they are complementary. It is a recommended exercise form in TCM and is taught widely as a healing art in China.

It is precisely the way TCM and qigong conceptualize the interconnectedness of body, mind, and spirit that I found useful in my attempt to restore the centrality of the body in teaching and learning. Since 1991, I have been experimenting with using qigong as a tool for cultivating critical inquiry that is at once embodied and reflexive—a mode of inquiry that is contemplative and dialogic and that acknowledges the equal participation of body, mind, emotion, and spirit in scholarly pursuit and in knowledge construction. This understanding underpins embodied learning.

Theorizing and Practising Embodied Learning

In addition to qigong theory and practice, I draw on Frantz Fanon's (1963, 1967) analysis of the psychology of the colonized and on Antonio Gramsci's (1971) notions of hegemony and common sense. Fanon's work is ground-breaking because he was one of the first social scientists to attempt to understand colonization as more than just a direct oppressive force. More profoundly, it is an attitude internalized by the colonized, so that she adopts the ideas and behaviour of the colonizer and acts, or regulates herself, according to the norms of colonial society. Similarly, Gramsci uses the term *hegemony* to explain how ruling ideas are shared by the dominant and working classes. He asserts that once a ruling idea becomes hegemonic, it becomes common sense. Common-sense thinking is uncritical, episodic, and disjointed, but it is also powerful because it is taken for granted (321–43). Applying Gramsci's historical discussion to racism in contemporary British society, Stuart Hall notes that ideologies "work most effectively when we are not aware that how we formulate and construct a statement about the world is underpinned by ideological premises; when our formulations seem to be simply descriptive statements about how things are (i.e., must be), or of what we can 'take-for-granted'" (Hall, quoted in Lawrence 1982, 46). Colin Leys suggests that when an ideology becomes completely normalized, it is embedded in language.[5] But ideology is not merely a set of ideas; it is a practice in that it shapes how we act, as well as how we think. I would extend Leys's observation to argue that once hegemonic ideas become common sense, they are *condensed* in our emotional and physical beings—in how we relate to women and minority

---

5 Leys made this observation in a seminar at OISE on 21 March 1993. The seminar, which Leys led, was organized by Tuula Lindholm on behalf of a Gramsci study group. I thank Tuula for inviting me to the seminar.

groups, for example, and in how we see and relate to ourselves.[6] In short, they become patterns of behaviour.

Elsewhere (Ng 2004), I have used my babysitter's attitude toward eating as an example to illustrate this force of habit. The example is worth repeating because it is clear and nonthreatening; its power as a message lies in its simplicity. My "babysitter," who looks after my animals when I am away, was eighty-two, going on eighty-three, when I first wrote about her. She doesn't cook, so I cook for her. She gulps down her food as soon as I put it in front of her, frequently finishing a whole dinner before I have a chance to sit down. When I asked her to eat more slowly, she would say: "I always had to eat fast when I worked at the hospital. We were only given half an hour for lunch." When I remind her that she has been retired since she was sixty-five, her rebuttal is inevitable: "I can't help it." It is the belief that "I can't help it" that locks people into fixed patterns of behaviour. So it is that my babysitter has developed a "habit" of eating quickly because of years of working in a place where she had to hurry or else her pay would be docked or she would be reprimanded. Gulping down her dinner is "natural" for her, taken for granted, not to be questioned. Thus, change is only possible if we can develop the capacity to examine our patterns of behaviour objectively, without attachment, in order to determine whether and how to change. This requires that we be reflexively critical, that we be open to examining the integrity of our being without guilt and judgment.

Using insights from Fanon, Gramsci, and Foucault, we can see how dominant and subordinate power relations are played out interaction-ally in "normal" and "natural" ways. Feminists have drawn attention to how patriarchy works in practice: men are listened to when they speak; women and minorities are not heard. My notion of embodied learning, which I am calling an "integrative critical embodied pedagogy" here, seeks to help us develop the capacity not only to reason critically but to see dis-passionately and to alter actions that contribute to the reproduction of dominant-subordinate relations. It is an attempt to close the gap between progressive theory and practice. To illustrate, I will describe briefly what I do in a course called "Embodied Learning and Qi Gong."

---

6 My characterization here resonates with Foucault's (1977) understanding of how the panopticon leads to self-regulation on the part of prisoners.

The course consists of three basic components. First, in addition to introducing students to TCM and qigong, I assign readings on different ways in which the body is conceptualized in different disciplines such as sociology, anthropology, and psychotherapy. The goal here is to expose students to the centrality of the body in academic and other writings—including what some sociologists have identified as the "absent body" in social theory (Shilling 1993; Turner 1991)—and to drastically different ways of constructing the body. Thus, they come to see that the boundaries of the body are by no means fixed; they are malleable. Understanding the diverse ways of perceiving and describing bodily experience raises questions about knowledge and power: about who has the power to define what constitutes illness, for example.

Second, at least one hour of this four-hour-per-week course is devoted to the practice of qigong as a form of mindfulness exercise. There are at least two objectives for this component of the course. Insisting that exercises be part of the curriculum reinforces the fact that we are embodied learners, that learning does not only involve the mind. It draws our attention to how the body, emotion, and spirit are involved in the learning process—and to what we embrace and resist, and why. Moreover, in many Eastern traditions, meditation is used as a discipline that focuses the mind, enhancing our capacity to reflect on our thoughts and actions without judging them—what Buddhism refers to as nonattachment, as opposed to detachment. An attitude of detachment is characterized by the absence of emotion when we are presented or confronted with something. In contrast, nonattachment consists in refraining from passing judgment on something in the first instance. It is a state of dispassionate observation, one that enables us to consider, objectively, how to interpret or act on something and to do so with understanding and compassion. The following journal description, written by one of my students, serves as an illustration:

> I felt my feet rooted to the floor. I sensed the movement of my limbs located in relation to the space I occupied. I sensed the tension and relaxation of my muscles as a physical experience of my tissues. I felt the flow of breath that was at one moment a part of me, inside my lungs, and at the next moment, a part of the air that surrounded me. I experienced these things with my body, that physical part of my self.

There were times when I was so involved in the physicality of the experience that my surroundings faded from my vision. I was aware of the professor's verbal instructions and my efforts to translate those instructions into coordinated physical movement. I was aware of concentrating on the cycle of my breathing. I knew these and other things from the cognitive part of my being. At times it was as if I were an outside observer watching the experience of my body. My mind, my body, and my breath were connected yet separate entities engaged in *qi gong*. It was like a revelation that day I was able to articulate a sense of body—my body from those oppositional and interdependent positions. Through repetition of body movement which replicates the cycles of breath I was echoing the rhythms of life and nature. . . .

. . . *Qi gong* training was embodied exploration of the invisible process of constructing knowledge of the body. (Gustafson 1998, 53)

While initially I took up qigong practice as a way of reducing stress and promoting health, with time and practice, I came to understand and appreciate how it is that qigong and other forms of meditation are spiritual, as distinguished from merely religious, practices. These practices enable one to develop the capacity to be *mindful* of one's thought and action, so that one does not go about one's daily business thoughtlessly and automatically as a matter of habit. They enable one to see how one's actions affect others, and whether and how one should change. They therefore give us the means, albeit not the only ones, to interrogate how our consciousness is developed and changed. The assumption here is that consciousness has both a mind-intellect and a body-spirit dimension. It is tangible because it is embodied. Understanding and analyzing the development of consciousness thus necessitates an interrogation of our being as sensuous living individuals, of the material conditions that enable and limit our bodily existence, and hence, of knowledge construction itself (which is accomplished by embodied subjects). Much like the call for starting with people's lived experience proposed by critical and feminist pedagogy, it is a mode of learning that grounds the knower in time and space and provides an anchor enabling us to see that thought processes are inevitably historically and spatially specific. This in turn allows us to see that, indeed, consciousness can be changed as we confront it and understand how it comes about.

The third component is journalling, which is included as part of the course requirement and as an accompaniment to the mindfulness exercises. Journalling has three purposes. First, as with many courses that require students to keep a reading journal, I ask students to summarize the major argument(s) of an assigned piece of reading to develop their comprehension and summary skills. Reviewing this part of the journal gives me a sense of whether students understand the materials and, if not, what remedial action I and they should take. Second, journalling is another tool that enables students to reflect on their reactions (feelings and emotions) to the course materials. I ask students to record and analyze their reactions, to trace how these feelings are triggered by what they've read, thus enabling them to use reactions as a starting point for reflection and analysis. Finally, students are required to keep a qigong journal, preferably on a daily basis, that describes their practice of and reaction to the practice of qigong.[7] The purpose here is to treat the body as a site for knowledge construction.

Risks and Possibilities of Embodied Learning

Practicing embodied learning by incorporating qigong in the university curriculum presents an invaluable and promising opportunity for me to interrogate Western knowledge-construction with like-minded, or at least curious, students. Not only have I learned tremendously from teaching embodied learning, but I have also changed my own praxis over time, to the point where I am now convinced that integrating body, mind, and spirit not only is disruptive to established educational conventions in North America but is a method of decolonizing—undoing—ways in which we have come to be in the world. Similarly, Deborah Orr has theorized and advocated for the use of mindfulness as part of anti-oppressive pedagogy in higher education. She claims that mindfulness practice is "a proven technique to address the non-cognitive forms of attachment to ideation that may remain in force despite the most thorough-going intellectual change" (Orr 2002, 477). In working with Aboriginal women who have experienced tremendous abuse

---

7 Indeed, students have to practice qigong and meditation for at least five minutes each day as part of the course requirement. The rationale is to make embodied learning part of their everyday lives so that mindfulness becomes a habit. From students' discussions, I have discovered that this is one of the most difficult aspects of the curriculum.

and violence, Alannah Young and Denise Nadeau argue strenuously for a multidimensional approach that uses songs, meditation, ceremonies, and other forms of embodied spiritual practice. In their view, "the transformation of the impacts of sexual, racial and colonial violence on Native women requires unlearning ways of thinking and being that have been etched onto the body" (Young and Nadeau 2005, 13), and thus one must decolonize the body in order to heal.

But what about the students? What do they get out of embodied learning in the classroom? Here, I want to report on three students' written reflections on embodied learning. These women took courses with me during different periods in my own development of embodied learning. Although my overall approach has remained fairly constant over the years, my own thinking and the course title, contents, and format have undergone many modifications. However, what can be gleaned from their writing is how they take up the notion of embodiment creatively in their own lives, thereby demonstrating the risks and possibilities of embodied learning. Their experience and work will be described in chronological order below. As much as possible, I will quote from their own writing in order to let them speak.[8] Even so, I vastly simplify the depth and poignancy of their analyses and narratives.

Si Transken was a student when I first offered the course "Health, Illness and Knowledge of the Body." I was both excited and apprehensive about introducing unconventional, specifically physical, movements in a graduate class. In retrospect, I had vastly underestimated the power of engaging the body explicitly in intellectual pursuit and what this might open up. Thus, Si's paper, "Reclaiming Body Territory," took me completely by surprise, as did the journal I required her to keep. In her paper, she detailed, for the first time, her experience of being sexually and physically abused for over a decade by her father and his friends, and her subsequent healing journey. The work she did in the course was part of this healing process, which involved a tremendous amount of emotional pain and physical discomfort. In the paper, she disclosed that she could not do the movement exercises because her method of survival throughout the abuse was to detach from

---

8 As we will see, the final term paper of one of these students, Si Transken, was subsequently published, and I am able to quote from that (Transken 1995). I have the permission of the other two students to use their names and to quote from their work.

her body; however, she also wrote succinctly and movingly about how she reclaimed her body during the course, which culminated in the writing of her final term paper. Below are excerpts from the conclusion of her paper, which was published in the Canadian Research Institute for the Advancement of Women's Feminist Perspectives series:

> I spent the first half of my life barely existing in my body. I have spent an equal number of years reclaiming my body. The remaining years of life I have available to me will, hopefully, be spent experiencing joy and peace in my body. I am attempting to be an active and vocal reclaimer and maintainer of my territory. One of the horrors of incest is the isolation and sense of aloneness in the world that the victim experiences.
>
> I am trying to reclaim all of my stolen self/body. While daring and reclaiming, I am also bearing witness and offering my testimony as a political act as well as a therapeutic act.
>
> The writing and the sharing of this story has been both excruciating and delightful and it has been an important part of that process of reclaiming. (Transken 1995, 28–29)

I remember clearly one of the questions posed by students in that course: "Are experiences always stored in the body?" My answer was "I think so." Since that time, I have learned a lot about embodiment and embodied learning. Now my answer would be "Absolutely," even when we have no active memory of the experience or event. In offering courses of this nature, I now warn participants about the risks of engaging the body in the learning process and provide resources for counselling and other help should painful memories arise for which they need support. If participants persist and work through their discomfort, the rewards can be satisfying, as Si Transken and Carrie Butcher discovered.

Carrie came into our program as a part-time mature student who had been active in the antiracism movement. She described herself as a "45-year-old woman of Hakka Chinese, African and Scottish descent" who "was born in the former British colony of Trinidad" (Butcher 2009, 2). While she originally returned to school to improve her professional knowledge and skills in organizational change and antiracism efforts, she found herself drawn to courses that focused on health, wellness, and creativity, which included "Embodied Learning and Qi Gong." After taking that course, she went on to enrol in my doctoral-level special topics course "Applications of Embodied Learning." In the beginning, her academic goal was to explore issues of resilience and decolonization of her body. Soon after the course began, her focus became much more practical and immediate: after doctors discovered fast-growing fibroids, she had to decide whether to have a complete hysterectomy.

Carrie's class presentation and her journal, which she continued to keep during her fairly lengthy hospitalization, documented her struggle with the decision. Her term paper (submitted two terms later, because she did undergo surgery) was an examination of how she applied embodied learning processes to prepare for the surgery and to aid in her recovery. In it, she reviewed various TCM, biomedical, and women-centred perspectives on uterine fibroids based on medical and popular writings, and she touchingly and candidly explored the connections among resistance, trauma, illness, and healing. She began the paper with her resistance to writing for an academic grade: "Reviewing my journal entry helped me to acknowledge and accept my resistance to writing about my surgery. . . . I came to see that my resistance to writing was a visceral message that it was time to care for myself before seeking to care for the world (through working with racialized communities)" (Butcher 2009, 5). She quoted from her journal to indicate how she worked through her resistance with the tools she learned from the class:

> Looking within—by this I mean bringing my attention, my consciousness, to my bodily feelings—I became aware of a feeling of resistance to writing followed by judgment of myself for not being able to write, and then a sense of panic. I gently brought my awareness to this energetic pattern of resistance, judgment and panic that had emerged within me. Employing the mindfulness practice of unattached observation, I was able to stand back in my observer self, and simply look at this energetic pattern. In so doing I was able to reframe my embodied inquiry. I reframed the judgmental question *"why can't I just write?"* to a more compassionate and simply curious question. It became *"what is this resistance about?"* This was an important shift, and one which finally allowed me to look at my resistance to writing. (7)

Through journalling and drawing, Carrie transformed fear and resistance into yielding and acceptance, thereby laying the foundation for her process of healing:

In the two days before my surgery I reflected on the transformational possibilities that severing ties with my fibroids and losing my uterus might hold. The image that follows is of a sketch from my new journal, created as I lay in my hospital bed about two days before my surgery. The sketch . . . [developed] into an abstract flower, to my surprise . . . [with] three distinct parts—root system, stalk and petals. (16)

These parts signified different things to Carrie: the root system represented stuck creativity, which was informed by some of the feminist spiritual writing on fibroids (see Northrup 1994) and by her African heritage, among other things. The vine-like stalk symbolized letting go, transformation, and "the body saying no to unhealthy patterns," in addition to ten other attributes (Butcher 2009, 18). At the centre of the petals is the word "possibility." For Carrie, they represent a number of "possibilities offered by the image of the flower head, located at the culmination of a period of illness" (19).

In her integrative paper for "Embodied Learning and Qi Gong," Carly Stasko recounted her resistance to the dominant definition and treatment of cancer and described how she applied the insights gained in the course to her work as a media literacy educator. Several years before she enrolled in the MA program in holistic education and took my course, Carly was diagnosed with Hodgkin's lymphoma, a form of cancer that affects young people. She wrote about how she survived the diagnosis and treatment process:

I began to resist what I saw as oppressive in the language and metaphors of cancer and reclaimed a place of authority for my own embodied wisdom. . . . I did not want to energetically claim the cancer. I saw it instead as a blockage that needed to transform and pass through me. . . . I saw healing in a way that more closely resembled the understandings of Traditional Chinese Medicine, TCM—such that energy flowed through my body in various patterns and that all "things are imbued with interactive qualities and dynamics in their relationships to the things around them" (Kaptchuk and Croucher 1986, p. 17). Through a form of daily mindfulness meditation I was able to . . . "develop an awareness of the corporeal and emotional responses that accompany ideas, opening up the possibility to more completely address their effects" in my life (Orr 2002, p. 492).[9] (Stasko 2009, n.p.)

The course and the work she did for it enabled Carrie to name her experience of recovery and healing and reinvigorated her already creative work in media literacy.

> Through my own process of embodied learning I've had to tune into my inner felt sense of power, energy and wellness, to have the courage to subvert a dominant narrative, and the creativity to generate a new narrative in which I had voice and could feel engaged in a meaningful and empowered way. This experience has reinvigorated my passion for embodied media literacy education because it showed me that processes learned in one context could be applied in unanticipated future ways. . . .
>
> By integrating embodied ways of knowing into media literacy pedagogy new ways of relating to learning and understanding can be established such that wisdom becomes rooted in the *felt sense of the body* so as to *ground a critical awareness* of the concepts that shape our ways of knowing. In this way the two forms of wisdom can become *integrated* through *engaged and embodied action* in the world.

While not all of these authors use the term *decolonization* explicitly, I argue that their analyses and narrations of their experience are concrete examples of decolonization that involves at least four elements: resistance, questioning, reclamation, and transformation (from negative to positive and from margin to centre). This progression, in turn, engages two critical acts: deep reflection and some form of embodied mindfulness practice that (re)integrates body, mind, and spirit.

Increasingly, therefore, I see embodied learning as a form of decolonizing pedagogy (see also Tejeda, Espinoza, and Gutierrez 2003). This contrasts with the common-sense use of the concept of "decolonization" to refer to a political and intellectual project having to do with the reclamation and

---

9 The references are to Ted Kaptchuk and Michael Croucher, *The Healing Arts: A Journal Through the Faces of Medicine* (London: British Broadcasting Corporation, 1986), and to Deborah Orr's "The Use of Mindfulness in Anti-oppressive Pedagogies" (Orr 2002).

reformulation of nationhood (see, for example, Duara 2004). For me, the notion of decolonization dissolves the boundaries between self and collectivity, between the individual and the system. It interrogates how we, as individuals living within and being part of collectivities, reproduce and sustain systems of oppression—the questions addressed by Fanon and Gramsci. Understanding the dissonance between body, mind, and spirit leads me to see that, regardless of whether we are the oppressor or the oppressed, the perpetrator or victim, we reproduce oppression through normalized patterns of behaviour that have developed over time and have become "natural," automatic, and unconscious actions and *ways of being* in the world. Thus, I use the notion of decolonization to indicate the practices in which we can engage to free us from ideas and ideology, on the one hand, and action and behaviour, on the other, that serve as sources of separation. A mindful and reflexive practice such as the incorporation of qigong into the classroom not only has the potential to extend the boundaries of Western knowledge construction but also helps us develop the capacity to transform our own bifurcated and compartmentalized way of being. It therefore holds the promise of facilitating personal as well as social transformation.

Final Question: Is Embodied Learning Interdisciplinary?

As commonly used, the term *interdisciplinary* refers to studies between or among disciplines as they emerged historically in the academy in Western societies. Strictly speaking, then, because TCM and qigong fall outside the disciplinary boundaries of the Euro-American construction of knowledge, my work on embodied learning is not interdisciplinary. However, if one adopts an expanded notion of interdisciplinarity as a crossing of boundaries, then one can say that my notion of an embodied critical pedagogy that combines Eastern mindfulness methods and Western critical analysis falls within the domain of interdisciplinary studies.[10] However, we are still left with the issue of how to distinguish between interdisciplinary, multidisciplinary, and integrated studies. The boundaries of interdisciplinary studies are still indeterminate and contested, and it is finally up to the reader to decide how she or he wishes to take up the ideas shared here.

---

10 All the same, during the symposium at which this essay was first presented, Julie Klein commented that embodied learning is a form of integrative study rather than interdisciplinary study.

References

Beinfield, Harriet, and Efrem Korngold. 1991. *Between Heaven and Earth: A Guide to Chinese Medicine*. New York: Ballantine Books.

Bordo, Susan. 1987. *The Flight to Objectivity: Essays on Cartesianism and Culture*. Albany: State University of New York Press.

Butcher, Carrie. 2009. "Telling My Story: How I Use Qi Gong, Mindfulness Meditation and Journaling in Preparing for a Total Abdominal Hysterectomy." Final paper, AEC 3131, 26 March. Ontario Institute for Studies in Education, University of Toronto.

Cohen, Kenneth S. 1997. *The Way of Qigong: The Art and Science of Chinese Energy Healing*. New York: Ballantine Books.

de Castell, Suzanne, and Mary Bryson, eds. 1997. *Radical In<ter>ventions: Identity, Politics, and Difference/s in Educational Praxis*. Albany: State University of New York Press.

Duara, Prasenjit, ed. 2004. *Decolonization: Perspectives from Now and Then*. London and New York: Routledge.

Fanon, Frantz. 1963. *The Wretched of the Earth*. Translated by Constance Farrington. New York: Grove Press. Originally published as *Les damnés de la terre* (1961).

———. 1967. *Black Skin, White Masks*. Translated by Charles Lam Markmann. New York: Grove Press. Originally published as *Peau noire, masques blancs* (1952).

Foucault, Michel. 1977. *Discipline and Prison*. London: Penguin.

Gramsci, Antonio. 1971. *Selections from the Prison Notebooks*. New York: International.

Gustafson, Diane L. 1998. "Embodied Learning About Health and Healing: Involving the Body as Content and Pedagogy." *Canadian Woman Studies / Le cahiers de la femme* 17(4): 52–55.

Hyde, Maggie, and Michael McGuinness. 1992. *Jung for Beginners*. Cambridge: Icon Books.

Kaptchuk, Ted. 2000. *The Web That Has No Weaver: Understanding Chinese Medicine*. 2nd ed. Chicago: Contemporary Books.

Lawrence, Errol. 1982. "Just Plain Common Sense: The 'Roots' of Racism." In *The Empire Strikes Back: Race and Racism in 70s Britain*, Centre for Contemporary Cultural Studies, University of Birmingham, 95–142. London: Hutchinson.

Marx, Karl, and Friedrich Engels. 1970. *The German Ideology*. New York: International.

McCarthy, Cameron. 1995. "Multicultural Policy Discourses on Racial Inequality in American Education." In *Anti-racism, Feminism and Critical Approaches to*

Education, edited by Roxana Ng, Pat Staton, and Joyce Scane, 21–44. Westport, CT, and London: Bergin and Garvey.

McLaren, Peter. 1995. *Critical Pedagogy and Predatory Culture: Oppositional Politics in a Postmodern Era.* London and New York: Routledge.

Ng, Roxana. 1993. "A Woman Out of Control: Deconstructing Sexism and Racism in the University." *Canadian Journal of Education* 18(3): 139–205.

———. 1995. "Teaching Against the Grain: Contradictions and Possibilities." In *Anti-racism, Feminism, and Critical Approaches to Education,* edited by Roxana Ng, Pat Staton, and Joyce Scane, 129–52. Westport, CT, and London: Bergin and Garvey.

———. 1998. "Is Embodied Teaching and Learning Critical Pedagogy? Some Remarks on Teaching Health and the Body from an Eastern Perspective." Paper presented at the presidential session on Critical Pedagogy and Cultural Difference, American Educational Research Association, San Diego, 13–17 April.

———. 2000. "Revisioning the Body/Mind from an Eastern Perspective: Comments on Experience, Embodiment, and Pedagogy." In *Women's Bodies, Women's Lives: Health, Well-Being, and Body Image,* edited by Baukje Miedema, Janet Stoppard, and Vivienne Anderson, 175–93. Toronto: Sumach Press.

———. 2004. "Embodied Pedagogy: New Forms of Learning." Workshop given in the Department of Sociology, Umea University, Umea, Sweden, 5 May, and presentation at Gavle University College, Gavle, Sweden, 10 May.

———. 2005. "Embodied Pedagogy as Transformative Learning: A Critical Reflection." In *Proceedings of the Canadian Association for the Study of Adult Education (CASAE) 24th Annual Conference,* edited by S. Mojab and H. Nosheen, 155–61. London, ON: University of Western Ontario.

Northrup, Christiane. 1994. *Women's Bodies, Women's Wisdom: Creating Physical and Emotional Health and Healing.* New York: Bantam Books.

Orr, Deborah. 2002. "The Use of Mindfulness in Anti-oppressive Pedagogies: Philosophy and Praxis." *Canadian Journal of Education* 27(4): 477–97.

Reid, Daniel. 1994. *The Complete Book of Chinese Health and Healing.* Boston: Shambhala.

Roman, Leslie G., and Linda Eyre, eds. 1997. *Dangerous Territories: Struggles for Difference and Equity in Education.* New York: Routledge.

Shilling, Chris. 1993. *The Body and Social Theory.* London: Sage.

Stasko, Carly. N. 2009. "Holistic Approaches to Embodied Media Literacy Education." Integrated paper, AEC 1181, 6 March. Ontario Institute for Studies in Education, University of Toronto.

Tejeda, Carlos, Manuel Espinoza, and Kris Gutierrez. 2003. "Toward a Decolonizing Pedagogy: Social Justice Reconsidered." In *Pedagogies of*

Difference: Rethinking Education for Social Justice, edited by Peter Pericles Trifonas, 10–40. New York and London: RoutledgeFalmer.

Transken, Si Chava. 1995. "Reclaiming Body Territory." Feminist Perspectives no. 25. Ottawa: Canadian Research Institute for the Advancement of Women.

Turner, Bryan S. 1991. "Recent Developments in the Theory of the Body." In *The Body: Social Process and Cultural Theory,* edited by Mike Featherstone, Mike Hepworth, and Bryan S. Turner, 1–35. London: Sage.

Young, Alannah Earl, and Denise Nadeau. 2005. "Decolonising the Body: Restoring Sacred Vitality." *Atlantis* 29(2): 13–22.

Zi, Nancy. 1986. *The Art of Breathing.* Toronto and New York: Bantam Books.

2 Embodying Indigenous Resurgence

"All Our Relations" Pedagogy

Alannah Young Leon and Denise Nadeau

We have collaborated for more than a decade in developing a pedagogy that is centred on restoring and facilitating relationships. We foreground Indigenous knowledge systems in both our education and advocacy work, as we continue to grapple with systems of knowledge that are both subjugating and privileged. Our intention has been to work from the wisdom of the body to explore educational tools for building Indigenous-settler relationships that support Indigenous resurgence. We work both inside and outside the academy and have developed a range of curricula and programs for Indigenous front-line workers, university and health institutions, and truth and reconciliation initiatives. In much of this work, we focus on Indigenous knowledge systems and, where appropriate, combine these with dance, somatic education, and expressive art practices.

Our purpose is to facilitate group work that supports the building of respectful relationships and Indigenous resurgence. We understand resurgence as the reaffirmation of a conceptual framework that, in the words of Leanne Simpson (2011, 31–32), "not only maps a way out of colonial thinking by confirming Indigenous lifeways or alternative ways of being in the world" but that ultimately "seeks to dismantle colonialism while simultaneously building a renaissance of mino bimaadiziwin"—that is, the living of a good life in accordance with ancestral teachings. We focus on the multiple interrelationships among relatives, or kin, in which human beings are embedded and on the responsibilities that arise from these relationships, or what we call "kinship relational responsibilities," as well as on the reciprocity implicit in these relationships. In doing so, we are supporting Indigenous lifeways and providing a decolonizing framework that involves the body at multiple levels.

In the opening section below, we describe how we begin our work and how the practice of following protocols sets the stage for embodied knowing that operates from within an Indigenous world view of an interconnected, interdependent universe. We then consider the centrality of ceremonial principles in relationship building and go on to explain how we approach decolonizing the body. In closing, we examine how "all our relations" pedagogy supports resurgence and decolonization.

Protocols: Getting Ready for Knowledge

Alannah. To show respect for the occupied territories of Coast Salish peoples, where I currently live and work, I introduce myself in the hən̓q̓əmin̓əm̓ language (one of the dialects of Halkomelem) when we are in their territories. Language is intimately connected to relationships with lands, waters, and territories, and to our corresponding responsibilities. Local Indigenous protocols remind me that I must acknowledge in whose territory I am situated and to locate where my people are from geographically. I have been a visitor to the unceded and occupied Coast Salish territories since 1990. My Indigenous diaspora and paternal location is as an Anishnabekwe Midewiwin woman. My matrilineal genealogy is Muskeg Inniwak, from the muskeg region located in the heart of Turtle Island, or in the central plain region of North America; I was born for the *amisk dodem*—the beaver clan. I acknowledge my place in Creation through my clan systems and the lifelong responsibility to live together on the land and to continually engage in reciprocal relationships consistent with the spirit of treaty laws. Radical Indigenism characterizes the scholarship within which I locate myself.[1]

---

1 In a review of Eva Marie Garroutte's *Real Indians: Identity and the Survival of Native America* (2003), Daniel Heath Justice (2005, 202) states that "radical Indigenism is posited on a reassertion of the central place of kinship, reciprocity, responsibility, and spirituality within the intellectual frameworks of American Indian scholarship." Our pedagogy focuses on providing embodied tools that link this to land relationships and responsibilities.

My declared social locations indicate my responsibility to Indigenous knowledge, resurgence, and kinship relational responsibilities. This pedagogical approach signals my ongoing commitment to live out the spirit of the treaties and to make visible or to embody concepts such as alternative nationhood-building that focus on sustainable relationships to lands—to live as a good relative so that our future generations can live in peace and prosper.

Denise. My name is Denise Marie Nadeau. I am originally from Québec, raised in Montréal, with family origins and ties in Gespe'gewa'gi, known as the Gaspé Coast, which is the territory of the Mi'gmaq peoples. I am a twelfth-generation Quebecer of French heritage, with some recent Scottish on my father's side and Irish and English on my mother's. There was some intermarriage with the Mi'gmaq on my maternal grandmother's side, however, this was soon forgotten or denied. When I researched my paternal ancestry in terms of colonial relations with the Mi'gmaq, I uncovered sawmill owners, a railroad-building contractor, a priest, an Indian Affairs superintendent, and even a cardinal. These men played a significant role in the material and cultural conditions that contributed to the displacement, impoverishment, and invisibilizing of the Mi'gmaq in the late nineteenth and twentieth centuries on the Gaspé Coast.

I now live as a visitor in the territory of the K'ómoks Nation, which is on the eastern coast of Vancouver Island, on the Salish Sea. I have lived on unceded Coast Salish territory for about thirty years. Over the years, working at the University of British Columbia (UBC) with Alannah, I have developed relationships with some of the peoples of the xʷməθkʷəy̓əm (Musqueam, "where the river grass grows") Nation.

I acknowledge the spirit and laws of treaty relationships; even as I currently live in these unceded territories. I have recently learned about my treaty relationships and responsibilities, defined by my ancestry, to the waters, lands, and peoples of the Gespe'gewa'gi region. For the Mi'gmaq, the treaties were *angugamgew'l*, adding to our relations, and *gisagnutmaqann*, what we agreed to (Mi'gmawei Mawiomi Secretariat 2009, 3). Elder Pnnal, from Gesgapegiag, further clarified the meaning of *angugamgew'l* as "to add in the process of negotiations," and *gisagnutmaqann* as "we have come to an agreement or mutual understanding." The Covenant Chain of

Peace and Friendship Treaties, which were signed in 1725, 1752, 1760–61, 1778, and 1779, were seen as "a way to extend family relations" (15). These covenants were based on the principles of reciprocity and mutuality. I return to Gespe'gewa'gi every year to maintain these relationships. As well, for several years I taught a course in Montréal at Concordia University every second fall called "Indigenous Traditions, Colonialism, and Women." For me, this is one way of living out my responsibilities that are entailed by my settler history in Québec.

This dialogue is about allowing and holding up our differences. Allowing our voices to be distinct is part of being who we really are. I remember Elder Pnnal reminding me that we need to honour ourselves and be honest with who we are if we are going to continue to coexist and work together for survival on this planet. If we erase our difference, which is a real temptation for settlers, we do not allow for the complexity of Indigenous-settler relationships.

Alannah. My decolonizing process involves accessing body wisdom and engaging blood memory and the multiple interdependent relationships it embeds and sustains. A term used by many Indigenous communities, blood memory refers to the knowledge that flows through our bloodlines, knowledge that we inherit from our ancestors and that connects us not only to all those with whom we share community but also to our ancestral lands (see Holmes 2001, 40, 41–44). By grounding us in a shared and living past, blood memory allows for the perpetuation of communal knowledge and traditions, both spiritual and intellectual. Pam Palmater (2011, 218) refers to it as the "deep connections with our past through our ancestors, with our present thorough our families and communities, and to our future through generations yet to come."

I came to the University of British Columbia to explore a master's degree in theatre and got involved with Full Circle First Nations Performance Society. Here, the Spakwus Slumlum Eagle Song Coast Salish Dancers taught us to embody the wisdom of animals. They had us move as animals in packs, and I experienced how the embodiment of animal wisdom reflects a kinship sensibility as well as a collective decolonizing and embodied approach. In effect, I experienced many other possibilities for how I could weave into my life and teaching embodied ways of engaging in the world from the peoples of this territory where I have been living as a guest for over twenty years. I saw the potential for how I could learn more from animals and apply this learning to other contexts, while embodying my responsibility to live my Indigenous clan and kinship teachings. More recently, I have been exploring how to embody relationships with plants, both on unceded and occupied Coast Salish territories and within my homelands. I travel home every year and embody my relationship to the plant medicines and engage in the ceremonial responsibilities for maintaining these relationships.

Since the mid-1980s, I have worked in the academy, developing decolonizing and culturally competent place-based pedagogies. I teach a course called "Cultural Competency and Protocols in Approaching Traditional Healing Modalities in Aboriginal Health" at the University of British Columbia. At the Justice Institute of British Columbia, I teach Aboriginal Focusing-Oriented Therapy. In these courses, I focus on decolonizing our health education practices by using Aboriginal holistic therapeutic modalities that teach people to reconnect to the land through the physical body, to begin to reclaim the senses, and to explore what it means to embody the term *all my relations*. As well, I have been working with Elder Jeri Sparrow, xʷməθkʷəy̓əm, and with the UBC Faculty of Land and Food Systems, Indigenous Research Partnerships and the Centre for Sustainable Food Systems to develop holistic practices on the UBC farm.

Denise and I met in a dance-therapy training program more than seventeen years ago. We came together so we could continue to deepen an embodied practice that reflected a commitment to our own ongoing decolonization process and our joint and separate teaching. In effect, my intention has been to embody the teachings and to develop a collective leadership of folks who could engage in this kind of work.

Denise. Our writing process around some of our earlier articles (Young and Nadeau 2005; Young and Nadeau 2006) was jagged as we tried to find a common language and meanings. Alannah had knowledge of Indigenous theory and practices; I was less aware of my colonial positioning, but I had more writing and activist experience. So we mentored each other. This dialogue represents the more balanced way we work together now. While my world view has become more Indigenized, the differences in our social locations, ancestry, and history has allowed for creative collaboration and sparking off each other. The dialogue format also illustrates more clearly where Euro-Western and Indigenous knowledge systems converge and construct each other.

My academic background has been in Christian theology and ministry. I identify as a Christian and hold the position that I need to take responsibility for the ongoing role of the Christian churches in the colonial project. For more than a decade, I have engaged with postcolonial feminist theology and worked in the interfaith arena, with a significant part of my focus being the impact of European Christianity on Indigenous traditions. After decades of engagement with Indigenous colleagues and friends, I situate myself with those whose involvement in interfaith relationships is connected to action for interfaith justice and the development of revolutionary spiritualties.

Over the years, I noticed that when I adopted a critical race-feminist analysis, which I viewed through an anticolonial lens, I was still operating out of a Euro-Western dualistic framework, even as I critiqued it. This is my critique of most postcolonial theory: it is still caught in oppositional dynamics with colonialism at its centre; it still isn't anticolonial or decolonizing. My intention with this work has been to develop a pedagogy that operates within an Indigenous world view and provides an embodied experience, a lived experience, of a cosmology that challenges both the material and social construction of colonialism. An "all our relations" pedagogy articulates, for me, the level of interconnection necessary to challenge imperial relations at all levels—body, mind, emotions, and spirit.

Identifying our social location and genealogy in relation to land is a first step in a decolonizing process. This helps us to know that there are particular knowledges and peoples in relationship within specific places. A second step is knowledge of local protocols. Engaging with Indigenous protocols informs both the process and product of our work. We braid them together here to share our experience in working with local Indigenous nations. Protocols help us to facilitate a respectful relationship with our implicit knowledge of where we are, what we value, and how we engage with other nations in whose territories we are visitors. Protocol principles inform how we engage in our homelands.

Denise. I remember when we were preparing a workshop on Truth and Reconciliation that was hosted by the United Church on the west side of Vancouver in xʷməθkʷəy̓əm territory. Alannah and I were following protocol and meeting with Elder Larry Grant, xʷməθkʷəy̓əm, to ask him to help with the work—to see if he was interested in contributing to the design. After he had agreed to participate and accepted our gift, I suggested that we do an introduction exercise in which we ask each person to identify his or her social location, including race and class background, and in whose territory she or he was living. Larry looked at me, chuckled, and then said, "You mean you want them to say where their granny is from."

I like to tell this story because it triggered my awareness of how understanding identity is different in European and Indigenous world views. A common trope of the dominant culture is to introduce yourself in terms of your work and, in academic and politically informed circles, in terms of your social location. In Indigenous cultures, what is important is to know the relationship network of which you are part, including your ancestry, genealogical lineage, and the community and land/territory to which you belong. Even the names of your family members are significant, as is that of your clan or house.

I now incorporate this "granny" activity into my university classes. I ask students to form small groups in relation to the four directions and to identify their family ancestry. (If they are adopted or fostered, we ask them to speak of the family to which they feel a connection now.) I ask them to identify the territories in which they grew up and in which they are now living. For students who grew up outside Canada, we ask them to identify the Indigenous territory of their homelands. I provide a map of the Indigenous language groups and nations of Turtle Island before 1492. This allows students to begin the process of seeing themselves as part of a web of relationships and connections and of understanding how the individualism of the dominant culture supports erasure of these connections, especially to land and place. The "granny" activity reveals how the dominant narrative of the land called Canada obscures the occupation of Indigenous homelands. It locates specific nations within specific territories and allows us to use this moment both to challenge pan-Indian notions of Aboriginality and to address the politics of naming—that is, how Indigenous peoples have been called Indians, First Nations, Aboriginal peoples, and so on to undermine and erase how each tradition is connected to a specific language, land, and place.

I remember hearing the late Mohawk scholar Patricia Monture comment that it is in white supremacy's interest to erase Indigenous history and ancestry. Educator David Greenwood has pointed out that the erasure of Indigenous presence on land and the history of the land is an intentional part of the placelessness of Euro-Western schooling. It is in the interest of the disembodying culture of global capitalism to undermine people's relationship to land and place so that the "breaking down of ties to home communities" can further the exploitation and extraction of human and natural resources (Greenwood 2009, 4). Greenwood's focus is on rural education, and though he calls for education about white colonization of Indigenous lands, he fails to mention how the capitalist value of "private property" as sacrosanct ensures that it is Native, not settler, land that is exploited. Part of our agenda is to expose settler complicity in the ongoing dispossession of Indigenous land.

Alannah. When we work with local Indigenous knowledge holders, it is important to follow their protocols and use oral citation as well as written citation to model mutually beneficent collaboration. In introducing an animal relations activity that we use in some workshops, for example, I acknowledge Bob Baker, from the Squamish Nation, and its youth group. I then indicate my clan locations, which inform my roles and responsibilities and are a signal to others that I know how I am related in a collective context.

I see my role as facilitating relationships with local community members and the Elders and the traditional knowledge keepers who are respected by community members and recognized as holders of cultural knowledge. As I learn from the ways in which the knowledge holders conceptualize and embody their roles and responsibilities, I deepen my understandings of my own genealogy, roles, and responsibilities. By locating myself as visitor, I look for ways to be a good relative. At a very basic level, to be ready for knowledge means that I first support local Indigenous initiatives. I learn how to support the ways in which knowledge holders conceptualize, embody, and transfer knowledge. I also learn how their particular pasts inform the present in the specific places where I am a visitor. When it is appropriate, I participate by using my privilege to support local Indigenous community initiatives.

Accordingly, in our work we consult as much as possible with local Elders in developing our programs. We do not believe in the practice of inviting a local knowledge holder only to give a welcome—an Elder is not simply an add-on or an afterthought. We learn from them along the way; our job is to make space for their voices, and we role model giving credit to them in the ways that are accepted and understood by both cultures. The practice of welcoming participants to a territory must always be accompanied by teachings from the Elders on the theme being explored. In our work with the LE,NONET Project (2010) at the University of Victoria, we developed and tested a curriculum with help from a team of Elders who guided us in following Coast and Straits Salish protocols from that region. These included incorporating and making space, as a pedagogical principle, for the Coast Salish witnessing practice; the use of a translator to translate the speaker's words from Hul'q'umi'num' into English; and the singing of appropriate public songs from that territory.

Denise. Sometimes when we are new to a territory, it takes time to form relationships with local knowledge keepers. I share my experience at Concordia University, where I taught a course called "Indigenous Traditions, Colonialism, and Women" for several years. Applying some of the local protocols was, at first, more difficult for me in Montréal because I had not yet formed relationships. I was able to bring in speakers through my relationships in Mi'gmaq and Anishinaabe territories, but it was critical that I teach the importance of respecting local protocols. Initially, I began the class by acknowledging the traditional territory of the Kanien'kehá:ka (Mohawk) peoples in whose territory Montréal is located. I briefly introduced myself, my ancestry, and the territory from which I come and that in which I presently live as a visitor. I explained how the practice of acknowledging territory affirms the connections among land, spirit, and culture and underlines the fact that the territory is a homeland that is occupied and, in many cases, unceded. As my relationships developed with the folks from the territory, I was able to incorporate Mohawk speakers into the first class and, eventually, the last class. These speakers welcomed the class to their territory; offered in Kanien'kéha and/or English the Ohenton Karihwatehkwen, the welcome address of the Haudenosaunee people; and shared some teachings from their tradition.[2]

Ceremony: Renewing Relationships

In modelling enactment of local protocols, we demonstrate a form of relational paradigm. We affirm that we are in relationship with the land and people of the local territory and that we have a responsibility to these relationships. Behind this is a larger commitment that frames our work—in acknowledging these relationships, we are affirming that the centre of our pedagogy is the well-being of the land, community, and future generations, within accountability to Indigenous laws. We name the practice of protocol principles and the affirmation of relationships as "getting ready for knowledge," because it establishes the relational framework in which we will learn. Throughout the work, we continue to focus on the well-being of land, community, and future generations, and this moves us out of a deconstructive agenda into a constructive one where we invite participants into a positive way of being. The role of ceremonial principles, then, becomes critical in our work, as it develops and affirms this relational way of being.

Denise. I learned about the meaning of ceremony through the discipline of attending specific ones over an extended period of time. Attending ceremony is not a drop-in activity but rather a commitment to relationship over time. I have attended the sweat lodge ceremony at First Nation House of Learning at UBC fairly regularly for over twelve years. It is an open teaching lodge that you, Alannah, have taken leadership in, and I felt welcomed there as someone active in interfaith work. But I quickly discovered that to commit to being there meant showing up in snow, rain, sleet, or hail, and often very early in the morning. It was only through repetition and through showing up with my body that I gradually developed a different relationship with the elements and plants—the fire, the water, the rocks, the cedar—and the people who were part of the ceremony. Slowly, I began to experience in

---

2 I acknowledge Orenda Boucher Curotte and Kahsennenhawe Sky-Deer for their contributions of Kanien'kehá:ka teachings and history to the course.

an embodied way that humans aren't the centre of the universe but rather just one part. I began to get a glimmer of what the expression "all our relations," said at the end of a prayer, song, or ceremony, might mean.

Alannah. For me, going to ceremony was primarily initially a responsibility. Then I realized that the ceremony looks after me. Ceremony helps me to renew my relationships and reminds me of the corresponding responsibilities I have to maintain these ceremonial renewal practices because they help my overall well-being. The ceremonies connect me to the seasons, the moon cycles, and the more-than-human beings. In effect, the ceremonies help me to decolonize my mind and body because I am reclaiming my relationship connections on multiple levels. This is my treaty responsibility—this is how I understand living the teachings or embodying the laws of reciprocal relationships.

Denise. I learned that ceremony involves the work of preparation, the work of setting up and taking down before and after, and the cleaning up after the feast that usually goes with it; all tasks are equally a part of ceremony. I remember my first sweat in 1990, when I was constantly looking at my watch, unhappy about how long it was taking, and leaving even before the feast. Later, I learned to put aside a whole day or series of days. As I began to engage with Indigenous colleagues in other milieus, I slowly shifted to the understanding that all of life is ceremony; all life involves enacting and recommitting to the rights and responsibilities of relationship. That insight affects how I teach. I now see the preparation for a course or workshop as ceremony, and I recognize the importance of bringing prayer and good intentions to all aspects of teaching and learning. I have had to acknowledge my responsibilities to the context in which I grew up in Québec, as well as to the peoples in whose territories I am living now—hence, my returning home to teach, to take seriously my responsibility to restore relationships with family and the land, and to support the Mi'gmaq struggles in Gespe'gewa'gi as part of ceremony.

Another critical turning point was when I was attending a Midewiwin ceremony in Wisconsin with you. You invited me so that I could be a witness and support you, but also so I could start to understand the level of embodiment in these ceremonies. I started asking you all these questions about what was going on. I remember you saying, "I can't answer you now. This is about group mind." Of course, I didn't get it then, but when I returned for the third time, again attending as a witness, and was there with a first timer who started asking me questions, I couldn't answer because I too had moved into group state of being. For me, these collective embodied states are where the spirit world is being accessed.

One challenge has been to translate some of the principles of ceremony into workshops and classrooms; we acknowledge that many ceremonies are site specific and not transferable to other contexts, so our task has become the exploration of how we can embody ceremonial principles in a workshop or classroom without "doing" a ceremony.

Alannah. One of the foundations of this work was developed when I did some informal research with the UBC student service unit called the First Nation Longhouse Community to develop the Longhouse Teachings information sheet.[3] I was asked to explore with students, staff, Elders, and child care workers what makes a healthy house or community. The Longhouse Community held a number of talking circles over two years, and we organized the findings. We developed a longhouse leadership program to reflect the values articulated by founding director Dr. Verna Kirkness, who, with Dr. Ray Barnhardt, wrote the seminal article on what is known as the Four Rs (Respect, Relevance, Reciprocity, Responsibility) of Higher Education (Kirkness and Barnhardt 1991). Respect, relevance, reciprocity, and responsibility are principles that guide our relational work at the First Nations House of Learning. As well, we work with Stó:lō scholar and educator Jo-ann Archibald's (Q'um Q'um X'iem) "storywork", research, values, and principles. Archibald (2008, 38) stresses that the "skills, knowledge, understanding and perhaps insight gained over a lengthy period must be shared in a manner that incorporates cultural respect, responsibility, reciprocity and reverence."

Denise. We always arrange seating in a circle. As Celia Haig-Brown (2010, 940) articulates so well, "the circle interrupts the assumptions of those other

---

3 *Longhouse Teachings: Respect, Relationships, Responsibility, and Reverence.* N.d. Pamphlet. Vancouver, BC: First Nations House of Learning. http://fnsp.arts.ubc.ca/files/2013/04/LonghouseTeachings2007.pdf.

heuristics—the line and the box, dualities and binaries." At different points and with different activities, we ask participants to reflect on their relationship to the seasons, to plant medicines, the cycles of life, the elements, the directions, the animals, and the ancestors, and we explore how they can embody and restore their connections to these relatives.

We state in the first session that racist, sexist, and colonial statements will not be tolerated. In addition to saying what's not acceptable, we say what is—that we expect them to demonstrate their learning within the framework of respect, relevance, reciprocity, and responsibility. I add reverence as a guideline, since I find that it helps students to know they need to treat all beings with reverence, including the person opposite them with whom they might disagree. I have chosen to respond to racism in the classroom with an I-statement that challenges what has been said or provides another perspective, without shaming or disrespecting the person. As well, I encourage moments of silence in the class and stress "deep observation" and listening. Lorna Williams (2008), a Lil'wat educator, explains how these latter skills support self-generated and self-motivated learning in Indigenous ways of knowing.

Alannah. By intentionally engaging with the values of respect, relevance, reciprocity, and responsibility and demonstrating how we embody these values, we can rearticulate our values in everyday acts of discipline. This is essential in living *mino bimaadiziwin*—the good lifeway, following our laws; the everyday acts that beckon us to sing the teachings, to embody, to live, to wear the teachings (Simpson and Manitowabe 2013). For me, the ceremonial principles call us to wake up in responsible and mutually beneficial ways to the connections inherent in our Indigenous knowledge lifeways, traditions and laws.

Denise. I'd like to mention here what is called the "spiritual bypass" in some psychotherapeutic circles. This refers to engaging in spiritual practices to avoid dealing with any painful situation (Masters 2010). What is usually bypassed in settler-colonial communities is doing the embodied work of processing the reality of one's historical and psychological relationship to colonialism. Many non-Indigenous individuals, especially white settlers, seek to experience Indigenous spirituality, specifically ceremony, without taking responsibility for the fact they are benefiting from the dispossession of Indigenous peoples. This is why it is important that we teach and approach daily living as ceremony and speak to living the values and traditions in daily practices of resurgence (Corntassel 2012). We encourage both white settlers and those from racialized groups to look at how they may be complicit in the social, economic, and political structures that dispossess Indigenous peoples. As Andrea Smith (2006, 89) argues, "It is not enough to understand or describe Native religious experience; it is also necessary to advocate for the survival of Native spiritual practices and an end to colonialism." The challenge for us has been to move people out of an intellectual understanding of colonialism to one that involves the realization that they need to make material changes in their lives. These can range from using one's privilege to unsettle colonial structures, to financially and physically supporting Indigenous land defenders, to, for those who have this option, giving back land.

Decolonizing the Body: Embodying the Teachings

While we consider all our work to be about decolonization, we intentionally involve the body and body awareness as central to the decolonization process. We have adapted some somatic techniques developed within Euro-Western psychotherapies, and we integrate them, when appropriate, with cultural teachings. At the same time, we draw on the reality that Indigenous cultural practices are embodied. Our intention is to provide participants with an introduction to a lived experience of embodying the teachings.

Denise. In bringing the body into our teaching, we move beyond what some call conscientization, which is the process of developing a critical awareness of oppression. It is easy to "facilitate settler innocence" by falling into the trap of what Tuck and Yang (2012, 9) call "decolonization as a metaphor." We are aware that changing one's thinking is not enough. Accordingly, we work at several levels: we include the spirit realm, we operate within the political project of Indigenism, and we prioritize Indigenous laws. For me, Indigenism is about Indigenous nationhood. Scott Lyons (2010, 64) defines it as a global political project that focuses on "promoting indigenous culture in opposition to neoliberalism and 'settler culture'" and "on ecological sustainability, collective land rights, the primacy of Indigenous ways of knowing and Indigenous values, and the political virtue of respectful co-existence." This project is contained within the framework of relationship. We believe that we are all in this together, that we have a responsibility to Indigenous law and values, and we strive to create what Willie Ermine (2007) calls the "ethical space of engagement" where two different world views meet.

The body cannot be separated from the whole person, so challenging and transforming the colonial project requires body awareness. Indigenous learning is holistic—body, mind, spirit, emotions—and includes working through all generations, as well as through the individual, family, community, and nation. We intentionally facilitate body awareness of both relationship and disconnection as central to this holistic learning.

Alannah. We start with one of the basic principles of dance therapy—if you move differently, you will think differently: that is, you can transform yourself through movement. This movement principle also applies to ceremonies. Ceremonies like the Sundance and the Midewiwin include embodied movement that has helped to transform and deepen my relationships to family, lands, and communities. My intention for our work has been to explore transformation through movement and to incorporate principles that work in multiple contexts.

Denise. I remember Stl'atl'imx Elder Gerry Oleman saying that the ceremonies that have been recovered from the past were developed in a time before colonialism and that additional tools are sometimes needed to address the terrible fragmenting impacts of colonialism on the body, psyche, and community. In our wellness group work, we incorporate resource development and presence skills drawn from Euro-Western somatic psychotherapy practices. Resource development involves building on the strengths and resilience of participants, as well as creating new approaches, some of which focus on enhancing our relationships with animals and finding an internal anchor or a specific place in nature that is experienced and felt in the body. Presence skills are specific body-based ways of increasing one's awareness of sensation and circulation of energy in the body in order to help process feelings and increase feelings of interconnection. The main function of these skills is to bring participants into the present moment and to help them become aware of their connection to place and people in the here and now. Guided imagery, music, drawing, and movement are some of the tools we use. These tools help us to express and enhance our connections with animals, stories, memories, or places. Many diverse cultural stories inform both the individual and the collective learning experience.

Alannah. This decolonizing embodied work includes reflecting back, through structured drawing and movement activities, participants' reconnection to their personal and collective relationships. For example, their dreams may be drawn as symbolic representations or expressed as a series of words strung together. These creative expressions are then grounded in the body through a participant's movement, with the rest of the group reflecting her physical movements back to her. If someone has drawn and danced an animal figure that has visited her in a dream, we give feedback to acknowledge that person's own self-determined bodily wisdom and interconnected relationships. We strive for a balance between relationship with self and relationship with others—developing our own self-determination in relationship to the collective is part of our responsibilities.

Denise. Another example is when we invite participants to connect the presence skill of centring by using belly button teachings in their respective traditions. This activity involves exercises that support the embodied exploration of the body's physical centre, followed by a sharing of navel and belly button teachings. We are careful to be respectful when participants are unable to share specific teachings for protocol reasons. We explore the relationship between the belly button, the umbilical cord, and the land, which, combined with a felt sense of a physical centre, provides a resource in the investigation of relational ways of being. This embodied reclaiming of relationship is decolonizing because the reference point is internally sourced and adds multiple cultural dimensions to our pedagogy of connecting.[4]

---

4 We acknowledge Meri Marshall (Māori), Norma Rose Point (xʷməθkʷəẏəm [Musqueam]), Lorna Williams (Lil'wat), and Evelyn Voyageur (Kwakwaka'wakw) for sharing with us their teachings about this intimate connection between the land and our bodies.

Alannah. Sharing some of my cultural practices reflects this pedagogical process and my ongoing understanding of how the body demonstrates our relationship to creation. The placenta and umbilical cord represent the Earth, which is our mother, and our connection to the moon, our grandmother, Nokomis. In my territory, my mother buried my daughter's placenta at the base of a tree in the area where I fasted as part of my coming-of-age ceremony. Such an embodied act signifies that we know how we are related to the Earth—and that the Earth is the mother that sustains life. The placenta feeds and nourishes us, so it also shows us our interdependent relationship with the plants, animals, and elements. Elder Norma Rose Point, xʷməθkʷəy̓əm (Musqueam), says that the MuXwuye—the belly button teachings—tell us about relationship and responsibility to Creation. They are very similar to my cultural understanding of the placenta as mapping the universe or stars. Many of our ceremonies are designed to demonstrate our relationship to Creation. In connecting or mapping these relationships, we are performing everyday acts of resurgence. I think one of the strengths of our work is how we make the transition from the individual to the collective.

Denise. This reminds me of Temitope Adefarakan's Yoruba teachings. In her chapter in this book, she describes how Yoruba "worldsense" challenges the Western understanding of the self by integrating individual and collective identity. She describes how the individual's body, mind, and spirit or soul is integrated and how one's integrated being is collectively connected and anchored in one's community and cosmology; there is a balance and unity among ancestors, the living, and the unborn. Like Temitope, our work is to explore pedagogical approaches that serve to develop embodied awareness that one is part of this web of relations, of the collective.

For me, part of the work of decolonizing the body involves transforming the theoretical bases of individualism that shape relationships in the dominant culture, in which autonomy is valued more than relationship. Underpinning individualism is the concept of the biological body, which is a unique historical construction of the past three hundred years in the West and, as Frédérique Apffel-Marglin (2011, 141) notes, is linked "to the separations among the realms of nature, the semiotic and the sacred." This conception of the solid body feeds the notion of the autonomous sovereign individual, which "necessarily makes of the individual one who dominates both non-human nature as well as those who do not fit its mold" (139–40). The deconstruction of the biological body is part of the task of decolonization.

Accordingly, we are building people's felt sense of connection to their relations, and in this way, we are moving out of individualism. We can begin to counter the impacts of the colonial past and present from an "all our relations" framework. Distorted family patterns, cultural violence and alienation, and oppression and dominance in relationships need to be resolved in a framework that is holistic—that includes not only mind, body, spirit, and emotion but also individual, family, community, land, and nation.

We don't often use the word *trauma* in our work because it frequently serves to pathologize victims and to individualize collective pain. In much of our work, our intention is to provide skills and resources that give a sense of inner authority, a positive sense of self, and to increase choices for individuals whose experiences of racist, sexist, and colonial violence have created self-destructive patterns. We teach embodiment practices and presence skills or use tools like the Life/Art Process (Halprin 2002) because we are supporting the ability to connect with relations in the present and to avoid getting caught up in the drama of one's individual story.[5] So we use the development of body-based skills to provide a bridge between individual and collective responsibility.

Alannah. We have created a workshop called "Moving with Water," the goal of which is to deepen participants' interconnection with and sense of responsibility to water, both to the water within our bodies and the watersheds around us. We begin with a welcome from people from the local territories, demonstrating the pedagogical principle of making their teachings central to the workshop. Then we open with a water song and teachings about water from my Anishinaabeg tradition, followed by teachings from Denise's tradition.

---

5 The Tamalpa Life/Art Process is a movement-based expressive arts practice that combines dance, visual art, and creative writing to explore and access the wisdom of the mental, physical, emotional, and spiritual body. "Tamalpa Life/Art Process," *Tamalpa Institute*, 2011, http://www.tamalpa.org/about/hlap.html.

Denise. We then provide an embodied experience of water's functions in our bodies. We do this by having participants move and dance with the rhythms of the different fluid systems in the body—the venous and arterial blood systems, the lymph system, the cellular and interstitial fluids, the synovial and cerebral spinal fluids. We describe the Blue Ecology water cycle articulated by Gitxsan artist and geologist Michael Blackstock (2013), which encompasses the movement of water between humans and the nonhuman world and includes five principles to support the protection of water: water as spirit, harmony, respect, unity, and balance. These principles concretize our connection to the waters outside of us and our option of listening to and respecting water. We can also choose to move more fluidly in our lives through accessing the water systems in our bodies.

Using the Life/Art Process, we have participants explore and listen for a message from a water body with which they have a relationship. This is done through drawing it, dancing their drawing, and then bringing to the group a movement phrase and message that represents their water body. In the final phase of the workshop, we bring participants together in a collective water ritual and dance. Here, we are drawing on the performative function of ritual, thus contributing to protecting the water at the level of the spirit realm. Often, we support group members to bring their movement piece, or performance ritual, to a public action to protect water. Inherent in this approach is the belief that, as relatives of water, we have obligations and responsibilities to the spirit of water and that our relationship to water is about more than a human right.

Alannah. What is decolonizing in this process is that we are affirming our interconnection with place and watersheds/water bodies. In this, we are supporting the experience of water as spirit enhancing and as kin. We are also inviting participants to see and listen to water bodies as living beings that need their own harmony and balance. Here, we challenge the colonial pattern of assuming that one knows best about the water. In effect, teaching people to see and to embody the resources available from the nonhuman relations has been, for me, a form of resurgence. For example, I continue to explore how I can remain connected to the waters through local language, ceremony, and song; what it means to live in the places where salt water meets fresh water; and how I can learn about this relationship together with local Indigenous knowledge holders. The daily practice of singing to the water, I believe, will help me, on my own terms, to map the paths that flow out of decolonization toward community regeneration while embodying respect for all the relatives who live in particular places.

Denise. This embodiment work has greatly aided my own decolonization journey. Much of antiracism and anti-oppression theory and practice, as well as critical whiteness theory, is experienced solely at the cognitive level by those with privilege. This is often accompanied by guilt, shame, anger, or a sense that one has "got it". and a belief that one can rise above it, now that one "knows." But translating that theory into embodied practice is difficult. Not only is the body a cipher or representation of one's privilege or lack of it, but the psychological processes inherent in colonial and racist attitudes are inscribed in the body.

In the work I have been doing in the past decade, I have been concerned to unmask the white helper—and in particular, the white helper woman (Nadeau 2005). As Daniel Heath Justice (2005, 144) has noted,

> The more superficial currents of liberal activism are posited on a model of "uplift"—that is, the idea that the downtrodden must be lifted up to the social status of the privileged but ostensibly sympathetic activist-observer. In such a model, there's no reflection on whether or not the observer's status quo standards hold any appeal for anyone else and no thought that those standards and values might be considered dangerous or even corrosive to those being "helped."

Not only must the notion of helper be dropped, but so must the subtle "one-up" position that is part of the one-up/one-down dynamic of unequal power relations. The "one-up" position of the helper can be expressed bodily in a moving out of inner awareness, losing contact with one's physical core or centre, and a hardening of muscles when constantly making judgments of the "other." The "one-down" position, which is often that of feeling like a victim, is lived in the body—in the shallow breath of someone who is always under siege and has to be vigilant.

I appreciate the description of the white helpers' "quick move to action" that is so well described in Randelle Nixon and Katie MacDonald's chapter in this book. They call for white settlers to look at the implications of their own affective relationship to the colonial project and to question the impulse to help. We have noted that sometimes white settlers also respond to decolonizing education with guilt and feeling bad about being white. Guilt is a form of disassociation and an indulgence of the privileged. Rather than a feeling of genuine sorrow, which can precede the desire to act to change things, the person mired in guilt experiences an energetic logjam in the body. In medieval Christian times in Europe, an embodied response of deep pain and sorrow in the recognition of one's complicity in evil was called compunction. Unless we allow ourselves to feel compunction and the pain of our complicity as ongoing beneficiaries of colonialism, we will either feel powerless or continue to be part of the problem. Compunction can lead to action based in compassion rather than the paralysis of guilt. As James Perkinson, a theologian of whiteness, states, "It is ultimately a matter of learning to live creatively out of one's own diverse genealogy and experiment with one's sense of embodiment gracefully—against the dominating structures and conforming powers of white supremacy that have already conscripted one's body for their service" (quoted in Budden 2009, 5).

Denise. I like how Nlaka'pamux lawyer Ardith Walkem (2007, 28), writing on water rights, quoted a Nlaka'pamux Elder who described the newcomers as famished: "newcomers never could stop eating away at the waters, at the trees, at the fish . . . they never feel full or satisfied." The colonial mindset supports a body caught up in grasping at the world—what we would call a developmental movement that is not completed—instead of allowing itself to receive, digest, and recognize fullness. I associate this with what I see as a gaping hole in the identity of whiteness. Whiteness constructs the autonomous self around hierarchies of comparison as opposed to a relational interconnected self. As Beenash Jafri (2013, 73) has noted, the desire of racialized subjects to be included in the colonial project, always "limited by processes of perpetual social, political and cultural misrecognition," complicates this understanding, yet alludes to how the embodied category of desire is central to settler colonialism.

Alannah. Disembodiment is reinforced through the colonial social institutions of religion, education, and the mass media. To embody connections is decolonizing only if the process is ongoing and is part of a political challenge to these structures. It takes commitment and practice, and for me, it is not enough to talk or write about it. So we structure our pedagogy in ways that build awareness, teach movement and resource development, and highlight the conscious intention of constructing relations and creative collective expression in the face of unjust structures. This includes supporting local community initiatives and taking the resource skills to the streets in order to support social movements such as Idle No More, Water Walks, and land reclamations.

Solidarity and Decolonization

Alannah. Our intention with this work is always to point a way toward action and building relationships for justice. Let's go back to the workshop we did for two United Churches—Ryerson and Knox—in the area of Vancouver that is situated in xʷməθkʷəy̓əm territory. This workshop about truth and reconciliation was an example of working together with local Indigenous Elders. We facilitated the building of relationship between the settlers and local nations through inviting Indigenous knowledge keepers Larry Grant, from xʷməθkʷəy̓əm, and Gerry Oleman, from Stl'atl'imx. These Elders each provided information about and told stories of the land around this neighbourhood and Vancouver that challenge the local "authoritative" narratives about those particular places. This allowed the participants to see the local land and relationships in a different way and to understand how the land has been occupied.

Denise. We then introduced an animal relations activity that challenged the non-Aboriginal participants' understanding of reconciliation. In this activity, each of the four directions in the room contained an image of an animal common to the xʷməθkʷəy̓əm territory in which we were working—an eagle, a deer, a snake, and a whale. We numbered off participants, placing them in four groups, each group with a different animal. First, we asked participants to share a story from their lives about their relationship with that animal. The Indigenous participants were able to share, in their small groups, cultural teachings about their animal. Then we invited people to embody their animal—to get into its skin in order to sense how it lives in the world. We next invited the animals to come together and explore how they related as a group—the whales to form a pod, the snakes to find their lair, the deer to move together as a family, and the eagles to fly in the same space. Each group performed for the other three, who witnessed in silence and then shared what they had observed and experienced. We asked participants to reflect on what they had learned about their animal and what wisdom it might contribute to the process of reconciliation.

In terms of the larger workshop, what was significant for me about this process was that we were focusing on the building of local relationships between settlers and the xʷməθkʷəẏəm as a crucial piece in a truth and reconciliation process.

Alannah. Later, we were able to build on the relationships made in this workshop by inviting the participants and others we had worked with to support c̓əsnaʔəm. This is an hən̓q̓əmin̓əm̓ term that refers to right relationships; it describes the name of a burial site and the call to support the xʷməθkʷəẏəm xwmuthkwey'um, Musqueam's aim to protect a sacred burial ground and heritage site from condo development (Boxberger 2007; Roy 2010).[6] Supporting resurgence, for me, includes restoring rightful relationships with local Indigenous peoples—just as the place name indicates. The struggle to recover c̓əsnaʔəm went on for several months and involved both a peace camp near the site and pressure on government. The non-Indigenous people who supported the camp were asked for specific forms of solidarity, such as letters of support, food, or presence at actions and at the camp. Our involvement in supporting this struggle was based on the long-term relationships we had developed with some of the xʷməθkʷəẏəm people.

Denise. This raises the issue for me of how we understand "Indigenous solidarity activism," a term I have trouble with since it takes the focus off the colonizers. The arena of non-Indigenous peoples supporting Indigenous struggles is a complex one to manoeuvre, whether the non-Indigenous are from European settler stock or are migrants of colour with a similar history of racism and colonialism. I agree with Zainab Amadahy (2010) that we need to move to a relationship framework in order to work together to support the sovereignty of all peoples: "Understanding the world through a Relationship Framework . . . we don't see ourselves, our communities, or

6 For information on the site and its history, see "c̓əsnaʔəm," *Musqueam: A Living Culture,* 2011, http://www.musqueam.bc.ca/c̓əsnaʔəm.

our species as inherently superior to any other, but rather see our roles and responsibilities to each other as inherent to enjoying our life experiences."

If we operate within an Indigenous framework of relations, we have responsibilities and obligations, such as treaty obligations, that are reciprocal. All of us, not just activists, need to engage with Indigenous legal traditions—that is, the Indigenous laws that are unique to each language group and territorial grouping. These traditions guide governance, family life, and relationship with the land and its creatures, as well as trade and relationships with other nations (Borrows 2010). Indigenous legal traditions were what guided the Indigenous leaders who signed peace and friendship treaties with the French and English. To understand our roles and responsibilities, we need to know the values and laws of the Indigenous lands that we occupy as uninvited visitors.

Alannah. This decolonizing embodied practice maps a way out of colonial thinking by affirming Indigenous lifeways while building a collective focus on what it means to live out, or embody, the spirit of the original treaty relationships. As Aimée Craft (2013, 92) notes: "The inaakonigewin, relationships, are strong indicators of normative expectations and obligations that exist between parties . . . and are based in equality and profound respect for all parts of creation." She goes on to explain that "the core purpose of treaty was to create relationships—not to cede land" (114). Relationships are understood as reciprocal and are based in kinship responsibilities (Justice 2005). Our approach and processes allow us the tools to explore diverse ways to embody both the spirit of treaty relationship with the peoples of these lands and the nonhuman relationships.

We seek to contribute to resurgence projects by striving to reflect what Indigenous terms and concepts mean in present-day contexts. By placing reciprocal relationships, for example, at the centre of political action to protect land and water, both individual and collective movements ensure the continuity of life and the sustenance of the lands (Young 2012). In retraining our senses to remember how we are related to the rest of creation, we provide an intervention that seeks to decolonize the body's sense of disconnection and provide an entry point to the principle, within Anishinaabeg legal tradition, of *nindinawemaganidog*—of interpenetration and interdependence. As James Sinclair (2013, 105) explains,

Nindinawemaganidog is the principle that the universe is a multi-dimensional web with entities that rely on each other to live.

Nindinawemaganidog is not the vague romantic chant of "we are all related" found in new-age books but is a binding, critical philosophy. It is, for most Anishinaabeg, a law devised through interactions between two Anishinaabeg philosophical principles: *enawendiwin,* the spiritual and material connections Anishinaabeg share with entities throughout Creation, and *waawiyeyaag,* a law of circularity that gives shape, meaning, and purpose to the universe.

Decolonizing the body requires a physical, social, and spiritual connection to Indigenous legal principles inherent in *nindinaweymaganidog.* These are lived out in creative, ongoing, everyday acts of relational resurgence—acts that seek to build new relationships, restore our medicine ways, and create and embody new dances.

Denise. This means engaging in personal and community decolonization. Harsha Walia (2012, 241) speaks to moving "beyond a politics of solidarity towards a practice of decolonization"—and this means being "active and integral participants in a decolonization movement for political liberation, social transformation, renewed cultural kinships, and the development of an economic system that serves rather than threatens our collective life on this planet." For me, it also means taking responsibility for our role in the many relationships we have in both the human and nonhuman world, living out reciprocity in our daily lives.

Alannah. Our focus on Indigenous land-based and embodied pedagogy aims to reconcile relationships. Relationship with lands is the foundation of this pedagogy, and decolonization means placing Indigenous resurgence at the centre of the endeavour. Resurgence, for me, means restoring Indigenous knowledge perspectives and articulating self-determined expression while maintaining responsibilities for the well-being of the collective. To access knowledge from the Anishinaabeg perspective, we have to engage our entire bodies (Simpson 2011). The core purpose of this pedagogy is to transform our ways of being by using our senses to embody an Indigenous resurgence that reflects living in relationships of good standing with all our relations.

References

Amadahy, Zainab. 2010. "Community, 'Relationship Framework,' and
  Implications for Activism." *Rabble.ca*, 13 July. http://rabble.ca/news/2010/07/
  community-'relationship-framework'-and-implications-activism.

Apffel-Marglin, Frédérique. 2011. *Subversive Spiritualities: How Rituals Enact the
  World*. New York: Oxford.

Archibald, Jo-ann. 2008. *Indigenous Storywork: Educating the Heart, Mind, Body,
  and Spirit*. Vancouver: University of British Columbia Press.

Blackstock, Michael. 2013. "Blue Ecology: A Cross-Cultural Ecological Vision
  for Freshwater." In *Aboriginal Peoples and Forest Lands in Canada,* edited by
  D. B. Tindall, Ronald L. Trosper, and Pamela Perreault, 180–204. Vancouver:
  University of British Columbia Press.

Borrows, John. 2010. *Canada's Indigenous Constitution.* Toronto: University of
  Toronto Press.

Boxberger, Daniel L. 2007. "The Not So Common." In *Be of Good Mind: Essays
  on the Coast Salish,* edited by Bruce G. Miller, 55–81. Vancouver: University of
  British Columbia Press.

Budden, Chris. 2009. *Following Jesus in Invaded Space: Doing Theology on
  Aboriginal Land.* Eugene, OR: Pickwick.

Corntassel, Jeff. 2012. "Re-envisioning Resurgence: Indigenous Pathways
  to Decolonization and Sustainable Self-Determination." *Decolonization*:
  Indigeneity, Education, and Society 1(1): 86–101.

Craft, Aimée. 2013. *Breathing Life into the Stone Fort Treaty: An Anishinabe
  Understanding of Treaty One.* Saskatoon, SK: Purich Publishing Ltd.

Ermine, Willie. 2007. "The Ethical Space of Engagement." *Indigenous Law Journal*
  6(1): 192–203.

Gespe'gewa'gi Mi'gmawei Mawiomi. 2009. *The Treaty Relationship Between
  Mi'qmaq of Gespe'gewa'gi and the British Crown and Its Implication for the
  Province of Québec.* Listuguj, QC: Mi'gmawei Mawiomi Secretariat Quebec.

Greenwood, David A. 2009. "Place, Survivance, and White Remembrance: A
  Decolonizing Challenge to Rural Education in Mobile Modernity." *Journal of
  Research in Rural Education* 24(10): 1–6.

Haig-Brown, Celia. 2010. "Indigenous Thought, Appropriation, and Non-
  Aboriginal People." *Canadian Journal of Education* 33(4): 925–50.

Halprin, Darai. 2002. *The Expressive Body in Life, Art, and Therapy: Working with
  Movement, Metaphor, and Meaning.* London: Jessica-Kingsley.

Holmes, Leilani. "Heart Knowledge, Blood Memory, and the Voice of the Land:
  Implications of Research Among Hawaiian Elders." In *Indigenous Knowledges
  in Global Contexts: Multiple Readings of Our World,* edited by George J. Sefa

Dei, Budd L. Hall, and Dorothy Goldin Rosenberg, 37–53. Toronto: University of Toronto Press.

Jafri, Beenash. 2013. "Desire, Settler Colonialism, and the Racialized Cowboy." *American Indian Culture and Research Journal* 37(2): 73–86.

Justice, Daniel Heath. 2005. Review of Eva Marie Garroutte, *Real Indians: Identity and the Survival of Native America. Wicazo Sa Review* 20(1): 201–3.

Kirkness, Verna, and Ray Barnhardt. 1991. "First Nations and Higher Education: The Four R's—Respect, Relevance, Reciprocity, Responsibility." *Journal of American Indian Education* 30(3): 1–15.

LE,NONET Research Project. 2010. *Staff and Faculty Aboriginal Cultural Training (SFACT): Building Respectful Relationships Curriculum.* Victoria, BC: University of Victoria.

Lyons, Scott. 2010. *X-Marks: Native Signatures of Assent.* Minneapolis: University of Minnesota Press.

Masters, Robert. 2010. *Spiritual Bypassing: When Spirituality Disconnects Us from What Really Matters.* Berkeley, CA: North Atlantic Books.

Nadeau, Denise. 2005. "Post-colonial Perspectives on the Church: A Euro-Canadian Position on Feminist Anti-colonialist Practice." In *Women's Ways of Being Church,* edited by Letty Russell, Aruna Gunardson, and Shannon Clarkson, 40–60. Geneva: World Council of Churches.

Palmater, Pamela. 2011. *Beyond Blood: Rethinking Indigenous Identity.* Saskatoon, SK: Purich Publishing Ltd.

Nadeau, Denise, with Alannah Young. 2008. "Restoring Sacred Connection with Native Women in the Inner City." In *Religion and Healing in Native America,* edited by Suzanne J. Crawford O'Brien, 115–34. Westport, CT: Praeger.

Roy, Susan. 2010. *These Mysterious People: Shaping History and Archaeology in a Northwest Coast Community.* Montréal and Kingston: McGill-Queen's University Press.

Simpson, Leanne. 2011. *Dancing on Our Turtle's Back: Stories of Nishnaabeg Re-creation, Resurgence, and a New Emergence.* Winnipeg: Arbeiter Ring.

Simpson, Leanne, and Edna Manitowabe. 2013. "Theorizing Resurgence from Within Nishnaabe Thought." In *Centering Anishinaabeg Studies: Understanding the World Through Stories,* edited by Jill Doerfler, Heidi Kiiwetinepinesiik Stark, and Niigaanwewidam James Sinclair, 279–93. Winnipeg: University of Manitoba Press.

Sinclair, Niigaanwewidam James. 2013. "Nindoodemag Bagijiganan: A History of Anishinaabeg Narrative." PhD diss., University of British Columbia.

Smith, Andrea. 2006. "Dismantling the Master's Tools with the Master's House: Native Feminist Liberation Theologies." *Journal of Feminist Studies in Religion* 22(2): 85–97.

Tuck, Eve, and K. Wayne Yang. 2012. "Decolonization Is Not a Metaphor." *Decolonization: Indigeneity, Education, and Society* 1(1): 1–40.

Walia, Harsha. 2012. "Moving Beyond a Politics of Solidarity Towards a Practice of Decolonization." In *Organize! Building from the Local for Global Justice,* edited by Aziz Choudry, Jill Hanley, and Eric Shragge, 240–53. Oakland, CA: PM Press; Toronto: Between the Lines.

Walkem, Ardith. 2007. "Water Philosophy: Indigenous Laws Treat Water with Awe and Reverence Rather Than as a Resource to Be Managed." *Alternatives Journal* 33(4): 28–31.

Williams, Lorna. 2008. "Weaving Worlds: Enhancing the Learning of Aboriginal Students." Minerva Lecture Series CCL CCA. http://en.copian.ca/library/research/ccl/minerva_lorna_williams/minerva_lorna_williams.pdf.

Young, Alannah Earl, and Denise Nadeau. 2005. "Decolonising the Body: Restoring Sacred Vitality." *Atlantis* 29(2): 13–22.

Young, Alannah Earl, and Denise Nadeau. 2006. "Educating Bodies for Self-determination: A Decolonizing Strategy." *Canadian Journal of Native Education* 29(1): 87–101.

Young Leon, Alannah. 2012. "Elders' Teachings on Indigenous Leadership: Leadership as Gift." In *Living Indigenous Leadership: Native Narratives on Building Strong Communities,* edited by Carolyn Kenny and Tina Ngaroimata Fraser, 48–63. Vancouver: University of British Columbia Press.

3   The Journey to You, Baba

Devi Dee Mucina

You, Baba, and I are like the sun and moon. We do not occupy the same space at the same time, but even the sun and moon have a special moment—the eclipse. Our family eclipse in 2008 was such a phenomenon; it brought our individual fragmented lives together. After being married for two years, I started having intense dreams about your death, and it was then that I came to realize that I needed to conclude certain affairs with you and also end our colonially imposed family fragmentation. To do this, I needed to come to Zimbabwe and find you.

My partner, Mandeep, who is of Punjabi descent, understood the significance of this journey because I was regenerating our African traditions as a way to decolonize my fragmented family. She also just wanted to meet you, her father in-law. When Mandeep's sister heard that we were going to Africa, she informed us that she was coming too. Fearing that Sanjit's decision would only put pressure on an already strained relationship with my in-laws, I tried to dissuade her. I told her about the hardships we would encounter on the trip, but she was set on going even though she knew that coming to Africa with us would not endear her to her parents and other members of the family.

When Renee, my adopted Black sister, heard about our trip, she asked if she could also come along. I immediately agreed, since I saw this as a great opportunity for her to connect with the mother continent and our people. Our shared Black racial embodiment is a site for shared love, while my connection with Mandeep's and Sanjit's Brown embodiment creates a racial and cultural threat for some of their family members.

The mixing of Black and Brown embodiment is another story, which I will tell at another time, but for now, Baba, I am proud to let you know that I remember the stories you told me about our people and that, as a son of the Ngoni, I hold South Africa to be our natal home. So our journey to you started in our ancestral homelands and loosely followed the Ngoni migration routes during the time of the Mfecane, the great displacement, now almost two hundred years ago. As we travelled north to you, I had a chance to engage with our African families in a changing southern Africa. But before I describe this journey, I want to say something about the method I have chosen to use.

Oral Storytelling: A Methodology That Honours *Ubuntu*

The storytelling methodology that I use has been regenerated from remembered fragments of African knowledge and from our collective expression of our lived experience. The oral transmission of stories and knowledge from past generations to current generations allows us to reflect critically on the political and cultural environment that brought our personal stories into existence. Storytelling is always relational. As the Ngoni say, "The story of one cannot be told without unfolding the story of many." So as more of us critically engage with our inherited philosophies and bodies of knowledge, we start to see that our fragmented individual efforts to decolonize are connected through our interdependence as human beings and our collective responsibility to care for one another—that is, our *ubuntu*.

The term *ubuntu* is related to the word *bantu*, which means "people." In Bantu languages, *ubuntu* is "humanness," that is, the quality of being human. But, in Ubuntu philosophy, it is more than just that. As Desmond Tutu (1999, 31) explains,

> When we want to give high praise to someone we say, "*Yu, u
> nobuntu*"; "Hey, so-and-so has *ubuntu*." Then you are generous,
> you are hospitable, you are friendly and caring and compassionate.
> You share what you have. It is to say, "My humanity is caught up, is
> inextricably bound up, in yours." We belong in a bundle of life. We
> say, "A person is a person through other persons." It is not "I think
> therefore I am." It says rather: I am a human because I belong. I par-
> ticipate, I share."

Ubuntu philosophy offers a philosophical and ethical system of thought that emphasizes the relational bonds and deep connectedness of all people and all things. Remembering that ideas and philosophies created in one language cannot always be adequately translated into another, let me offer some of the Ubuntu philosophical principles taught to me by my family and community:

> I am a reflection of the existence of my ancestors. I exist because they exist or, as the Zulu saying goes, "Umuntu ngumuntu ngabantu"—"A person is a person through other people."

> We come from the energy flux, and we are the energy flux. This is why the circle is important in Ubuntu spirituality. The circle shows that we are one.

> We respect and give thanks for all of our relations because all elements are part of the energy flux that makes up life.

> We try to live with the aim of finding integrity and wholeness in the balance of nature and to recognize the energy flux in everything.

> To acknowledge the reciprocity fundamental to the web of life, we ask permission of each person, place, animal, or object before taking anything, and then we give thanks.

> We honour, through ceremonies and rituals, the spirit of the land, water, and all other elements. The specific experiences we have with these elements teach us to understand and respect all our relational connections.

> We honour the dead because they live in a world parallel to that of the living. (Mucina 2013, 24)

Much of the knowledge I have of Ubuntu teachings came to me in the interactive context of oral storytelling. Storytelling engages both the teller and the listener in specific performative functions, which promotes active, co-created learning rather than passive reception.

In oral cultures, storytelling is essential to the transmission of knowledge, and, even in the age of print, it continues to be a popular mode of instruction.[1] Permit me to demonstrate the teaching power of oral storytelling among the Bantu-speaking peoples of southern Africa.[2] If a storyteller utters the following priming words—in Shona "Paivapo," in Ndebele "Kwakukhona," in Zulu "Kwesukasukela" ("There once was" or "Many, many millet granaries ago")—people, old and young, begin to draw nearer to the speaker. These idioms are very precise in that they let us know that the story to unfold is based on historical facts. In response to the storyteller's prompting of "Paivapo" ("Many millet granaries ago"), in Shona, the audience replies, "Dzepfunde," which is to say, "I am ready to absorb" or "I am ready to accept your lessons." Each time the speaker introduces the audience to a new location, or different characters, or a new philosophical idea, she appeals to them by chanting "Paivapo." The audience's response of "Dzepfunde" is an active acknowledgement that they are attuned to the oral teaching methodology of the person speaking. So, at this point, I, as the speaker, say to you, the reader, "Paivapo," and I invite you to respond in your own language or in a manner that communicates to you that we are synchronized for this storied engagement.

The ability of storytelling to teach through interactive performance, in which the speaker and the audience actively co-create the teachings that emerge from the story, is one of the distinctive qualities of an oral methodology. Another is the repetitive quality of the storytelling, which provides the audience with clues that enable them to identify important teachings. Yet, in the following pages, I will share our journey to my Baba in writing, through what might be called the "written oral" approach. I am aware that writing down my words undermines the interactive nature of oral storytelling. Through my use of writing, I lose the lived performativity and the reciprocity, but I gain the ability to talk globally to a broader and more

1 On the centrality of oral storytelling to everyday discourse in Africa, see Finnegan (2007). For more on the relationship between African storytelling and knowledge production, see Mucina (2011).

2 Bantu languages (of which there are hundreds) are widely spoken throughout southern Africa. Bantu-speaking peoples include the Zulu, Ndebele, and Swazi, who live primarily in the northeastern region of South Africa, as well as in Zimbabwe and Swaziland, and the Xhosa, whose traditional lands lie further south. The Sotho, who live in both South Africa and Lesotho, are also Bantu-speaking, as are the Shona, a major ethnic group in Zimbabwe and also in Mozambique. In addition, Swahili—the lingua franca in Kenya—is a Bantu language.

diverse audience without compromising my highest obligation, which, for me, is engaging the global Black communities through a resurgence of the Ubuntu world view. This is the irony of writing about performative oral discourse as a form of reciprocal engagement in a global context dominated by neocolonial methodologies that encourage each of us to speak in monologues (Okri 1997, 46). The former honours *ubuntu*; the latter does not.

From the perspective of African oral storytelling, how I interpret these stories as I tell them—the meanings I take from them in the present moment—is not meant to imply that this is the only way in which to analyze these stories. I offer my analysis simply as a way of reflecting my learning in a specific context at a specific time in my life, while remembering that an analysis of the same story at a different time may produce a different meaning, because meaning is made in the context of the knowledge we have. For this reason, the most important interpretation is the one given by the audience, which in our case is you, the reader, because your understanding reflects your learning in your precise context. Oral storytelling affirms the value of all our critical analyses through open dialogue, making space for all our relational engagement.

All the same, as committed as I am to social and political truth in our quest to reintegrate our fragmented families and selves, the emotional impact of sharing stories may limit my engagement—there are some things I will not talk about because it hurts too much to remember and I would rather forget. Yet what I can give, I give freely. This decolonizing work I perform in much the same way that the "ritual age" stories were told to me by Baba Mukulo, a Ngoni elder. In his stories about coming of age, ritualism marked the time of individual self-discovery, away from community. In those moments of seclusion, one begins to reflect on one's relational connections. I see my work on Ubuntu as a ritual that is directing me toward my embodied Black self-discovery as performed away from my African home and community.

Johannesburg

Dear Baba, each history that I have is a story that has been burnt into my memory bank among many silent stories at this particular time. It is possible that at another time, another story from these experiences would stand out more. But for now, here is what stands out for me.

A medium-sized African man in his early fifties comes up to us and asks in a South African accent, "Waiting for Diamond Digger Lodge?" In an unrehearsed reply, in unison, some of us say, "Yes," and others say, "Right." The man says, "Let's get your stuff and go. By the way, I am Madiba."

"Madiba is your name?" I ask.

The man: "Yes, like Nelson Mandela."

As we start to talk about his name, he also begins to lead us to the vehicle. As we near the vehicle, Madiba switches into his tour guide/operator role and says in his official voice, "Welcome to South Africa. Is this your first visit?"

I say, pointing to the others: "For them, yes, but not for me."

Madiba: "Where are you from?"

Me: "I was born in Zimbabwe."

Madiba: "Mugabe, that old man is too much. So you are my brother. What about them?"

Sanjit says: "We are from Canada."

And Renee adds: "But my parents are from Grenada."

As if not to be outdone, Mandeep adds: "Our parents are from India."

And, just like that, we have all marked our racial embodiments with specific geopolitical locations as a way of belonging and claiming space. For the rest of the drive, we talk easily with Madiba, who shifts from being informal in one conversational exchange to being very formal in the next. I wonder if it is always like this for him or if it is different today. I wonder how he views his brother travelling with three women, two Indian and one Black. Does he wonder which one of these three is with me or has he generously considered me a polygamist? My act of questioning the marking of our embodiment is embedded in the fact that South Africa is still a deeply racist and sexist society.

As I go to register for our lodgings, I cannot help but notice that all the domestic workers are Black and all the administrative staff are White. This is a colonial legacy that privileges White people over Black people and, in our case, make for some interesting engagements. For example, when the Black staff see us, they greet us very politely. This engagement changes with the first White staff we encounter, who is painting in front of the car park area where we left our bags. His nonverbal behaviour makes it very clear that he does not wish to engage us or demonstrate any politeness toward us. Yet when any White tourist walks by the same White painter, he demonstrates great interest in them by offering them greetings with a warm smile and showing clear verbal expressions of polite communication. At some point, the White painter becomes aware that we have noticed his racist behaviour and he turns toward his work with a sour-faced expression, which communicates to me: "There is no smile or anything for you here, darky."

While walking toward the accommodation registration office, I see a Black sister working with tears running down her face. In this situation, the first thought that comes to me is that I am still in colour-conscious South Africa, where to embody Whiteness is to embody racial privilege while to embody Blackness is to embody the racial scorn of Whiteness. The trauma of our colonial experience has misguided some of our political leaders to mistakenly view our decolonization as the act of replacing white bodies with black bodies within colonial governance structures (Fanon 1963, 35). Yet the hearts and the minds of our people struggle with internalized oppression. This is why it seems to me that Desmond Tutu's rainbow nation still operates on a colour-ranking system.

Cape Town

Dear Baba, we are in Cape Town, your favourite city. Our White cabdriver says: "Watch out for these buggers, they can steal you blind." He is talking about a young Black man who is looking tired and hungry.

Our White cabdriver adds: "You can find accommodation that suits your needs within this one block. Just make sure that only one of you guys goes to look for a place while the others stay with the bags."

The Black street brother says: "Don't worry brother; I'll take care of you. I know all the hotels around here. I will take you to a very good cheap place. Don't worry brother, I've got you covered. But brother, I need something. I have not slept in two days. I'm hungry and tired. I don't need much, just a little. Can you help?"

I say to my street brother: "I'll see what we can do. But first help me. Just to be clear, I am not promising you anything. Are we clear about that?"

Street brother says: "Yes brother, I understand, whatever you can give me. It is all up to you."

"Okay," I say.

I do not know why I am tipping this cabdriver, because I am sure he is a racist. I have not yet quite figured out the currency exchange rate, and I give the cabdriver a tip of about seventy rand. I can tell from the smile on his face that it was not as low as he was expecting. To show his gratitude as he helps unpack our bags, he says, "Keep an eye on these Blacks. Sorry, I mean blocks."

With a hint of sarcasm, I say to the cabdriver, "Don't worry, I think my brother will take care of us."

As the cabdriver gets back into his vehicle, he mumbles, "Your problem," before driving away.

Street brother says to me, "Brother, come, everything is very close here. You don't have to go very far."

Mandeep says, "Go ahead, babe, and we will watch the baggage."

Street brother says, "Let us start with this place across the road; all kinds of people like it and it is also called Ubuntu. I will wait for you here."

I ask, "Why?"

Street brother replies by saying, "If they see me with you on the security camera, they won't open the door for you. I am a street man; they don't like us, better you go alone." The clothes he wears, his cultural mannerisms, and most importantly, his Black embodiment mark him as a street man who threatens what, for the most part, is White business.

The man at reception says they are all booked up for the week, and I am sad because this place has a great feel to it and the guests sitting around are indeed a reflection of the South African rainbow nation. As a result, everyone wants to be here. Hence, there are no rooms left. Street brother takes me to three other places, all of which will not open their security gate and inform me through their intercom system that they have no rooms available. I wonder if there is no room because I am a Black African man. I am starting to get frustrated when my street brother says, "Try this place; it is very good but is a little more expensive than the other places I have shown you." He leads me to a Daddy Long Legs Independent Travellers Hotel and I ring the security bell. I know that the receptionist on the other side can see me, so I am surprised when I hear a very pleasant-sounding woman say, "Please come in, sir. You will find me at reception if you walk up the stairs."

As I am walking up the stairs, I tell myself that this pleasant-sounding woman must be a Black woman, but when I arrive at the reception desk, I see a tall, striking, slim brunette. She says, "Can I offer you a drink before I attend to your other needs?" I decline the offer of a drink because I want to settle my family, but I am impressed with how compassionately she engages with me. Does more money buy you a race-free engagement, or is this one human engaging another human? South Africa is a country full of contradictions; one minute you're being despised for your racial embodiment and in the next engagement you are being treated like a king, yet you are still in the same Black body. The spirit of *ubuntu* among White people in South Africa is still a hit-and-miss affair. This being said, the hotel crew from Daddy Long Legs took such good care of us; we all became good friends and still keep in contact via Facebook.

Baba, as these are journal entries, I am only giving you the facts that stand out for me, which means that dates and times become compressed or flattened. Point in case—the rest of the story of the street brother has no time indicators to convey the passage of time, because we met when we did and it was never planned. We never knew when we would meet our street brother, but when we did meet, we tried to take care of each other. Our street brother was generous with his information and made sure we were safe. For example, the women were out one night on the streets and a group of guys blocked their path, making it hard for them to get back to the hotel. Being well known on the street, our street brother gently intervened by making it clear that these were his sisters, and the harassment stopped right away. For our part, we tried to give our street brother as much as we could, but sadly, after the women's harassment, we saw him only one other time. To this day, I still hope that our street brother's luck changed and that he found that job he was looking for. I want to be hopeful about the fact that our street brother was nowhere to be found during the last few days before we left Cape Town. We never got to say goodbye to him and I still find this sad, because he reflected a part of South Africa's Black embodied challenge in a changing world.

To Durban on the Shosholoza Meyl Railway Train

Dear Baba, the train should have left fifteen minutes ago, but we haven't started loading yet. I am a little anxious, as I am not sure if we are on the right platform. I have been assured that we are, but I have seen many people coming and going, and we are still here. The Congolese man who cut my hair yesterday when we came to buy our train tickets warned me that this is the place where thieves make their fortune. He told me not to allow anyone to take any of our bags out of our sight. When we left our hotel, the staff warned us about the high level of robbery that takes place here in the train station. After checking in, the desk clerk warned us to watch our baggage. She advised us to only get direction and assistance from official customer representatives, who were wearing uniforms and were situated strategically throughout the train station.

After such cautioning, Baba, I see myself scrutinizing every young Black man who comes to stand near us. Through my colonial lens, I see the distance between myself and what I perceive as the other young, poor Black males. As I stand there, I become the Black colonizer who fears his own reflection (Fanon 1963, 18). I notice two Black youths pushing the biggest load of luggage I have ever seen. I wonder where the luggage owners are. Whoever they are, they seem to be ignoring all the warnings we have been given about caring for our luggage. From the direction that the young men have come from, an elderly grandfather of mixed race (coloured), out of breath from trying to keep up, yells: "That is the right place, you can offload." The elderly grandfather asks the official if the young men can help get the luggage on the train, and the official informs him that it will not be possible but offers to get some attendants to help.

Grandfather turns toward the direction he has come from and nine or ten coloured elderly grandmothers are descending upon him in the most jovial manner. They are laughing, giggling, and joking with each other. Their mischievous, girlish behaviour seems to contradict their elderly status. As I watch them, I see their inner child that has been oppressed by the many years of adult responsibility. Their joy and carefree behaviour is as fresh as morning dew on a blade of grass. Their smiles and joviality is beginning to infect my overly alert and anxious behaviour. They are all talking at the same time, and when they notice this, they begin to laugh at each other. I am quietly laughing at the drama that they are creating, and I see that my companions are doing the same. Some of the women notice us laughing at them, and they wave, smile, or say hello and then return to engaging each other in loud, friendly banter. This is *ubuntu*; this is love.

Baba, you will not believe that their mere presence has changed everything. These elders have taken the fear away and replaced it with love. I have no anxiety or worry about losing anything. These elders are helping me see all the other smiles on all the other people. Across from me on the furthest platform, I see a young man holding a newspaper. He is pretending to read it. Two other well-dressed young men approach him with two large bags, and one of them whispers something in his ear. Slowly, he closes his paper up and scans the area before getting up. For a brief moment, our eyes meet and he smiles at me, and I cannot help but smile back. I turn to see if anyone else in our group has seen him, but the women are engaged with watching the antics of the Gogos (grandmothers). When I look back again, the young men have vanished. I say nothing to anyone, but I keep wondering—did I just witness a robbery? Yet no one seems to be complaining about missing bags. Could it be that the young men were bootleggers selling something illegally on the train station premises? Whatever the case was, Baba, I am no longer scared of our embodied Black reflections, thanks to the jovial manner of those grandmothers. Regardless of race, poverty creates violence, and regardless of the racist fear tactics used in South Africa, a smile can win you over or it can distract you.

As White People Come Home, Black People Leave

Dear Baba, we see it—we feel it—yet I force my family to keep silent until the pain is too much; then we fight among each other. This, indeed, is a peculiar experience. Colonial history makes it possible; I am told it is over, but my experience and my feelings communicate otherwise. I am in my friend's home en route to Swaziland. He lives in a beautiful neighbourhood with his beautiful White family. Like him, his neighbours are White. As we were driving up to his house in our rented car, an armed security truck passed us on patrol, and as we were parking the car, a police truck slowed down to check us out. It was just before 5:00 p.m. and we were observing a Black exodus.

Mandeep says, "Why are all the Black people leaving?"

I say, "Because they are the domestic workers."

Renee asks, "Is it okay for us to be here?"

Sanjit does not say a word but I can see that she is very uncomfortable. I tell everyone that it will be okay because this is a very good friend. Our gracious hosts welcome us into their home. I am trying to get my family to relax in a colour-conscious South Africa, but it is not working. The next day, a Black maid arrives and, on seeing visitors, makes a request for a uniform; we are all shocked into silence. Although we are all familiar with families hiring people to help with domestic work, we wondered whether the maid's demand for a uniform was meant to underscore her position of servitude and to distance herself from these White people, these people we called our friends. We questioned whether we were positioning ourselves on the wrong side of the colour conscious South Africa.

Sanjit makes her discomfort known by asking when we are leaving. I tell everyone that we will be leaving in three days. I tell everyone that our hosts are doing everything they can to make us comfortable and therefore, we need to make the best out of a bad situation. To some extent, I was reconnecting with the racial injustice and inequity of Southern Africa, which even among so-called friends, affected and directed our interactions. We spent the next few days at the beach, and in the evening, we hung out on the shore of the river, drinking and eating, conversing in very formal and limited ways with our White hosts. My friend and I reminisce about our youthful experiences, but even there, Baba, I see the race lines. I am now aware, Baba, that my friend's memories are of a different Zimbabwe than mine. A colour-conscious South Africa reminds me that what we appreciated of our friendship was limited to small moments of shared humanity, but the White racism was always there. I guess if you experience racism all the time, you have to ignore it sometimes to give yourself some relief. Is this how we have survived, Baba?

On a Friday, two nights before we leave, our hosts want us to meet their friends at a costume party. Renee and Sanjit make it clear that they cannot handle any more of this White gated community and have no desire to meet another White racist. I think to myself that they are being a little melodramatic but agree that they should stay back if they are not up to it. Mandeep does not want to go but she feels obliged, as my partner, to come. I try to tell her that she does not need to go to the party, but she will not put this burden down, so we go together. The first thing we notice, as soon as we get to the party, is that there is no other visible race except for Whiteness. Most people are speaking English or Afrikaans. We are introduced to a few of our hosts' friends, and it is painfully clear that we do not belong here. One of the guests comes up to us and says: "So how did you guys get into this party? You couldn't have gate crashed. Are you the servers?" This is meant to be a joke, but it is only funny to them. We meet the host of the party and she introduces us to her parents.

The father settles down to speak to us as his wife and daughter leave. He starts by posing the following question: "So how do you like South Africa?"

I say, "It is a beautiful country."

And he says, "But crime is destroying it." I take his statement to mean that Black people are destroying the country.

To this, I say, "How would you know when you live in a fortified White community?"

For no reason, he switches subjects: "So you agree with the government, that I should sell forty percent of my farm to the Indigenous?"

I say, "If you accept the fact that the land was stolen from them in the first place, then this is a small price to pay." Our heated discussion is starting to create a sour taste for other White guests, and our hosts intervene with the excuse that they would like to introduce us to some other people. As we are all walking away, my old White friend says, "It looked like you needed some saving." He and his wife offer to drive us back to their house right away. As they are offering their farewells to their friends, Mandeep and I wait for them by ourselves. I look at Mandeep and I question myself. How have I got my family into this racial nightmare? Where is the rainbow love in this wealthy White haven of South Africa? After spending three nights in my friend's White haven in our Black Africa, I felt grateful for having the resources that allow us the freedom to leave their White haven, but like you, Baba, there are brothers and sisters who cannot escape this neocolonial reality. For them, surviving neocolonialism means suppressing their Ubuntu knowledge so that they do not feel so acutely the pain of neocolonialism. As much as I may hate how these White racist communities exploit our people's labour, we in southern Africa have not come up with better employment solutions or investments that help our people, who have little or no education.

You, Baba, were like many of these brothers and sisters who entered these unwelcoming White racist communities on a daily basis in order to sustain your family on the margins; I do not need to make you understand the value of choice denied to these brothers and sisters in South Africa. Let us, as Ubuntu Africans, develop and invest in our own sustainable economic structures so that we can offer our own people the choice to work in environments where their dignity and self-respect is honoured.

Swaziland

Dear Baba, we are at the border crossing between Swaziland and South Africa. The customs officer gives us a broad smile and says, "Welcome to Swaziland." As he looks at my passport, he says, "Brother, you look Swazi and you have a Swazi name, so how did you end up being born in Zimbabwe?"

I chuckle and say, "This is why I have come here. I am hoping I can use my name to help me connect with my ancestral roots."

The customs officer shakes my hand and says, "Welcome home, brother. If you go to the parking area, I will take my break now so I can give you directions to your people." To my own research, the customs officer adds detailed maps and directions. I thank him and as I start to drive toward our ancestral home, my sister Renee says, "This is a real homecoming."

Mandeep says, "I didn't like the racial tension in South Africa. It made it impossible to relax." We are all in agreement about feeling more relaxed in Swaziland. They tell us that apartheid is over in South Africa, but it did not feel like it for us.

We are staying at a guest house in Manzini, and our host is very excited to hear about my efforts to connect with my ancestral home and people. She gives us more detailed directions to Mdzimba, which is the ancestral home of many Maseko Ngoni. Being here in Swaziland feels so liberating. For the first time, no one is asking me where I am from. I feel genetically connected to everyone around me.

As we are driving into the Mdzimba Mountains, I see the stone-built *munzi*s (villages) of Sotho peoples who belong to the Mnesi (or Mnisi) and Mncina *mafuko*s (clans). I had read about the Mnesi and Mncina when I was doing research for my master's thesis, so I knew about their tradition of collective self-governance (see Mucina 2006, 70). When, sometime around 1820, the Ngwane ruler Sobhuza set out to conquer the central part of Swaziland, the Mncina were among the few who resisted (Bonner 1983, 31). The name Mncina can also be rendered Macina or Mucina. Embedded in this name is a continuum of shared experience that joins past to present to future and that links me to Swaziland and to this Sotho community.

At the top of the mountain, I become aware of feeling relaxed and in no rush, and I say out loud, "I can feel that I belong here." I remove my shoes and let my feet connect with the soil. I feel grounded for the first time. I only wish you were here, Baba, to experience this wonderful moment with us. I rub my hands and feet into the soil and say a prayer to our ancestors for both you and me, because I want our ancestors to know that I have touched the soil of the place I belong and that the soil and I are one. Knowing that we will return to Swaziland in the near future, we leave for Durban so that Renee can catch her flight back to Toronto and the rest of us can catch a bus to Botswana.

Botswana to Zimbabwe

Baba, we have been informed by our friends that there is no food in Zimbabwe and that even if we can find food, it will be too expensive. So they make us buy absolutely everything before leaving Swaziland, and we end up carrying two very large grocery bags. We go to the local bus station to catch a bus to Zimbabwe. We see a luxury bus going to Zimbabwe, but I am informed that all the seats have already been sold and that the bus will not be back for another two days. I do not want to wait for two days, since I am feeling a sense of urgency about getting to you. Thinking that it would be a good experience for Mandeep and Sanjit to get acquainted with the local African transportation system, I buy tickets for a local bus leaving that evening at six o'clock.

The bus conductor has anticipated our inexperience in travelling on local buses and so has kindly reserved a bench seat for the three of us in the middle of the bus. However, it is very difficult to get to our seats because all the floor space has been taken up. To get to our seats, we have to step on people's luggage. I am aware that fire regulations in this situation do not apply, so we make ourselves as comfortable as possible. Six o'clock rolls around and the bus is still being loaded. At eight o'clock, we still have not moved and I ask the bus conductor when we are leaving. He replies, "Very soon my friend, don't worry." The family behind us communicates to me in Shona that this means we are now officially on African time. At ten o'clock, the bus starts to move but the conductor informs us that we are going to a gas station to fill up with diesel. This takes over an hour. When our bus starts to leave the gas station, some locals in their cars begin yelling,

"Zimbabweans go back home." As our bus bound for Zimbabwe passes local communities, people throw up the insulting middle finger and openly jeer us. They have forgotten the history of Ubuntu love that binds our people.

Since the bus is so overloaded, every time it goes over a bump, the frame rubs against the tires; soon we can smell them burning. Fearing a blowout, some passengers demand that the bus driver slow down, and, as a result, we do not get to the Zimbabwean border until seven o'clock in the morning. At the border crossing, the bus conductor informs us that we may need to put a little money together to placate the Botswana customs officials. After about an hour, the bus conductor returns to the bus and informs us that his efforts have not yielded positive results and we must unload the whole bus. With everyone helping, the process takes about two hours, and then everyone has to stand in a queue with all their belongings. The customs officials keep making everyone line up again because they claim the queues are disorderly. As I observe these tactics, I am reminded that we have replaced Whiteness with Blackness, but the White structure of control still dominates us as Black bodies.

An hour goes by while the customs officers switch from insulting us to ignoring us. After some time, three customs officers approach us and announce in military style that they are taking over our situation. They tell us that our cooperation will speed up our leaving. For some reason, the customs officer who is speaking notices me and comes over and asks for my passport. I give it to him and while he is looking at it, he asks whether Sanjit and Mandeep are with me. I respond in the affirmative and he says, "Why are you doing this to yourself? Why do you not fly to Zimbabwe or take the luxury bus system? You would save yourself all this hassle."

I respond by stating that this is the cheapest and fastest way to Zimbabwe. The customs officer laughs and says, "In my opinion, this experience is not worth having because it is not a lot of fun. I will make sure you guys go in first." He then yells to everyone else, "The queue starts behind this gentleman," and everyone rushes over to be behind me. Everyone wants to be processed as quickly as possible so that their journey home can continue. A few people with very large loads are disgruntled with how badly they are being treated and refuse to move. On seeing this open challenge, one of the officers starts using violent tactics. He throws people's belongings onto the road, which forces people to rush over and try to rescue them. One woman seems to be unwilling to be intimidated, or perhaps she is just overly exhausted and cannot move. The customs officer approaches her with great haste, but she cannot see him as he is in her blind spot. He slaps her violently across the face and the woman doubles over in pain, but no one moves to help her. Somehow, the woman manages to move toward us.

Sanjit, who is standing next to me, says, "I can't believe that man has just hit that woman." As she is saying these words, we both realize that Mandeep is standing in the area where the woman was attacked. The officer is heading toward Mandeep and the rest of us freeze. The officer raises his hand to slap Mandeep hard on her back, but when he realizes that she is not African, he turns his slap into a forceful pat on the back. He says, "Madam, you'll have to move to where the others are. Do you understand?" I sigh in relief, and the man behind me puts his hand on my shoulder and says in Shona, "Do not worry, they can still see her humanity, but for some reason, they cannot see our humanity even though this black skin binds us as family." The actual processing by customs takes less than five minutes, and I cannot understand why we went through hours of unnecessary suffering. I can only speculate that absolute power corrupts when it is being applied to the poor and vulnerable because the chances of consequential action by the poor and vulnerable is greatly diminished when they are focused on trying to survive.

The Zimbabwean customs officials inform us that we each need a visa for US$60, and the customs officer informs us jokingly that all this could have been avoided if Canada had not imposed a visa requirement on Zimbabweans. The easygoing nature of the Zimbabwean customs officials is relaxing everyone, but some of the bus passengers are trying to take advantage of this. Those who had bought large flat-screen TVs, refrigerators, car parts, bicycles, and other nonessential goods are refusing to identify themselves as the owners of these goods, so as to avoid having to pay duty on them, and this is wasting our time. The bus driver threatens to leave these unclaimed goods and simply drive away, but the bus conductor informs him that all will be resolved in good time. So we wait and quietly complain.

At three o'clock, we start loading the bus again, but three hours later one of the back tires explodes because the frame of the bus has been rubbing against it. There is no spare tire on the bus, as it had been removed to make more space for goods. Luckily, we are near the town of Gweru, where the bus was scheduled to stop at a gas station in the town centre. At this point, we have been on the bus for more than twenty-four hours, so when we get to the Wimpy outlet (a fast-food, hamburger outlet, which served local traditional cuisine at better prices than their hamburgers) in Gweru, we are so hungry that we pay a lot of money to treat ourselves to good local cuisine, thus distracting ourselves from our ongoing bus problems. By now, the bus passengers have all become quite familiar with one another. Political issues have been discussed; feminist ideas about power, equality, and sexism have been thoroughly debated, as have various forms of Christianity—although, in my view, traditional religion has been quietly left out. After an unbelievable thirty-eight hours, we unload from the bus, having travelled from Gaborone to Harare, a trip that should have taken only five to seven hours.

The Land of My Birth, Zimbabwe

Innocent, our Zimbabwean friend whom we had met in South Africa, came to pick us up at the bus station and took us to the apartment that Kevin, another friend from South Africa, was allowing us to use. At the apartment, we met two other young men who were also staying there—Oliver, from the Democratic Republic of the Congo, and Joe, the younger cousin of Innocent. Joe worked for a company as a computer technician, so we saw very little of him. Oliver, like most of our Zimbabwean friends, was trying to make his fortune in Zimbabwe, through trading in illegal diamonds. All were good people involved in shady business dealings in order to survive. The elder of this group of men was a man whom we had dubbed Uncle Munya. It was Uncle Munya and his business associates who took us in an open pickup truck to the township of Mbare for a barbecue feast. As we drank beer and ate meat and a thick cornmeal porridge called *sadza,* I became aware that many people had a link to what was termed the green market (that is, illegal business trading), garnering their main income from that activity. Failure to participate in the green market meant that you could not savour the wonderful barbecue we were enjoying. The truth is that many—like you, Baba—could not dream of taking pleasure in such luxuries.

Unbeknownst to me, a five-minute walk from where we were enjoying our barbecue, my maternal family members were trying to sell vegetables in order to survive. They were so poor that if the police raided them and took away their vegetables, they would struggle to replace them, and at times, this meant going without food. In contrast, the butcher store that operated the barbecue was the meeting place for high-end illegal traders, and it was situated right next to the police station. As good as the barbecue was, I could not fully enjoy it, because about sixty metres away from us, kids were feeding on our leftover bones on a rubbish heap. These beggars and food scavengers were intermittently kept at bay by other children who were hired to do so. The colonial strategy of divide and conquer, which had been applied to us using racial markers, we had now modified and were applying along class lines. The envious stares of the poor confirmed that we had escaped poverty—perhaps by being the inheritors of our families' breakthrough into the new Black wealth. Yet I still remember how I used to forage for food in garbage heaps just like the kids I was watching. I was one of them, and now I am seated on the other side. I want to identify with their struggle so that I can help, but I do not want to be in their position because I remember how hard it is. It is this memory of hardship and the stories that I have heard from kids who have foraged for food in garbage heaps that motivates me to tell stories about why we need to make change.

The next day, I took Mandeep and Sanjit to see the orphanage where I grew up. The place looked rundown. There was mould on the walls, windows were broken, electrical wires were exposed, and there was no running water in the bathrooms. I recognized some of the boys in the orphanage from five years earlier, when I did some outreach work as part of my Child and Youth Care degree. Langara College had funded the development part of my work, the main aim of which was to offer the staff of the orphanage current resources and training materials on residential child care. I also offered workshops to the boys in the orphanage, in which I addressed their fears about leaving the orphanage and described the actions that had allowed me to be successful beyond the orphanage. In addition to providing funds so I could give professional and personal advice, Langara College's student union body had also donated many computers for the boys and had given me money to purchase food for them.

So you can see how the boys in the orphanage were surprised to learn that I had come empty handed. As I was leaving, I heard one of the boys say, "Where is the money and computers?" I pretended not to hear, because if I had answered it truthfully, I would have said, "I am sorry, this trip is about connecting with my father; my focus is mainly on this and nothing else."

To find you, Baba, I needed the help of Baba Colin (the orphanage cook), who had helped me track you down in 2003. Baba Colin had learned that you were not staying with the young family who had been caring for you when I left you. After a day of searching, he found an address for where you were staying. Again, our friend Innocent drove us there, but no one could track you down. However, everyone we talked to had a story to share about how poverty and homelessness threatened your life every single day. On hearing these reports, I felt guilty for not having taken better care of you as your firstborn son.

That night, I led our family in a discussion about how we could care for you. Our total savings at that moment was around five thousand dollars, and we also had an emergency fund of about two thousand dollars. To me, this meant that we could afford to buy some land in the townships or rural communities and still have enough money to build a very small house for you on that property. The problem was that you would not have your family or community around you. In the midst of my planning, Mandeep asked, "Do we know if this is what Baba wants?" Not wanting to impose anything on you, we decided to suspend everything until we met you the next day.

The next day, Joe kindly offered to drive us to the place you were staying, and when we found you, I was shocked with how emaciated you were. I remember you telling us that you were having stomach problems and were unable to digest certain foods. As you were speaking, I kept asking myself, How have I let this happen to you, my own Baba? How will I explain this to our ancestors? Oh, Baba, I felt great shame and you only made my shame even greater when you started to share the little we had given you. How is it that with so little to your name, Baba, you were so generous? I see now that your generosity was not limited to family members. You were the love that was *ubuntu* and this is why you were never a stranger in unfamiliar places.

Baba, through you, I have learned that *ubuntu* means that if I see a person next to me starving, then I must share that little piece of bread that I was saving for tomorrow. After I have saved the person next to me, then we, together, can worry about tomorrow. Your Ubuntu practice is hard to follow, Baba, and I still have a lot to learn. As we were talking, I watched you create a pile of things you wanted to give to my brothers and another pile of food that you wanted to share with your community. As you were making your sharing piles, you told me your stories about your struggles, your farming activities, planned future business adventures, and hopes for the family. As I listened, I felt that your stories had a common theme of finding final settlement, and so I asked you if you wanted to take us home to our family community of Lizulu. Thoughtfully, you informed us that you were ready to go home, but you were afraid that everyone you knew was dead and no one would know you. You were also afraid that you would not fit in with the community after being away for so long. You had been separated from your family for so long, you even suggested that we could go alone while you stayed in Zimbabwe. I assured you that we would not leave you in an environment in which you did not feel safe or happy. With this promise from us, you hesitantly and cautiously agreed to take us home to Lizulu. At the age of thirty-five, I was so excited to be going home with my Baba. I was a little kid again in your care, and at the same time, I was an adult who was caring for you.

My excitement about going home began to infect you too, and you suggested we leave right away. I reminded you that we needed travel visas for us and an emergency travel document for you. You laughed at this. "Who will stop me from travelling on our soil? These are all my people, my lands, and I have worked the soil from here to home. I know all the languages and the names of all the places," you told me confidently. Philosophically and politically, I agreed with your position, but we were running out of time as we could not change our travel plans because of a lack of funds and our schooling commitments. Wanting to get you home for the first time with as little problem as possible, I told you that we were going to the Malawian Embassy to get you a travel document. I remember what you said in response to my authoritative direction, and the weight and responsibility of what you said still haunts me. You placed your right hand on my shoulder as if you were transferring the burden of family responsibility to me and then simply said: "Baba, the sun is rising to your authority; I support this and will not get in your way." Until now, I have not shared with anyone the heaviness of these words that you gave me.

Zimbabwe to Malawi

As we went to the Malawian Embassy, you behaved like a little child who had new toys. You wanted to stop and show us off to your community of friends, and I behaved like a strict parent. I kept telling you, "Sorry, we need to leave;

sorry, we do not have time to meet other people because we are late and we need to go now if we are to get your emergency travel document before the embassy closes for the day." We arrived at the embassy during lunch, so we had to wait for an hour before they reopened. However, the security man informed us that the embassy on that day closed at three o'clock and there was a long line of people ahead of us. I can still remember hearing the security man speculate that we may have to come back another time. I told the security man that I did not want to wait another day because for the first time in my thirty-five years of being on this planet, I was going home. The security man asked why this was so and you gave him our family story about our fragmentation. When the other embassy workers heard our story, they made it clear that we would get your emergency travel document that day. And to help speed up the process, the security man offered his professional photography services for your identification photo. This service, he offered at a cost calculated in US dollars.

The next day, early in the morning, we caught the bus going to Malawi at the Mbare bus stop. I noticed that you were not talking with any of us, so I engaged you in light conversation until we neared Nyamapanda, which is just before the border with Mozambique. Nyamapanda is also the home of Lee and Simba, my two half-brothers from your last partner, to whom you were not traditionally married. If the bus had run this route more than once a week, I would have suggested we stop and see them, but we were running out of time. To ease my conscience, I asked you when you had last seen my brothers. I was expecting you to tell me that you had seen them about a month ago, but you replied, "In 2005, Lee came to see me for some money because he needed shoes, but his younger brother, Simba, will not talk to me because he feels I have abandoned him, which makes him very angry. How do I explain to him that I cannot present myself to his mother's family when I have nothing to offer them? I am the hunger created by a lack of food in abundance and I am poverty beyond the comfort of measure. I am silent because I cannot find the words that stop my suffering."

Your truth created an uncomfortable silence. I wanted to offer you some comfort, but blame kept making its way toward my lips, so I too kept silent because this was what I could offer as support without projecting my judgment. I am sorry now that I did not break the silence of our suffering when you were offering me the opportunity that day. I hope it is not too late to start following your lead of breaking the oppressive silence that continues to fragment our family.

The Malawi we took you to, Baba, was not the Malawi you left. The city of Blantye impressed you so much that you told us you were willing to live there if things did not work out at home in Lizulu. You were so proud of this new Malawi that had blossomed while you were away and you said, "I will stay here and die in my own country among my own people." We spent two nights and two days in Blantye before going to Zomba, where a friend lent me his car. As we were driving to Lizulu, you started to get sick. You complained of abdominal pain and reported that your stomach felt sour. I had to stop the car a few time so you could throw up or so we could prevent you from throwing up. Travelling at a much slower speed, we got into Lizulu around three in the afternoon. As soon as we arrived in Lizulu, we presented ourselves to the chief, who informed us that our family lands and properties were in Mozambique, so we would need a letter of clearance from the police, which the chief assured us would take less than five minutes. The more important task was to find a family member who could take us home. Within half an hour, the chief's staff had found one of your nephews, Fixon.

Fixon informed us that most of your family members had passed on from this life to the world of the ancestors. I could not help but watch the facial expressions you made as you heard about the death of each family member you inquired about. Just before we left for our motel, you asked Fixon very reluctantly, as if you did not want to hear the answer, "What of my sister, Janet?" Fixon flashed a huge smile and told you that your sister was doing very well in Lilongwe, the capital city of Malawi. She had built her own house there, had two living children, Moses and Regina, and from her children who had died, she had many grandchildren. Your eyes reddened with tears as you told us that you wanted to go to your sister right away; you made it clear that you had no interest in meeting any other family members.

At this point, we would have left if it had not been for the wise counsel of the chief and the persistence of Fixon. I remember the two of them making the point that you needed to take us to our home village so that our ancestors could connect with us. To this, you retorted by saying that our ancestors were always with me and that I did not need to go to a village full of the offspring of those who had caused you so much pain. The chief wisely told you that your retort was good but that if you took us to our home village, you would be showing respect for our ancestors. The chief added that your father had ensured that you had walked on the soil that held the remains of our ancestors, as a way of making sure you were connected to our lands and people. "Will you deny your son this connection?" he asked. Under such pressure, you agreed to go to our home village the next day.

About forty family members were at the home village to welcome us home, and they kept apologizing that they had not had time to inform other family members who were in schools or working in other parts of the country. I could not believe that so many people were related to me. Regardless of how poor they were, I felt wonderful belonging to them and they to me. I am not sure whether you felt the same connection that I felt to all these family members. I have learned that your smile and sweet words can hide your true feelings, so I wondered how you felt being welcomed by some family members whose parents may have had a hand in your leaving. Yet by the time we left, I could see a new level of strength and pride that I had never seen in you, and from that moment, your joy was mine and your problems were mine. Baba, I am still trying to find ways to connect with my brother Simba, who I am told is in South Africa. I am also very sorry that I never got to build a stronger relationship with my brother Lee before he passed on from this life to the world of the ancestors.

Fixon offered to take us to Baba's sister, Dadakazi Janet, in Lilongwe. (The kinship term *dadakazi* literally means "female father": in the context of our Ngoni culture, everyone from my paternal family is identified as masculine.) I was a little frustrated with Fixon's directions because he was directing us by memory and could not give us reference points to help map our trip. His way required us to trust him, while our Western academic training required us to depend on evidential data. With no other choice, I was forced to trust and depend on Fixon totally, and my discomfort with that kept me questioning and challenging Fixon's directions, which made him nervous and led to small directional errors. When I realized that I was subjecting Fixon to Western ways of knowing, I stopped and apologized. It was not easy for me to let him lead us, but needless to say, he got us to Dadakazi Janet as soon as I stopped my judgmental commentary about his navigational methods. Interestingly, I now only know directions to Dadakazi Janet's home through memory and not through the conventional Western way of using street names. The lesson here for me is that if we want the outcome of a specific knowledge, we must honour its rightful process.

On arrival at Dadakazi Janet's home, we were informed by the neighbours that she had gone to church. So we went to her son and daughter's home nearby, but her son, Moses, was away on business and her daughter, Regina, was at church with her. Luckily, a niece informed us that she would send a message to Dadakazi Janet and cousin Regina to inform them that they had visitors at home. Regina and a nephew by the name of Joseph, were the first people to come back from church. After exchanging a formal greeting, Fixon informed Regina as to who you were. On hearing that you were Dadakazi's brother, Regina started laughing so hard I thought she would start crying. While still laughing hard, she got up and gave you a big hug and then told us that she had seen many things but she had never believed or dreamt that she would see us. Regina informed us that Dadakazi had named one of her children after your memory, but unfortunately the child had died. Looking at me, Regina told me that Dadakazi had had a hard life, but even at her lowest point, she had never stopped wondering about her brother, Peter Dee. As Regina was talking, more family members were coming in. In all this excitement, I remember Regina hugging me while telling me that we were family. I can remember Sanjit saying to Regina and me, "Yes, you are of the same blood line. I see it in your face and body structure." Within a few minutes, we were all talking over each other in a spirit of familial love. By the time Dadakazi Janet arrived, the room was full of family and communal laughter.

As soon as Dadakazi walked into the room, we all went quiet but our hearts' excitement kept dancing in the room. Dadakazi was about to ask who the visitors were when she locked eyes with you, Baba. As she stared into your eyes, she seemed to lose her voice. Regina then asked, "Who is that?" And Dadakazi, after a moment of disbelief, said, "This is my brother who has been lost in some foreign lands. I have wondered for many years if he was dead, yet I could not explain why I felt that he was still alive. I have missed you, my king. My heart is full of love and pain at the same time, and I have no words to share. Now let me meet my family." Lovingly, Dadakazi welcomed us home with hugs, but as soon as she was done, she raced over to you and locked her arm with yours. Looking at me, she said with deep, slow, emotional excitement, "Baba, thank you for bringing my brother back to me." I was speechless. After some time, you, Baba, broke the silence by saying, "We should also thank my daughter in-law, because I believe she is the one who pushed your son to come find me." Dadakazi gave Mandeep a quiet word of thanks before she focused back on you again, Baba. The two of you were inseparable from that moment on.

As news of your arrival spread, Dadakazi's friends began arriving to witness this extraordinary happening. If Dadakazi was sugar then her friends were her salt, because they lamented how you had abandoned her in this lonely world. Dadakazi's friends conveyed to you how much she had lost and how much she had worried about you. In all these discussions, you remained silent, and at times when things got heated beyond my comfort, I defended you by reminding people that you were now here and the important thing was for us to start building our family as a whole. I told the family and Dadakazi about how you were living in Zimbabwe and asked them if you could stay with them while we tried to find you a place near Dadakazi so that you would not be separated from your sister again. As we were looking for a place for you, Regina called us to a family meeting. At this meeting, Regina informed us that if we made you and Dadakazi live apart, we would embarrass ourselves before the community. People would ask why we were keeping two old relatives apart who had found each other in old age after being separated a long time ago by colonial and familial fragmentation. Regina then informed us that, instead of buying a place for you, the family wanted to use the money to upgrade Dadakazi's house so that you could both live there. In the meanwhile, the two of you could live in her house.

On hearing the family's decision to keep Dadakazi and you together, I felt comforted and relieved about your safety. The little savings that we had, we handed over to the family for building our home extension. Knowing you were in safe hands, we returned to school in Canada in late August 2008. One year later, in August 2009, Khumalo, your grandson, was born, and four months later, on 6 December 2009, you left this living world for the world of the living dead ancestors. Sister Regina, on 5 June 2010, also left this world to be with you among our ancestors. Baba, take care of Regina and help Dadakazi have some peace, because she has dealt with too much loss for one person. In 2011, we were given another child, Nandi. She and her brother, Khumalo, are loved very much and we are working on building a strong physical and spiritual *ubuntu* home. I want you to know that I have not forgotten my responsibility toward Dadakazi Janet; right now, our support is nothing because we are struggling, but I see the light coming by the end of 2014. In reference to your death, Baba, I am not sad in any way because you are with our ancestors and the healing of our family, broken from colonial fragmentation, has started. You have left me the thread to continue connecting our family beyond fragmentation, and for this and other lessons that you have given me, I thank you. I have said many things, Baba, but now I clap my hands as a way of welcoming and honouring your spirit. I am now listening, so please inscribe your *ubuntu* spiritual wisdom in these blank pages. But be warned that if your spiritual wisdom does not honour our Black Ubuntu embodiment, then I will reject it.

Respectfully, your son Khomba,
Dr. Devi Dee Mucina

References

Bonner, Philip. 1983. *Kings, Commoners and Concessionaires: The Evolution and Dissolution of the Nineteenth-Century Swazi State.* Cambridge: Cambridge University Press.

Fanon, Frantz. 1963. *The Wretched of the Earth.* Translated by Constance Farrington. New York: Grove Press. Originally published as *Les damnés de la terre* (1961).

Finnegan, Ruth. 2007. *The Oral and Beyond: Doing Things with Words in Africa.* Chicago: University of Chicago Press.

Mucina, Devi Dee. 2006. "Revitalizing Memory in Honour of Maseko Ngoni's Indigenous Bantu Governance." Master's thesis, University of Victoria.

———. 2011. "Story as Research Methodology." *AlterNative: An International Journal of Indigenous Peoples* 7(1): 1–14.

Okri, Ben. 1997. *A Way of Being Free.* London: Phoenix House.

Tutu, Desmond. 1999. *No Future Without Forgiveness.* New York: Doubleday.

4 Being Moved to Action

Micropolitics, Affect, and Embodied Understanding

Randelle Nixon and Katie MacDonald

> Let's face it. We're undone by each other. And if we're not, we're missing something. . . . One does not always stay intact. It may be that one wants to, or does, but it may also be that despite one's best efforts, one is undone, in the face of the other, by the touch, by the scent, by the feel, by the prospect of the touch, by the memory of the feel. (Butler 2004, 19)

In the above passage, Judith Butler poignantly describes the inherent relationality of identity and the way in which both real and imagined affective encounters with others have the capacity to "undo" us. In this chapter, we emphasize the vital role of embodiment, emotion, and affect in how we come to know others and ourselves and point to how affect surpasses the intentionality and control of individual subjects. We, like many others, argue that rational thought does not occur through a repression or domination of our affective responses; rather, what we understand to be rational relies and draws on our bodily feelings and knowledge. Thus, we are seeking here to collapse several dualisms that continue to structure Western culture: mind and body, reason and emotion, thinking and doing.

In the following pages, we use the video that formed the centrepiece of Invisible Children's Kony 2012 campaign to explore the ethical politics of being undone and to examine the multiple forms of coming undone in the context of the West, where affective and emotional responses are a tool for profit, used to spark political mobilization. When interrogated, however, these responses can be deep sources of knowledge that have the potential to spark social change. In what ways did *Kony 2012*, the video at the centre of the campaign, "undo" individuals? What kinds of histories of feeling and acting does *Kony 2012* evoke? What are the effects of this kind of being undone? And finally, what are the implications of not reflecting on how being undone is inextricable from specific genealogies of (inter)subjectivity (Heyes 2007)? Before beginning our discussion, though, we want to be explicit about what, in this chapter at least, is *not* our problem: Invisible Children, the complex issues surrounding development and international aid, and Joseph Kony.

The Kony 2012 campaign debuted on YouTube on 5 March 2012. The video (https://www.youtube.com/watch?v=Y4MnpzG5Sqc) was released by Invisible Children, a charitable organization founded by filmmaker Jason Russell, with the aim of raising public awareness of the atrocities committed by the militia group Lord's Resistance Army (LRA) operating in central and northern Africa; the ultimate goal was to bring its leader and an international war criminal, Joseph Kony, to justice. Within days, the video went viral, and at the time of writing, it has been viewed over 101 million times on YouTube. With the help of his young son, Russell introduces the audience to Joseph Kony and gives an artfully arranged and affectively compelling synopsis of the LRA and Joseph Kony, along with a detailed explanation of how the Kony 2012 campaign will lead to his eventual capture; through a poster campaign, the distribution of a $30 Action Kit, and pressure on American politicians to encourage and continue intervention, Joseph Kony will be "made famous."

Kony 2012 opens with the written words "Nothing is more powerful than an idea whose time has come, whose time is now." An image of the earth appears, and we hear a voice talking about the human desire to belong. Rapid images of traffic and loved ones hugging and connecting through social media whip by as we are told about the power of social media to connect people and to "change the way the world works." One-second clips of recognizable and heartwarming viral videos are shown—a clueless white elderly couple tries to use a webcam; an overzealous inspirational white child gives a short pep talk ("If you believe in yourself, you will know how to ride a bike. Rock and roll!"); a white twenty-nine-year-old woman hears for the first time after receiving a hearing device. We're hooked—we've laughed, we've experienced extensive visual stimulation, and our heartstrings have effectively been pulled by videos and narratives we already know. As more images of scrolling tweets and sharing videos flash before our eyes, we listen to an ominous script telling us that the world is changing, that older genera-tions are concerned, and that essentially, because the world is out of control, anything is possible. As we are beginning to wonder what this was all about (after all, our late modern minds have an attention span not much longer than one minute), a slow, clear, and straightforward voice tells us: "The next twenty-seven minutes are an experiment. [pause] But in order for it to work, you have to pay attention."

Kony 2012 can be examined from several angles. The lens through which we will examine this short documentary focuses on the interwoven layers of affect, embodiment, politics, and suffering. Specifically, we explore the relationships among Western subjectivity, affect, and the video's reliance on familiar narrative forms to trigger its Western audience affectively. We argue that the comfortability, predictability, and oversimplified nature of this narrative functions to keep the stability, innocence, and superiority of the Western subject intact; perhaps more problematically, the video forecloses (at the level of affect and bodies) a reflective engagement with the affective politics of difference. By exposing this narrative and the very familiarity of its characters and elements, we hope to push the reader (and ourselves) into a space of affective reflection—a space where what we feel is neither good nor bad, right nor wrong, but is nevertheless loaded with epistemic significance; where what we feel in our bodies is understood not only as an individual expression but as a deeply historical product of collective ways of knowing and feeling. Thus, we do not prescribe other avenues on how to find Joseph Kony or on what should be *done*. One of the central points we seek to make is the need to reimagine thinking *as* a kind of doing.

Repositioning thinking as doing is not an elaborate evasion of responsib-ility or a suggestion to do nothing in the face of suffering and injustice. On the contrary, we want to push against and probe the impulse to help others before knowing how our own affective and political histories are implicated in the kinds of actions we feel moved to take. We want to reflect on a wildly unsuccessful (predominantly white) Western history of helping in both global and local contexts (from colonization to international aid) and to question deeply the implications of the unreflected-upon moves to action that have shaped this history. Thus, rather than emphasize the specificities of the Kony 2012 campaign, or Invisible Children, we will use the video not only to push against the anxious desire to know and to save but also to explore how this desire is wrapped up in colonial histories. To do so, we consider how "international norms" hail Western subjects into this narrative (in this case, with the imagined Ugandan child and the imagined Ugandan warlord) as the bearer of knowledge and truth. We will examine the embodied and political aspects of the "knowing" Western subject, keeping at the forefront the inextricable relationship between power and knowledge.

We want to think through precisely why *Kony 2012* moved so many people. While the role of social media and the heated debate that followed the video are obvious contributors to its viral popularity, there is something very specific about the narrative and affective structure of the video that enabled it to resonate through, across, and between so many bodies. We argue that what was specific or unique about *Kony 2012* was the way it compacted so many elements common to stories of development, colonialism, and the industrial saviour complex in a very short, visually stimulating way. The video not only made us feel but also told us how to feel and what to do with those feelings. It demanded a seemingly intuitive action that made thinking about or reflecting upon this action counterintuitive or potentially unethical. In the face of overwhelming suffering and violence, the impulse of most people is to want to do something, to help, to stop it. However, that impulse—the embodied energy and intensity that one feels in the face of massive injustice—is not enough on its own. As we will discuss later, ethical and political transformation lies in the painful pedagogical work of processing and translating affective energy.

We begin our exploration of the video with a discussion of our methodology and the theoretical concepts upon which we draw to unpack the way bodies, identities, politics, and learning are all implicated with and through one another. Among those theoretical ideas are our conceptualizations of affect and emotion as they relate to bodies, power, and the embeddedness of ethics and politics in every encounter. We discuss how affective encounters are (re)produced within specific embodied histories of structural violence and oppression. We rely heavily, explicitly and implicitly, on the resonances between feminist philosopher Alexis Shotwell and antiracist feminist scholar Sara Ahmed, each of which draw heavily on the work of second-wave feminist Audre Lorde, whom we consider a precursor to many contemporary discussions surrounding bodies, politics, and pedagogies. What these thinkers bring to the fore is how embodiment and feeling (sensation and emotion) are inextricable from histories of domination and deeply sedimented structures of inequality and how these structures are manifested again and again in our daily interactions. Put another way, these thinkers point to the ways in which material practices and structures have a dynamic and co-constitutive relationship with the materiality of bodies and feelings: our feelings are literally shaped by these structures but they also reinforce and continue to reshape and reform these same structures. We draw from these insights to suggest that the stories told in *Kony 2012* are not only about what we "learn" but about the shape, movements, and reactions of our bodies.

In the second section, we use this theory to examine the highly emotional and moralistic responses to *Kony 2012* and the way in which these responses reaffirm Western subjectivity yet largely fail to interrogate the affective structure of the typical Western body-subject. In the video, Jason Russell shows a picture of Joseph Kony, the "bad guy," to his five-year-old son Gavin and explains to him that Kony "has an army," "takes children from their parents," "gives them a gun to shoot and he makes them shoot and kill other people" and "forces them to do bad things." When asked by Russell what he thinks, Gavin replies, "Sad" (9:30–10:38). The narratives told by the video are so simplistic that even a child can point to the "bad guy." Furthermore, the panic and hype caused by the video works to obscure the rampant systemic racism(s) that routinely occur on domestic soil. For example, in the Canadian context, the presence of sympathy toward child soldiers and the (fleeting) desire to capture Joseph Kony exists in stark contrast to the affective and political numbness toward the suffering of First Nations people, including the atrocities and treaty violations at the hands of the Canadian government and the historical and ongoing apathy and inattention toward missing and murdered Aboriginal women.

We conclude this chapter by discussing possibilities that can emerge from experimenting with our affect and cultivating new embodied practices—practices that can foster learning, unlearning, and relearning at the level of the body. We frame this discussion with Angela Davis's (1997, 318) notion of "basing identity on the politics rather than the politics on identity," which challenges the dominance of identity politics and focuses on political and ethical praxis. We give concrete examples of what Deleuze and Guattari's (2004, 149–166) conception of the "body without organs" might look like when put into practice; this conception points to how experimenting with bodily intensities has transformative political potential and can bring to consciousness the ways in which the body and bodily processes are politically and historically organized.

Methodological Approach and Theoretical Framework

Affective and Decolonizing Methodology

In this chapter, we centre decolonization not only as a change of framework synonymous with coalition politics but also as a process through which the complications of land, governance, and the lives of both colonized and settlers materialize. We take seriously Tuck and Yang's (2012, 21) call to their readers "to consider how the pursuit of critical consciousness, the pursuit of social justice through a critical enlightenment, can also be settler moves to innocence—diversions, distractions, which relieve the settler of feelings of guilt of responsibility, and conceal the need to give up land or power or privilege."

Following Tuck and Yang (2012), we consider decolonization as a more complicated process than the conscientization that Freire (2000) suggests is a mode of cultivating new ways of seeing the world. As Fanon (2004, 36) argues in *The Wretched of the Earth:*

> Decolonization, which sets out to change the order of the world, is, obviously, a program of complete disorder. But it cannot come as a result of magical practices, nor of a natural shock, nor of a friendly understanding. Decolonization, as we know, is a historical process: that is to say that it cannot be understood, it cannot become intelligible nor clear to itself except in the exact measure that we can discern the movements which give it historical form and content.

Thus, we seek to contribute to a decolonizing methodology that is, in many ways, impossible to define in advance, since it will take shape differently depending on local contexts and is inarticulable from the place we stand. For us, a decolonizing methodology accompanies a refusal to forget that the dominance of certain types of methods (modes of data collection), methodologies (modes of data analysis and interpretation), and epistemologies has played a massive role in the displacement and erasure of Indigenous peoples and ways of knowing.

The Kony 2012 campaign video aimed to mobilize American intervention and consumerist practices as a way of both stopping Kony and stopping child soldiers. This move to justify American imperialism and position the American government as the helper of those in the Global South, particularly through the infantilizing focus on children, necessitates a decolonizing lens that not only asks how we perceive and think about others but also how we position ourselves in relation to others and their land. A decolonizing method takes seriously a critical consciousness, but it also retains a focus on land, power, and privilege rather than simply being a move to reflect on and cultivate the self.

We understand affect to be the unconscious intensities we feel in our bodies; in contrast, emotion is the verbal expression of those intensities. Following several feminist, postcolonial, antiracist, and critical theorists and philosophers, we want to destabilize the dominant understanding of affect and emotion as individual and natural (and therefore indisputable) and to resituate affective encounters as sociohistorical. Patricia Clough (2010, 228) points out that since affect is felt on the unconscious register, "affect studies calls for experimentation in methodology." Given that our analysis of *Kony 2012* is primarily concerned with the affective politics of the video and how it moved bodies, our methodological approach is one attempt to meet this call for experimentation.

Drawing on feminist media analysis (Currie 1999; Jiwani 2009; Stabile and Kumar 2005), we look to *Kony 2012* for which narratives are being (re) told about the world. We suggest that these discourses reveal different ways of making meaning of the world (Weedon 1997, 23). We draw from critical discourse analysis to consider how ideology is at play in representations and the context of discourses—we examine the video for both what is said and what is not said, and we also attempt to read in the framing and affective pull of the video the ways in which bodies are being moved. We pay attention to camera angles: for example, when the viewer is positioned as "above" those in the screen, this conveys a sense of power and superiority (Jewitt and Oyama 2001, 135).

Following Nancy Armstrong's (2002) work on photography, we suggest that visual representations (including video) do epistemological work for the viewer, based on already existing categories and ideas. We read *Kony 2012* for the epistemological work that is accomplished and for how these representations compel particular affective responses. Thus, rather than doing a visual or discursive analysis, we take *Kony 2012* as an opportunity to consider how affect structures not only the framing of the campaign but also what viewers learn—bodily and intellectually. We ask what position the viewer is put into through camera angles and voiceovers, what is present and absent in the video, what viewers are asked to do, what the tone of the video is, who is speaking, and who is asked to act.

In our reading of the video, we found that tropes of hero or saviour, alongside of victims or innocents as well as villains or "bad guys," were deployed, with the viewer being ushered into the position of "hero." We ask what this may mean for orientations toward the stories of Invisible Children: How are bodies shaped and moved? What does the narrative propel bodies to do, or not do?

Our analysis of *Kony 2012* employs a critical, decolonizing framework that explores the possibilities and consequences of intervention, imperialism, and invasion. We turn now to the theoretical framework that enables an affective deconstruction of *Kony 2012*, suggesting that the video frames viewers as saviours, without attention to land, rather than enabling a reflexive engagement of consciousness and embodied relationality.

Theory, Thought, and Feeling

We draw on various theoretical traditions and concepts to think through the affective impact of, and responses to, *Kony 2012*. We use these concepts to examine how the video deploys familiar historical narratives; this examination moves us toward a space of critical reflection on how we might begin to work through feelings such as the ones evoked by the video and how these sorts of feelings tell us more than that Joseph Kony is bad and scary and that children getting kidnapped is sad. We want readers to engage seriously with the reality that in conjunction with deliberate rational thought, patterns of feeling structure our political and ethical actions and identities. Given this reality, thinking about how one feels, what it feels like to believe in something, how it feels to identify with something or someone, and, perhaps more pertinently, how it feels when one *cannot* identify with someone or something becomes an entry point into both embodied learning and complex political and ethical engagements with difference. However, because this is not how most of us are trained to learn and because feeling is so ubiquitous and involuntary, reflecting on our sensory habits can be a very emotionally draining and intellectually challenging process.

Discussing the embodied roots of subjectivity and the politically vital process of disidentification, Rosi Braidotti (2012, 35) states:

> Disidentification involves the loss of cherished habits of thought and representation, a move that can also produce fear and a sense of insecurity and nostalgia. Change is certainly a painful process, but this does not equate it with suffering. . . .
>
> Changes that affect one's sense of identity are especially delicate. Given that identifications constitute an *inner scaffolding* that supports one's sense of identity, shifting our imaginary identifications is not as simple as casting away a used garment. [emphasis added]

What Braidotti describes is the way in which affective patterns "constitute an inner scaffolding" that supports the self and how one makes sense of the world. Thus, changing these "cherished" habits is painful, because shifting how we think and feel not only inevitably alters how we perceive the world and, as such, is accompanied by a loss of parts of ourselves, but also potentially changes our relationships, career choices, patterns of speech, behaviours, and so on. The process of disidentification is "delicate" in that feeling stable grants us a certain amount of control and security in a world that can seem chaotic. Disidentification asks us to feel unstable in reflecting on our inner scaffolding.

Rather than destabilize or interrogate how our "inner scaffolding" is constituted by potentially oppressive patterns of thought and feeling, *Kony 2012* relies on well-known narratives that work to restabilize (rather than interrogate) the structure of Western subjectivity as the agent of historical change. Through a series of affective strategies, the video evokes intense emotions that at first glance appear to come from a place of genuine engagement but actually reinscribe Western identity at the expense of African bodies that have been discursively produced by the overdeveloped world.

Affect, Emotion, Intensity

At this juncture, it is important to explain how we define *affect* and to understand the difference between affect and emotion. According to Spinoza, *affect* refers to a force or felt intensity that impinges upon the body as well as to the idea that the affect evokes (cited in Massumi 2002, 31). This definition encapsulates both the intersubjective and embodied aspects of affect and its inextricability from thinking and ethical practice.

We follow Brian Massumi (2002, 27–28) in his understanding of affect as bodily intensity registered below or prior to subjective qualification. Emotion, in contrast, is determined by the extent to which a subject consciously narrates the affective experience of intensity into historically specific sociolinguistic discourses. In other words, emotion is the attempt to make sense of and capture affect within language. It is our interpretation and expression of our bodily intensity according to dominant social and political categories.

In *Foucault,* Deleuze (1988, 60–61) discusses the relationship between power (relations) and affect, explaining that exercised power is affective and that force is defined by its power to affect and be affected. Drawing heavily on Spinoza's parallelism (i.e., the idea that mind and body are not separate but rather act in parallel), Deleuze states that one's capacity *to be affected* and one's capacity *to affect* occur simultaneously. Since power and affect are physical, in that they literally shape and move bodies, doing the work of exploring our bodily capacities and "to learn to be affected" (Latour 2004, 205) becomes a political task. Learning to be affected, or to be more attuned to our sensual capacities, by unpacking both the meaning and histories embedded in our everyday encounters and the ways in which we narrate them can enhance our power to act and can also become an ongoing embodied, pedagogical, and ethical practice.

Deleuze and Guattari's (2004, 149–66) concept of the "body without organs" is one entry point into thinking through how this learning process can be undertaken; the authors discuss how experimenting with intensity, or affect, can enable us to challenge the established patterns of feeling through which the self is structured. For Deleuze and Guattari, the body is politically organized according to historically specific ideas about what is "normal" and "proper." The "normal" body-subject, which Deleuze and Guattari refer to as the "organism," regulates and controls its body, feelings, and desires according to these pregiven ideas about what is right, productive, and possible. The organism demands interpretation and organization from the body, with the goal of extracting embodied and affective labour for a higher "cause," be that capitalism, patriarchy, the nation, heterosexuality, or God (Protevi 2009, 94–101). The organism channels its bodily intensities into productive (capitalist social relations, proper labour practices) and reproductive (the species, proper sexual practices) labour because of the social stigma attached to "doing" the body otherwise (unproductive labour, nonreproductive sex, etc.).

In contrast to the heavily regulated bodily patterns of the organism lies the "body-without-organs"—the "body" whose conditioned habits have been released from its controlled form, thus leaving thoughts, feelings, and desires totally open to any and all possible connections (Deleuze and Guattari 1987, 30). The body-without-organs does not interpret anything—it is driven by desire. It is a body-subject without a social filtration system that tells one what is and is not right, what should and should not be said, felt, eaten, or done.

To clarify, the body-without-organs and the organism are both *limits* on a spectrum (no one is a perfect organism or a completely disorganized body-without-organs). Through consistent and careful experimentation, however, one can become conscious of the ways in which the body is politically organized according to truths (given by God and/or experts) that have been absorbed into our embodied and emotional habits.

The project of experimenting with, asking after, and working to become aware of our affective and emotional habits is a never-ending practice. It is a process that can often be incredibly difficult and dangerous; Deleuze and Guattari (1987, 160) caution us to use the "art of dosages" in order to keep ourselves safe and intact: "You don't do it with a sledgehammer, you use a very fine file." They use the drug addict and hypochondriac as examples of those who have gone too far in their experimentation and have become unrecognizable to themselves and the social world (163). Being open to thinking through our bodies and with our affect then becomes vital to living an ethical life. This requires the work of moving through our feelings and through the possible thoughts, norms (clothing, eye contact, gender expression, sexual orientation), beliefs (about God, nature, society), and affects (these tears welling up in me mean that I am sad) that contributed to the manifestation of that particular feeling. Cultivating practices that seek to bring to awareness how our bodies are vital to learning can aid in the process of integrating our minds and our bodies.

The creators of *Kony 2012* relied on historically produced differences between the viewers and subjects of the video in order to maximizing the affective response. We believe that the visceral response to the video was exacerbated by the fact that YouTube is often watched voluntarily and in solitude, thereby maximizing a certain level of attention and minimizing the chance of a mediated response; in addition, the "comments" section was turned off, further exacerbating the solitude of watching and foreclosing the possibility of meaningful dialogue. Our problem with the outpouring of emotion that the video evoked is not the reaction itself but the fact that the intensity of this affect obscured many of the difficult realities of this sort of suffering, including the contexts of the conflict that have sustained it and Western implication in this conflict. The affective response was directed to an emotional narration that affirmed separateness between the presumed viewers and the subjects of the video.

Despite the seeming ethical simplicity of the video, the visceral responses to it were not necessarily right, true, or ethical. Affect is about style, colour, texture, speed, culturally specific images, narration, tonal vibrations, and how these elements move our bodies in ways that are below conscious awareness. Instead of opening a space where a critical engagement with "cherished habits" of feeling could occur (Braidotti 2012, 35), the *Kony 2012* creators artfully and intentionally arranged all of these elements in order to ensure a high-impact affective result and then provided outlets for this affect. Intense feelings, in that they come from our bodies, are involuntary and are generally considered "natural"; thus they are often interpreted as a sort of truth. One might think: How can anyone *not* be appalled by the fact that this is happening in our world? How can any caring, conscientious person *not* want to do something about this? The video relied on feelings alone as enough. However, feelings alone are not always enough; they have a long history of being created by and reproducing incredibly violent and oppressive power inequalities. For example, take a mundane racial encounter. A white woman walking alone at night passes a group of young black men; she may experience embodied triggers that signal fear and, based on that feeling, may come to a seemingly rational and intuitive conclusion that there is in fact something inherently dangerous about black men. She came to this conclusion based on the *effect* the encounter had on her body. However, if she had probed the *cause* of that feeling, she may have questioned the extent to which the history of slavery and mass media representations of black men as dangerous and sexually predatory structured her initial and seemingly natural feelings of fear.

Recognizing the Villain: Affective Encounters and Racialized Histories

Sara Ahmed's work on histories of encounters with difference is very useful for exploring racialized histories in the context of *Kony 2012*. As evidenced by never-ending debates on comment threads, Facebook sites, and blogs, virtual or "imaginary" encounters are enfleshed and literally move bodies. We assert that *Kony 2012* triggered histories of black-white racial violence and the familiar figures of the dangerous black man and the innocent child, alongside that of the white saviour, all of which ensured the affective impact on its viewership.

A long history of racial encounters helped to make Joseph Kony a recognizable (online) stranger who had already been pseudo-materialized through viewers' local (real-life) encounters. Due to the "racialized fear that the perception of blacks" evokes in many white people (Protevi 2009, 174), the image of the black man is a loaded signifier with a history of being used for specific purposes, often with the intention of striking fear into the white population in order to garner political support and ensure white economic and political dominance (Westen 2007, 60–68). Affective responses to loaded images are particularly potent in the political realm because the impact often occurs below conscious awareness. In *Kony 2012*, the images are intended to hail white subjects into a particular relation to, and history of, racial encounters. In Ahmed's interpretation of Louis Althusser's theory of subject formation, she considers hailing as a simultaneous recognition of the self and the stranger (Ahmed 2006, 107). That is, one becomes a subject through ongoing judgments of difference between the self and the stranger both consciously and subconsciously. The process of subject formation is thus inherently intersubjective and collective; the "I" can only take shape as it moulds itself into a larger (and in the case of the Kony campaign, predominantly white and Western) "we," in contrast to a pseudo-materialized "them." Recognizing the stranger and then taking action to remove and punish him (in this case, Joseph Kony) provides Western subjects with a needed mechanism to reassert and stabilize a (civilized, moral, good) "we" in opposition to an uncivilized, immoral, inhuman "them." However, and this is particularly true in the case of Kony, the distance of the stranger shifts its function from an actual to an imaginary, fairy-tale–like monster from which we derive pleasure. Much like the pleasure in watching a thriller or horror movie, the "Third World" monster functions to distract from, yet reinforce, real-life spatial negotiations that accompany encounters with bodies read as different at "home."

Embodied encounters are the raw material of subject formation, and therefore, thinking through our feelings and feeling through our thoughts as we encounter difference is an ongoing pedagogical process. Ahmed (2000, 7) contends that the process of recognition operates as a visual economy, since it relies on seeing difference. What might it look like to decentre the reliance on sight—on the seemingly unavoidable capacity to see difference—in order to bring into focus other sensory experiences evoked by strange encounters? And in the context of late modernity, what would it mean to think through the implications of intersubjective encounters in the context of online publics and to reflect on the way these encounters interpellate and thus constitute and produce new subjectivities into and through processes of differentiation? Since the rapid and ongoing decisions that fuel processes of subject formation are made below explicit patterns of thinking, their vast pedagogical possibilities often remain unacknowledged.

Kony 2012 leaves its viewers with an intense affective charge that could have pedagogical potential; however, what is masterful about the video is its (albeit implicit) built-in pedagogy. Rather than leaving with a sense of dis-ease, a sense of questioning, and a desire to learn more about the context of the conflict, viewers leave affectively satisfied and content with the knowledge of how to do their part. In other words, the video does not require the viewer to engage with the history and ongoing practices of colonialism and with the way in which Western subjects are directly implicated in these processes. Rather than feeling ashamed of being implicated in the suffering of others, the viewer leaves feeling benevolent and satisfied. We feel that this is another major failure of *Kony 2012*, and we want to follow Alexis Shotwell's (2011) exploration of the potential productivity of white shame. Sparing a white viewership of responsibility relies on the all-too-common assumptions that white people "feeling bad" is the wrong way to go about achieving antiracist goals and that positive feelings (happiness, pride, excitement) are intrinsically innocent and conducive to building solidarity. In terms of the Kony 2012 video and campaign, the potential of white people engaging with their "bad feelings" associated with historical and current colonialism was obscured by a positive (and historically constituted) feeling of helping. The affective identifications that uphold unjust gender and racial formations were relied on rather than challenged, leaving the embodied, historical, and economic structures that reproduce inequality, and the Western subjectivities that rely on and benefit from those structures, more secure than ever.

Cultivating Practices and "Identifying into" Politics

> Our seldom-inspected common sense posits a separation—or even an opposition—between thought, understood as cerebral reflection, and action, understood as embodied engagement with the world. This makes it hard to see thinking itself as a kind of action—that we are *doing thinking*, in other words, touching the world and being touched by it and in the process things (and we) are changing. (Gibson-Graham 2006, xxix)

In a "risk society" where society is increasingly oriented to towards identifying and managing risk (Beck 1992), our bodily capacities and emotional energies are increasingly expected to be under our control. They are simultaneously being used and exploited for political and economic gain in relation to risk and safety; doing the work of sorting through our affects is therefore an ethical necessity for feminist, queer, antiracist, and anticapitalist struggles. In this section, we give concrete examples to prompt affective experimentations. We do not provide "rules" on how one should feel but rather attempt to develop a guide to open up the reader to the plethora of ways in which we can actively and thoughtfully engage with our bodily sensibilities and capacities.

Here we move from thinking in particular about the Kony 2012 video to thinking broadly about practices that may challenge common responses to witnessing suffering. Following Angela Davis's (1997, 318) desire for folks to work at "basing the[ir] identity on politics rather than the[ir] politics on identity," we suggest some practices that may help to cultivate new affective and emotional responses that push at, rather than reinforce, liberal forms of identity politics. Several scholars and philosophers have addressed the role of bodily experimentation in better understanding how we relate to and are composed through our encounters with the external world (Deleuze and Guattari 2004; Connolly 2002), and in that spirit, we have constructed several scenarios to help prompt such affective experimentation. The types of experimentation we are imagining here are not of the scientifically rigorous sort. Rather, we imagine experimentation within an ethos that is mindful, playful, and gentle; one that is not invested in obtaining particular results or the Truth but that seeks to push against taken-for-granted and often unreflected-upon patterns of thought and feeling. The purpose of such experimentation is to open up possibilities for new insights, which, "once developed, can inform the reflective techniques we apply to ourselves to stimulate thought, complicate judgment, or to refine ethical sensibility" (Connolly 2002, 13). The scenarios that follow are structured around questions rather than prescriptions because of the necessity that they remain open to subjective reflection rather than foreclose what possible affects should be.

While recognizing that the word *experimentation* can evoke negative affect because of the ways in which colonizing and Western science have and continue to use "experimentation" as a guise to construe subjects as objects (including nonhuman animals), we continue to use the term for an important reason. *Experimentation* is a term in the literature in relation to the project of changing embodiment, relation to others, and thought *through* action with the hope of cultivating a different future, but with unpredictable "results." While terms such as *reflection* and *inquiry* may be offered as synonyms, we feel that *experimentation* signals the embodied component of this engagement. Reflection and inquiry are often imagined as cognitive processes, but the processes that we are suggesting emphasize the embodied and material components of thought, as well as affect and matter. We maintain concerns about the use of the word *experimentation* because of these histories, but we also use it with the hope that this experimentation can be seen in a different light, in that it isn't searching for truth, nor for a way to fix things; rather, it is conducted in the spirit of cultivating open futures without a predicted ending.

PRACTICE #1: *Experimenting with Anger*

In "The Uses of Anger," Audre Lorde (1997 [1981], 280) states that

> anger expressed and translated into action in the service of our vision and our future is a liberating and strengthening act of clarification, for it is in the painful process of this translation that we identify who are our allies, with whom we have grave differences, and who are our genuine enemies.
> Anger is loaded with information and energy.

For Lorde, anger is a tool that can be used to combat both personal and institutional oppression and is perhaps our most powerful energy source for political change. Lorde clarifies, however, that it is in the "painful process" of translating anger into action that the potential for change lies. Directing our bodily intensities, such as anger, into intentional and careful ethical thought and action can provide the initial motivation to gain a deeper understanding not only of systems of power but of one another. As stated above, *Kony 2012* does this translation for us. The pain that inevitably accompanies the process of translating our rage, grief, or love into action will certainly be reduced in having a third party do it for us, but the comfort this grants us evacuates our capacity to be intentional with our thoughts and feelings (even if we ultimately decide that our translation was mistaken). To be clear, thinking of anger as politically and epistemologically useful does not mean that being angry at or toward others is useful. Reflecting on and converting our bodily intensity into political energy is a learning process that gives us the tools to work through not only our own anger but also the anger of others.

Example: As rape cases come up in the media, we are constantly confronted with discourses of "victim blaming." Women are blamed for what they were wearing, how they were acting, who they were with, and their sexual histories. Men's potentially altered futures are lamented and the media suggests that their "loss" is more poignant than the loss of survivors. Our rage fills us. How does our anger move us? At whom is our anger directed? On what basis are those around us angry? How can we channel our rage into something intentional, political, and ethically poignant?

PRACTICE #2: *Experimenting with Comfort*

In discussing the relationships among comfort, normativity, and heterosexual privilege, Ahmed (2004, 147) states that comfort suggests "well-being and satisfaction" as well as "ease and easiness." She goes on: "To be comfortable is to be so at ease with one's environment that it is hard to distinguish where one's body ends and the world begins. One fits, and by fitting, the surfaces of bodies disappear from view" (148).

Following Tuck and Yang's (2012, 3) assertion that a consideration of land is central to the project of decolonization, we suggest using Ahmed's definition of comfort to consider the ways we move through space. Are there places we do not go to? Are there places we love to go to? Why do we love going there? Where are the places we only drive through? Who lives there? Who walks through this space? Are there spaces where we feel we do not belong, where our body comes into view—what does this feel like, why is our body brought into view, by whom and how? Are there ways to escape this, to become comfortable once again? Are there places where we feel "at home" where other bodies are brought into our view—which bodies, and what kind of view?

Example: Walking from the east end of Toronto to the west end of Toronto, I passed through various neighbourhoods—Leslieville (up and coming), Riverdale (wealthy), Regent Park (notorious), the Eaton Centre (touristic), Bay Street (financial), Kensington Market (community-focused). I paid attention to which sorts of bodies filled which spaces, whether I felt "at home" or "in view" in neighbourhoods and why. What were the things I had heard about Regent Park? The Eaton Centre?

PRACTICE #3: *Experimenting with Solidarity*

In explaining the genealogical method, Foucault (2003, 361) states that, as genealogist, one need not separate oneself from one's corporeality (as positivism demands); on the contrary, genealogy narrows "its vision to those things nearest to it—the body, the nervous system, nutrition, digestion, and energies" and approaches the most taken-for-granted and seemingly private and natural inclinations with a "joyous" suspicion (361). Dominant conceptions of the body posit it—and especially its processes, whether biological, physiological, or neurological—as natural, stable, and, most significantly, passive. What happens when we shift our thinking and draw our attention to the vital aspects of our bodies? What does it mean to think of our biology as socialized and historical? What would it look like to actively work on anxiety triggers that have been established through not only a personal but also a racial and colonial history?

Example: As white Canadian women, we may think through the implicit understandings (see Shotwell 2011) that inform both our emotional and affective resistance to finding solidarity with the Idle No More movement and our trust in the Canadian government. We might ask ourselves these questions: How much knowledge do I possess about treaty agreements and violations? Do I believe that the Canadian government is working toward the same social justice goals that I am? How do racial stereotypes about Canada's First Nations people foster this resistance to solidarity? What habits (spending habits, habits of speech, eating habits, and so on) may be threatened by discussing the extent to which my (white) privilege has been and continues to be made possible by past and present colonialisms? What taken-for-granted personal or cultural skills (such as driving, taking transit, doing homework, or getting to school on time) might I possess that make suggestions of assimilation seem nonviolent or even practical? To what extent do I feel the weight of the history of colonialism in my body as I walk through my day? What does this weight (or lack of weight) tell me about my experience of oppression, and thus my capacity to fully understand it?

PRACTICE #4: *Experimenting with Violence and Grief*

Judith Butler (2004, 20) argues that liberal versions of politics and personhood fail "to do justice to passion and grief and rage, all of which tear us from ourselves, bind us to others, transport us, undo us, and implicate us in lives that are not our own, sometimes fatally, irreversibly." With an eye to international relations, and particularly through *Kony 2012,* we have examined which subjectivities are capable of action and what images and figurations move us to particular modes of action. Butler suggests that "international norms . . . insist that certain kinds of violences are impermissable, that certain lives are vulnerable and worthy of protection, that certain deaths are grievable and worthy of public recognition" (32). In the Kony 2012 campaign, the figure of the child soldier makes invisible not only the adult soldier but also the context of the conflict, and it hampers our ability to see ourselves as implicated in these conflicts. Rather than encourage a move to imagine ourselves (or our children) in the place of the other, we suggest that we must ask through which frames these images become understandable, moving, and grievable. What images are erased through these framings, and how do they reaffirm our subjectivity rather than undo us?

Example: In compelling campaigns for girls' education, girls are figured as vulnerable and fragile and are presented as objects to invest in for the good of the future of families, communities, and the men in the girls' lives. How does this framing ignore the desires and motivations of girls? What is it about education that compels us to fund programs in ways that, for example, complicated narratives of schooling and gender inequality do not? What are the framings that move us to donate, and how does the movement for girls' education maintain a particular subject position? What are the futures made possible for us and for girls through this framing? How much do I know about the educational system in any of the countries discussed in campaigns and how do particular assumptions about the Majority World inform my understanding of "need"? How do I conceptualize learning and education? How does donating money bring me into relation with others?

Conclusion

We chose to focus on the Kony 2012 campaign video not because it is unique but because it is symptomatic of our contemporary political and emotional climate and its distancing from critical, embodied pedagogies. Like the creators of most images, films, commercials, and documentaries, the makers of *Kony 2012* deployed familiar narratives that resonate with racial and colonial histories. The effectiveness of the video relied on a lack of critical, embodied thought about the video itself or the issues it presented. *Kony 2012* moved so many bodies because it was built upon the scaffolding of internalized, uncanny narratives about race, gender, and class that are so common that their implications or validity are rarely questioned. Why people were moved in particular ways by the representation of Joseph Kony—the villain—in this video is a key question that partially (if not entirely) speaks to the ways in which discourses of racialization are organized into one's being. What was it about the plight of Ugandan children that moved us into an enraged frenzy? How does being the ones doing the saving make us feel, and what histories (and presents) continue to place us, structurally, as the savers and others, somewhere else in the world, as needing to be saved? And, lastly, the Foucauldian question: Who benefits?

We argue that being undone, as Butler describes it, is to be undone internally—that *who I am* and the patterns of thinking and feeling I use to navigate the world are troubled and shaken. This undoing is material as well as discursive in that the affective and emotional impact of an undoing is felt but its quality and intensity is contingent upon the social, historical, political, and economic ways of knowing that structure our bodies and minds. We have a strong sense that it is highly unlikely that *Kony 2012* made people come "undone" in this way; rather, it tightened and strengthened inner scaffoldings along with existing structures of inequality. That being said, what makes *Kony 2012* an important site for thinking through the ethical politics of affect is that the documentary highlights precisely how moving feelings and bodies is vital to the reinscription of difference and the reinforcement of dominant ways of knowing. It shows us the material impact of intense emotions and thus the exciting and unpredictable poten-tiality of embodied intensity. However, our main point is that because it is impossible to do one or the other in isolation, thinking and feeling through intense encounters (with people, inanimate objects, YouTube videos, ads, books, scholarly material, etc.), while not a smooth or comfortable process, is of vital ethical and political importance in a contemporary global climate characterized by expanding entities that seek to squash uncertainty, risk, and critical engagement with *the way things are*. The kind of learning we encourage is characterized by careful and active engagement with the kind of undoing that makes one question oneself (in relation to others, to land, to economic policies, to official national or regional discourses) through relat-ing immediate affective and emotional responses to histories of oppression as they are lived in our present.

References

Ahmed, Sara. 2000. *Strange Encounters: Embodied Others in Post-coloniality.* London: Routledge.

———. 2004. *The Cultural Politics of Emotion.* New York and London: Routledge.

————. 2006. *Queer Phenomenology: Orientations, Objects, Others*. Durham: Duke University Press.

Armstrong, Nancy. 2002. *Fiction in the Age of Photography: The Legacy of British Realism*. Cambridge, MA: Harvard University Press.

Beck, Ulrich. 1992. *Risk Society: Towards a New Modernity*. New Delhi: Sage.

Braidotti, Rosi. 2012. "Interview with Rosi Braidotti." In *New Materialism: Interviews and Cartographies*, edited by Rick Dophijn and Iris van der Tuin, 19–37. Ann Arbor, MI: Open Humanities Press.

Butler, Judith. 2004. *Undoing Gender*. New York: Psychology Press.

Clough, Patricia. 2010. "Afterword: The Future of Affect Studies." *Body and Society* 16(1): 222–30.

Connolly, William E. 2002. *Neuropolitics: Thinking, Culture, Speed*. Minneapolis: University of Minnesota Press.

Currie, Dawn. 1999. *Girltalk: Adolescent Magazines and Their Readers*. Toronto: University of Toronto Press.

Davis, Angela. 1997. "Interview With Lisa Lowe—'Angela Davis: Reflections on Race, Class, and Gender in the USA.'" In *The Politics of Culture in the Shadow of Capital*, edited by Lisa Lowe and David Lloyd, 303–23. Durham, NC: Duke University Press.

Deleuze, Gilles. 1988. *Foucault*. Edited and translated by Seán Hand. London: Athlone Press. Originally published in French as *Foucault* (1986).

Deleuze, Gilles, and Félix Guattari. 2004[1987]. *A Thousand Plateaus: Capitalism and Schizophrenia*. Translation and foreword by Brian Massumi. Minneapolis: University of Minnesota Press. Originally published as *Capitalisme et schizophrénie*, vol. 2, *Mille plateaux* (1987).

Fanon, Frantz. 2004. *The Wretched of the Earth*. Translated by Richard Philcox. New York: Grove Press. Originally published as *Les damnés de la terre* (1961).

Foucault, Michel. 2003. "Nietzsche, Genealogy, History." In *The Essential Foucault: Selections from Essential Works of Foucault, 1954–1984*, edited by Paul Rabinow and Nikolas Rose, 351–69. New York: The New Press.

Freire, Paulo. 2000. *Pedagogy of the Oppressed*. Translated by Myra Bergman Ramos. Thirtieth anniversary edition. New York: Continuum. Originally published as *Pedagogia do oprimido* (1968).

Gibson-Graham, J. K. 2006. *A Postcapitalist Politics*. Minneapolis: University of Minnesota Press.

Heyes, Cressida. 2007. *Self-Transformations: Foucault, Ethics, and Normalized Bodies*. London: Oxford University Press.

Jewitt, Carey, and Rumiko Oyama. 2001. "Visual Meaning: A Social Semiotic Approach." In *Handbook of Visual Analysis*, edited by Theo van Leeuwen and Carey Jewitt, 134–56. London: Sage.

Jiwani, Yasmin. 2009. "Helpless Maidens and Chivalrous Knights: Afghan Women in the Canadian Press." *University of Toronto Quarterly* 78(2): 728–44.

Latour, Bruno. 2004. "How to Talk About the Body? The Normative Dimension of Science Studies." *Body and Society* 10(2–3): 205–29.

Lorde, Audre. 1997 [1981]. "The Uses of Anger." *Women's Studies Quarterly* 25(1–2): 278–85.

Massumi, Brian. 2002. *Parables for the Virtual: Movement, Affect, Sensation.* Durham, NC: Duke University Press.

Protevi, John. 2009. *Political Affect: Connecting the Social and the Somatic.* Minneapolis: University of Minnesota Press.

Shotwell, Alexis. 2011. *Knowing Otherwise: Race, Gender, and Implicit Understanding.* University Park: Pennsylvania State University Press.

Stabile, Carol A., and Deepa Kumar. 2005. "Unveiling Imperialism: Media, Gender, and the War on Afghanistan." *Media, Culture, and Society* 27(5): 765–82.

Tuck, Eve, and K. Wayne Yang. 2012. "Decolonization Is Not a Metaphor." *Decolonization: Indigeneity, Education, and Society* 1(1): 1–40.

Weedon, Chris. 1997. *Feminist Practice and Poststructural Theory.* Oxford: Blackwell.

Westen, Drew. 2007. *The Political Brain: The Role of Emotion in Deciding the Fate of the Nation.* New York: Public Affairs.

5 Volatile Bodies and Vulnerable Researchers

Ethical Risks of Embodiment Research

Carla Rice

Feminist methodology as it has developed over the past thirty years offers a critical response to conventional research, which is seen by some to carry the risk of exploiting participants. Although feminist researchers have envisioned more self-conscious and accountable ways of doing research, many acknowledge the potential for abuse inherent in researching other and/or othered people's lives. This is particularly true for feminists researching groups less powerful than those to which they belong (Brown and Strega 2005). In this chapter, I draw on critical feminist theories of the body (Fausto-Sterling 2000; Grosz 1994), feminist disability studies (Garland Thomson 1997; Shildrick 1997, 2002), and postconventional and postcolonial research methodologies (Hesse-Biber 2007; Naples 2003; Rice 2009) to consider ethical dilemmas in critical research focused on women's accounts of embodiment.

My analysis in this chapter is founded on two qualitative research projects, both with a focus on embodiment—an arts-based project, titled Envisioning New Meanings of Disability and Difference, that used digital storytelling to consider the efficacy of the arts in challenging misperceptions of women and gender variant people, and an earlier project in which I interviewed a diverse group of women about their experiences of embodiment. Drawing on examples from this research, I reflect on what I regard as a central ethical challenge of critical embodiment research:

the need for all researchers, including those with and without embodied differences, to maintain self-reflexivity and vulnerability with regard to their embodied experiences and histories when conducting research with groups whose bodies are socially constructed as anomalous. These groups include people with mobility and sensory disabilities, people with chronic illness, people whose faces, physical attributes, and/or body sizes fall outside the range considered to be normal, and LGBTQ people, especially those who may not neatly fit into categories of masculine/male or feminine/female and whose gender presentation may confound onlookers, as well as those perceived as racially or ethnically different from the dominant unmarked norm. In analyzing the experience of the differently bodied, I necessarily also examine the ways in which my own body history has influenced my interpretative process.

Envisioning New Meanings

The two research projects on which I will draw below both explore the influence of cultural meanings on women's embodiment. Beyond the body beautiful, they consider the significance of messages about the "abject body" in shaping each woman's sense of body self. Julia Kristeva (1982, 1–2) defines the abject as the "twisted braid of affects and thoughts" that overwhelms us when we are confronted with "the jettisoned object," that is, with something that is neither us nor not-us—some aspect of ourselves that we have rejected. In particular, we experience the abject when we encounter bodily fluids, open wounds, diseased or dying bodies, corpses, and other evidence of the unwanted aspects of our embodiment. People whose bodies remind us of the unknowability and uncontainability of our own bodies, of our vulnerability to injury and disease, and of the certainty of our death are therefore rejected—jettisoned from the social body.

While women in proximity to the ideal may become objects of the gaze, those who inhabit abject bodies are, according to disability theorist Rosemarie Garland-Thomson, subjected to "the stare." Staring, for Garland-Thomson, involves our urgent compulsion to look at disaster, or what Mike Ervin calls "the car wreck phenomenon" (quoted in Garland-Thomson 2009, 3); the double take we do when an ordinary look fails and we want to know more about something different; and the intense visual exchange between people when we can't pull our eyes away from the unfamiliar, the unexpected, the strange. Since staring often defines the relationship between disabled and nondisabled people, it is a primary site through which those who embody difference face the curiosity, fear, and hostility of nondisabled others (Tregaskis 2002, 461). Although staring is most often a voyeuristic, dominating act, Garland-Thomson argues that the stare has the potential to transform perceptions and create possibilities for mutual recognition, especially when mediated by the arts. In what follows, I outline how disability is typically represented in mainstream culture and then turn to how disability studies and the arts represent disability differently. Before returning to Garland-Thomson's point later in this section, I briefly discuss how some scholars are applying decolonizing theory to representations of, and responses to, disability.

Representations of disability, by shaping people's taken-for-granted understandings and expectations, also inform the ways in which currently nondisabled folks perceive and treat those who embody difference.[1] The representational history of disabled people can largely be characterized as one of being put on display or hidden away (Eliza Chandler, pers. comm., 3 November 2012). According to disability scholar Eliza Chandler, people living with disabilities have been, and continue to be, displayed in freak shows, in medical journals, in charity campaigns, and as evil or pitiable figures in novels and films. At the same time, disabled bodies have generally been removed from the public eye, hidden in institutions, hospitals, and group homes. Even today, disability continues to be interpreted in our medicalized culture as the polar opposite of health and is thought of in terms of deficiency, limitation, or flaw (Metzl and Poirier 2004).

Solutions to the "problem" of disability can take a number of forms and—in our highly medicalized, technologized, and individualized world—tend to entail elimination, cure, or the will to overcome. While people sometimes seek out cures and are relieved to find them, it is also true that many impairments aren't curable, so to perceive all disability as something that needs to be cured discounts the human experience of living with disability (Chandler and Rice 2013, 5). This view also elides the reality that because of economic and political barriers in Canada and beyond, many people with

---

1 Since disability is a temporal condition that is both dynamic and emergent over the lifespan, I use the term "currently nondisabled" to capture the reality that almost all nondisabled people will become disabled if they live to old age.

disabilities simply do not have access to treatments and supports that could improve the quality of their lives.

Efforts to eliminate disability through genetic screening or prenatal testing (which often results in aborting disabled fetuses) ignore the reality that most people acquire disability not genetically but through living in the world (Chandler and Rice 2013, 6). This suggests that the making of disability is strongly influenced by people's social conditions, a point I take up below. And since most of us, if we live long enough, will undergo the gradually disabling process of aging, disability should not be seen as exclusive to a small number of people but rather as a central part of the human condition (Garland-Thomson 1997, 13). Finally, the "overcoming" narrative that is common in disability sports and in popular films assumes that one must surmount disability to achieve and thus that disability is antithetical to achievement. By turning those with disabilities into heroes, these larger-than-life portrayals also give viewers little space to make sense of the nuances of and contradictions within the experience of living with disability and hence can erase people's humanity (Rice, Renooy, and Odette 2008, 7).

It is important to note that in addition to age, dimensions of social position and power such as race and class strongly influence who might acquire a disability. Structured by legacies of colonialism and the logics of capitalism, contemporary global power relations sanction dangerous working conditions and unhealthy living environments and fuel wars that disable millions worldwide (Meekosha 2011). Poor and racialized people living in the Global South and in polluted and unsafe areas in the Global North, as well as Indigenous peoples living on poorly resourced reserves, are especially vulnerable to impairment. Here, the conditions wrought by colonialism and capitalism not only produce impairment but also privilege certain bodies (such as physically "fit" bodies) over others, thus fuelling discrimination against those with disabilities (Rice 2014, 101). Put differently, race- and class-based oppressions that impair bodies (among them unregulated global capitalism, colonial histories, and legacies that have rendered some groups more vulnerable to impairment) intersect the oppression of disabled bodies (through high unemployment or by being seen as frightening and "other" or as childlike and expendable, to name a few forms of disability oppression), resulting in the production of disability as a problem.

In addition, just as social location influences who acquires disability, it also strongly impacts how different groups of disabled people are represented and treated in society. For example, racialized and poor folks with disabilities, especially those with learning disabilities or mental health issues, are often assumed to be lazy, angry, criminal, and drug/alcohol addicted. Nirmala Erevelles and Andrea Minear (2010, 127) analyze the case of Eleanor Bumpurs, "a poor, elderly, overweight, disabled black woman" who was murdered by police officers as they attempted to evict her from her apartment. The authors question whether a rich, white, and thin disabled woman would be similarly treated and then go on to argue that many critical feminists who embrace analyses of race, class, and gender often fail to engage with disability as a determinant of social location in their research.

In the Canadian context, it is worth considering the treatment of Kimberly Rogers, a poor, white, disabled college student and mother-to-be who, in 2001, died by suicide in her Ontario apartment while under house arrest for welfare fraud. This young woman, who was suffering from severe depression, was pushed into suicide by moralistic public opinion and punitive social policies that treated her as a criminal simply for having received a student loan while living on welfare (Landsberg 2003). Here, marginalization based on social class may have played a part in the production of Kimberley's disability (assuming that the economic crisis she faced contributed to her depression), and social perceptions of her class affiliation may have influenced the court's punitive response to her. At the very least, it is likely that Kimberley would have been treated with more respect by health and welfare systems had she been middle class and partnered, and she probably wouldn't have been criminalized.

These examples show that while disability is represented and treated in complex and contradictory ways, in mainstream culture, the underlying message remains the same: that disability is undesired and that those with disabilities lack capability and vitality (Chandler and Rice 2013, 8). Recognizing the paucity of powerful stories about disability and difference that circulate in our society, I am guided by the insights of Nigerian novelist Chimamanda Ngozi Adichie. She reminds us of the danger of relying on only one story: "The single story creates stereotypes, and the problem with stereotypes is not that they are untrue, but that they are incomplete. They make one story become the only story" (Adichie 2009).

Disability studies teaches that disability can be represented otherwise: as a life worth living, as an identity, and as a culture. It argues that to achieve full rights, people with disabilities must be represented as fully human and that embodied difference must be seen as an integral part of human diversity rather than simply tolerated. In recent years, a generative disability arts movement has developed a new genre that aims to give expression to disability experience and to reimagine bodily difference (Allan 2005; Roman 2009a, 2009b). The racially and culturally diverse San Francisco-based performance troupe Sins Invalid, for example, revisions imperfect bodies as aesthetically interesting, exciting, and vital through cutting-edge performances that challenge medical and cultural paradigms of normal and sexy, "offering instead a vision of beauty and sexuality inclusive of all individuals and communities."[2] Disability arts can offer a powerful counternarrative to mainstream cultural practices, which assume that disability makes life not worth living and which proliferate biotechnologies and bioethics (genetic testing, physician assisted suicide) that eliminate disability from populations. One way to take up the challenge posed by disability justice activists is through telling and listening to stories that represent disability in new ways. This is where the first research project I wish to discuss, Envisioning New Meanings, comes in.

The power of the arts to enhance understanding, open possibilities, and break down barriers is indisputable (Cole et al. 2004; Gallagher 2009). However, there is little research that has examined the impact when misrepresented groups seek to generate and communicate their embodied experience and knowledge directly and creatively. In response to this gap, I became involved in Envisioning New Meanings of Disability and Difference, an arts-based research project with women living with disabilities and differences. The aim of Envisioning was to uncover and address the gaps in how women with disabilities and differences see themselves and are seen by others. In intensive workshops that taught the fundamentals of representation, storytelling, and filmmaking (Lambert 2010; 2013), participants from diverse locations had opportunities to make digital stories (first person films that pair narratives with visuals) in order to speak back

---

2 "About Us: Our Mission," *Sins Invalid: An Unshamed Claim to Beauty in the Face of Invisibility,* n.d., http://sinsinvalid.org/mission.html.

to dominant representations about their bodies and lives (Rice et al. 2015; Rice, Chandler, and Changfoot 2016).

Creating space where disability was welcomed allowed artists to tell complex and nuanced stories about their embodied experience. Working in groups designed and led by facilitators living with disabilities and differences also gave participants the opportunity, individually and collectively, to challenge outsiders' perceptions and to explore alternative ideas of difference. The digital storytelling genre, with its unique emphasis on image and narrative, enabled storytellers to represent their sensory worlds in new ways, conveying the volatility and instability of human embodied experience and opening possibilities for intimate encounters with difference. Recall that Rosemarie Garland-Thomson (2009) understands staring as a complex response to difference, one that can bring about domination or mutual recognition. She suggests that the stare is productive when the starer is open to being changed and the staree is able to wield some control by telling her story in a way that enables both parties to recognize each other's personhood.

In their piece, *Body Language,* Envisioning filmmaker Jes Sachse dares viewers to look at their body and think about how it feels to look like them, thus illustrating Garland-Thomson's point about how intense looking can remake viewers' perceptions (http://www.youtube.com/watch?v=Vyk48Nc-a9o). Lindsay Fisher, another Envisioning artist, does more in her video, *First Impression,* than grant people permission to look intently at her. In her search to discover what onlookers see when fixing eyes on her difference, she asks audiences to see beyond first impressions to find value in difference (http://www.youtube.com/watch?v=ER_jE51g6II).

By inviting us to look intensely and question our urge to stare, these filmmakers challenge us to acknowledge our responses to difference—and, ultimately, become conscious of our own embodiment. Through this refraction, they refocus our collective gaze into societal views of difference and illuminate the myriad ways in which we share the experience of what it is to be vulnerable, flawed, and embodied—and hence, to embody "difference," at least in relation to the culturally idealized mode of embodiment, which is imagined as invulnerable, autonomous, and always in control. The works of Sachse and Fisher offer audiences important insights into how disabled artists themselves learn, even as they teach others, to sense difference differently. Put differently, the self-learning that the artists share is inextricably connected to the teaching they offer us as viewers.

Volatile Bodies and the Vulnerable Researcher

The Envisioning project grew out of earlier narrative research on the bodily experiences of a diverse group of women, published as *Becoming Woman: The Embodied Self in Image Culture* (Rice 2014). Because most existing research in the area of embodiment and body image focuses on average-sized, non-disabled, white women's weight problems, I decided to interview diversely embodied women to learn more about similarities and differences in their experiences. The narratives were told by almost a hundred women from all walks of life and diverse racial and ethnic backgrounds, of varying sizes, and with and without disabilities. Included were participants perceived as attractive or normative as well as those deemed to inhabit bodies rendered as abject in our culture.

During the interpretation phase of this project, I became acutely conscious of my positionality in relationship to participants' diverse embodiments. This consciousness brought me to consider questions of intersectionality and embodied self-reflexivity in analysis (see Burns 2006). Through intersectionality and self-reflexivity, I came to think about the significance of vulnerability in embodiment research, especially with populations positioned historically and socially as "vulnerable." We can think about concepts of vulnerability, self-reflexivity, and intersectionality as integral to critical feminist approaches and as related to and dependent on one another. For example, researchers can practice self-reflexivity only if they are willing to make themselves vulnerable, to share and analyze something difficult or discomforting about themselves as a way of deepening understanding about an issue. Moreover, an intersectional analysis entails self-reflexivity, since self-reflexivity requires researchers to subject their positionalities to the same analyses as they do participants. Self-reflexivity thus enables them to raise questions of power and difference that need to be posed in order to do intersectional research.

Intersectionality is both a concept and an approach to understanding the experiences of individuals and groups in their diversity and complexity (Hobbs and Rice 2013). Emerging as a theoretically important term in the work of African American feminists and critical race scholars such as

Patricia Hill Collins (1990) and Kimberlé Crenshaw (1994), it has since been adapted and developed by other feminist researchers. Intersectionality describes the idea that people live multiple layered identities and encounter shifting privileges and oppressions (Canadian Research Institute for the Advancement of Women 2006). It critiques the limitations of perspectives that look narrowly at social relations through a gender lens alone, encouraging a wider view focused on the multiple components of identity and intersecting axes of power that constitute individuals' experiences in the world (Karpinski 2007; Yuval-Davis 2006).

Intersectional theories and methods work to explore ways in which factors such as gender, sexuality, Indigeneity, class, race, disability, geography, refugee and/or immigrant status, size, and age interact to shape people's social positioning. Such differences are also examined in the context of colonialism, neoliberal globalization, and other historical and political forces that create unequal access to power and privilege. While I acknowledge that the concept of intersectionality emerged from Black feminist thought and that scholars continue to debate whether intersectionality theory should be applied to other aggrieved groups (see Alexander-Floyd 2012; Anthias 2012), in my view, the concept is flexible enough to be applied broadly in order to better understand the diverse ways in which power and oppression operate across social situations. As intersectionality theorists Sumi Cho, Kimberlé Crenshaw, and Leslie McCall (2013, 787) write, "Intersectionality's insistence on examining the dynamics of difference and sameness has played a major role in facilitating consideration of gender, race, and other axes of power in a wide range of political discussions and academic disciplines." This does not mean that researchers must include in their research all people across all differences. Instead, researchers study how the complexities and specificities of their own and participants' particular embodied identities and social locations play an important part in shaping their research and knowledge production.

This discussion brings us to the significance of self-reflexivity in critical research. Self-reflexivity—an ongoing critical reflection on the self and how the self is influencing the research—is a key component of postconventional and postcolonial feminist research, both of which are methodologies developed as a critical response to conventional research (Ghorashi 2005; Henry 2003; Rice 2009). Here, the term "conventional research" refers to research methodologies rooted in positivism and in some earlier interpretive paradigms such as grounded theory and phenomenology. Conventional methodologies encompass all research approaches premised on epistemologies (theories of knowledge) and ontologies (theories of reality, subjectivity, and the world) that privilege a Western scientific world view over other ways of knowing and being in the world, researcher detachment and transcendence over researcher interconnectedness and embodiment, knowledge as universal and fixed over knowledge as unstable and situated, and the researcher as impartial observer over the recognition of a researcher's embeddedness in knowledge production and social conditions (Bell 2012; Haraway 2000, 2003; Shildrick 1997, 2004). In conventional research, for example, the self is seen as insignificant—at best, an unwelcome influence and, at worst, an outright obstacle to the acquisition of reliable knowledge, as something that has to be ignored or transcended in order to produce unbiased results.

Poststructuralist and postcolonial theories have posed serious challenges to the notion of the unbiased observer who faithfully records reality. Unlike conventional science, which looks to the external world for answers to research questions, postconventional research looks both outward and inward for its answers, investigating how researcher subjectivities also influence what knowledge gets produced. Although postconventional researchers harness a diversity of methodologies ranging from the qualitative to the quantitative, their aims are quite different from those of conventional research: they seek to "de-territorialise" knowledge and reality (Shildrick 1997, 3) by challenging the myth of objectivity inherent in the positivist paradigm; to reconceptualize subjectivity as embodied, interconnected, and interdependent; to revalidate lived and local knowledge; and to recognize the social context from which knowledge originates and the implications of knowledge claims for social justice aims (Bell 2012).

In postconventional research that attends to power relations, including the impacts of colonial histories on subjectivities and social relationships, interrogation of one's positionality is critical. Here, researchers examine the significance of the self to all stages: how our subjectivities influence our choice of topics, the methods we choose, what we hear and don't hear in our data, and how we analyze our results. The self can't be separated but is integral to what knowledge gets produced. We can't escape our selves, but we can account for and critically analyze the influence of our selves in our research. For many of us, postconventional and postcolonial methods require unlearning conceptual frameworks that we as Indigenous and non-Indigenous teachers and learners in postcontact settler societies have been inculcated into. Because postconventional and postcolonial methods have as an aim to reframe whatever the "problem" is and to repurpose the methods for researching it, the research process itself becomes educative as much as an explicit pursuit of social justice.

The willingness to turn the gaze on one's self even when this may lead to discomforting and unsettling truths thus requires that critical researchers make themselves vulnerable. Yet vulnerability is defined very negatively in our society: it is conventionally described as a susceptibility to being wounded or hurt and an openness to criticism or attack. Vulnerability is also associated with the feminine, the disabled, the aged, the marginalized, the weak, and all groups seen as more prone or susceptible to harm due to their embodiment (illness, disability, pregnancy) or social disadvantage (poverty); this is especially so in the Western world, which privileges self-contained, autonomous, and independent selfhood. But while vulnerability can increase people's susceptibility to suffering and inequality (since groups marked as vulnerable are socially rendered violable), it is also the ground for human exchange, empowerment, and growth. It is necessary for human being and human understanding. It is fundamental to relationship and to social life. It is, finally, a condition for learning and for transforming our world views and taken-for-granted ways of sensing the world.

Legal scholar Martha Fineman (2008, 8) seeks to rescue the term *vulnerability* from its purely negative associations, emphasizing instead its potential for re-thinking what constitutes "the human" and for enacting more inclusive social policies and justice if understood as a "universal, inevitable, enduring aspect of the human condition." Recognizing both the negative and positive dimensions of vulnerability is important, she argues, since together they capture the inherent interdependence that underpins human existence. Fineman's understanding of vulnerability as something shared by all human beings challenges the myth of the invulnerable autonomous self that is the basis of Western legal systems and social policies (including education practices such as standardized testing) and enjoins us to rethink these by taking the vulnerable self, our shared common human experience, as our starting point for building a more equitable society.

Anthropologist Ruth Behar coined the term the "vulnerable observer" as a way of talking about the value of vulnerability to research. Here, researchers make themselves vulnerable in the sense of sharing something about themselves that sheds additional light on the subject being discussed—in the same way that they write about "other" people's lives to shed light on a topic. According to Behar (1997, 14), "Vulnerability doesn't mean that anything personal goes. The exposure of the self who is also a spectator has to take us somewhere we couldn't otherwise get to. It has to be essential to the argument, not a decorative flourish, not exposure for its own sake." Being a vulnerable researcher means being present and honest with ourselves throughout our projects—namely, with our contradictory, uncomplimentary, or difficult thoughts and emotions, including our fears and desires and our implicatedness in others' suffering. At the same time, it requires a willingness to be present to others' emotions and experiences, to approach respectfully and tread carefully.

Because our culture associates vulnerability with cultural abjection and social exclusion, it is difficult for people to be vulnerable. Some groups are forcibly positioned as vulnerable. People also learn that they may be violated if they show vulnerability. But when people decide to make themselves vulnerable, this can interrupt prevailing norms and provoke personal and collective transformation. This is especially true when individuals in privileged positions unmask their vulnerabilities in an effort to deepen understanding and expose the operations of power surrounding constructions of vulnerability. For example, in opposition to the culturally sanctioned understanding of researchers as disembodied experts, those who write from their body histories insist on revealing the vulnerability they share with others, animating Fineman's definition of the term and blurring boundaries between bodies that are forcibly positioned as vulnerable and those that intentionally position themselves as vulnerable. Granted, the consequences of vulnerability for those on whom it is imposed differ considerably from the consequences for those who choose to become vulnerable. All the same, a researcher's articulation of vulnerability in the context of the cultural imperative to be (or at least appear to be) "all knowing" challenges expectations of who is vulnerable.

Being vulnerable challenges research conducted through imperial eyes, a perspective that Linda Tuhiwai Smith (Maori) (1999), Kathy Absolon

(Anishinaabe) (2011), Eve Tuck (Aleut) (Tuck and Yang 2012), and other Indigenous scholars have thoroughly critiqued. Vulnerability directs researchers to turn the gaze on themselves to attend to the partiality and cultural specificity of their knowledge claims. Insofar as it "unsettles" idealized notions of the self-contained, autonomous Western self, vulnerability also aids in decolonizing ways of knowing and generating knowledge. By decolonization, I mean the broad project of critiquing Western world views and challenging oppressive power structures that they uphold. According to Tuhiwai Smith (1999, 98), decolonizing, "once viewed as the formal process of handing over the instruments of government, is now recognized as a long-term process involving bureaucratic, cultural, linguistic, and psychological divesting of colonial power," including within the academy and other sites of learning. For Dawn Rae Davis (2010), decolonization means displacing white, Western subjectivities and world views from the centre of teaching and research and disrupting Eurocentric, First World privilege through an examination of colonial relations from the perspectives of colonized others.

In decolonizing approaches to research specifically, the connection between teaching and research is inescapable, since researchers must unlearn Western ways of knowing in order to contribute to the decolonization of knowledge itself. According to Eve Tuck and Wayne Yang (2012, 7), "decolonization is not a metaphor" for the liberation of all oppressed groups but a specific process that involves "the repatriation of land simultaneous to the recognition of how land and relations to land have always already been differently understood and enacted" by Indigenous and non-Indigenous peoples. Thinking with these writers, I understand decolonizing research as research that aims to understand Indigenous experiences of colonization and to revalue Indigenous knowledges as a way of reclaiming Indigenous lives, lands, languages, and world views. I see researcher vulnerability as a potentially "unsettling" process that supports decolonization because it means continuously working to divest myself of the masks of white, ableist, and settler privilege and power that uphold colonial and other oppressive histories and legacies. In my work, I strive to enact decolonizing methodologies by prioritizing process and relationship—by working to ensure that the participants gain something valuable from the research experience, that they come to see themselves as knowledge producers in the process, and, perhaps most importantly, that they are self-determining throughout it.

Ethical Risks of Self-Reflexivity in Embodiment Research

In this final section, I share my research as an example of how one research-er's embodied identities and experiences have influenced her research process and the knowledge she produces. I use my research to take up how we can use our selves in an ethically transparent way. My point is not to priv-ilege or centre the self but to develop a consciousness of the self so that we can see how the self impacts on our projects: What am I both seeing and not seeing because of the positions I occupy? I begin by discussing my embodied difference and a digital story I made about embodied self-reflexivity called *The Elephant in the Room*. I then analyze what I had chosen to conceal about my bodily experiences and look at some of the ways in which my body secrets influenced my interpretation of the accounts told by women participating in my research. I conclude by thinking critically about the risks and rewards of embodied vulnerability and self-reflexivity in research.

In the past twenty years, feminist researchers concerned about ethics in representation have advocated a range of practices, including the following: building researcher accountability through checking interpretations with informants and consequences of representations for researched groups (Cos-grove and McHugh 2000; Lather 1991); increasing researcher responsibility through immersing oneself in the experiences, world views, and challenges of communities under investigation (Merrick 1999); enhancing researcher advocacy through commitment to producing knowledge with possibilities for improving people's lives (Fine et al. 2003); and engaging in researcher self-reflexivity through interrogating the researcher's emotions, embodi-ments, identities, and allegiances that affect research processes (Deutsch 2004; Hoskins and Stoltz 2005; Johnson-Bailey 1999; Reger 2001). While I have used all of these methods and strategies, I have also struggled with the challenges that they each pose, especially embodied self-reflexivity. To shed light on why turning the gaze on myself has been difficult, I examine how secrets in my body story simultaneously complicated my understanding of participants' accounts and provided important entry points into them.

My own account of my relationship to this research topic is heavy with secrets and silence (see Rice 2009). Before outlining my body history, I want to give some background on the digital story I made about it (view at carlarice.com/carla-rice/, password: abc123). While I created this video as a self-reflexive exploration for the Envisioning project, it captures the dilemmas I encountered throughout the earlier Becoming Women project. Since I was asking women involved in Envisioning to expose their vulnerabilities, I knew that I wanted to acknowledge my own. I intended the film as a tool for calling attention to power relations based on appearance and difference, analyzing shared vulnerabilities across differing experiences of body privilege and abjection, and blurring boundaries that exist in our culture between categories of normal and abnormal and male and female, as well as between the disabled and nondisabled worlds.

The first body secret explored in the digital story is that I am a former fat girl. This embodied identity still haunts me. As the Becoming Women research progressed, my body shifted from a comparatively large to a culturally acceptable size. Although I lost weight gradually over a long period of time, as I move through space today, I still imagine my bodily boundaries to be much larger, carrying body memories of my fat embodiment. My body secrets do not stop at my former fat girl identity. I am also a woman with facial hair. This aspect of my embodied identity I have hidden through electrolysis and other efforts at hair removal. As with fat, anxieties about exposing this devalued difference continue to plague me. For example, I have wondered: Would unmasking my fatness or facial hair invite others' pitiful or critical gaze? Increase my vulnerability to harsh assessments that I have "failed" as a feminine, or as a feminist, woman? I see similar dilemmas represented on the Post Secret website (www.postsecret.com), a site to which people anonymously mail handcrafted post cards revealing closely guarded secrets. The site's popularity might reveal something about how people in our society are subjected to rigid standards of normal and how failure to live up to rules for normalcy can open up space to see the constructedness of these categories.

During data collection for Becoming Women, I confronted situations in which my own and others' queries about my appearance sharpened these inner conflicts. One example of self-questioning arose in an interview with a young South Asian Canadian woman who I'll call Erum. While many women identified body hair as a problem trait, Erum emphasized that facial hair was especially frightening because it was read as a sign of biological maleness, undermining her sense of security in her sexed identity, by eliciting the intensely anxiety-provoking sensation that she was not really a woman. As Erum spoke about her fears of feeling "other than female," I identified strongly with her sense of difference. When she spoke about the ways in which racialized women are imagined as hairier and more masculine, I began to understand how this abject—the image of the dark, hairy other—works to uphold a white body ideal. Reflecting on Erum's comment about how these notions about the bodies of racialized women had to be grounded in "stereotypes" because "Italian women are hairy too," I realized that she was drawing on a cultural imaginary that sees women from the Global South and from southern Europe as dark others who deviate from northern European ideals of femininity.

There is a colonial basis for this sort of racist extrapolation. Historically, certain groups of racialized women, including darker-skinned African and South Asian women, as well as Indigenous South American women and, to a lesser extent, those from southern Europe, were perceived to have more hair than northern European women. (I am of both Scottish and Italian ancestry, and others invariably associate my hairiness with my Italian heritage.) In the service of British and European imperialism, this presumed difference was incorporated into a culturally constructed hierarchy of beauty and femininity that nineteenth- and early-twentieth-century scientists created to support colonial policies of subjugation. In the nineteenth century, for example, Julia Pastrana, an Indigenous woman from Mexico, became a freak show performer in Europe owing to her excess facial hair, the result of a rare condition called hypertrichosis. Hypersexual advertising presented her in highly exaggerated ways as a cross between male (with a full beard) and female (wearing a knee-length dress), and as a human-animal hybrid (with a supposedly ape-shaped skull and body) (Browne and Messenger 2003; Garland-Thomson 1997, 73).

Controversy surrounding the Art Gallery of Ontario (AGO) exhibition that featured the work of Mexican artist Frida Kahlo, suggests that the depiction of racialized Indigenous women as hairy and masculine is a practice not relegated to our colonial past.[3] Believing that audiences knew little of Kahlo save for her iconic "unibrow," AGO marketers initiated a scheme inviting

---

3 The exhibition, "Frida and Diego: Passion, Politics and Painting," ran from 20 October 2012 to 30 January 2013.

patrons to take self-portraits sporting stick-on unibrows in photo booths installed in front of the gallery (Mortimer 2012). The resulting photos of people with felt unibrows making funny faces, later printed in local newspapers, suggest that rather than raising awareness, the gimmick tended to provoke public ridicule because it drew on old ideas about Indigenous women as unfeminine and ugly. The AGO tried to defend its stunt by asserting that Kahlo aggressively challenged these associations in her art. However, it is questionable whether the gallery would promote an exhibition featuring a revered white male artist that poked fun at attributes (such as penis or skull size) similarly weighted with historical meanings. In the wake of recent bullying-related suicides in North America and an antibullying law passed by the Legislative Assembly of Ontario, it strikes me as particularly ironic that one of the province's major cultural institutions would pursue a marketing scheme that teaches children that it is permissible to mock others' bodies and perceived differences.

I respected Erum for revealing her experiences. Yet, during our interview, I concealed my own similar struggles. Over time, I have become uncomfortably aware of the ways in which my secrecy, by contributing to silence about white women's hairiness, also reflects the racially based assumption that there is something wrong with body hair—that, as a quality associated with the dark-skinned other, it renders a woman something other than female. In other words, my silence about white women's facial hair simply acquiesces in, and thus reinforces, a racial hierarchy of beauty and femininity.

Throughout this process, not only did I privately question my capacities to analyze informants' accounts, but such questions were also raised during public lectures about this research. For instance, after one talk, a young academic asked me how I could name so many bodily differences and affinities between myself and participants while ignoring what she perceived to be the "elephant in the room": that I was "an attractive woman." At that moment, I realized the impossibility of removing my bodily struggles from interpretation. As I scrambled to compose an answer, I once again confronted my duplicity. Reflecting on my self-questioning and the audience's queries that culminated with this woman's question, I began a searching examination of my critical intentions, including my role in upholding or interrupting processes of "othering" throughout the research. I began to appreciate the privileges of passing as a conventional woman: from the safe space of the unmarked centre, I could theorize about other/ed women's lives. This is what finally galvanized me to turn the gaze on myself.

As a result of internalizing dominant ideas about what counts as knowledge, I had removed myself from my analysis. In so doing, I suppressed a source of insight into theorizing women's narratives. Some feminists have argued that sexist, racist, and consumerist interests push women into appearance alteration (Bordo 1999, 33–65; 2009). Others contend that women are not "cultural dupes" but "secret agents" who strategically alter their appearance in their best interests (Davis 1995, 159–81). My body secrets, considered in conjunction with informants' stories, suggest to me that appearance alteration might encompass both positions—that body modification may signify women's capitulation to ideals and their opposition to being othered. Analyzing my experiences alongside those of other women also reveals how body secrets work to sustain our sex/gender system. For example, keeping secrets such as hair removal serves to uphold sex categories as "natural" and suppresses knowledge about the ways in which so-called natural sex differences are socially produced. Keeping body hair removal a secret also upholds racial categories as "natural" by reinforcing the myth that certain groups of racialized women are more hairy and hence less female. Revealing these practices further reveals the gendered racism that reinforces hierarchies among different groups—namely, the sliding scale of beauty, femininity, and femaleness that positions white northern European women on the highest rung. In this way, self-reflexivity has allowed me to deepen my own understanding and analysis of corporeal power relations underpinning this research.

I now turn to "embodied engagement" and my ongoing examination of the ways in which my body history has influenced research activities. The strategies I began to use in an attempt to do research differently included decentring my bodily self, revisiting my story, and imagining the experiences of others. Because I was interviewing across and about differences, I tried to pose questions that facilitated exploration without making assumptions about participants' experiences. For example, the question "What is an early, or perhaps your earliest, memory of your body?" called to mind, for some, memories of sexual abuse and its consequences for embodiment. For others, this probe elicited accounts of bodies as vehicles for their active exploration of the world. By centring each woman's story while bearing in mind my own and other women's points of connection with her account, I was able to craft new questions that considered commonalities across differences. Questions that emerged—such as "When, if ever, did you begin to feel like a woman?"—invited participants to reflect on the idea of "qualifying" as a woman and/or to consider how differences have disqualified them.

I knew from the beginning that I did not want to appropriate others' stories to tell my own. Conducting a self-interview at the beginning of my project (when I was fat) allowed me to add my own voice to those of participants without centring myself. After spending time immersed in other women's stories (and having lost weight), I was shocked to discover, upon returning to my own, that I had become "other" to myself. When I reread my transcript, I encountered a familiar yet foreign self whom I recognized but no longer regarded as me. It was difficult to stay present with the pain and anger that made her story simmer. For the first time, I understood how narratives capture ephemeral moments in individuals' lives. Surprised by the forceful emotions that gripped me when I encountered this other who had been displaced by subsequent selves, I inferred that some participants might have similar responses to their stories. I began to view analysis as a relational process that occurs between investigator and informants and between a researcher's (and participants') past and present selves.

I also came to understand how my embodiment at the time of my self-interview had significantly contoured my interpretation of the memories told. Revisiting this previous bodily self enabled me to see how my interpretations shifted and changed at different times because of my changing embodiment. The rage and shame I had felt because of others' disparagement of my body gradually decreased along with my diminishing weight, but reconnecting with this "other within" helped me to relate to the strong emotions that inflected other women's accounts. Through appreciating this other within, who was displaced by subsequent embodied selves, I could begin to acknowledge the unbridgeable space between self and other, and other in the self. I came to see how re-encountering this former self could bring me closer to others' accounts of embodiment, even though that prospect frightened me. Expressed differently, confronting difficult emotions of shame and rage became a productive move during analysis, since it propelled me to question my shifting shades of body abjection and privilege relative to others' embodiments and to my current and former bodily selves.

Feminist researchers have critiqued the idea that you can know or become an authority on someone else's experience. However, some have argued that women can traverse differences without assuming an arrogant "all knowing" role. Nira Yuval-Davis (2006) proposes a transversal approach that combines "rooting" in one's own situation (understanding one's own history and implicatedness in conditions) with "shifting" to the position of the other (understanding the other's history and current conditions) as a method for difference-sensitive feminism. According to Yuval-Davis (1997, 125), a transversal politics replaces feminist claims to, or aims of, unity and sameness with dialogues that recognize women's situated differences; it strives to find or forge common values from divergent positions. While feminists have since advocated taking a transversal approach for crossing borders of ethnicity, nationality, history, and place (see, for example, Archer 2004), such a method could also be used by those seeking to traverse boundaries of subjectivity, body, and physical space.

This crossing does not replay what Mary Louise Fellows and Sherene Razack (1998, 335) call the "race to innocence" or what Tuck and Yang (2012, 10) refer to as "settler moves to innocence"—strategies or positionings wherein researchers from privileged locations cast off their subjectivities, embodiments, histories, and cultural legacies to fantasize merging with a mythical other. Nor does it involve taking up the stance of what Susan Dion (2009, 179) calls "the perfect stranger," the position of false innocence achieved through non-Indigenous people's claims to ignorance and denial of the enmeshed histories of Aboriginal and non-Aboriginal people in Canada. Rather, I came to see what I now call "embodied transversalism" as a method that acknowledges the unbridgeable space between self and other, that approaches rather than appropriates others' experiences, and that invites generative engagement with, rather than denial of or disengagement from, questions of privilege and difference. This method also resonates with Roxana Ng's (2011, 347) "integrative critical embodied pedagogy or embodied learning," an approach to decolonizing teaching and learning that highlights the importance of the learner's interrogation of the social and sentient experience of self and other throughout the learning process. Central to an embodied transversal interpretive approach is shifting between empathically interpreting my own body history and empathically imagining others' embodied lives. Moving beyond empathy alone, this approach combines empathic with informed imagining by immersing me in my own perspectives and histories as well as in those of research participants. Significantly, the method enabled me to recognize differences and affinities while respecting the incommensurability, indeterminacy, and asymmetry of my own and other women's embodied accounts.

Conclusion

In this research, I used embodied reflexivity and vulnerability as a way to risk fathoming, while resisting mastery over, other women's experiences. Had I not analyzed my body secrets, I might have missed how appearance is an important social category that intersects and overlaps with, but is not reducible to, more familiar categories such as gender, race, Indigeneity, disability, or class. In this analysis, I centred my own bodily struggles not to decentre others' stories of injustice or to appropriate their suffering but to bring to the surface another axis of power and oppression that functions through bodies in our homogenized, biomedicalized Western world: bodily difference, normalization, and norms. Had I not acknowledged the elephant in the room, I might also have missed the shared vulnerabilities and experiences of abjection underpinning my own and participants' accounts. In this way, attending to power relations operating through bodies in this research offered insights into the intrapsychic and social relations of appearance and difference that regulate our lives.

In the wake of completing the Becoming Women project and this work, however, I am left with an unsettling question regarding the perils of traversing the space between self and other in feminist-informed social justice and decolonizing research. I worry about "playing in the dark," to extend writer Toni Morrison's (1992) metaphor (about the ways in which white writers historically have projected their culturally shaped anxieties and desires onto the racialized characters they create) beyond the literary to the researcher's imagination: I'm concerned about how my leap into other women's lives might embody my own fears and desires. I worry, too, about "playing Indian," as Philip Deloria (1998, 7) has put it, about how exposing vulnerability may be a way of disguising myself as other to evade my implicatedness in colonial, ablest, and other processes of othering. Methods of decentring myself, revisiting my body story, and imagining others' embodiments have made possible more faithful accounts that come closer to informants' experiences. At the same time, I have learned that difference can't be fully known, for to claim that one can know the other is to collapse difference and absorb it into the self. In teaching me that difference cannot be mastered or overcome then, these methods of traversing positionalities have also taught me to shoulder responsibility for my privilege and to honour the space in-between.

References

Absolon, Kathleen. 2011. *Kaandosswin: How We Come to Know*. Black Point, NS: Fernwood Publishing.

Adichie, Chimamanda Ngozi. 2009. "The Danger of a Single Story." *TED Global Talks*. http://www.ted.com/talks/chimamanda_adichie_the_danger_of_a_single_story.html.

Alexander-Floyd, Nikol G. 2012. "Disappearing Acts: Reclaiming Intersectionality in the Social Sciences in a Post-Black Feminist Era." *Feminist Formations* 24(1): 1–25.

Allan, Julie. 2005. "Encounters with Exclusion Through Disability Arts." *Journal of Research in Special Educational Needs* 5(1): 31–36.

Anthias, Floya. 2012. "Hierarchies of Social Location, Class, and Intersectionality: Towards a Translocational Frame." *International Sociology* 28(1): 121–38.

Archer, Louise. 2004. "Re/theorizing 'Difference' in Feminist Research." *Women's Studies International Forum* 27(5–6): 459–73.

Behar, Ruth. 1997. *The Vulnerable Observer: Anthropology That Breaks Your Heart*. Boston: Beacon Press.

Bell, Karen. 2012. "Towards a Post-conventional Philosophical Base for Social Work." *British Journal of Social Work* 42(3): 408–23.

Bordo, Susan. 1999. *Twilight Zones: The Hidden Life of Cultural Images from Plato to O.J.* Berkeley: University of California Press.

———. 2009. "Not Just 'A White Girl's Thing': The Changing Face of Food and Body Image Problems." In *Critical Feminist Approaches to Eating Dis/orders*, edited by Helen Malson and Maree Burns, 46–59. New York: Routledge.

Brown, Leslie, and Susan Strega, eds. 2005. *Research as Resistance: Critical, Indigenous, and Anti-oppressive Approaches*. Toronto: Canadian Scholars' Press.

Browne, Janet, and Sharon Messenger. 2003. "Victorian Spectacle: Julia Pastrana, the Bearded and Hairy Female." *Endeavour* 27: 155–59.

Burns, Maree. 2006. "Bodies That Speak: Examining the Dialogues in Research Interactions." *Qualitative Research in Psychology* 3(1): 3–18.

Canadian Research Institute for the Advancement of Women. 2006. *Intersectional Feminist Frameworks: An Emerging Vision.* Ottawa: Canadian Research Institute for the Advancement of Women.

Chandler, Eliza and Carla Rice. 2013. "Revisioning Disability and Difference." Faculty of Health Sciences, University of Ontario Institute of Technology, Oshawa, Ontario.

Cho, Sumi, Kimberlé Crenshaw, and Leslie McCall. 2013. "Toward a Field of Intersectionality Studies: Theory, Applications, and Praxis." *Signs* 38(4): 785–810.

Cole, Ardra, Lorri Neilsen, Gary Knowles, and Teresa Luciani, eds. 2004. *Provoked by Art: Theorizing Arts-Informed Research.* Toronto: Backalong Books.

Collins, Patricia Hill. 1990. *Black Feminist Thought: Knowledge, Consciousness, and the Politics of Empowerment.* Boston: Unwin Hyman.

Cosgrove, Lisa, and Maureen McHugh. 2000. "Speaking for Ourselves: Feminist Methods and Community Psychology." *American Journal of Community Psychology* 28(6): 815–38.

Crenshaw, Kimberlé. 1994. "Mapping the Margins: Intersectionality, Identity Politics, and Violence Against Women of Color." In *The Public Nature of Private Violence,* edited by Martha Fineman and Roxanne Mykitiuk, 93–118. New York: Routledge.

Davis, Dawn Rae. 2010. "Unmirroring Pedagogies: Teaching with Intersectional and Transnational Methods in the Women and Gender Studies Classroom." *Feminist Formations* 22(1): 136–62.

Davis, Kathy. 1995. *Reshaping the Female Body: The Dilemma of Cosmetic Surgery.* New York: Routledge.

Deloria, Philip Joseph. 1998. *Playing Indian.* New Haven: Yale University Press.

Deutsch, Nancy. 2004. "Positionality and the Pen: Reflections on the Process of Becoming a Feminist Researcher and Writer." *Qualitative Inquiry* 10(6): 885–902.

Dion, Susan. 2009. *Braiding Histories: Learning from Aboriginal Peoples' Experiences and Perspectives.* Vancouver: University of British Columbia Press.

Erevelles, Nirmala, and Andrea Minear. 2010. "Unspeakable Offenses: Untangling Race and Disability in Discourses of Intersectionality." *Journal of Literary and Cultural Disability Studies* 4(2): 127–45.

Fausto-Sterling, Anne. 2000. *Sexing the Body: Gender Politics and the Construction of Sexuality.* New York: Perseus Books.

Fellows, Mary Louise, and Sherene Razack. 1998. "The Race to Innocence: Confronting Hierarchical Relations Among Women." *Journal of Gender, Race, and Justice* 1(2): 335–52.

Fine, Michelle, Lois Weis, Susan Weseen, and Loonmun Wong. 2003. "For Whom? Qualitative Research, Representations, and Social Responsibilities." In *The Landscape of Qualitative Research: Theories and Issues,* 2nd ed., edited by Norman Denzin and Yvonna Lincoln, 167–207. Thousand Oaks, CA: Sage.

Fineman, Martha. 2008. "The Vulnerable Subject and the Responsive State." *Yale Journal of Law and Feminism* 20(1): 1–22.

Gallagher, Kathleen, ed. 2009. *The Methodological Dilemma: Creative, Critical, and Collaborative Approaches to Qualitative Research.* London: Routledge.

Garland-Thomson, Rosemarie. 1997. *Extraordinary Bodies: Figuring Physical Disability in American Culture and Literature.* New York: Columbia University Press.

———. 2009. *Staring: How We Look.* Toronto: Oxford University Press.

Ghorashi, Halleh. 2005. "When the Boundaries Are Blurred: The Significance of Feminist Methods in Research." *European Journal of Women's Studies* 12(3): 363–75.

Grosz, Elizabeth. 1994. *Volatile Bodies: Toward a Corporeal Feminism.* Bloomington: Indiana University Press.

Haraway, Donna. 2000. *How Like a Leaf: An Interview with Thyrza Nichols Goodeve.* New York and London: Routledge.

———. 2003. "Situated Knowledges: The Science Question in Feminism and the Privilege of Partial Perspective." In *Turning Points in Qualitative Research: Tying Knots in a Handkerchief,* edited by Yvonna Lincoln and Norman Denzin, 21–46. Walnut Creek, CA: AltaMira Press.

Henry, Marsha. 2003. "'Where Are You Really From?' Representation, Identity, and Power in the Fieldwork Experiences of a South Asian Diasporic." *Qualitative Research* 3(2): 229–42.

Hesse-Biber, Sharlene Nazy, ed. 2007. *Handbook of Feminist Research: Theory and Praxis.* Thousand Oaks, CA: Sage.

Hobbs, Marg, and Carla Rice. 2013. "Mapping the Terrain of Gender and Women's Studies in Canada." In *Gender and Women's Studies in Canada: Critical Terrain,* edited by Marg Hobbs and Carla Rice, xvii–xxiv. Toronto: Women's Press.

Hoskins, Marie, and Jo-Anne Stoltz. 2005. "Fear of Offending: Disclosing Researcher Discomfort When Engaging in Analysis." *Qualitative Research* 5(1): 95–111.

Johnson-Bailey, Juanita. 1999. "The Ties That Bind and the Shackles That Separate: Race, Gender, Class, and Color in a Research Process." *International Journal of Qualitative Studies in Education* 12(6): 659–70.

Karpinski, Eva. 2007. "'Copy, Cut, Paste': A Reflection on Some Institutional Constraints of Teaching a Big Intro Course." *Resources for Feminist Research* 32(3–4): 44–53.

Kristeva, Julia. 1982. *Powers of Horror: An Essay on Abjection.* Translated by Leon S. Roudiez. New York: Columbia University Press. Originally published as *Pouvoirs de l'horreur: Essai sur l'abjection* (1980).

Lambert, Joe. 2010. *The Digital Storytelling Cookbook.* San Francisco: Digital Diner Press.

———. 2013. *Digital Storytelling: Capturing Lives, Creating Community.* New York: Routledge.

Landsberg, Michele. 2003. "Let's Keep Fighting the System for Kim Rogers' Sake." *Toronto Star,* 25 January.

Lather, Patti. 1991. *Getting Smart: Feminist Research and Pedagogy With/in the Postmodern.* New York: Routledge.

Meekosha, Helen. 2011. "Decolonising Disability: Thinking and Acting Globally." *Disability and Society* 26(6): 667–82.

Merrick, Elizabeth. 1999. "'Like Chewing Gravel': On the Experience of Analyzing Qualitative Research Findings Using a Feminist Epistemology." *Psychology of Women Quarterly* 23(1): 47–57.

Metzl, Jonathan, and Suzanne Poirier. 2004. "Difference and Identity in Medicine." *Literature and Medicine* 23(1): vi–xii.

Morrison, Toni. 1992. *Playing in the Dark: Whiteness and the Literary Imagination.* New York: Vintage Books.

Mortimer, Sarah. "Frida's Unibrow Was a Statement, Not a Gimmick." *Huffington Post,* 9 November 2012. https://www.huffingtonpost.ca/sarah-mortimer/frida-kahlo-ago-unibrow_b_2100916.html.

Naples, Nancy. 2003. *Feminism and Method: Ethnography, Discourse Analysis, and Activist Research.* New York: Routledge.

Ng, Roxana. 2011. "Decolonizing Teaching and Learning Through Embodied Learning: Toward an Integrated Approach." In *Valences of Interdisciplinarity: Theory, Practice, Pedagogy,* edited by Raphael Foshay, 343–65. Edmonton: Athabasca University Press.

Reger, Jo. 2001. "Emotions, Objectivity, and Voice: An Analysis of a 'Failed' Participant Observation." *Women's Studies International Forum* 24(5): 605–16.

Rice, Carla. 2009. "Imagining the Other? Ethical Challenges of Researching and Writing Women's Embodied Lives." *Women and Psychology* 19(2): 245–66.

———. 2014. *Becoming Women: The Embodied Self in Image Culture.* Toronto: University of Toronto Press.

Rice, Carla, Eliza Chandler, and Nadine Changfoot. 2016. "Imagining Otherwise: The Ephemeral Spaces of Envisioning New Meanings." In *Mobilizing Metaphor: Locating Artistic and Cultural Interventions,* edited by Christine Kelly and Michael Orsini, 54–75. Vancouver: University of British Columbia Press.

Rice, Carla, Eliza Chandler, Elisabeth Harrison, Kirsty Liddiard, and Manuela Ferrari. 2015. "Project Re•Vision: Disability at the Edges of Representation." *Disability and Society* 30(4): 513–27.

Rice, Carla, Lorna Renooy, and Fran Odette. 2008. "Talking About Body Image, Identity, and Difference." Workshop and paper presented for the Envisioning New Meanings of Disability and Difference Project. York Institute for Health Research, York University, Toronto.

Roman, Leslie. 2009a. "Disability Arts and Culture as Public Pedagogy." *International Journal of Inclusive Education* 13: 667–75.

———. 2009b. "Go Figure! Public Pedagogies, Invisible Impairments, and the Performative Paradoxes of Visibility as Veracity." *International Journal of Inclusive Education* 13: 677–98.

Shildrick, Margrit. 1997. *Leaky Bodies and Boundaries: Feminism, Postmodernism, and (Bio)ethics.* London: Routledge.

———. 2002. *Embodying the Monster: Encounters with the Vulnerable Self.* London: Sage.

———. 2004. "Genetics, Normativity, and Ethics: Some Bioethical Concerns." *Feminist Theory* 5(2): 149–65.

Smith, Linda Tuhiwai. 1999. *Decolonizing Methodologies: Research and Indigenous Peoples.* London: Zed Books.

Tregaskis, Claire. 2002. "Social Model Theory: The Story So Far." *Disability and Society* 17: 457–70.

Tuck, Eve, and K. Wayne Yang. 2012. "Decolonization Is Not a Metaphor." *Decolonization: Indigeneity, Education, and Society* 1(1): 1–40.

Yuval-Davis, Nira. 1997. *Gender and Nation.* London: Sage.

———. 2006. "Intersectionality and Feminist Politics." *European Journal of Women's Studies* 13(3): 193–209.

6 Resistance and Remedy Through Embodied Learning

Yoga Cultural Appropriation and Culturally Appropriate Services

Sheila Batacharya

In Canada, health research addressing Indigenous and other racially subordinated women identifies violence, social inequity, and lack of access to social and health services as primary concerns (Amnesty International 2004, 2009; Federal/Provincial/Territorial Working Group on Women's Health 1990; FORWARD 2006; Harding 2005; Khanlou and Hadjukowski-Ahmed 1999; Khosla 2003; McKenna and Larkin 2002; Native Women's Association of Canada 2004). Young women face increased exposure to violence and their experiences of systemic oppression, especially racism and colonialism, not only compromise their options for support but may profoundly damage their sense of identity and hamper their strategies to resist, cope with, and recover from abuse (Ali et al. 2003; Czapska et al. 2006; Handa 2003; Jiwani 1999, 2002, 2005; Rice and Russell 1995a, 1995b; Shakti Kee Chatree Collective 1997). With regard to health policy and programming, this body of research further suggests the need for greater attention to the strategies that young women use to resist and cope in contexts of violence and oppression.

In 2004, I facilitated twelve yoga workshops addressing health, healing, violence, and oppression for young South Asian women living in Toronto. I then conducted individual interviews with fifteen workshop participants and three yoga teachers that same year. Participants theorized yoga as a

resource for addressing mental, physical, emotional, and spiritual consequences of violence and oppression. In this project, spirit and spirituality
were described as experiences of deep respect, a sense of humility, and
awareness of one's connection with other beings and with nature in general.
Although yoga is the framework used in this study, it is not privileged by
the researcher or the participants as a superior form of spiritual knowing
or practice.

Identity and critiques of social relations of power are salient themes
that emerged in the interviews. In particular, participants objected to New
Age reinterpretations of yoga and cultural appropriation. However, their
critiques of New Age yoga are not easily remedied by recourse to definitions
of authentic South Asian culture. The young women indicate that it is not
sufficient to frame yoga as authentic and therefor a culturally appropriate
resource if it is presented using orthodox religious, nationalistic, patriarchal,
colonial, or other hegemonic tropes. Similarly, the yoga teachers discussed
how they meet the challenge of supporting students who have experienced
violence and oppression. They also highlighted the importance of addressing identity and social relations of power.

The workshop participants and the yoga teachers offered insightful considerations and recommendations for using yoga as a counterhegemonic
healing strategy grounded in "ethical cultural connections" (Kadi 1996, 125).
I argue that the counterhegemonic healing strategies used by participants
disrupt dominant healing and embodiment discourses such as New Age
romanticism and "somatophobia" (Davis 2007, 53) in critical theory. Said
differently, participants illustrate how sentient-social embodied learning is
an important form of resistance to violence and oppression.

Doing Embodiment Research

Theorizing sentient-social embodied experience within critical Western
scholarship carries certain challenges. As a researcher, I have undergone
extensive training about how social relations of power operate and I have
practiced methodologies that identify lived experience as an important
source of knowledge. However, to write about lived experiences of mind,
body, breath, emotions, and spirit in academia is venturesome, despite the
existence of research that addresses these topics in interesting and provoca-
tive ways. Scholars, notably Roxana Ng (2000b, 2011) and the contributors to

this collection, ask why embodiment *feels* out of place in academic forums, and in doing so they produce varied responses (Alexander 2005; Frankenberg 2004; Graveline 1998).

When the body is understood as inextricable from perception, rather than as an obstacle to it, embodiment can be understood as the "worldsense" (Oyěwùmí 1997) of an individual and a collective—an understanding that Temitope Adefarakan explains in her chapter in this collection as "how life is understood from this multisensory position." However, in critical antiracist and feminist studies, sentient embodiment remains a tricky topic despite widespread acknowledgement of lived experience as a valued source of knowledge. "One of the most unfortunate legacies of poststructuralist and postmodern feminism," notes Stacy Alaimo (2008, 237), "has been the accelerated 'flight from nature' fuelled by rigid commitments to social constructionism and the determination to rout out all vestiges of essentialism. Nature, charged as accessory to essentialism, has served as feminism's abject." Indeed, discursive inquiries about the body have at times obscured the material concerns that were central to these insights in the first place (Bordo, 2004, 282). However, this was not always the case. Susan Bordo (2004, 16) argues, the body was at the centre of women's liberation and black power movements long before it was addressed in poststructuralism.

Critical feminist scholarship that privileges mind over body in the repudiation of the physical body, along with nature, dovetails with hegemonic denials of lived experiences of subordination. The retreat from the material body, or "somatophobia" (Davis 2007, 53), is rooted in the objection to a biological determinism that assigns intrinsic characteristics to dominant and subordinate people, the latter of whom are positioned on the body side of the mind-body dichotomy. Like Bordo (2004), Kathy Davis (2007, 53) argues that many critical feminist investigations of social embodiment do address both the material and discursive aspects of lived sentient experience. As she points out, numerous theorists—among them Evelyn Fox Keller, Sandra Harding, Patricia Hill Collins, and Dorothy Smith—situate "sentient, embodied experiential knowing as a resource for unmasking the universalist pretensions of science and for providing the basis for an alternative, critical epistemology, which would be grounded in the material realities of women's lives."

Situating "sentient, embodied experiential knowing" as a source of knowledge features prominently in antiracist and feminist scholarship, and, despite the discursive turn in Western knowledge-production, scholars continue to assert that lived experience is an important source of knowledge about social systems and inequities. I, too, am interested in research that goes beyond cognitive ways of knowing—in other words, research that addresses how embodiment is a social experience but one that is not fully explained by social theory and is not reducible to thinking. Embodiment is surely experienced through discourse, but the story does not end there.

In response to the problem of dichotomous thinking in terms of a sentient body versus a socially constructed body, science studies scholar Elizabeth Grosz (2008, 24) asks, "How does biology, the bodily existence of individuals (whether human or nonhuman), provide the conditions for culture and for history, those terms to which it is traditionally opposed? How does biology—the structure and organization of living systems—facilitate and make possible cultural existence and social change?" Attending to the body as "organized by processes that are living systems" (24) and examining how these systems interlock with social systems have been central concerns in both my work as a yoga teacher and my research about embodiment and embodied learning. When I teach about the relationships among body, mind, breath, emotions, and spirit, I do so by drawing attention to the body and sentient experiences; however, sentient experiences occur symbiotically with social experience. As Zainab, a twenty-seven-year-old youth counsellor and graduate student, said during an interview,

> I think remembering moments of, like, positive experiences away
> from those destructive situations, when you had moments of insight,
> when you felt peace flooding your body, when you've been sensitive
> and flexible and open, help keep you human when you are faced with
> that violence and oppression. 'Cause I'm not reducible to this, I'm not
> reducible to this situation or my response to it.[1]

Many of the participants in my study described sentient experiences of body, breath, and spirit as providing an important opportunity to

---

1 All the participants in my research study have been given pseudonyms. I extend my thanks to them all for their insights and for allowing me to quote their comments.

theorize and respond to social experiences. As the comment above suggests, sentient-social embodied awareness provides an important perspective from which to respond to social inequity and its consequences. Zainab acknowledges social experience but refuses to be reduced to it. In identifying moments of embodied insight as a resource for contending with violence and oppression, she expresses embodied awareness as sentient and social.

The ways in which sentience and perception have been avoided as a result of the mind-body dualism are being rethought in embodiment studies. "To explain or analyse perception," notes Elizabeth Grosz (1994, 94), "requires an understanding not only of physiological and psychological processes but above all the ways in which each is mutually implicated with the other." Wrestling against dismissals of lived experience and sentient knowledge that include but are not limited to cognitive knowing is a very difficult project within academia. Lived experience is, and should be, subject to critique; however, experience (often that of marginalized persons) can also be dismissed as suspicious because of the belief that it is discursive and subject to infinite interpretations. In other words, perceptual knowing may be defined as nothing more than the result of discourse on an inert body-object. The contradiction here is stunning in that there can be no material body in a discursive universe, yet an inert body as object must exist for discourse be applied to. Ultimately, both sentient and social experience have at times been disdained and dismissed as unknowable—as fragmented or essentialist. Needless to say, these dismissals have also been resisted.

Antiracist feminism provides an important lens through which to understand how the participants in my research are positioned in society and how they negotiate their experiences of social hierarchies as interconnected and mutually constituting (Bannerji 1993; Calliste and Dei 2000; Hill Collins 1998; Lorde 1984; Mohanty, Russo, and Torres 1991; Ng 1986, 1993; Razack 1998; Stasiulis 1990). It also supports my investigation of sentient-social embodiment and "transformative possibilities beyond the frame" (Calliste and Dei 2000, 12) of dominant ways of knowing. As noted in the introduction to this collection, anticolonialism and decolonization are social movements and constitute a historicized approach to theory and practice with the aim of ending colonial power relations; it "can only be engaged through active withdrawal of consent and resistance to structures of psychic and social domination" (Mohanty 2003, 7). Importantly, anticolonialism and decolonization provide frameworks that expose and challenge the histories and legacies of colonialism from the perspectives and knowledges of Indigenous peoples (Dei and Asgharzadeh 2001, 298).

Framing yoga teachings as an Indigenous knowledge in my research is a decolonizing move, but it is only so when specific and situated forms of colonization, such as the distinction between settler colonialism on Turtle Island and exploitation colonization in South Asia, are confronted (Tuck and Yang 2012, 4). Yoga teachings offer important strategies for engaging in decolonization by preparing one to unlearn ways of being and thinking that one has been inculcated into and takes for granted. Yoga provides training for witnessing oneself and others with discernment; this skill is important for avoiding guilt and the manifold ways in which those in positions of settler, racial, gender, class, and ability privilege seek innocence by way of resisting or embracing positions of superiority and/or victimhood (Lawrence and Dua 2005; Razack 1998). Roxana Ng (2011, 352) insists on both the discursive/symbolic understanding and the material/praxis of embodied learning, "not only to reason critically but to see dispassionately and to alter actions that contribute to the reproduction of dominant-subordinate relations." Yoga teachings may be used to challenge hegemonic thinking, but they only become anticolonial when reconciled with actions that contribute to both discursive and material decolonization.

Antiracist feminism frameworks illustrate how race and gender interlock with other social categories of difference, such as ability, sexuality, class, religion, ethnicity, and age. However, these insights must be considered in terms of anticolonial and decolonization critiques that identify how colonialism grants privilege to differently situated settlers (Lawrence and Dua 2005; Tuck and Yang 2012). Drawing on antiracist feminism, anticolonial and decolonization frameworks provide perspectives through which to address historical processes that have led to and shaped the establishment of a South Asian diaspora in Toronto (Brah 1996; Handa 2003; Grewal 2005; Rajiva 2004, 2006; Razack 2002; Thobani 2007). Furthermore, using these frameworks help to contextualize yoga—a knowledge that is historically and culturally associated with South Asia, although it is practiced and produced in settler societies such as Canada.

Kathy Absolon and Cam Willett (2005, 98) discuss what it means to "put ourselves forward" by addressing colonial history as an important aspect of self-location in the research process—by thinking of location as "more than simply saying you are of Cree or Anishinaabe or British ancestry; from Toronto or Alberta or Canada." Rather, one's location is defined by relationships, not only to land and language but also to "spiritual, cosmological, political, economical, environmental, and social elements in one's life." Described as part of the challenge to "unlearn colonial research agendas and processes" and the need to "be creative in revising research methodologies to make our research more Indigenous and counter-colonial" (106), locating oneself is identified as central to resisting Eurocentrism and ethnocentrism by countering the idea of objectivity and the process of objectification (107). Absolon and Willet explain that self-location also helps readers identify the vested interests of the researcher and calls her to be accountable in her relationships. Keeping this in mind, I try to write as an embodied subject "and to show how such an account can be written not merely as a self-absorbed autobiography" (Ng 2000a, 185).

I have lived and travelled through the territories of Haudenosaunee, Anishinaabeg, and Wendat nations since my birth. My mother's paternal forbears arrived as colonial settlers in the mid-1800s from Britain to the Anishinaabeg territories of the Mississauga peoples.[2] They purchased land through the process of colonial land theft and the illegal appropriation of Mississauga territory through the Toronto Purchase—a deed that was blank between 1787, the year of its inception, and 1805, when the Mississauga peoples were coerced into signing a new deed.[3] My mother's maternal lineage includes French settlers in the territory of the Mohawk people of the Haudenosaunee Confederacy in the early 1700s.[4]

---

2 I am grateful to relatives Jane (née Rundle) Barnacki and Theresa Faubert who shared research about our family history with me.

3 The Toronto Purchase is currently being challenged by the Mississaugas of the New Credit in land claims negotiations with the Canadian government. See Mississaugas of the New Credit First Nation, *Toronto Purchase Specific Claim: Arriving at an Agreement,* n.d., http://www.newcreditfirstnation.com/uploads/1/8/1/4/18145011/torontopurchasebkltsm.pdf.

4 Haudenosaunee are the people of the longhouse. The Haudenosaunee Confederacy includes the Cayuga, Mohawk, Oneida, Onondoga, Seneca, and Tuscarora peoples (Sunseri 2011, 9). See *Kanesatake: 270 Years of Resistance*, directed by renowned filmmaker Alanis Obamsawin (1993), for a detailed history of the

Linda Tuhiwai Smith (1999) explains that colonial settlers engaged in the process of claiming Indigenous status after several generations of land occupation. This, she argues, was made possible by the erasure of colonial violence underpinning such claims (7). I, along with my maternal family, never questioned our sense of entitlement and belonging in the Canadian nation, and despite my experiences of racism, I too grew up claiming Canada as my "home and native land," as declared in the Canadian national anthem. Also factoring into our settler entitlement were the unremitting crises that my mother's family members faced, all of which, I believe, contributed to our unquestioned sense of belonging to the nation, as compensation for our hardships, and thus to the complicity with the inequities that underpin it. I would even argue that these crises fuelled our identification with whiteness and all other markers of elite citizenship, despite experiences of subordination violence in a white settler capitalist society. Sunera Thobani (2007, 21) explains nonelite claims to Canadian citizenship as a process of exaltation: "Exaltation enables nationals with even the lowliest 'internal' status to claim civilizational and existentialist *parity* with privileged insiders and civilizational *superiority* in their daily encounters with outsiders. . . . It enhances the social and moral being of all those included within the national enterprise and promotes aspirations of acquiring greater nationality among even the most despised of insiders." In other words, I and my maternal family demonstrated a settler mentality based on a strong sense of entitlement to the privileges we possessed by virtue of having worked hard and having suffered for them.

My paternal ancestry is South Asian. My father was born near Kolkata in West Bengal, India, in 1930. My father's elders were persecuted during the Indian independence movement. However, my father came from a family of propertied Brahmins, and his class location and access to education allowed him to study and work in Europe and then eventually to immigrate to Canada, in the mid-1960s. This coincided with what antiracist historians have referred to as a period of "paki-bashing"—a time in which increased South Asian immigration was met with pervasive racist violence perpetrated by Canadian citizens who may or may not have had a significantly longer settler presence but were economically and culturally threatened by these

Mohawk peoples and documentation of the 1992 Oka "crisis" as a continuation of anticolonial struggle for self-determination.

newcomers (Bolaria and Li 1988; Thobani 2007). My father was an immigrant from postcolonial India and a settler. His immigration to Canada was shaped by colonization in both countries, and although not an elite beneficiary, he, like my mother's family, enjoyed the rewards of living in a settler society. As Sunera Thobani (2007, 16–17) argues,

> Propelled into the circuit of migration by structural conditions within the global economy, as well as by their desires for economic advancement, migrants have been party to the ongoing colonization of Aboriginal peoples.
> . . . Although the suffering of immigrants cannot be minimized neither can their participating (and benefiting from) the ongoing cultural and material domination of Aboriginal peoples.

With this in mind, I consider my situated and specific racialized and gendered experience as the result of my marginalization and privilege within a white settler nation.

Paying attention to my location requires more than cognitive theorization. Emotional, physical, and spiritual aspects of my lived experience and family relationships are critically important in my endeavour "to understand how oppressions, as well as privilege, intersect and how these affect interactions between people" (Batacharya 1994, 183). This is where my yoga practice has been helpful. Having a way to engage emotional, psychic, and "spirit wounding" (Wing 1997, 28)—a way that attends to breath, body, and spirit—has been an important part of my practice of self-location. While the teachings of yoga in and of themselves offer remedies to damages caused by violence and oppression, in my case, yoga is also a way to think about culture, history, and community and how these shape identity; in many respects, it has been a way to locate oneself using spirituality (Absolon and Willett 2005, 112).

However, social location also changes in response to context. "We each locate ourselves differently at various points in our lives. As our recovery from colonialism progresses, we speak about our past and present experiences with more awareness, understanding, and knowledge, and we revise the stories of our lives" (Absolon and Willett 2005, 112). When I reflect on my experiences and observe how I write about them now compared to twenty years ago, I see new offshoots rather than hard breaks. These shifts debunk the idea that research is objective or that research can be anything but a process characterized by change and context. I agree with Sandra Harding (1993, 65), who argues that communities, not individuals, produce knowledge because it is only through community that the knowledge I claim can be challenged or legitimated.

Healing Discourses and Yoga: Cultural Appropriation and Culturally Appropriate Services

It is important to address the ways in which embodiment and healing are discoursed in order to distinguish between hegemonic and counter-hegemonic meanings and practices. Just as the material dimension of social inequity has embodied consequences, so too does discourse. Susan Hekman (2008, 100) writes that "the goal of Foucault's analyses of discourses in all of his works is to reveal how discourses shape the material reality in which we live." She argues that "bodies are crafted by discourse and that this crafting has very real consequences for how those bodies inhabit cultural space" (101). If healing is an important response to the embodied consequences of violence and oppression, as the South Asian women and yoga teachers whom I interviewed claimed, what kinds of discursive approaches to embodiment and healing help or hinder that healing? What is meant by "healing" in different historical contexts and frameworks? What are the different understandings of embodiment that underpin healing discourses?

New Age discourses inform popular understandings of embodiment and healing. Yet although New Age attends to mind, body, emotions, and spirit, social relations of power are often effaced. Furthermore, New Age knowledge production provides many examples of how Western cultural dominance, appropriations, and reinterpretations of Indigenous knowledges are not acknowledged or critically engaged, despite the widespread recourse to Indigenous knowledges for teachings about embodied learning and holistic healing. By examining New Age discourses, it is possible to trace both social relations of power and their effacement in hegemonic discourses pertaining to embodiment and healing.

Despite claims to novelty, New Age discourse is consistent with other developments in Western thought, particularly those that occurred during the Enlightenment and its offshoot, Romanticism (Hammer 2001; Tumber 2002). The Enlightenment is generally understood as a late-seventeenth- and eighteenth-century movement characterized by specific trends in knowledge production in England and France that privileged rationalism, absolute and universal truth, positivism, and materialism with the aim of dispelling religious superstition and ushering in an era of liberty, freedom, democracy, and reason (Hammer 2001, 4; Zeitlin 1990, 1–6). The ability to reason, however, was considered to be the exclusive domain of men of European ancestry, who were also the subjects to which notions of liberty and freedom applied; race and gender, important categories in the Enlightenment world view, were presented as purely factual when used to justify and organize colonial projects (Loomba 1998, 64). Reacting to Enlightenment priorities, Romanticism did not challenge a hierarchical world view or the rationalist aims of the Enlightenment. It did, however, emphasize passion, creativity, and the "inner quest" as a means of privileging the individual and utopian notions of fulfilling man's destiny of mastering the physical world (Hammer 2001; Tumber 2002). As Raymond Williams (1996, 53) notes in *The Politics of Modernism*, the Romantic movement was characterized by a fascination with folk art, which was "seen as primitive and exotic" and was made widely available through European imperialism. Williams argues that "these appeals to the 'Other'—in fact highly developed arts of their own places— are combined with an underlying association of the 'primitive' and the 'unconscious'" (53). In other words, the Romantic spiritual inner quest into the unconscious is inextricable from the fetishized and racialized "other."

Cultural appropriation has been theorized as a form of violence. For example, Kadi (1996, 116) defines cultural appropriation as "taking possession of specific aspects of someone else's culture in unethical, oppressive ways." Furthermore, Kadi argues that "what passes for multiculturalism is actually covert and overt cultural appropriation, actually a form of cultural genocide. As dominant white society casually buys and sells our symbols/ realities, their cultural meaning is watered down and their integrity diminished" (120). While opposing the "imperialist attitude in which privileged people want to own segments of other people's cultures" (117), Kadi is not simply opposed to people participating in traditions other than their own. Rather, "ethical cultural connections" have the potential for building solidarity and fighting oppression:

> Ethical cultural connections are comprised of respect for the community involved, a desire to learn and take action, an openness to

being challenged and criticized, a willingness to think critically about personal behavior, and a commitment to actively fighting racism. These cornerstones remain the same whether I'm getting to know one Native person or buying a carving from a Native museum. They apply to people of color and white people. (125)

Kadi theorizes a protocol that challenges New Age cultural appropriation and objects to the ways in which tradition is sometimes evoked within communities in the name of cultural nationalism in order to entrench social hierarchies. Traditions, Kadi argues, are negotiated, not static, and oppressive traditions "need to be kissed goodbye" (124).

New Age discourses and practices are constructed as an opposition to dominant Western religious, medical, and political institutions. However, despite this claim to marginality and counterculture status, New Age discourses are inseparable from European colonialism and Western knowledge production. Linda Tuhiwai Smith (1999, 1), a scholar of Maori descent, writes as one of the colonized whose Indigenous knowledge has been appropriated: "It appalls us that the West can desire, extract and claim ownership of our ways of knowing, our imagery, the things we created and produce, and then simultaneously reject the people who created and developed those ideas and seek to deny them further opportunities to be creators of their own culture and own nations." Cultural appropriation is not merely an exchange of cultural knowledge. It occurs within asymmetrical social relations of power and involves attempts to erase the historical, political, and cultural experience of the subordinated group. This is not only discursive but is inextricable from material realities.

Yoga provides a framework for participants' embodied learning in this study. When referring to Indigenous knowledges, I am aware of the problems associated with collapsing differences and distinctions between peoples and their knowledges and practices by way of generalizations, homogenization, and the failure to acknowledge power differentials and relationships among peoples. However, it is possible and useful to note commonalities among Indigenous knowledges and practices. I agree with George Dei, Budd Hall, and Dorothy Rosenberg (2000, 6), who write:

This body of knowledge is diverse and complex given the histories, cultures, and lived realities of people. . . . Indigenous knowledges are emerging again in the present day as a response to the growing awareness that the world's subordinated peoples and their values have been marginalized—*that their past and present experiences have been flooded out* by the rise in influence of Western industrial capital.

Importantly, "counter colonial" (Absolon and Willet 2005, 106) aspects of Indigenous knowledges include a high regard for process, for relationships among all things, and for lived embodied sentient-social experience as inextricable components of knowing and being.

Diverse yoga teachings have evolved over millennia. The term *yoga* is derived from the Sanskrit root *yuj,* which signifies union, and is broadly used to define concepts in religious, scientific, astronomical, philosophical, spiritual, and physical knowledges (Banerji 1995, 1). The various exegetic texts associated with yoga may be addressed as reflective of the epistemo-logical, cosmological beliefs and practices of some South Asian peoples. However, these knowledges are neither static nor homogeneous. Rather, they have been transformed by many transitions and upheavals within the extremely diverse part of the world defined as South Asia. These knowledges reflect power dynamics within communities and other social formations. Furthermore, Hinduism, with which yoga is associated, is not an easily reconciled religious category (Chakraborty 2011, Doniger 2009; King 1999). Richard King (1999, 98) notes that "the notion of 'Hinduism' is itself a Western-inspired abstraction, which until the nineteenth century bore little or no resemblance to the diversity of Indian religious belief and practice."

Yogic knowledge, like other forms of knowledge production, is hetero-geneous. It is diverse, sometimes contradictory, and is found in different schools of thought and religious frameworks developed over the span of more than three thousand years. Texts that focus on yoga are legion and will not be reviewed in this chapter. However, by acknowledging the specificity and complexity of yogic knowledges, I maintain that yoga is socially con-structed through power relations at the same time as it references a distinct "worldsense" (Oyěwùmí 1997) that contrasts with and challenges hegemonic Western ways of knowing, particularly in terms of embodiment. Roxana Ng makes a similar observation and argument about traditional Chinese medi-cine (TCM) as a style of medical knowledge and practice synthesized from diverse local practices and knowledges. Although TCM is subject to power relations and historical formations, it nonetheless reflects a distinct and cohesive way of knowing that contrasts with allopathic medicine and dominant Western knowledge production (see Ng's chapter in this collection).

Discussions about yoga as it relates to consumerism, appropriation, intellectual property patents, authenticity, reinterpretation, and charlatanism are increasingly common. A plethora of journalistic forums—such as the website *Decolonizing Yoga, Assent Magazine,* and documentaries including *Yoga, Inc.* (Philp 2007) and *Who Owns Yoga?* (Bhanu 2014)—testify to a concern about social relations of power with respect to yogic knowledge and its applications. Many have attempted to engage with yogic knowledge in terms of political and material realities, some examples being yoga instructors such as Krishna Kaur, of the American Black Yoga Teachers Association (Chavis 1998); Tawanna Kane, executive director of the Lineage Project in New York (Neilson 2004); and Jade Harper, owner of Spirit Fusion, a mobile yoga studio in Winnipeg that combines Cree and Ojibwe teachings with yoga (Harper 2016); writers and scholars such as Marina Budhos (2007a, 2007b), Retiki Vazirani (2001), Barbara Stoler Miller (1995), and Shola Arewa (1998) can be added to the list.

Farah Shroff (2000) contends that yoga and Ayurveda were suppressed during the colonial occupation of South Asia by the British because of the anticolonial implications of this medical knowledge and practice. She argues that "the struggle to reclaim holistic health care involves decolonizing the mind, which is a political benefit; at the same time, it has the potential to offer valuable therapeutic contributions to health care" (217). However, as demonstrated by Indian Prime Minister Narendra Modi (MacAskill 2015) and the popular yogi Swami "Baba" Ramdev (Nelson 2009), yoga may also be discoursed in the service of promoting religious communalism and homophobia. Understanding yoga requires addressing its Indigenous context as well as how it is influenced by, and reinterpreted through, colonialism and Western imperialism, including current neoliberal formations. That said, a nuanced approach values yogic knowledge as not reducible to hegemonic interpretations. Attention to the therapeutic benefits of yoga, including its countercolonial applications, reveals the complex material and discursive aspects of this knowledge (Budhos 2007a, 2007b; Chavis 1998; Grewal 1996; Shroff 2000). Reetika Vazirani (2001, 133) observes that

> by turning at critical junctures to the East—to the stereotype that
> in Indian philosophy, truth has no context, that oblivion is the

geography of wisdom, that nirvana is emptiness, that nonattachment means we can forget about other people, and about race, class, and gender—America supplies itself with the anesthesia it craves to numb itself from the pain of its history: the pain of stolen land and labor, the outrageous waste.

Vazirani suggests that this "forgetting" has consequences: "In our insatiable drive for ownership and the future, we lose the advantage of the present tense. Thus, we wreck our breathing. Our bodies click out of joint" (133). She articulates an understanding of yoga through her experiences of racism, the confusion and grief she felt after her father committed suicide when she was ten years old, and her difficulties developing her yoga practice within a context of American appropriations and reinterpretations (121). She elaborates on her sentient-social embodiment from her location as a South Asian woman; her yoga practice includes being aware of self-location, nation making, and the colonial history of the United States.

Embodied learning has and continues to be an important resource in healing from violence and oppression. Somatic therapies are gaining greater recognition in clinical health fields at a time when researchers and therapists are acknowledging that solely cognitive-based counselling may not always be effective when addressing trauma (Baranowsky and Lauer 2012; Battell et al. 2008; Haskell 2001; Nadeau and Young 2006; Rai 2009). However, a crucial contribution of feminist therapy is the assertion that therapeutic approaches that neglect the social context of trauma perpetuate oppression for women in recovery (Burstow 1992; Lamb 1999). While addressing sentient-social embodiment as an important strategy for recovering from violence and oppression, "it is only by changing the social relations between colonizer and colonized that psychosocial trauma can be alleviated" (Nadeau and Young 2006, 91).

The individual subjective aspect of embodied learning accommodates an examination of oneself but need not devolve into a New Age individualistic pursuit. In fact, approaches to embodied learning that keep hold of both individual experience and social context posit an interdependence of self, other, and environment: "Self-sufficiency is important to health, but its necessary condition is relationality, a concept that illuminates meanings of health as regards person, species, environment, and community" (Fields 2001, 69). Relationality and self-determination are important teachings in many Indigenous knowledges. As Patricia Monture-Angus (1999, 8) explains, "Self-determination begins with looking at yourself and your family and deciding if and when you are living responsibly. Self-determination is principally, that is first and foremost, about our relationships." She also points out that "living in peace is about living a good life where respect for our relationships with people and all creation is primary" (41).

Yoga—when framed by antiracist feminist, anticolonial, and decolonization scholarship and practice—encourages healing in terms of sentient-social embodiment. Understanding yoga in this way has three significant advantages. First, it challenges New Age individualism and dominant discourses of healing by insisting on the acknowledgement of historical specificity and social relations of power. This is important to circumvent victim blaming toward those who suffer poor health and are unable to thrive because of social determinants of health. Second, it challenges the Cartesian mind/body dichotomy, making room for a sentient-social embodied approach to healing and learning. Third, in practice, Indigenous knowledges such as yoga are important resources, often supplementing limited state medical care and services or, in some cases, replacing it when it is inaccessible or ineffective (Rai 2009; Shroff 2000; Waldron 2005).

Resistance and Remedies: Situated, Strategic, and Transcendent Identity

This study illustrates the social differences of birthplace, language, class, education, and sexual identity within a grouping such as "young South Asian women" in a diasporic setting such as Toronto. For example, ten of the fifteen participants were born in Canada: five in Toronto and five in Edmonton, Moncton, Calgary, Vancouver, and Victoria, respectively. Five women were born abroad: two in Sri Lanka, one in Saudi Arabia, and two in the United Arab Emirates. Languages other than English spoken by individual women are Arabic, Baluchi, Bengali, French, Gujarati, Hindi, Karachi, Persian, Punjabi, Sinhalese, Spanish, Tamil, Telegu, and Urdu. All participants spoke English, two spoke only English, and seven spoke three or more languages besides English. English was not the first language of six women in the group.

The young women, aged from nineteen to twenty-six, use nuanced strategies to access spaces and resources that acknowledge their lived experiences and identities. Amrit, Sarah, Zainab, Mina, and Maya wanted to participate because the class was free of charge, specifically designed for young South Asian women, and combined yoga instruction with discussion about social issues. For example, when asked what stood out for her in the workshops, Sarah replied that discussions about the murder of Reena Virk, the suicide of Hamed Nastoh, and how South Asian youth are gendered and racialized were memorable.[5] Furthermore, many of the women commented on self-location in relation not only to communities to which they belong but also to those with which they express solidarity (e.g., Indigenous, black diasporic, and LGBTQ communities). Although being with other young South Asian women in this project was important, none of the women expressed an exclusive affiliation with this social group. Participating in the yoga classes was expressed as an interest in discussing social relations of power and how this shapes community, culture, and identity rather than because of any presumed sense of sameness within the group. Rania, a twenty-three-year-old community worker and consultant, described the experience of being with other young South Asian women as a means of support that did not presume friendship:

> I think on a very small scale like just the act of us coming together every Wednesday as South Asian women and sharing, like we're not friends but that's the space that we need and then doing yoga and the session afterwards just kinda allows us to open up and talk about experiences that we have on a daily basis and how being South Asian women, how that affects us.

Shared identity was significant for the participants not because of assumed homogeneity but because of the potential to have a conversation about commonalities and differences. As Maya, a twenty-four-year-old nursing student said, "You don't know their stories, you don't know even if they have a story, but you know that we are all living in this world together and we've probably all encountered some sort of situations being South Asian."

---

5 Reena Virk was a fourteen-year-old South Asian girl who was murdered on 14 November 1997 by two white youth, a young man and woman, who had never met her before the night she was killed (Rajiva and Batacharya 2010). Hamed Nastoh, a young South Asian man, committed suicide on 11 March 2000. He experienced homophobic torments from his school peers (Walton, 2005).

A space for young South Asians does not ensure affinity; however, it can be a useful space to investigate identity, as articulated by Rekha, a third-year university student:

> I've never felt like, oh, okay, I'm South Asian so I need to practice yoga, although I feel that sometimes that's the way other people may look at me. I don't think you have to be from South Asian descent to practice, but I do sometimes feel closer to the spirituality of it because I'm Hindu. I wanted to experience being with all brown women and doing yoga. Second, all these topics have such an importance to me and now just learning more has drawn me in even further. I knew that I wanted to be educated more about certain things, and I still do want to explore more.

Participants articulated a nuanced understanding of culture as fluid and as an important resource in knowledge production and identity making. Amrit, a mental health coordinator, addressed cultural stereotypes:

> I think that probably in the Western world there is absolutely that "oh cool, she's like that new wave artsy fartsy type and she's in the helping profession and she does yoga"—there is that whole image and stereo-type. I'm probably viewed that way, so that probably does impact or change my relationships with people. But I also think that there is that substantive quality of, like, I'm nicer, I'm much more mellow, I have a spiritual understanding of things and so I'm a lot less cruel to people. . . . I'm less openly argumentative about things because I understand that there is this mysticism in this world that I wasn't open to before.

Amrit, while suggesting that her yoga practice may position her as a respect-able New Age consumer, asserts that her interest in the practice is due to the substantive benefit to her lived experience and engagements with others.

The participants objected to the manner in which yoga is fetishized and commodified. They criticized the use of images of Hindu deities as decora-tions, the whiteness of yoga magazine imagery, and the economic and class aspects of yoga fashions exemplified by boutique yoga mats and pants. Some claimed that they avoid yoga studios because of the race and class dynamics they observe. However, none made the claim that only South Asians have a right to practice yoga. Furthermore, they claimed that it is inaccurate to assume that yoga is a culturally appropriate teaching and practice that resonates for all South Asians. Given the diversity of their social locations and identities, it is perhaps not surprising that participants challenged the idea that young South Asian women necessarily have familiarity with or an interest in yoga. When asked if yoga is part of her identity, Rania replied:

> No, and I say no because there is this whole thing of, oh, you're Indian, you must know how to do yoga. When I think of yoga, like I said before, I think of something Hindu, and I'm not Hindu. So that's like a false assumption that all Indians practice yoga. And I think yoga practiced here is very different from the way it is practiced in India. So, I mean, I don't see it as something specific to my identity at all.

Yoga is not part of her identity, but interestingly, the yoga workshops were an opportunity to explore it.

While some of the women in the project critically engaged yoga as culturally and historically situated, others saw it very much in the context of a health practice and as one of many options available to them. Shallini, a human resources professional, saw it from both perspectives:

> I have West Indian background; there are few people [with that background] that are Hindu, and there is a majority that are Christian and their ancestors were Hindu. I know my great grandparents were. I think also that makes me want to learn about my culture, my background. . . . In all the magazines, you see that so and so is practicing yoga, Madonna, Sting, and they have excellent form, excellent shape. If you practice yoga, you can be like them.

Similarly, Zahra commented, "I didn't have so much exposure to yoga, but I had an idea that it was becoming more popular. . . . I got really interested and I wanted to try it. It was exotic in its own way, and I decided I would give it a try. And I started." Later, when asked if she reflected on her experience as a South Asian woman while learning yoga, Zahra said she did not. She was referred to the yoga workshops by her counsellor, and her understanding of yoga is in relation to health and healing rather than culture. She laughed when she described yoga as exotic, thereby implying its otherness; however, she also chose to participate in the workshop because it was for young South Asian women. Both Shallini and Zahra described yoga as a practice akin to other lifestyle and fitness commodities in the dominant culture, but issues of identity and culture figured in the subtext of their discussion.

The finding that young South Asian women are interested in yoga coincides with other research indicating that South Asians in Toronto turn to traditional healing practices when they have mental health needs that are not met by Western counselling practices (Rai 2009). My research indicates, though, that this is not without complex considerations. In addition to expressing an aversion to New Age yoga studios, some participants also said they avoid traditional healing resources offered in their communities. Amrit commented, "I'm not really down with organized religion. I don't feel that our temples are places that are really inclusive and equitable." Rekha similarly recounted, "I went through a period of time where I said, no, I don't want to go to this religious place." Zainab told of having abandoned her spiritual practice long ago: "Aspects of the ritual corrupted it for me so that I could no longer engage in it. And I've missed that for the years and years and years since I've stopped praying." Amrit, Rekha, and Zainab indicate a wariness of religious institutions and teachings that efface social relations of power. Aanchal Rai (2009, 27) explains that within South Asian healing traditions, ideas such as karma (the result of past actions), God's curse resulting from wrong deeds or lack of devotion, and destiny are prevalent. These teachings may efface social determinants of health such as social inequities (Wilkinson 2005). While Amrit, Zainab, and Rekha were referring to religious organizations, I argue that their comments are also applicable to yoga studios and ashrams, which are often institutional and hierarchical in structure and are didactic in a way that precludes critical engagement with yoga teachings and society at large.

I asked the women about their participation in healing traditions and knowledges other than yoga. The critique of how yoga has been culturally appropriated was reflected in comments about Indigenous teachings that are not part of their own cultural heritage. Mina, a graduate student, remarked:

I guess I find safety in practicing yoga because it does come from a place where I identify with and a culture that I can connect with. And I think I'm very wary of and I'm very conscious of cultural appropriation, particularly with Indigenous knowledge within North America and how that's been taken and ripped apart and mainstreamed in the same sort of way that parts of yoga have.

Zainab expressed similar concerns:

> I have been thinking of doing drumming as something similar but
> I have a lot of reservations and worries about cultural appropriation
> and appropriateness and how things can get captured. . . . I was wary
> about coming into some other culture's practice and saying, like, okay,
> this seems to be more flexible and open so I can get in on it.

Rekha, on the other hand, explained how her yoga practice provides a foundation for understanding and participating in other healing traditions:

> I think through practicing yoga, which has come from India, I've felt
> a desire to learn about other Indigenous cultures in Canada and in
> South Asia. . . . I feel very interested and drawn towards natural heal-
> ing throughout all cultures. I think it also has to do with yoga and the
> way I've been brought up, being able to respect other people's cultures
> and wanting to learn about them as well.

Rekha then described her experience attending a sweat lodge and how her
yoga practice prepared her to "stay in the moment and challenge myself . . .
to breathe and focus on not just the physical body and what you're experiencing, because it's so much more than that." I asked Rekha about how the
sweat lodge was conducted and by whom. She replied that it was conducted
in a traditional way; however, the woman who conducted the ceremony
was Croatian. Rekha explained that this woman has a deep respect for the
ceremony and the culture from which she learned it and that an elder gave
her permission to conduct the sweat lodge. Rekha also commented on the
presence of an Indigenous man at the sweat lodge:

> He was teaching us a lot, and he kept telling us that this woman
> knows so much about this culture. That was really important and
> really refreshing to see as well. I also appreciated the fact that the
> Native man was there to bring us through his own perspective and to
> sing prayers in his own language and allow us to experience the actual
> roots of what we were doing.

Rekha made several notable comments about her engagement with yoga
and sweat lodge teachings. She explains how her yoga practice provided a
framework for learning about and respecting the sweat lodge ceremony. She

also explains that the ceremony was conducted by a Croatian woman who, Rekha said, was given permission by an elder to conduct the sweat lodge ceremony. This is, of course, controversial because many Indigenous people assert that given the past and current levels of colonialism and genocide, ceremonies should not be performed by non-Indigenous peoples (Smith 2005). However, Rekha reconciles her concerns about cultural appropriation by attributing authenticity to the Indigenous man who shared teachings at the sweat lodge ceremony. Rekha signals her concern with cultural appropriation and her account conveys the difficulty of negotiating participation as a cultural visitor in contexts where authenticity, ethics, and community consent and permission are complex and likely contested.

Candace, one of the yoga teachers I interviewed, self-identifies as a Cree woman with French ancestry. Like Rekha, she seeks permission and validation in her bid to avoid cultural appropriation. Speaking of an exchange between herself and an activist scholar and yoga practitioner visiting Toronto from India, Candace remarked:

> She was really encouraging 'cause I felt somewhat, like, I know how it is being an Aboriginal woman and dealing with appropriation, and I felt very—I'm aware of that and I try not to pretend like I'm original to these instructions. I think that's a really important thing, that us in the West, we tend to forget and not acknowledge, and it's really important to acknowledge. So [she] really kind of made me feel at peace with just being here. She said something—really, I can't remember exactly the words, but just she reminded me, you're teaching here on Turtle Island and you are teaching to your people and you know it is okay.

Rekha and Candace both expressed concern about permission and guidance with regard to participating in a tradition to which they are visitors. On the surface, this raises the issue of tokenism and looking to "native informants" (Trinh 1989) for validation and proof of authenticity. Arguably, it also speaks to a politics of "ethical cultural connections" (Kadi 1996, 125) by acknowledging the importance of where traditions come from and whose ancestors carried them. However, other issues must be considered as well, such as how the difference between exploitation and colonization in South Asia affects yoga knowledges and practices, on the one hand, and the genocidal settler colonization in the Americas and how this has impacted the knowledges of Indigenous peoples of Turtle Island, on the other. For example, the protocols for participating in yoga studios are framed through neoliberal markets; participation is based on tuition fees. While the practice of initiation and mentorship may have been protocol for transmitting yoga teachings in the past, and may still figure in different (sometimes abusive) ways now, for the most part, the ability to pay for instruction is the determining qualification for learning yoga in the West—and increasingly in South Asia as well, since yoga teachings have become centralized through the ashram model and commercialization. Protocols for participating in Indigenous ceremonies such as the sweat lodge are not the same as those for studying yoga. While one can always find opportunities to attend a sweat lodge, marketing this experience to settlers should be approached with as much skepticism and critical thinking as one would approach naked or surfboard yoga instruction. Interestingly, Rekha and Candace expressed similar concerns about cultural appropriation; however, their comments also raise questions about differences in knowledges and practices. Similarities in yogic and sweat lodge teachings pertain to the material body in terms of breath and emotions, but discursive practices and knowledge production within different traditions will vary widely, especially with respect to New Age reinterpretation, neoliberal commercial practices, and colonial contexts.

While examples of people (including people of colour) appropriating and commercializing Indigenous and traditional health knowledges abound, many others are held accountable and act responsibly regarding membership and participation in cultural and community spaces where these knowledges are taught and practiced. The spread of yoga is a good example of this: yoga has been reinterpreted for commercial gain and in support of New Age ideologies, but it has also been used in activist communities as a response to the consequences of social inequities, with only some of these initiatives led by South Asians. For example, people of African descent, many of whom see the roots of yoga as African as well as South Asian (Shola Arewa 1998), and other racially marginalized communities have integrated yoga into their protocols and goals (Chavis 1998).

Reinterpreting yogic knowledge as a resource for challenging social inequities is a very different project than adapting yogic teachings to support New Age consumption and neoliberal individualism. The latter effaces social relations of power while the former aims to correct power imbalances. "The difference between appropriation and proliferation," notes Gloria Anzaldúa (1990, xxi), "is that the first steals and harms; the second helps heal breaches of knowledge." The pertinent question regarding the Croatian woman who conducts the sweat lodge that Rekha attended is whether it is an appropriation, and if not, what criteria are met to ensure that the ceremony she conducts helps rather than harms. This is an important consideration given her social location. However, it is a criterion that is also required of Indigenous people conducting ceremonies. Jade Harper (2016), an Indigenous woman who teaches yoga in Winnipeg, carefully considers how to integrate yogic, Cree, and Ojibwe teachings. She comments on the importance of building relationships with elders and yoga instructors with whom she works:

> I build relationships with people, and to me, that is really important because when I started learning my traditional ways when I was seven years old, that was the first time I went to a lodge. I learned that learning our teachings is a part of who we are and using them is a part of our inherent right. And so, I think that through building relationships, people get to know me and understand that my intentions with sharing this information or sharing our traditional ways is coming from a good place. It is not about being a commodity as much as, I think, that it is a part of also bridging.

When asked about how she would respond to challenges about presenting Indigenous teachings in yoga classes, Jade responded:

> It is more about a conversation. To be honest, I don't really look forward to it, but I do look forward to that conversation happening at some point [laughs]. I know that I'm treading on—I'm embarking on something a bit new. It's not out of ill intent or that I am trying to sell ceremony or trying to exploit an entire ancient tradition of yoga, which is not a part of my culture, and that is something I am actually learning about. I am very committed to learning about Indian culture and yoga because I know that there are so many other connections beyond yoga, like colonization.

While some yoga schools tend to claim an original authentic yoga, the diversity of teachings complicates this assertion. This is not to say that yoga teachings are, in the postmodern sense, open to any and all interpretations, devoid of history and context. Rather, it is a matter of yogic knowledge being created in the context of community instead of in the domain of any one individual or group. Yogic knowledge is subject to exegetical debate and contestation, ideological tensions, and a wide range of practical applications. I argue that talking about what yoga is may be less productive than theorizing "how we live our yoga" (Jeremijenko 2001) and how we engage in critical dialogue about it, including discussions about how to practice yoga in counterhegemonic ways that defy cultural appropriation. The interviews with Candace and Rekha may be read as both a critical and an unresolved attempt to think about what it means to teach yoga as a First Nation woman and to participate in a sweat lodge ceremony as a young South Asian woman on Turtle Island. In their work with Indigenous women, Denise Nadeau and Alannah Young (2006, 97) address the issue of cultural appropriation and make the point that negotiation and attention to power relations are crucial considerations: "Negotiating ceremonies and protocols is a co-creative process that reflects and maintains equitable power dynamics. The appropriate protocol is to acknowledge historical relationships and identify how to demonstrate power-sharing and enhance community vitality in accordance with the traditional teachings." Participants in my study struggle with cultural appropriation and power relationships when learning Indigenous knowledges as insiders and outsiders.

Anne-Marie, a yoga teacher of African, South Asian, European, and Caribbean Indigenous ancestry, commented on a different aspect of the ethics of cultural appropriation. She is frustrated when subordinated peoples are denied, or deny themselves, teachings that could benefit them.

> You know if there is anything that gets my back up against a wall, it's when people can't even choose something. They must be able to make that choice. I feel really badly in the sense that there's all these people, these Caribbean people, suffering, and when other groups of people who have more privilege suffer, they feel fine about going here, getting this kind of healing, going over there and getting that kind of healing, and [if] all that didn't work, I'll go do acupuncture. . . . They think about all of the things, as long as they can get to know about them,

they just include all of these modalities as, like, a big buffet and that it is their right to go and try them and see how it works. Then you have this group who are suffering, and they are allowed by their religious leaders only one thing. That, to me, is the saddest thing. It is just so sad because what it actually does, and it's really opposite to what they want it to do, what it actually does is reinforces the slave mentality of being regulated and confined and not allowed to try these things. It's actually so reinforcing of the mindset, the cultural mindset of slavery that I actually find it scary that it's not understood that way. But they can't see what it's actually doing to that group of people what has always been done to them.

Anne-Marie asserted that it is important to acknowledge where yoga comes from, especially when teaching South Asian women. However, as the quotation above indicates, she also feels that everyone should be able to access remedies that will help them, especially those who have suffered oppression. She commented that in the Caribbean community in which she works, Christian prayer is prescribed as the only option for healing. In attempting to work around this, she finds ways to adapt teachings—for example making connections between yogic teachings and the experiences of her students.

I'll talk about the idea of kundalini and that the literal translation as I received it is the lock of the hair of the beloved. And that is, for the Caribbean person coming from Christianity who can't hear about snakes and women without having alarm bells going off—to have a coil of love at the base of the spine seems to be okay. I also sometimes will talk a little bit about how in Egyptian pyramids—in papyruses, those kind of things—there were also images of shoulder stands and energy wheels for the body, and all of those things, to try to bring yoga through India back to Africa if I feel that it's going to help.

Similarly, Candace makes links between yoga and Indigenous knowledges in North America:

I find that there is a strong connection to the land with yoga, and even if you go to Ayurveda, which is an extension of yoga—I mean, you know, the elements, and I mean there are many connections. Well, obviously, with the fasting—fasting is a ritual or a practice among Indigenous people. . . . I could definitely see the links there. And meditation, I mean, vision quests are meditative, whether they have a certain technique, it is a little bit different but it's experiential basically. When it gets right down to it, that's the fundamental similarity I think between Indigenous ways, First Nations or North America, and Eastern philosophy and yoga is experiential learning.

Similar to Anne-Marie's adaptation of yoga teachings to suit the context she works in, Candace recalled that during a yoga class, one of her students became triggered by the sound of a chime, commonly used in yoga classes to signal the end of the class, because it reminded him of bells used in residential school.

> I've had questions about are you going to be indoctrinating, because it is a Hindu belief system and people are aware of that, and I think there are a lot of sensitivities, particularly with the Aboriginal community because of residential schools and, you know, assimilation policies and that sort of thing. There are those, you know, people are, have their guards up in some cases, so I think that's probably the biggest concern that I face presenting and offering this to Aboriginal communities.

Anne-Marie and Candace remarked that teaching yoga in their communities is not without challenges related to culture and history, particularly the history of slavery, colonialism, and cultural assimilation. Despite these complexities, they remain committed to the pursuit of practices such as yoga because of its health benefits.

The young women and yoga teachers interviewed claim yoga as an important resource; however, they also problematize hegemonic approaches to yogic knowledge production and practice. They address the paradoxes arising from cultural appropriations and the notion that yoga is culturally appropriate for anyone who is of South Asian ancestry; they object to the idea that cultural spaces where yoga may be offered are necessarily accessible and/or helpful. Pursuing these themes further, Mina's thoughts on identity and embodied experience are worth quoting at length.

> If you ask me who I am, I'll say I'm a South Asian woman, I'm Punjabi Sikh, and I'm a student, and this is who I am. And I guess yoga would be more sort of removing yourself from that and looking at yourself

as I am, a whole person . . . like, I don't know how you would describe that. But it is another way of approaching how we look at who we are ourselves and how we build that notion of that. . . . And it [yoga] humbles you and it sort of removes yourself from that and [you] are maybe able to look at yourself just for your own spiritual, emotional, and physical self as opposed to all these other trappings. And physical in a very, sort of, these-are-my-legs sort of way, not just in an appearance sort of way. . . . I've sort of been struggling with the identity game in a lot of ways. I do take a lot of power and I do think there are a lot of positive things that can come out of your identity, but I also think that even intellectually, I've reached a point where I'm finding that a bit limiting. And it seems the politics in this sort of area, like the lefty politics and in academia, is based solely around the identity games and using those to sort of state your case. . . . And then there's the horrible tokenism that comes out of that. So I guess I'm just personally trying to struggle with that.

Here, Mina addresses the importance of a strong social identity as well as its limits. Violence and oppression impact individuals in every way—mind, body, emotions, and spirit, as well as self-perception and identity. While acknowledging the need to address this in, for example, identity-based group work with young South Asian women, Mina suggests that it is important to understand ourselves as more than socially constructed beings. Without privileging one over the other or seeing these concerns in conflict with one another, Mina struggles to acknowledge both. Given that binaries and dichotomies underpin many forms of oppression, this acknowledgement is useful in asserting that one need not be forced to choose between healing and social engagement or between social identities and practices that allow for strategically transcending the artifice of social divisions, despite their very real consequences.

Sonia, a yoga teacher who identified as a Punjabi Sikh woman and whose ancestry is from the Pakistan region of pre-partition Punjab, stated,

I believe fundamentally in personal responsibility and I am in no way suggesting that people ask for violent situations or anything like that. I mean, no way am I even going there . . . I mean, there is no denying that the options are ultimately limited, but I do feel, I guess this is my spiritual belief, that each person has a tiny window of opportunity to find a sense of peace and a sense of happiness in whatever situation that they are in. . . . I just feel, ultimately, I don't want people to feel disempowered. That's where I'm coming from in my heart, is that I don't want anyone to feel like they have no options.

Sonia will not let go of the importance of personal responsibility, not because she underestimates the consequences of violence and oppression but because she sees individual agency as a crucial resource for overcoming victimization. Although her belief in personal responsibility could be taken to resonate with health-promotion discourses of New Age, neoliberalism, and behaviour modification, I would argue that her acknowledgement of the potential misunderstanding of how she takes up individual agency constitutes a counterhegemonic approach to healing. Patricia Hill Collins (1990, 237) has similarly theorized that

the existence of Afrocentric feminist thought suggests that there is always choice, and power to act, no matter how bleak the situation may be. Viewing the world as one in the making raises the issue of individual responsibility for bringing about change. It also shows that while individual empowerment is key, only collective action can effectively generate lasting social transformation of political and economic institutions.

The struggle to reconcile individual agency with the need for structural social transformation is complicated by the ways in which agency and systemic determinants of health are dichotomized. For example, to regard individual agency as important coincides with New Age and health-promotion discourses that efface social inequities. However, to deny the importance of individual agency is also to deny the importance of that window of opportunity so crucial to healing as a form of resistance. Participants suggest that acknowledging and challenging the structures of social inequity need not dismiss the importance of individual agency, resistance, and creative actions. Finding a window of opportunity does not dismiss the reality that some windows are very small and difficult, if not impossible, to access. However, survival often depends on individual agency. As Sara Ahmed (2004, 201) argues,

For those whose lives have been torn apart by violence, or those for whom the tiredness of repetition in everyday life becomes too much to bear, feeling better does and should matter. Feeling better is not a sign that justice has been done, and nor should it be reified as the goal of political struggle. But feeling better does still matter, as it is about learning to live with the injuries that threaten to make life impossible.

Attunement to sentient-social embodiment becomes a counterhegemonic healing strategy when women participate in identity formation and use their agency to feel better by "making sense" of their experience, "not covering over" the wounds they have incurred living through violence and oppression (197).

Roxana Ng (2011, 351) explains that observing ourselves, what we do and who we present ourselves as, involves recognizing deeply ingrained patterns that may go unnoticed. "Once hegemonic ideas become common sense," she contends, "they are *condensed* in our emotional and physical beings—in how we relate to women and minority groups, for example, and in how we see and relate to ourselves. In short, they become patterns of behaviour." Countering hegemonic ideas involves attending to perceptions about who we are in relation to others and what we do in our interpersonal interactions. Furthermore, as Ng explains, change is not only a matter of thinking differently but also involves emotional and physical transformation: "It draws our attention to how the body, emotion and spirit are involved in the learning process: what we embrace and resist, and why" (353).

In Denise Noble's (2005) discussion of the Sacred Woman program, a self-help Afrocentric healing program for women of African ancestry, she argues that "critiques of essentialism must be historicised and contextualised, for there are no identities devoid of essentialist elements and moments" (151). As with Noble's research participants, the young women in my study convey an "engaged cultural criticism," which Noble describes as consideration of "whether there may paradoxically be emancipatory elements in moments of essentialism, which can be brought to give voice to criticism from within" (151). The young South Asian women in my study exhibited a complex and strategic understanding and use of identity. They claimed a racialized and gendered location in opposition to racism and sexism; however, they also resisted essentializing definitions of South Asian experiences. As Mina suggested, the limiting aspects of identity categories must be addressed, including the ways that "people reify binaristically constructed concepts of self, gender, race, and a host of other categories with which they identify and to which they become deeply attached at the same time that they assign the oppositional terms to others" (Orr 2002, 491). The young women and yoga teachers attest that this can only be accomplished through a sophisticated approach to embodiment rather than through renouncing or dismissing it as essentialist. Additionally, transcendence is not understood as an escape or a place in which to permanently reside. Rather, it fosters nonjudgment and the opportunity to observe more deeply the contours of our sentient-social embodiment. Putting this awareness to use in everyday life is an important aspect of resisting and finding respite from violence and oppression.

Conclusion

The women I interviewed affirmed that sentient-social embodied attunement is an important strategy for contending with social inequity and its impacts on health and healing. They considered how yoga can be used as a counterhegemonic healing strategy through a careful critique of cultural appropriation. I address New Age, neoliberal, and colonial reinterpretations of yoga in the context of settler colonialism in Canada in order to consider the experiences of participants in this study. Identity is discussed at length as an important resource and many of the women explained how they rely on it when coping with and resisting social inequities. However, they also expressed interest in knowledges and practices that examine the socially constructed aspects of identities. They explore yogic teachings not as an escape or denial of identity and social context but rather as a resource for understanding and contending with material realities. Furthermore, their interviews offer a critique of essentialist notions of identity—and indeed, of yoga itself. In other words, the young South Asian women and yoga teachers explored social identities to counter racism and colonialism and as a challenge to cultural essentialism. In doing so, they contributed to the ongoing discussion about cultural appropriation and culturally appropriate services through a nuanced and critical examination of social relations of power and strategies for resisting violence and oppression.

References

Absolon, Kathy, and Cam Willett. 2005. "Putting Ourselves Forward: Location in Aboriginal Research." In *Research as Resistance: Critical, Indigenous, and Anti-oppressive Approaches,* edited by Leslie Brown and Susan Strega, 97–126. Toronto: Canadian Scholars' Press / Women's Press.

Ahmed, Sara. 2004. *The Cultural Politics of Emotion.* New York and London: Routledge.

Alaimo, Stacy. 2008. "Trans-corporeal Feminisms and the Ethical Space of Nature." In Alaimo and Hekman, *Material Feminisms,* 237–64.

Alaimo, Stacy, and Susan Hekman, eds. 2008. *Material Feminisms.* Bloomington: Indiana University Press.

Ali, Alisha, Notisha Massaquoi, and Marsha Brown. 2003. *Racial Discrimination as a Health Risk for Female Youth: Implications for Policy and Healthcare Delivery in Canada.* Toronto: The Canadian Race Relations Foundation and Women's Health in Women's Hands Community Health Centre

Alexander, M. Jacqui. 2005. *Pedagogies of Crossing: Meditations on Feminism, Sexual Politics, Memory, and the Sacred.* Durham, NC: Duke University Press.

Amnesty International. 2004. *Stolen Sisters: A Human Rights Response to Discrimination and Violence Against Indigenous Women in Canada.* Ottawa: Amnesty International. https://www.amnesty.ca/sites/amnesty/files/ amr200032004enstolensisters.pdf.

———. 2009. *No More Stolen Sisters: The Need for a Comprehensive Response to Discrimination and Violence Against Indigenous Women in Canada.* London: Amnesty International. http://www.amnesty.ca/sites/amnesty/files/ amr200122009en.pdf.

Anzaldúa, Gloria, ed. 1990. *Making Face, Making Soul / Haciendo Caras: Creative and Critical Perspectives by Feminists of Color.* San Francisco: Aunt Lute Foundation Books.

Banerji, Sures Chandra. 1995. *Studies in the Origin and Development of Yoga.* Calcutta: Punthi Pustak.

Bannerji, Himani, ed. 1993. *Returning the Gaze: Essays on Racism, Feminism, and Politics.* Toronto: Sister Vision Press.

Baranowsky, Anna, and Teresa Lauer. 2012. *What is PTSD? 3 Steps to Healing Trauma.* CreateSpace Independent Publishing Platform.

Batacharya, Sheila. 1994. "In a Complex Weave." In *Resist! Essays Against a Homophobic Culture,* edited by Mona Oikawa, Dionne Falconer, and Anne Decter, 179–85. Toronto: Women's Press.

Battell, Evelyn, Shayna Hornstein, Jenny Horsman, Christianna Jones, Judy Murphy, Ningwakwe / E. Priscilla George, Kate Nonesuch et al. 2008. *Moving*

Research About Addressing the Impacts of Violence on Learning into Practice. Edmonton: Windsound Learning Society.

Bhanu, Bhatnagar. 2014. "Who Owns Yoga?" *Al Jazeera*, 27 November. http://www.aljazeera.com/programmes/aljazeeracorrespondent/2014/11/who-owns-yoga-20141117114315748275.html.

Bolaria, B. Singh, and Peter S. Li. 1988. *Racial Oppression in Canada.* Toronto: Garamond Press.

Bordo, Susan. 2004. *Unbearable Weight: Feminism, Western Culture, and the Body.* Berkeley: University of California Press.

Brah, Avtar. 1996. *Cartographies of Diaspora: Contesting Identities.* London: Routledge.

Budhos, Marina. 2007a. "Culture Shock." *Yoga Journal*, 28 August. http://www.yogajournal.com/article/lifestyle/culture-shock/.

———. 2007b. "Out of India." *Yoga Journal*, 28 August. http://www.yogajournal.com/article/lifestyle/out-of-india/.

Burstow, Bonnie. 1992. *Radical Feminist Therapy: Working in the Context of Violence.* Newbury Park, CA: Sage.

Calliste, Agnes M., and George J. Sefa Dei. 2000. *Anti-racist Feminism: Critical Race and Gender Studies.* With the assistance of Margarida Aguiar. Halifax: Fernwood Publishing.

Chakraborty, Chandrima. 2011. *Masculinity, Asceticism, Hinduism: Past and Present Imaginings of India.* New Delhi: Permanent Black.

Chavis, Melody Ermachild. 1998. "In the Eye of the Storm." *Yoga Journal* 138 (March/April): 65–71, 142–44, 149.

Collins, Patricia Hill. 2000. *Black Feminist Thought: Knowledge, Consciousness, and the Politics of Empowerment.* New York and London: Routledge.

———. 1998. *Fighting Words: Black Women and the Search for Justice.* Minneapolis: University of Minnesota Press.

Czapska, Asia, Annabell Webb, Angela Sterritt, and Nura Taefi. 2006. *Submission to the United Nations Commmittee on Economic, Social, and Cultural Rights at Its 5th Periodic Review of Canada.* Vancouver: Justice for Girls.

Davis, Kathy. 2007. "Reclaiming Women's Bodies: Colonialist Trope or Critical Epistemology?" In *Embodying Sociology: Retrospect, Progress, and Prospects*, edited by Chris Shilling, 50–64. Malden, MA: Blackwell.

Dei, George. J. Sefa, and Alireza Asgharzadeh. 2001. "The Power of Social Theory: Towards an Anticolonial Discursive Framework." *Journal of Educational Thought* 35(3): 297–323.

Dei, George J. Sefa, Budd L. Hall, and Dorothy Goldin Rosenberg, eds. 2000. *Indigenous Knowledges in Global Contexts: Multiple Readings of Our World.* Toronto: University of Toronto Press.

Doniger, Wendy. 2009. *The Hindus: An Alternative History.* New York: Penguin Press.

Federal/Provincial/Territorial Working Group on Women's Health, Conference of Deputy Ministers of Health. 1990. *Working Together for Women's Health: A Framework for the Development of Policies and Programs.* With the assistance of Anne Rochon Ford. [Ottawa]: Federal/Provincial/Territorial Working Group on Women's Health.

Fields, Gregory P. 2001. *Religious Therapeutics: Body and Health in Yoga, Āyurveda, and Tantra.* Albany: State University of New York Press.

FORWARD. 2006. *Burned by the System, Burned at the Stake: Poor, Homeless, and Marginalized Women Speak Out.* Report to the United Nations on Violations of the International Covenant on Economic, Social, and Cultural Rights in Canada. Toronto: FORWARD. http://www2.ohchr.org/english/bodies/cescr/docs/info-ngos/forward.pdf.

Frankenberg, Ruth. 2004. *Living Spirit, Living Practice: Poetics, Politics, Epistemology.* Durham, NC: Duke University Press.

Graveline, Fyre Jean. 1998. *Circle Works: Transforming Eurocentric Consciousness.* Halifax: Fernwood Publishing.

Grewal, Inderpal. 1996. *Home and Harem: Nation, Gender, Empire, and the Cultures of Travel.* Durham, NC: Duke University Press

———. 2005. *Transnational America: Feminisms, Diasporas, Neoliberalisms.* Durham, NC: Duke University Press.

Grosz, Elizabeth. 1994. *Volatile Bodies: Toward a Corporeal Feminism.* Bloomington: Indiana University Press.

———. 2008. "Darwin and Feminism: Preliminary Investigations for a Possible Alliance." In Alaimo and Hekman, *Material Feminisms,* 23–51.

Hammer, Olav. 2001. *Claiming Knowledge: Strategies of Epistemology from Theosophy to the New Age.* Boston: Brill.

Handa, Amita. 2003. *Of Silk Saris and Mini Skirts: South Asian Girls Walk the Tightrope of Culture.* Toronto: Women's Press.

Harding, Sandra. 1993. "Rethinking Standpoint Epistemology: What Is 'Strong Objectivity'?" In *Feminist Epistemologies,* edited by Linda Alcoff and Elizabeth Potter, 49–82. New York: Routledge.

Harding, G. Sophie, ed. 2005. *Surviving in the Hour of Darkness: The Health and Wellness of Women of Colour and Indigenous Women.* Calgary, AB: University of Calgary Press.

Harper, Jade. 2016. "Jade Harper and Spirit Fusion Yoga." *Unreserved.* CBC Radio, 17 April. http://www.cbc.ca/news/jade-harper-and-spirit-fusion-yoga-1.3536456.

Haskell, Lori. 2001. *Bridging Responses: A Front-Line Worker's Guide to Supporting Women Who Have Post-traumatic Stress.* Toronto: Centre for Addiction and Mental Health.

Hekman, Susan. 2008. "Constructing the Ballast: An Ontology for Feminism." In Alaimo and Hekman, *Material Feminisms,* 85–119.

Jeremijenko, Valerie, ed. 2001. *How We Live Our Yoga: Teachers and Practitioners on How Yoga Enriches, Surprises, and Heals Us.* Boston, MA: Beacon Press

Jiwani, Yasmin. 1999. *Violence Prevention and the Girl Child.* London, ON: Alliance of Five Research Centres on Violence.

———. 2002. "Race, Gender, Violence, and Health Care." In McKenna and Larkin, *Violence Against Women,* 223–54.

———. 2005. "Walking a Tightrope: The Many Faces of Violence in the Lives of Racialized Immigrant Girls and Young Women." *Violence Against Women* 11(7): 846–75.

Kadi, Joanna. 1996. *Thinking Class: Sketches from a Cultural Worker.* Boston: South End Press.

Khanlou, Nazilla, and Maroussia Hadjukowski-Ahmed. 1999. "Adolescent Self-Concept and Mental Health Promotion in a Cross-Cultural Context." In *Women's Voices in Health Promotion,* edited by Margaret Denton, Maroussia Hadjukowski-Ahmed, Mary O'Connor, Isik Urla Zeytinoglu, and Karen Williams, 138–51. Toronto: Canadian Scholars' Press.

Khosla, Punam. 1991. "With My Heart in My Mouth: Keynote Address at the South Asian Women's Community Centre Conference." *Resources for Feminist Research* 20(3/4), 80–81.

King, Richard. 1999. *Orientalism and Religion: Postcolonial Theory, India, and "the Mystic East."* London: Routledge.

Lamb, Sharon. 1999. "Constructing the Victim: Popular Images and Lasting Labels." In *New Versions of Victims: Feminists Struggle with the Concept,* edited by Sharon Lamb, 108–38. New York: New York University Press.

Lawrence, Bonita, and Enakshi Dua. 2005. "Decolonizing Antiracism." *Social Justice* 32(4): 120–43.

Loomba, Ania. 1998. *Colonialism/Postcolonialism.* New York: Routledge.

Lorde, Audre. 1984. *Sister Outsider: Essays and Speeches by Audre Lorde.* Freedom, CA: Crossing Press.

MacAskill, Andrew. 2015. "India Hindu Nationalist Jibe at Muslim Vice-President Disturbs Yoga Calm." *Reuters: World News,* 23 June. http://www.reuters.com/article/2015/06/23/us-india-yoga-iduskbnop316r20150623.

McKenna, Katherine M. J., and June Larkin, eds. 2002. *Violence Against Women: New Canadian Perspectives.* Toronto: Inanna Publications and Education.

Miller, Barbara Stoler. 1995. *Yoga: Discipline of Freedom*. New York: Bantam Books.

Mohanty, Chandra Talpade. 2003. *Feminism Without Borders: Decolonizing Theory, Practicing Solidarity*. Durham, NC: Duke University Press.

Mohanty, Chandra Talpade, Ann Russo, and Lourdes Torres. 1991. *Third World Women and the Politics of Feminism*. Bloomington: Indiana University Press.

Monture-Angus, Patricia. 1999. *Journeying Forward: Dreaming First Nations' Independence*. Halifax: Fernwood Publishing.

Nadeau, Denise, and Alannah Young. 2006. "Educating Bodies for Self-determination: A Decolonizing Strategy." *Canadian Journal of Native Education* 29(1): 87–148.

Native Women's Association of Canada. 2004. *The Native Women's Association of Canada Background Paper: Aboriginal Women's Health, Canada—Aboriginal Peoples Roundtable, Health Sectoral Session*. Ottawa: Native Women's Association of Canada.

Neilson, Leslie Marion. 2004. "Personal, Political, Everyday Yoga: Tawanna Kane Reflects on Diversity, Access, and Yoga as a Grassroots Movement." *Ascent* 23: 12–16.

Nelson, Dean. 2009. "Hindu Guru Claims Homosexuality Can Be 'Cured' by Yoga." *The Telegraph*, 8 July. http://www.telegraph.co.uk/news/worldnews/asia/india/5780028/hindu-guru-claims-homosexuality-can-be-cured-by-yoga.html.

Ng, Roxana. 1986. "The Social Construction of 'Immigrant Women' in Canada." In *The Politics of Diversity: Feminism, Marxism, and Nationalism,* edited by Roberta Hamilton and Michèle Barrett, 269–86. London: Verso.

———. 1993. "Sexism, Racism, and Canadian Nationalism." In *Feminism and the Politics of Difference,* edited by Sneja Gunew and Anna Yeatman, 197–211. Halifax: Fernwood Publishing.

———. 2000a. "Revisioning the Body/Mind from an Eastern Perspective: Comments on Experience, Embodiment, and Pedagogy." In *Women's Bodies, Women's Lives,* edited by Baukji Miedema, Janet M. Stoppard, and Vivienne Anderson, 175–93. Toronto: Sumach Press.

———. 2000b. "Toward an Embodied Pedagogy: Exploring Health and the Body Through Chinese Medicine." In Dei, Hall, and Rosenberg, *Indigenous Knowledges in Global Contexts,* 168–83.

———. 2011. "Decolonizing Teaching and Learning Through Embodied Learning: Toward an Integrated Approach." In *Valences of Interdisciplinarity: Theory, Practice, Pedagogy,* edited by Raphael Foshay, 343–65. Edmonton: Athabasca University Press.

Noble, Denise. 2005. "Remembering Bodies, Healing Histories: The Emotional Politics of Everyday Freedom." In *Making Race Matter: Bodies, Space and*

Identity, edited by Claire Alexander and Caroline Knowles, 132–52. New York: Palgrave Macmillan.

Obamsawin, Alanis. 1993. *Kanesatake: 270 Years of Resistance.* Written and directed by Alanis Obomsawin. Montréal: National Film Board of Canada.

Oyěwùmí, Oyèrónké. 1997. *The Invention of Women: Making an African Sense of Western Gender Discourses.* Minneapolis: University of Minnesota Press.

Orr, Deborah. 2002. "The Uses of Mindfulness in Anti-oppressive Pedagogies: Philosophy and Praxis." *Canadian Journal of Education* 27(4): 477–90.

Philp, John. 2007. *Yoga, Inc.* Written and directed by John Philp. Brooklyn, NY: Bad Dog Tales.

Rai, Aanchal. 2009. "Bridging the Gap: Western Counselling and South Asian Mental Health Needs." In *Within and Beyond Borders: Critical Multicultural Counselling in Practice,* edited by Olga Oulanova, Isaac Stein, Aanchal Rai, Maya Hammer, and Patricia A. Poulin, 24–35. Toronto: Centre for Diversity in Counselling and Psychotherapy, Ontario Institute for Studies in Education, University of Toronto.

Rajiva, Mythili. 2004. "Racing Through Adolecence: Becoming and Belonging in the Narratives of Second Generation South Asian Girls." PhD diss., Carleton University, Ottawa.

———. 2006. "Brown Girls, White Worlds: Adolescence and the Making of Racialized Selves." *Canadian Review of Sociology and Anthropology* 43(2): 165–83.

Rajiva, Mythili, and Sheila Batacharya. 2010. *Reena Virk: Critical Perspectives on a Canadian Murder.* Toronto: Canadian Scholars' Press Inc.

Razack, Sherene. 1998. *Looking White People in the Eye: Gender, Race, and Culture in Courtrooms and Classrooms.* Toronto: University of Toronto Press.

———. 2002. *Race, Space, and the Law: Unmapping a White Settler Society.* Toronto: Between the Lines.

Rice, Carla, and Vanessa Russell. 1995a. "Embodying Equity: Putting Body and Soul into Equity Education—Part 1: How Oppression Is Embodied." *Our Schools / Our Selves* 7(1): 14–36.

———. 1995b. "Embodying Equity: Putting Body and Soul into Equity Education—Part 2: Strategies for Change." *Our Schools / Our Selves* 7(2): 42–54.

Shakti Kee Chatree Collective. 1997. *Shakti Kee Awaaz: An Anthology by Emerging Young South Asian and Indo-Caribbean Women Writers and Artists.* Toronto: Ontario Women's Directorate.

Shola Arewa, Caroline. 1998. *Opening to Spirit: Contacting the Healing Power of the Chakras and Honouring African Spirituality.* London: HarperCollins.

Shroff, Farah M. 2000. "Ayurveda: Mother of Indigenous Health Knowledge." In Dei, Hall, and Rosenberg, *Indigenous Knowledges in Global Contexts,* 215–33.

Smith, Andrea. 2005. *Conquest: Sexual Violence and American Indian Genocide.* Cambridge, MA: South End Press.

Smith, Linda Tuhiwai. 1999. *Decolonizing Methodologies: Research and Indigenous Peoples.* London: Zed Books.

Stasiulis, Daiva K. 1990. "Theorizing Connections: Gender, Race, Ethnicity, and Class." In *Race and Ethnic Relations in Canada,* edited by Peter S. Li, 269–305. Toronto: Oxford University Press.

Sunseri, Lina. 2011. *Being Again of One Mind: Oneida Women and the Struggle for Decolonization.* Vancouver: UBC Press.

Thobani, Sunera. 2007. *Exalted Subjects: Studies in the Making of Race and Nation in Canada.* Toronto: University of Toronto Press.

Trinh, T. Minh-Ha. 1989. *Woman, Native, Other: Writing Postcoloniality and Feminism.* Bloomington: Indiana University Press.

Tuck, Eve, and K. Wayne Yang. 2012. "Decolonization Is Not a Metaphor." *Decolonization: Indigeneity, Education, and Society* 1(1): 1–40.

Tumber, Catherine. 2002. *American Feminism and the Birth of New Age Spirituality: Searching for the Higher Self, 1875–1915.* Lanham, MD: Rowman and Littlefield.

Vazirani, Retki. 2001. "The Art of Breathing." In *How We Live Our Yoga: Teachers and Practitioners on How Yoga Enriches, Surprises, and Heals Us,* edited by Valerie Jeremijenko, 120–34. Boston: Beacon Press.

Waldron, Ingrid. 2005. "African Canadian Women Resisting Oppression: Embodying Emancipated Consciousness Through Holistic Self-Healing." In *Surviving in the Hour of Darkness: The Health and Wellness of Women of Colour and Indigenous Women,* edited by G. Sandra Harding, 13–31. Calgary: University of Calgary Press.

Walton, Gerald. 2005. "Homophobia Overlooked as Cause of Bullying." *SFU News Online,* 28 April. http://www.sfu.ca/sfunews/sfu_news/regular_features/comment04280501.htm.

Wilkinson, Richard G. 2005. *The Impact of Inequality: How to Make Sick Societies Healthier.* New York: The New York Press.

Williams, Raymond. 1996. *The Politics of Modernism.* London: Verso.

Wing, Adrien Katherine. 1997. "Brief Reflections Toward a Multiplicative Theory and Praxis of Being." In *Critical Race Feminism: A Reader,* edited by Adrien Katherine Wing, 27–34. New York: New York University Press.

Zeitlin, Irving M. 1990. *Ideology and the Development of Sociological Theory.* Englewood Cliffs, NJ: Prentice-Hall.

7 From Subjugation to Embodied Self-in-Relation

An Indigenous Pedagogy for Decolonization

Candace Brunette-Debassige

Wabun Geezis nindishnikaas. Muskego iskwew endow. My Cree name is Morning Light and I am an *Ininew iskew* (a Cree woman) of James Bay Cree, French, and Métis heritage. I was born and grew up off-reserve in the small town of Cochrane in northeastern Ontario; however, my Cree lineage traces to Fort Albany First Nation, about 350 kilometres north of Cochrane, an isolated community near the shores of James Bay—a place where the stories of my ancestors continue to live beneath the landscape that I also call home. By beginning this chapter with sharing my cultural identity and ancestral lineage, I am both locating myself and grounding my work in an Indigenous epistemology. In Indigenous research methodologies, self-location is a significant entry point (Absolon and Willet 2005); it has also been recognized as "important in terms of being able to make research an embodied journey" (Batacharya 2010, 162). Indigenous research is becoming commonly seen as a "methodological approach that welcome[s] a more holistic, kinesthetic and soulful way of knowing" (Ritenburg et al. 2014, 69).

My story is unique but also akin to the stories of other Indigenous peoples. In fact, I have heard variations of my story many times from other Indigenous artists who have experienced the transformative impacts of learning through the body and expressing oneself through movement and story in the context of Indigenous performing arts. These artists, like myself, have awakened their bodies through embodied knowing and found in creative expression a means to release the internalized systemic silencing of colonization. Their experiences, along with my own story, have led me to recognize that embodied practices in Indigenous performing arts can contribute in essential ways to the growing discourses on embodied learning and can function as a decolonizing tool for Indigenous peoples.

Learning to Be Disembodied: My Story

For me, the shackles of colonialism began to lift over fifteen years ago when I first took up the embodied practices of hatha yoga and meditation as a way to cope with my stress. As a new yoga practitioner, I cultivated inner faculties of awareness that supported me in renewing my relationship with my body from disembodied subjugation toward holistically embodied "self-in-relation" (Graveline 1998). The concept of being embodied was initially so foreign to me that I experienced a strong reaction to it, but after some time, I slowly began to feel safe, unravel, open up, and learn a different and more empowering way of being—embodied in my own Indigenous presence.

Until I began practicing yoga and meditation, I lived in a relatively disembodied way. It was a familiar place for me—a survival mechanism that helped me cope with the pain and trauma of my history. Like many Indigenous people, my family has endured poverty and violence connected to the fragmenting effects of colonialism and residential schools in Canada. My grandmother was apprehended from her family, community, and muskeg land at the age of seven and forced to attend an Anglican-operated and government-legislated residential school in Moose Factory for nine years. During that time, she was prohibited from seeing her family and was physically beaten for speaking her Cree language. She was coerced into abandoning her "heathen" and "savage" ways and forced into adopting the "superior" English language and dominant European Christian values. These early childhood experiences left devastating imprints on my grandmother and have had intergenerational impacts on my mother and all her sixteen siblings, as well as on the grandchildren, the location from which I speak.

As a result of family breakdown and cultural dislocation connected to this colonial history, my grandparents struggled with parenthood; my mother ran away from home at the age of fifteen and soon after became pregnant with me. In grade ten, she dropped out of high school to care for me and, like many young single mothers without an education, ended up on social assistance for a period of time. More than thirty years later, I still vividly remember the mistreatment that my mother experienced on the "welfare system," which was laden with stigma, discrimination, racism, and social rejection associated with ingrained societal ideologies about social assistance.

As I grew into adolescence and became more independent, I often found myself negotiating my mixed identity in relation to social pressures imposed by my environment, including my non-Indigenous peers, by the dominant culture's expectations of me, and through the settler government's narrow gendered and racialized definitions of "Status Indian" which excluded me for many years. Nonetheless, I was always aware of my Cree ancestry, but I often struggled to fit into colonial definitions of "Indian" and reconcile my tenuous connections to my faraway coastal First Nation community as a "mixed-blood," "off-reserve," and "non-Status" Indian.[1] Despite the colonial pressures within our small town to assimilate into the dominant settler norms, my mother encouraged me and my sister to learn about our Cree culture and language and to connect with the local Indigenous community. I always felt more connected to my Cree culture and identity, since the large role played by my mother and maternal grandmother in my early development greatly shaped my sense of self.

While my mother did her best to instill a sense of pride in our Cree identity, I grew up in a small rural community where the acceptable and dominant culture was, at best, English, at worst French Canadian, and certainly never First Nation. I quickly learned that it was dangerous to express my Cree identity, and silence soon became a coping strategy. My discomfort increased after I left my ancestral territory and moved to the urban landscape of Toronto. My fairer complexion marked me as the target of assaults on my identity by non-Indigenous people who were disappointed because I did not meet their expectations of what a "real Indian" should look like. At the same time, my lack of government authentication, in the form of a "Status Indian" card, enabled certain members of the Indigenous community to reject me on the grounds that I wasn't "Indian enough." Indeed,

---

1 In the eyes of the government, I was a "non-Status Indian" until 2010, when the Gender Equity in Indian Registration Act was passed. Only then was I able to register with my Fort Albany band.

for most of my life, I have felt as if my sense of self has been regulated by colonial constructs of "Indianness," by how others perceive me through colonial definitions, making it challenging for me to attend to who I actually am—my lived experiences, my ancestry and connections to land, and how I feel inside.

As a Cree woman, I have also been subjected to intolerable attitudes against Indigenous women, a combination of gender discrimination and colonial sexual violence. Early colonial writing represents Indigenous women as "Indian princesses," "traitors," "whores," and "squaws" and denigrates them as dirty, sexually deviant, and uncivilized, judgments that are still rampant in dominant societal perceptions and subconscious attitudes (Lawrence 2004; Anderson 2000). As a result, Indigenous women are disproportionately affected by violence and are at greater risk of experiencing sexual and physical assaults (Amnesty International 2004; Pearce 2013). My mother was a victim of sexual violence, and despite her vigilant efforts to protect me as a young girl, I was sexually abused at the age of five by a babysitter. Through this confusing and shameful experience, I was taught that my body was an object to be manipulated for sexual gratification. I also learned not to trust my body and to keep secrets, thus silencing my expressive life. I grew up with a skewed perception that a young woman's worth is measured by another's desire to be with her. As a survivor of sexual abuse, I embodied this belief. In this sense, I related to my body in terms of how it was objectified by others rather than how I felt inside.

Without a balanced sense of "self-in-relation," an understanding of the interdependence between self and community that provides a place from which to view "life, the natural world, and one's place in it" (Graveline 1998, 57), I turned to drugs and alcohol to cope. In my early teenage years, my parents broke up and my father passed away suddenly of alcohol-related issues. This only exacerbated my own substance abuse. During this vulnerable stage of my life, I spun out of control, weaving a complex web of dysfunction around me. At the age of thirteen, in an effort to reshape my body to accord with the ideals of femininity imposed by hegemonic Eurocentric and heteropatriarchal norms, I began a five-year battle with bulimia. Bulimia stole my relationship with food and land, transforming it from a form of nourishment and sustenance to a foreign substance to be controlled and disembodied. I regarded my body in terms of how it looked from the outside rather than how it felt on the inside—a result of an "objectified body consciousness" rooted in sexism, oppression, and trauma (McKinley 1998).

Through the privileges afforded to me in my many formal educational and embodied training opportunities, I have learned to understand how power and privilege shaped my past circumstances, choices, and sense of agency. I also recognize that all experience is connected to complex interlocking systems of power based on one's gender, race, age, sexual orientation, class, religion, dis/ability, embedded in an overarching structure of settler colonialism. These social hierarchies all too often serve to subordinate Indigenous people, especially Indigenous women. It is clear that many Indigenous women have internalized the effects of colonization. The very notion of Indigenous as other is a subordinating position that reinforces the perception of one's self as an object judged from the outside by external authorities rather than as a subject experienced within a holistically embodied (mind-body-spirit) centre of knowing. The creation of other is deeply embedded in the imperial-colonial enterprise, firmly entrenched in the white European gaze of the nineteenth century. This othering is reinforced in education and mainstream media and through Canadian government legislation that has regulated Indigenous identity and that, for hundreds of years, prohibited Indigenous people's free expressions through ceremonies, song, and dance (Murphy 2007). Consequently, Indigenous people's relationships with our bodies have been socially manipulated and habituated; we have been taught to ignore our internal bodily messages, to hold our breath, and to bite back our words and not express our truths. This systemic and oppressive approach by governments and institutions has fragmented many Indigenous people internally and has affected individuals, families, and communities intergenerationally. The impacts of colonization have created a sense of disembodiment at both individual and collective levels.

Awakening Embodied Knowing Through Yoga

Certainly, all of my difficult experiences as an Indigenous woman and my understandings of colonialism have informed my decolonizing research and pedagogical interests. More than anything, though, my everlasting passion for embodied learning emanates from my ongoing practices of hatha yoga and meditation and their imprints on my way of being. Turning inward through yoga and meditation helped me restore my relationship with my body-mind-spirit and cultivate an inner awareness, a sense of relaxation, and a trust in the present moment. As the dominance of my conditioned mind began to wane, I discovered inner silence and gained the ability to listen to my body's many messages with curiosity. The constant negative and paranoid chatter of my mind from years of internalized colonial narratives and oppressive beliefs, subordinating positions, rationalized and judgmental thinking eventually quieted. The repetition of gently returning my awareness to my breathing nurtured a sense of safety, expansiveness, and curiosity. I can now observe my mind without judgment and can recognize that my mind is deeply influenced by its exposure to external messages. This was something that I had been incapable of doing because I believed every stereotype and had internalized the master colonial narrative that "Indians are not good enough." By learning to be in my own presence and sit with difficult emotions, I began to understand and disassociate from the colonial messages I had internalized and the years of tension absorbed by my body unraveled. The sense of liberation that ensued is impossible to convey in the confines of an academic paper, but the impacts are lived and have been transformative in my life.

Through the embodied practices of hatha yoga and *vipassanā* meditation, I also began to hear my inner voice, and as my intuition and body-spirit connections grew, I became more interested in Cree spirituality, from which I had distanced myself during my teenage years. I began to see how, for the most part, I identified being Cree/Indigenous with the oppressive narratives of victimhood rather than associating my Cree identity with the strength, resiliency, and beauty of my culture. Together with my academic learning in university, my yoga and meditation practices began to generate within me a strong desire to reconnect with Cree teachings and ceremonies. I also recognize that this desire to connect spiritually was first awakened through the embodied practice of yoga and that my disconnection from Cree spirituality had been reinforced by a lack of access to Elders and knowledge keepers. This lack reflected the general loss of culture linked to residential schools, but it was partly the result of my feeling that I wasn't "Indian enough" to deserve to access my own ancestral knowledge. These internalized feelings of not belonging are connected to a genocidal violence that has attempted to erase Indigenous people (Lawrence 2004). Thankfully, I mustered up the courage to source out and reconnect with Elders and ceremonies, both of which have nurtured a stronger sense of self-identity and connection to community. I still recognize, however, the role that embodied learning played in opening me up to a deeper sense of spirituality. My experiences with yoga were so transformational that I had to keep on learning, and eventually, I became a yoga teacher.

While yoga training supported the development of my personal practice, it often left me wanting more, since I felt that many of the training programs were not critical and did not take an approach that recognized the history of yoga or the impacts of oppression on the body. I also found that too many yoga teachers were on a quest for self-realization in the absence of community, society, and critical reflection around issues of privilege, oppression, colonial violence, and cultural misappropriation. As an Indigenous woman, I was also sensitive to the problems with taking up yoga in a New Age boutique approach, especially when teaching yoga within an Indigenous community context. I often criticized the larger yoga community for being overly commercialized, inaccessible to marginalized groups, and uncritical of its scientific or fitness approaches to teaching about the body. These tensions, which I found myself negotiating in isolation, became so intense at one point that I took a hiatus from teaching yoga altogether. While I have since returned to teaching yoga, the distance and time for deep reflection allowed me to process my experiences and develop a personal pedagogy and teaching practice that incorporates decolonizing approaches to taking up Western yoga along with critical understandings of the body, embodiment, healing, and well-being.

Finding My Voice Through Indigenous Theatre

When I first began teaching yoga, I was completing my undergraduate degree in Indigenous studies. My journey of finding my voice and expressing myself through Indigenous performance writing began during a summer course on Indigenous theatre in which I was introduced to plays written by Indigenous female artists like Maria Campbell, Thomson Highway, Marie Clements, Yvette Nolan, Spiderwoman Theater, Monique Mojica, and the Turtle Gals. These oral-based texts spoke to my experiences in deep and complex ways. In the play *Princess Pocahontas and the Blue Spots,* Monique Mojica resists the misrepresentations of Aboriginal women as "traitors and whores"—stereotypical labels that I too clearly understand. Like my grandmother and my mother, I was often called "squaw" on the playground by my white male counterparts. These oral counternarratives resisted Western misrepresentations of Indigenous women and talked back to colonial narratives, in turn undoing the silencing of my own experiences.

The course was taught by an Anishinaabe/Ashkenazi theatre practitioner and scholar, Jill Carter, who nurtured her students' voices and provided them with a safe space to write and share their stories through monologue. I responded enthusiastically to this Indigenous approach to teaching and learning. I chose to write/tell the story of my birth—a deeply personal story about my mother running away from violence in the home, living on the streets, and getting pregnant with me at age fifteen. The opportunity to explore my place in the world and to share my story through breath and body in an oral performance strengthened my inner voice and ignited within me a burning desire to continue expressing myself through orality and embodied ways of writing.

Weeks after my performance in the Indigenous theatre course, I approached Jani Lauzon, a Métis performer and playwright, and invited her to work with me in an independent study course. This course not only provided me with an opportunity to explore Indigenous theatre but also introduced me to theatre methods and helped me gain some experience in scriptwriting, rehearsal, and performance. Jani, whose mantra is "our bodies are our books," spent time teaching me practical approaches to writing that privileged the body. This independent study culminated, in April 2005, with my performance of a forty-minute work-in-progress titled *Wandering Womb*—a play that explored my disenfranchised history, mixed-blood ancestry, and tenuous connection to my First Nation community.

My undergraduate theatre studies left me thirsty for more. In the summer of 2005, I participated in a Storyweaving program with Muriel Miguel that was offered through the Centre for Indigenous Theatre (CIT) in Toronto. In January 2006, I joined the Young Voices Program with Native Earth Performing Arts (NEPA), also in Toronto. Both CIT and NEPA offer emerging Indigenous performers and writers opportunities to develop and showcase creative work. With the direction and support of Anishinaabe/ Cree dramaturge Lisa Ravensbergen, I wrote *Old Truck*, a story inspired by real-life experiences that examines the effects of alcoholism on family. This second play-in-progress was presented at the Weesageechak Festival in 2006 and 2007. Since then, I have further developed *Old Truck,* with the support of Muriel Miguel (of the Kuna and Rappahannock nations) and the Ontario Arts Council, and I continue to complete theatre projects. In my graduate work, I furthered this passion by looking at the role of Indigenous theatre in my own healing journey of decolonizing and re-membering myself to narratives from family, community, Elders, land and place, as well as to those embodied within. In this scholarship, I explored the experiences of six collaborators involved in a community theatre project that involved returning to land and place and Elders to gather stories in order to create a play.

Until my exposure to Indigenous theatre, my inner truth was stifled and my self-expression was filtered through the lens of the colonized other. I walked through life trying to be what I was taught I should be, based on dominant Eurocentric prescriptions. I rarely expressed my inner truth, and I hid facets of my cultural and personal identity out of fear of not belonging. I did not acknowledge my inner voice, follow my intuition, or explore creative impulses. Instead, I was subdued by the oppressive conditioning of the colonizer's inherent subjugating and silencing nature. I recognize now, however, how systems of power reinforced and stifled my own voice and how these disembodied ways of being served the colonial project by subordinating my agency, reinforcing conformity and assimilation, and preventing freedom of expression—all of which perpetuates the cage of oppression (Frye 1983, 5–8).

A Decolonizing Embodied Pedagogy for Indigenous Peoples

As my embodied knowing expanded through my yoga and Indigenous theatre practices, I began to recognize the value of bringing embodied learning and creative expression together to formulate an Indigenous decolonizing and embodied pedagogical approach. My experience of decolonization in postsecondary education was entirely theoretical, consisting of reading, writing papers, and participating in discussions about the politics of knowledge production, the philosophical and theoretical underpinnings of colonialism, and the need to dislodge the universality of Western knowledge production and its inherent assumptions. But the theory alone always left me wanting more and feeling frustrated and disempowered. Like many Indigenous scholars, I wanted to live decolonization rather than simply, talk about it within the confines of a Western academic institution. A handful of professors supported students like me, offering us a space to share and reflect upon our decolonizing practices that were happening both within and outside the institution.

One of these professors was Roxana Ng, whose course on embodied learning nurtured a space for students to take up the practice of qigong, her own ancestral knowledge, and to reflect upon our embodied learning through journalling. According to Ng (2011), embodied learning challenges the primacy of mind over body in education, disrupting the normative epistemological assumption that the mind, as the seat of rational thought, is the only legitimate gateway to knowing. Especially in the post-Enlightenment academy, the body has been positioned as unreliable. This lack of respect for lived experience as a source of knowledge lies at the heart of the tension between Indigenous ways of knowing and Western paradigms, and the ongoing failure to recognize the epistemological value of lived experience is arguably the greatest obstacle to fully Indigenizing the academy.

Outside the classroom, I gravitated toward Aboriginal student services and the Indigenous theatre community to do my community decolonizing work, which often merged my two passions—embodied learning and embodied writing. In "Embodied Knowledge and Decolonization: Walking with Theatre's Powerful and Risky Pedagogy," Shauna Butterwick and Jan Selman (2012) describe theatre as a process of decolonization that connects mind, body, and emotion through embodied activities that contribute to naming oppression; when facilitated effectively, they argue, this process can lead to enfranchisement and action. Butterwick and Selman also identify the need for pedagogical and ethical frames for educators to use to guide the risky processes of naming oppression and dealing with fears and triggered emotions that subsequently surface. The call for ethical guidelines is based on the need to keep participants safe in the theatrical process. The concerns identified by these authors are similarly noted by Jill Carter in "Towards Locating the Alchemy of Convergence in the Native Theatre Classroom," where she addresses ethical conundrums when taking up Indigenous theatre in a university context. Carter (2012, 82–83) poignantly states that "grief is unavoidable" and that, in the intercultural and interdisciplinary exchanges, "there be landmines." I agree with Carter that the project of decolonization should be shared by Indigenous and non-Indigenous peoples. I think that when intercultural exchanges are necessary, it is essential for a decolonizing framework to be introduced up front to help contextualize Indigenous experiences within a historical context that disrupts Western hegemonic thinking. I also believe that Indigenous ways of knowing can support the emotional triggers associated with the inevitable grieving that surfaces in this healing work.

In a decolonizing framework, I echo Alannah Young and Denise Nadeau's recommendation that an embodied spiritual pedagogy be utilized as a strategy for decolonization. In their work, Young and Nadeau (2005, 2) not only identify the body as a site for decolonization but also emphasize the need for "tapping into our natural spiritual resilience" through connection to identity, community, and earth. Similarly, Roxana Ng (2011, 344) advocates for embodied-learning practitioners to "turn to and incorporate other epistemological and philosophical traditions" in the process of decolonizing and recovering the mind-body-spirit connections. Ng herself, as a visible immigrant and scholar in Canada, returned to her Chinese lineage and the practice of qigong to recover from the effects of colonialism. While Butterwick and Selman (2012) do not focus on the body-spirit interconnections within their proposed decolonizing and embodied pedagogy in theatre, they do recommend that future research focus on the use of Indigenous ways of knowing to identify ethical guidelines in decolonizing approaches.

It should be noted that while Indigenous ways of knowing is an important facet of a decolonizing framework for Indigenous people, we must also take up Indigenous ways of knowing in critical and respectful ways (Battiste and Henderson 2000). Because Indigenous knowledge has so often been misappropriated, Indigenous people must be at the forefront of this reclamation and integration movement. Without Indigenous knowledge keepers and scholars, leading the development of decolonizing and embodied pedagogies for Indigenous peoples, we risk the continued misinterpretation, misrepresentation, and misappropriation of Indigenous ways of knowing.

As a Cree yoga teacher from Turtle Island, I have struggled with teaching a practice that is rooted in a tradition from South Asia and is considered by some people to be an Indigenous knowledge that is outside of my cultural and ancestral background. At the same time, I recognize the diversity of modern yoga practices, and while yogic knowledge can be contextualized as originating within Hinduism, Jainism, and Buddhism, it is, like my own culture's Indigenous ways of knowing dynamic and constantly evolving. To complicate matters further, yogic knowledge has been shaped by colonial powers stemming from Britain's colonization of India. Modern-day yoga has been further influenced by its importation to the West and by New Age social movements. Rather than avoid teaching the contemporary practice of yoga altogether, I have, at least in part, reconciled my own tensions by taking up some of these historical and political issues in my approaches to teaching yoga. I acknowledge my self-location and the tensions of taking up the contemporary practice of yoga in the West. Sheila Batacharya's (2010) research helped me reflect on my own teaching position and to better understand and articulate some of the problematic tendencies of taking up yoga in the West (see Batacharya's chapter in this collection).

Reflecting on My Teaching Practice

In 2008, I taught a noncredit course titled "Decolonizing the Body Through Yoga," which was offered through the student services division of the university I attended. This was followed, in 2009, by a course called "Introductory Movement," which I taught in an Indigenous community-based theatre setting. In my evaluation of my own teaching in these courses, I applied Cole and Knowles's (2000) model of "reflexive inquiry" by using daily and weekly journal reflections to critically examine my teaching philosophy in relation both to classroom practices and to student experiences. Both courses were created with a decolonizing methodology in mind (see Smith 1999; Battiste 2013): the purpose was to guide the Indigenous student participants through processes of embodied learning with the goal of challenging the kinesthetic reality of colonization. My course objectives focused on providing Indigenous students with embodied-learning frameworks and tools that would promote self-determination (Nadeau and Young 2006). My methodology was also based on an Indigenist approach that acknowledges a personal and subjective relationship to knowledge and "focuses on the lived, historical experiences, ideas, traditions, dreams, interests, aspirations, and struggles" of Indigenous peoples (Rigney 2006, 45).

In 2010, after reading Batacharya's (2010) PhD dissertation, I was inspired to reflect further on my teaching practice. My decision to examine my teaching was also greatly influenced by the internal tensions I endured being both an Indigenous woman and a yoga teacher in the West. I felt the responsibility to reflect critically upon my teaching in relation to the history and globalization of yogic knowledge(s). My hope was that through reflexive inquiry, I would grow professionally and develop a more critical pedagogy. My goal was to decolonize and develop a teaching practice that was more congruent with my epistemological and ethical values and political goals. I also wanted to challenge myself to begin incorporating more critical theories and learning strategies into my yoga classes, including embodied-learning theories that challenged the positivistic notions of learning and included sociological understandings of the body through social and cultural dimensions of health, healing, and embodiment.

As a teacher working with Indigenous people in an urban context, I understood first-hand the health conditions prevalent in the population I was working with. I was working with a segment of the population who, because of complex historical and social factors, were sometimes struggling with being embodied. By modifying my pedagogy, I learned that it was helpful to talk about the kinesthetic realities of colonialism and make connections to its impacts of disembodiment. I also learned that integrating Indigenous notions of health, healing, and wellness were useful and that I was not the only one who found that yoga's innately embodied and spiritual nature complemented an Indigenous paradigm. In order to bridge different understandings and privilege Indigenous epistemologies and knowledge, I worked with Elders to share traditional teachings about holistic understandings of health and relationship to land.

Offering yoga classes to Indigenous university students called for a more critical engagement with yoga and its history and with contemporary realities, which also greatly enhanced my critical pedagogical approach. Early on, students expressed concerns about melding different traditions (yoga and smudging) and about taking up cultural practices outside their own belief system, voicing apprehension about New Ageism and cultural misappropriation. Through reflection, I aimed to privilege these issues—to integrate readings about them and make time in my classes for dialogue about New Ageism and misappropriation. These experiences have helped me grow and have informed my critical teaching philosophy and practice.

Teaching Philosophy and Theories

I wish to continue to work with Indigenous people, sharing practical and theoretical ways to help mend the mind-body-spirit fractures of colonialism and repositioning the body as a holistic source of knowing and a pathway for decolonization. I recognize that our experiences are encoded in our bodies in complex ways that are linked to historical, political, and social dimensions of embodiment and experience. And while these experiences and centres of knowing have been impacted, fragmented, and silenced by colonialism, I understand through personal experience that embodied learning offers pathways to healing.

I draw from many theoretical frameworks including Indigenous ways of knowing, decolonizing methodologies (Nadeau and Young 2006; Smith 1999), embodied learning (Batacharya 2010; Johnson 2007; Ng 2011), and critical pedagogy (Freire 1970; hooks 2003). I am also influenced by my first-hand storied experiences as a survivor of various forms of colonial violence and historical trauma and by my transformative embodied experiences in yoga and theatre.

As an adult educator, I recognize the complex nature of adult learners, who bring with them rich experiences and understandings of the world; their ability to engage with new understandings is sometimes challenging. My critical pedagogical approach recognizes the value in unlearning, learning, relearning, reflecting, and evaluating (Freire 1970). I apply this critical framework by sharing various understandings of the body and embodiment, along with embodied practices that facilitate self-awareness and new ways of being that, in turn, can dislodge internalized hegemonies embedded in the body from past experiences of oppression. Through embodied unlearning and relearning, I believe that we can awaken and liberate ourselves from being continuously revictimized from past colonial oppressions.

My embodied teaching repertoire draws primarily from the practices of hatha yoga (Sivanada and Iyengar-Scaravelli yogic lineages), Indigenous theatre approaches (for example, Indigenous Storyweaving (Carter 2010), as well as Augusto Boal's Forum Theatre and Image Theatre (2002, 1979), and other somatic techniques (for example, Laban/Bartenieff movement). In hatha yoga philosophy, I have been taught that there are six limbs of yoga (areas of knowing), which are commonly referred to in Sanskrit as āsana (postures), *prāṇāyāma* (breathing techniques), *pratyāhāra* (ability to withdraw from external world stimuli and step back to look at oneself), *dhāraṇā* (single-focused concentration of the mind on a specific energy centre or sound), *dhyāna* (meditation without focus), and *samādhi* (transcendence from self and interconnection with all living things). As a lifelong yoga practitioner, I am still learning to embody these limbs through a regular personal practice. I also believe that the yoga limb framework offers a set of learning outcomes that can support holistically embodied pedagogies for Indigenous people.

Eleven Pedagogical Principles

I have reflected on and distilled eleven key principles to consider when taking up a decolonizing embodied-learning pedagogy. These principles—along with their purposes, underlying theories, and some practical applications—are outlined here.

1. *Activate Indigenous pedagogies.*

First and foremost, it is helpful for embodied-learning educators, when working with Indigenous people, to take up Indigenous pedagogies that privilege Indigenous ways of learning. Indigenous ways of learning inherently recognize the holistic nature of knowledge and its relationship with mind, body, emotions, and spirit within a powerful embodied centre of knowing. Indigenous approaches support students in coming from this subjective centre whenever possible, often through stories and sharing. Indigenous pedagogies are experiential in nature, often allowing for activities connected to or on the land; they extend learning outward to one's relationship with family, community, and nation, honouring the significance of community and social responsibilities. Sharing and giving back to the collective is a significant facet of Indigenous ways of knowing. Indigenous pedagogies also recognize the history of colonization and its impacts on Indigenous peoples in a contemporary context.

Embodied-learning educators play a powerful role by telling their own personal stories, locating themselves through sharing their identities and connections to land and place. Indigenous educational strategies like Fyre Jean Graveline's (1998) "circle teaching format" are useful in nurturing a sense of community and encouraging students to share subjectively and collectively. Especially for Indigenous people, who have learned silence, the act of sharing can be essential to processing experience. If time is limited, teachers can ask learners to share only a word, an image, or an idea that resonates with them. Augusto Boal's Image Theatre techniques are helpful in unlocking hidden messages of the body in nonverbal ways, thus dislodging the culture of oppression. Sound and movement techniques used in Indigenous Storyweaving approaches also provide powerful mirroring effects that privilege the body's centre of knowing. The purpose here is to give Indigenous learners space to be and to be heard or witnessed collectively.

2. *Foster interconnections with land and cosmos.*

Traditional Cree people have a deep respect for the bush and for our spiritual relationship with animals, who, in our understanding, sacrifice their lives for humans to live. The subsistence cycle of the Cree hinges in complex ways on respect, understanding, and communion with the movement of animals in relation to our six seasons (fall, freeze-up, winter, break-up, spring, and summer), which are influenced by larger cosmological factors, including the earth's relationship with the sun, moon, and stars. This understanding among Cree people has been transmitted orally through stories since time immemorial, passing on mythologies, teachings, language, and histories from generation to generation. Cree mythological narratives often centre on human-animal relationships and position animals as no less significant than human beings. While oral traditions have been impacted by colonialism, storytelling today continues to be a pathway for igniting the "learning spirit" (Battiste 2013) among Indigenous peoples. Many Indigenous stories of being alive and well involve listening and moving in balance with and in relation to the land, which is seen as integral to our collective survival as human beings.

The interconnections among humans, animals, and the land is a key principle and underlying theme to teaching an Indigenous embodied approach to decolonization. For that reason, yoga sequences like the sun, moon, fire, and water salutations; postures like mountain and tree pose; and asanas like the eagle, crow, pigeon, and turtle, to name a few, have always resonated deeply with me. Exploring aspects of nature in the body was what initially engaged me and drew me into yoga practice. Strengthening interrelationships to land and place is a foundational aspect of Indigenous knowing and learning. For instance, Indigenous powwow dances embody and strengthen human, animal, and land relationships.

3. *Understand the kinesthetic impacts of colonialism.*

It is also essential to teach Indigenous learners about the kinesthetic and embodied nature of colonialism and oppression. By introducing, examining, and reflecting on colonial histories and their impacts on our bodies, minds, and spirits, embodied-learning educators can help students unearth their lived experiences and dislodge colonial hegemonic ways of being. When settler-colonial ideologies about Indigenous people go undisrupted they form hegemonic thinking. Antonio Gramsci (1971), a Marxist scholar was one of the first to introduce the concept of hegemony which he related to the ways that the ruling class impose their values, beliefs, and perceptions onto society in a way that becomes assumed and common sense. From my perspective, hegemonic thinking about Indigenous people has been created by settler society and imposed onto Indigenous people. Teaching about how colonial narratives reinforce disembodied ways of being in the world and become internalized helps Indigenous learners not only to recognize colonial hegemonic silencing patterns in themselves but also to recover their own presence, voice, and agency, in turn opening themselves up to possibilities for change and transformation.

It is also critical for embodied-learning instructors to adopt trauma-sensitive approaches when working with Indigenous students. In the realm of psychology, the existence of traumatic experiences has been recognized since at least the late nineteenth century, and we have since gained a better understanding of the chemical and neurological impact of certain experiences on the brain. Feminist approaches to critical traumatology recognize that oppression is traumatic and often criticize psychology for its pathologizing tendencies (Burstow 2003). Critical pedagogies of embodied learning are well positioned to teach learners about the embodied impacts of trauma and oppression such as disassociation or alienation from the body, body shame, heightened startle responses, hyperarousal of the sympathetic system, bodily memories, and avoidance of stimuli. Rae Johnson (2007), in her doctoral work, uncovered three primary embodied responses to oppression and the embodied impact of trauma: embodied memories, somatic vigilance, and somatic withdrawal and alienation.

Within Indigenous scholarship, historical trauma has been linked to residential schools in Canada, the effects of which have been passed on intergenerationally (Wesley-Esquimaux and Smolewski 2004). The experience of colonization and residential schools has also been characterized as a form of "ethno-stress," or what Eduardo Duran (2006) calls a "soul wound," that has engendered a deeply ingrained lack of trust. While this wariness serves as a social coping mechanism, it also contributes to diminished health and well-being. The embodied nature of historical trauma, I believe, leads many Indigenous people to disembodied ways of being, manifesting in chronic tension, breathing and muscular holding patterns, and other forms of dis-ease that wreak havoc in our relationships with our own bodies and with others through inter-embodied relationships. In *Overcoming Trauma Through Yoga,* David Emerson and Elizabeth Hoper (2011) outline four key themes to a trauma-sensitive approach: experience the present moment, provide opportunities to make choices, talk about effective actions, and create rhythms to foster a sense of connection. These approaches may be helpful to those working with Indigenous people who have experienced trauma.

Critical theories also help educate students about how power, privilege, and systems of oppression are embodied and inter-embodied and, more importantly, how the body is simultaneously a site of both personal agency and social power that can help one cope with one's experience of oppression. In this sense, embodied learning can be considered a practice leading to self-determination that counters internalized oppression through raising one's consciousness and embodied presence.

4. *Know through experience.*

As the living libraries in Indigenous communities, Elders play a central role in Indigenous ways of knowing and learning. Indigenous ways of knowing, therefore, inherently honour the experiential way of knowing, recognizing that knowledge is not merely about content or conceptual learning but is activated through the process of life experience. Embodied learning educators can inherently honour Indigenous ways of knowing; they respect the learners' journeys by helping them to come back into their bodies to experience their own knowing. It is integral to begin a teaching session almost immediately by bringing Indigenous students back inside their bodies to experience their own sensations as reliable sources of knowledge. This practical work directly counters and resists the normative tendency of Western thought and education to privilege mind-intellect over mind-body-emotion-spirit centres of knowing.

Early scientific philosophers such as Plato, Socrates, and Descartes all asserted that the body was unreliable in perceiving objective truth. These dominant Western positivistic assertions have positioned the body at an inferior level, closer to animals, in the hierarchy of Western intelligence. The reorientation of becoming our own authorities according to our bodily sensations rather than relying on external objective truths can be foreign territory for many people, since in formal education in the West, we are taught from *outside of* our bodies. Bringing marginalized peoples who have been bombarded by external authorities speaking for them back into their bodies is critical in empowering them to discover their personal power and agency.

This can be a radical paradigm shift for Indigenous people and requires unconditional, gentle, and ongoing practical work, with reminders for students to listen to, experience, and open up to the subtle nuances of their bodily messages. The dominant mind will inevitably want to analyze and categorize sensations, but this experiential practice is simple and requires the temporary suspension of the mind. The purpose is to develop inner faculties that are nondiscursive (preverbal, with no need to search for cause or give title). It is simply to experience sensations and open up an expansive space of limitless possibilities inside.

5. Breathe.

Heightening one's awareness of one's breathing cycle is a freeing practice and a primary principle of a decolonizing embodied pedagogy. Frantz Fanon, the notable anticolonial scholar, famously linked the effects of colonization to breathing patterns of the colonized: "There is not occupation of territory, on the one hand, and independence of persons on the other. It is the country as a whole, its history, its daily pulsation that are contested, disfigured. . . . Under these conditions, the individual's breathing is an observed, an occupied breathing. It is a combat breathing" (Fanon 1965, 65).

Fanon shone a light on the damaging effects of colonization on one's breathing cycle. The focus on breathing is therefore foundational when addressing the effects of colonization for the oppressed. Since breathing generally happens at the perimeter of our consciousness, students can become greatly empowered by learning more about their own breathing patterns, especially in terms of how to release "combat breathing" through embodied techniques. Embodied-learning educators can provide students with various active and passive breathing techniques as tools for calming and energizing. Many yoga practices offer myriad breathing techniques connected to a long-held *prāṇāyāma* practice, which is meant to purify the complex meridian energy channels.

From a more scientific perspective, the reduction of autonomic stress responses through active breathing can be incredibly powerful, especially for Indigenous peoples, who have often experienced violence and oppression. Recent research has shown that yoga—including meditation, relaxation, and physical postures—can "reduce autonomic sympathetic activation, muscle tension, and blood pressure, improve neuro-endoctrine and hormonal activity, decrease physical symptoms and emotional distress, and increase quality of life" (Emerson et al. 2009, 124). As students become aware of and reflect on their own unconscious breathing patterns, they can begin to examine the ways in which they may interfere with their own natural breathing cycle during times of stress.

6. *Relax.*

As part of an embodied-learning approach to decolonization, fostering the ability to relax is crucial. Educators can also share the theory behind this practice to help facilitate and integrate the learning. Yoga has greatly contributed to my appreciation for conscious relaxation at the beginning and end of one's embodied practice. In hatha yoga, this form of relaxation is called *śavāsana* (resting pose) and is believed to be integral to a healthy and balanced practice. Conscious relaxation is believed to help process information and learning and to facilitate deep integration of knowledge. In our society, we often move from activity to activity quickly without much time for repose, and through this orientation, reinforced via societal norms and educational approaches, we become socially conditioned to do rather than to be. This way of being can be unlearned through the practice of relaxation. Until the mind-body-spirit can rest, the integration and mending of disconnections caused by colonization cannot occur. Through various embodied techniques including yoga, meditation, or just simple breathing in silence, educators can help students recover from the withdrawing and alienating effects of colonial oppression.

7. *Ground yourself.*

The technique of grounding, or relating our bodies to the earth's gravitational pull, is a paramount principle in a decolonizing embodied pedagogy. This interaction initially happens physically and energetically by consciously and intentionally releasing one's weight, energy, and intention into the earth—exhaling, giving, releasing, and letting go into gravity and then waiting for the spontaneous, natural, and reciprocal response of inhaling and rising. Students of yoga can learn to embody this concept of grounding in nearly every movement, every breath, and can reflect upon it in relation to their embodied reality and orientation toward others.

My former teacher Roxana Ng challenged us, her students, to consider this energetic relationship in our personal and professional lives and in our activist work. As a result, I often find myself coming back to grounding when I find myself in a difficult dynamic with others, and students can learn to do the same in their own difficult experiences. I find this concept philosophically compelling, since I have spent much of my life in unconscious states of resistance. The resistance became lodged in my body, resulting in a disembodied way of being. I find it empowering to notice when my energy shifts from being in strong opposition to others to trusting the earth beneath me to support me. I have discovered that the act of grounding is both embodied and inter-embodied. A striking example of embodied forms of resistance came with the Idle No More movement of 2014, when Indigenous people across Canada activated their embodied and inter-embodied ways of being through collective round dances.

It is especially important for colonized peoples—who, for complex reasons, are forced into states of resistance—to practice grounding in their personal and professional lives. For me, the purpose of grounding through yoga is not to ignore the colonial past or become complacent in the ongoing colonial present; instead, grounding provides me with a pathway to become aware of my disembodied states of being and, more importantly, to choose to create a more embodied way of being and living in the present. Grounding is also an excellent way to support survivors of historical trauma in self-care and self-determination. I do believe that there are times when Indigenous peoples need to resist in order to protect the earth and our sovereign rights; at the same time, I also believe that we need to have embodied learning processes in order to come back into our holistic bodies and Indigenous presence for the well-being of ourselves, our families, and our communities.

8. *Release tension and obstructions.*

It is helpful to recognize how tension, or the absence of relaxation, is embodied and constricts and inhibits the free flow of energy, breath, and bodily fluids, causing internal blockages. Many somaticists assert that muscular tension not only obstructs energy flow but also affects attitudes, thoughts, and feelings (see, for example, Green 1993). These obstructions need to be released. The release of tension absorbed in the fascia can happen in different ways, including muscle and fascia lengthening, yawning, sighing, voicing, spontaneous tears, and/or even spontaneous acts of creativity. The key for embodied-learning educators is to become stewards of a safe space where students can feel free to relax, let go, and release without having to understand, explain, or rationalize their experiences. Indigenous practices such as drumming, singing, sharing circles, and smudging can promote the releasing processes in culturally relevant ways (Nadeau and Young 2006). In my experience, relaxation and releasing go hand in hand and are greatly enhanced when a teacher can step back and allow learners to do their own embodied work in their own time. The role of the educator in these sacred moments is to act as a witness and hold a safe space. There is nothing more respectful of a person's learning journey than to be present and share the space in a non-interfering and compassionate way. Noninterference is an Indigenous ethical practice.

9. *Unlearn and relearn movement patterns.*

Our bodies move, act, and react in relationship to experiences, other bodies, and the environment (Johnson 2007). Every person's body has a somatic memory and develops its own habits, patterns, and tendencies of moving, which come to acquire hegemonic force, such that our movements become automatic. Somatic practitioners see their role as helping learners to become more aware of their movement patterns and, more importantly, to unlearn them and learn healthier, more conscious and empowering ways of being and moving. Many somatic techniques guide students through slow movements that identify individual patterns. Somatic education comprises a growing group of bodywork disciplines that tend to privilege the internal subjective experience of the body, including yoga, Laban/Bartenieff fundamentals, mind/body centring, the Feldenkrais method (1991), and Alexander techniques. Many somatic techniques are experiential approaches to movement that support self-observation and movement enquiry. Somatic techniques generally allow students to experience their bodies in space and to re-educate themselves into more conscious ways of moving.

In my opinion, a teacher's pedagogy plays a paramount role in guiding learning and supporting conscious self-exploration. I have attended many different classes that involve movement (including yoga classes) in which teachers approach the body from the outside, as an object that students learn to manipulate, while also encouraging a competitive atmosphere among the students. Such an orientation is antithetical to both the spirit and the goals of embodied learning and, from that perspective, tends to produce counterproductive results. In my experience, it is helpful to expose students to various techniques and provide them with opportunities to explore what works for their subjective bodies and to reflect on their experiences and responses (for example, their holding patterns, breathing responses, emotional responses, preferences and tendencies, challenges and abilities in moving freely and maintaining focus). Being aware and observing consciously without judgment are critical to raising our embodied consciousness. It is also sometimes helpful to have a teacher as an external witness who can provide gentle feedback about learners' patterns of movement. Sometimes instructors can mimic students' movement back to them in a mirroring way or offer new ways of moving that allow students to shift holding patterns.

10. *Develop embodied consciousness.*

It is transformative for students to develop their embodied consciousness—the ability to be a witness to their own mind, body, and spirit connections. Meditation techniques offer gateways to developing this introspective embodied consciousness. The practice of meditation in the West draws primarily from the Buddhist *vipassanā* tradition. Mindfulness meditation has been introduced by Jon Kabat-Zinn (2003) as a form of stress reduction to treat anxiety, pain, stress, and illness in hospitals and health and medical centres around the world.

Meditation is also increasingly being practiced by a growing number of Indigenous scholars—including Bonnie Duran (2017) and Michael Yellow Bird (2013)—who recognize meditation's congruence with Indigenous epistemological frameworks. Deborah Orr (2002) considers mindfulness meditation to be a tool in an anti-oppressive pedagogy, and Renita Wong (2004) encourages bringing mindfulness approaches into the classroom when educating social workers about power and privilege. In Australia, mindfulness practices have been introduced as a part of curriculum in Indigenous educational contexts—drawing comparisons between mindfulness and the Aboriginal concept of *dadirri*, or deep listening.[2] Michael Yellow Bird (2013) also positions meditation as an Indigenous form of decolonizing the mind. In the United States, mindfulness approaches have also been implemented as a preventive intervention for suicide among American Indian youth populations, resulting in "positive indications in terms of better self-regulation, less mind wandering, and decreased suicidal thoughts" (Le and Gobert 2013).

Embodied consciousness helps students develop internal capacities, including the ability to witness their thoughts and feelings without judgment. This internal space within each of us is where our true willpower lives. As we learn to witness our thoughts, we realize that regardless of our social conditions, we always have a choice in our reactions, an understanding that is often extremely empowering. While distinct from mindfulness meditation practices, which are based in Buddhism, Indigenous spiritual practices support introspection while seeking guidance from the Great Spirit, or Creator, through fasting, dreams, and other types of meditative approaches.

11. *Find your voice and express your truth.*

The final principle in my decolonizing embodied approach is to help students find their voice and express their truth freely. To be silenced is to be unable to speak or be heard. Paulo Freire (1970) was one of the first scholars to articulate the silence of oppression, linking it to a culture of fear. The culture of fear plays out when the colonized refrain from speaking their truths. Silence, therefore, can become a learned behavioural pattern that is reinforced by institutions in government, education, and the media (Dunlap 2007). Silence manifests in many forms, from not having a political voice within larger

---

2 See, for example, "Working Together: Module 2—Mindfulness," esp. 6–7. Available at "Working Together: Intercultural Leadership—Program Resources," *Curtin University,* n.d., http://academicleadership.curtin.edu.au/IALP/program/program_resources.cfm. Click on "Module 2 Resources" and then "Module 2: Mindfulness, File Notes."

governmental structures to not feeling worthy to express our own feelings out loud in smaller circles. This kind of silence creates knots and blockages among oppressed people that need to be unlearned and released.

Decolonizing approaches to theatre provide powerful mechanisms for releasing the voice. Augusto Boal's *Theatre of the Oppressed* (1979) provides pedagogical and dramaturgical approaches to social action. In a similar way, Spiderwoman Theater's Indigenous Storyweaving technique undoes the silencing nature of colonization by combining storytelling, acting, and writing to create theatre in response to Indigenous people's real lives (Carter 2010). Releasing the voice is an inherent part of Indigenous performing arts training. Indeed, voice work is a part of most quality theatre training programs. It usually begins by working at the impulse level and recognizing the role that inner impulses play in stimulating our breath. Kristen Linklater (2006, 13), a well-known voice teacher, describes the physiological mechanics of speaking in her book *Freeing the Natural Voice* and provides exercises that help people to release their voice and understand the complex relationship among impulse, breath, sound, and body. According to Linklater, the voice is an instrument of truth in that the natural voice makes direct contact with emotional impulses, which are natural reflexes powered by breath. Through relaxation, the muscular system loosens up, allowing energy to channel emotional impulses throughout the body. Linklater notes that, sadly, many people have been socialized to control the primary emotional reflex of their natural voices (19–20). The habit of restraining our emotional impulses can become so deeply engrained that it functions as form of social conditioning. I believe that Indigenous practices such as traditional singing, drumming, and dancing, as well as various other forms of creative expression such as poetry, monologues, journalling, and collage or vision boards, can serve to undo the silencing nature of colonialism.

The collective sharing process of our creative truths is an equally important facet of a decolonizing process. Educators may wish to facilitate a final culminating activity that involves a presentation of students' work to their family and community, which can further support students in undoing the silencing of oppression and in developing their agency and power. Through the collective sharing process, one's self is turned outward into the larger community (Nadeau and Young 2006) and thus can engage others in education.

Final Thoughts

My experience of recovering from the kinesthetic impacts of colonialism through the embodied-learning and storytelling practices of yoga and theatre taught me that embodied learning can be a powerful tool for healing. When combined with critical and decolonizing pedagogical approaches, embodied learning can be transformative for Indigenous people, helping them to unlearn the internalized forms of oppression. However, the work of decolonization does not take place simply at the individual level; instead, it must involve a multidimensional, inter-embodied approach in which many players work from at various levels to unravel the complex effects of colonialism. Clearly, this is not to say that work at the level of individual embodiment is unimportant, but as the impacts of colonization continue to rage on inside many bodies of the oppressed, embodied-learning and decolonizing educators need to work on all fronts to support affected individuals and communities.

My proposed pedagogy does not impose change on others or the world from the outside. Instead, it offers a safe space in which to encourage individuals to embark on their own embodied journey, whether alone or with the support of a community and alongside embodied-learning educators. It is important to recognize, however, that, from the standpoint of decolonization, individual embodied work does not exist in isolation but rather acquires its power in relation to others. Through the sharing process, individual transformation can be extended beyond the borders of self and serve as a model for inspirational change. In other words, individual work must be connected to a systemic process of decolonization that challenges settler colonialism and works toward the political repatriation of Indigenous lands and the restoration of Indigenous rights and Indigenous ways of being. It is my hope that the pedagogy presented here will be considered by decolonizing educators who are searching for embodied approaches to education with the aim of fostering self-determined communities.

References

Absolon, Kathy, and Willett, Cam. 2005. "Putting Ourselves Forward: Location in Aboriginal Research." In *Research as Resistance: Critical, Indigenous, and Anti-oppressive Approaches,* edited by Leslie Brown and Susan Strega, 97–126. Toronto: Canadian Scholars' Press.

Anderson, Kim 2000. *A Recognition of Being: Reconstructing Native Womanhood.* Toronto: Sumach Press.

Amnesty International. 2004. *Stolen Sisters: Discrimination and Violence Against Indigenous Women in Canada—A Summary of Amnesty International's Concerns.* London, UK: Amnesty International. http://www2.uregina.ca/resolve/assets/pdf/StolenSisters.pdf.

Batacharya, Janet Sheila. 2010. "Life in a Body: Counter Hegemonic Understandings of Violence, Oppression, Healing, and Embodiment Among Young South Asian Women." PhD diss., Ontario Institute for Studies in Education, University of Toronto.

Battiste, Marie. 2013. *Decolonizing Education: Nourishing the Learning Spirit.* Saskatoon: Purich.

Battiste, Marie, and James (Sákéj) Youngblood Henderson. 2000. *Protecting Indigenous Knowledge and Heritage: A Global Challenge.* Saskatoon: Purich.

Boal, Augusto. 1979. *Theatre of the Oppressed.* London: Pluto.

———. 2002. *Games for Actors and Non-Actors.* New York: Routledge.

Burstow, Bonnie. 2003. "Toward a Radical Understanding of Trauma and Trauma Work." *Violence Against Women* 9: 1293–1317.

Butterwick, Shauna, and Jan Selman. 2012. "Embodied Knowledge and Decolonization: Walking with Theatre's Powerful and Risky Pedagogy." *New Directions for Adult and Continuing Education* 134: 61–70.

Carter, Jill. 2010. "Repairing the Web: Spiderwoman's Children Staging the New Human Being." PhD diss., Graduate Centre for Study of Drama, University of Toronto.

———. 2012. "Towards Locating the Alchemy of Convergence in the Native Theatre Classroom." *Canadian Theatre Review* 149: 82–84.

Cole, Ardra and J. Gary Knowles. 2000. *Researching Teaching: Exploring Teacher Development Through Reflexive Inquiry.* Boston: Allyn and Bacon.

Dunlap, Louise. 2007. *Undoing the Silence: Six Tools for Social Change Writing.* New York: New Village Press.

Duran, Bonnie. 2017. "Indigenous Presence: Decolonizing our Minds and Cultivating the Causes of Happiness." National Indigenous Women's Resource Center. Wellness Webinar, 22 February.

Duran, Eduardo. 2006. *Healing the Soul Wound: Counseling with American Indian and Other Native Peoples.* New York: Teachers College, Columbia University.

Emerson, David, and Elizabeth Hopper. 2011. *Overcoming Trauma Through Yoga: Reclaiming Your Body.* Berkeley, CA: North Atlantic Books.

Emerson, David, Ritu Sharma, Serena Chaudhry, and Jenn Turner. 2009. "Trauma-Sensitive Yoga: Principles, Practice, and Research." *International Journal of Yoga Therapy* 19: 123–28.

Fanon, Frantz. 1965. *A Dying Colonialism.* Translated by Haakon Chevalier. New York: Grove Press. Originally published as *L'an V de la révolution algérienne* (1959).

Feldenkrais, Moshé. 1991. *Awareness Through Movement.* London: Thorsons.

Freire, Paulo. 1970. *Pedagogy of the Oppressed.* Translated by Myra Bergman Ramos. New York: Herder and Herder. Originally published as *Pedagogia do oprimido* (1968).

Frye, Marilyn. 1983. *The Politics of Reality: Essays in Feminist Theory.* Trumansburg, NY: Crossing Press.

Gramsci, Antonio. 1971. *Selections from the Prison Notebooks of Antonio Gramsci.* Translated by Quintin Hoare and Geoffrey Nowell Smith. New York, NY: International Publishers. Originally published as *Quaderni del car cere* (1948–1951).

Graveline, Fyre Jean. 1998. *Circleworks: Transforming Eurocentric Consciousness.* Halifax: Fernwood Publishing.

Green, Jill. 1993. "Fostering Creativity Through Movement and Body Awareness Practices: A Postpositivist Investigation into the Relationship Between Somatics and the Creative Process." PhD diss., Ohio State University.

hooks, bell. 2003. *Teaching Community: A Pedagogy of Hope.* New York: Routledge.

Johnson, Rae. 2007. "(Un)learning Oppression Through the Body Toward an Embodied Critical Pedagogy." PhD diss., University of Toronto.

Kabat-Zinn, Jon. 2003. "Mindfulness-Based Interventions in Context: Past, Present, and Future." *Clinical Psychology* 10(2): 144–56.

Lawrence, Bonita. 2004. *"Real" Indians and the Others: Mixed-Blood Urban Native Peoples and Indigenous Nationhood.* Lincoln: University of Nebraska Press.

Le, Thao, and Jen Gobert. 2013. "Translating and Implementing a Mindfulness-Based Youth Suicide Prevention Intervention in a Native American Community." *Journal of Child and Family Studies* 24(1): 12–23.

Linklater, Kristen. 2006. *Freeing the Natural Voice: Imagery and Art in the Practice of Voice and Language.* London: Nick Hern Books.

McKinley, Nita Mary. 1998. "Gender Differences in Undergraduates' Body Esteem: The Mediating Effect of Objectified Body Consciousness and Actual/Ideal Weight Discrepancy." *Sex Roles* 39(1–2): 113–23.

Murphy, Jacqueline Shea. 2007. *The People Have Never Stopped Dancing: Native American Modern Dance Histories.* Minneapolis: University of Minnesota Press.

Nadeau, Denise, and Alannah Earl Young. 2006. "Educating Bodies for Self-Determination: A Decolonizing Strategy." *Canadian Journal of Native Education* 29(1): 87–101.

Ng, Roxana. 2011. "Decolonizing Teaching and Learning Through Embodied Learning: Toward an Integrated Approach." In *Valences of Interdisciplinarity: Theory, Practice, Pedagogy*, edited by Raphel Foshay, 343–65. Edmonton: Athabasca University Press.

Orr, Deborah. 2002. "The Uses of Mindfulness in Anti-oppressive Pedagogies: Philosophy and Praxis." *Canadian Journal of Education* 27(4): 477–90.

Pearce, Maryanne. 2013. "An Awkward Silence: Missing and Murdered Vulnerable Women and the Canadian Justice System." PhD diss., University of Toronto.

Rigney, Lester. 2006, "Indigenist Research and Aboriginal Australia." In *Indigenous Peoples' Wisdom and Power: Affirming Our Knowledge Through Narrative*, edited by Nomalungelo I. Goduka and Julian E. Kunnie. Burlington, VT: Ashgate.

Ritenburg, Heather, Alannah Earl Young Leon, Warren Linds, Denise Marie Nadeau, Linda M. Goulet, Margaret Kovach, and Meri Marshall. 2014. "Embodying Decolonization Methodologies and Indigenization." *AlterNative* 10(1): 67–80.

Smith, Linda Tuhiwai. 1999. *Decolonizing Methodologies: Research and Indigenous Peoples.* London: Zed Books.

Wesley-Esquimaux, Cynthia C., and Magdalena Smolewski. 2004. *Historic Trauma and Aboriginal Healing.* Aboriginal Healing Foundation Research Series. Ottawa: Aboriginal Healing Foundation.

Wong, Yuk-Lin Renita. 2004. "Knowing Through Discomfort: A Mindfulness-Based Critical Social Work Pedagogy." *Critical Social Work* 5(1). http://www1.uwindsor.ca/criticalsocialwork/knowing-through-discomfort-a-mindfulness-based-critical-social-work-pedagogy.

Yellow Bird, Michael. 2013. "Neurodecolonization: Applying Mindfulness Research to Decolonizing Social Work." In *Decolonizing Social Work,* edited by Mel Gray, John Coates, Michael Yellow Bird, and Tiani Hetherington. Burlington, VT: Ashgate.

Young, Alannah Earl, and Denise Nadeau. 2005. "Decolonising the Body: Restoring Sacred Vitality." *Altantis* 29(5): 1–13.

8   Integrating Body, Mind, and Spirit Through the Yoruba Concept of *Ori*

Critical Contributions to a Decolonizing Pedagogy

Temitope Adefarakan

> *My fullest concentration of energy is available to me only when I integrate all parts of who I am, openly, allowing power from particular sources of my living to flow back and forth freely through all my different selves, without restrictions of externally imposed definition.*
>
> Audre Lorde (1984, 120–21)

Achieving self-integration is a complex challenge for any human being. But this struggle is especially difficult for those of us who are marginalized and oppressed—those of us marked by race or ethnicity, gender, religion, and/or socioeconomic class, whose humanity is persistently questioned or denied in a world dominated by Western values and ideologies. We live in a world bent on having us remain colonized, disintegrated, and disembodied, a world in which we are taught the supremacy of whiteness, of maleness, of heterosexuality, and of the able body, as well as the importance of surrounding our bodies with material symbols of middle-class affluence. And yet we also live in a world that, despite its obsession with the body, paradoxically equates power and privilege with intellectual activity, with the *absence* of body—a world in which we are taught the deeply entrenched view that the mind is superior to the body. In the passage quoted above, Audre Lorde speaks of the challenge of acknowledging and living the *wholeness* of our humanity, especially in the face of the colonizing definitions thrust upon us. What she suggests is the possibility of arriving at an embodied consciousness that does not fragment the body, mind, spirit, and soul—an emotional, cognitive, physical, and spiritual awareness that allows for the integration of all parts of who we are.

The challenge of embracing an embodied wholeness and humanness is rarely engaged within the institutional spaces of Western education, a system founded on the familiar split between mind and body. Especially in the domain of higher education, learning is assumed to take place in the mind, which is understood as the seat of intellect, the source of the human capacity to reason. In this elevation of rational thought processes over other ways of learning and knowing, the spirit (or soul) is, more often than not, silenced, dismissed or ignored, while the body is habitually rendered invisible—as if, in keeping with the Cartesian binary, the mind can exist in separation from matter. This disintegrated framework was imposed on Indigenous peoples in the course of their colonization by European powers, and it continues to dominate Western pedagogical models. In this chapter, I share how I came to discover the decolonizing possibilities of the Yoruba concept of *ori* (that is, one's destiny, purpose, or calling). I argue that, as a counterhegemonic concept, *ori* subverts conventional Cartesian frameworks by encouraging the reconceptualization of the self as the fusion of body, mind, and spirit, an empowering shift of embodied consciousness that can help to counteract the dislocation and oppression prevalent in mainstream teaching and learning.

As an Indigenous Yoruba woman who addresses embodiment from the standpoint of a Yoruba conception of the world, or worldsense, I acknowledge that the discussion here raises questions about what it means to teach and practice Indigenous African concepts and ways of knowing in a North American Indigenous context. More specifically, it raises questions around what it means to be an Indigenous African on land to which one is not Indigenous. While this is not my central focus here, I discuss how a Yoruba worldsense can assist learners in thinking about and working through the relationship between diasporic Africans and the Indigenous peoples of North America. I have grappled with these questions elsewhere (Adefarakan

2015), arguing for more flexible imaginings of Indigeneity, especially where diasporic Africans are concerned, so that the particularities of our history and circumstances can be effectively theorized on our own terms and from the entry point of our own experiences.

The Yoruba Community

Known for their complex divinatory and religious systems, political and religious institutions, urban centres, and ancient art (Warner-Lewis 1997), the Yoruba are one of the most familiar ethnic and linguistic groups in West Africa. Numbering more than 40 million, the Yoruba live primarily in a region known as Ile Yoruba, or Yorubaland, which extends from southwestern Nigeria into the neighbouring countries of Togo and Benin. According to archaeological excavations carried out in the spiritual and political city centres of Ile-Ife and Oyo, the Yoruba urban presence in this region dates as far back as 800 to 1000 CE (Drewal and Pemberton 1989, 13). While the theory of Yoruba-migration has been traced to Egyptian origins by scholars such as Samuel Johnson (1921, 5–7), it is a theory that remains contested. Considerable Yoruba communities also exist as part of the African diaspora, the descendants of Yoruba who were enslaved and transported across the Atlantic. These communities exist principally in Trinidad and Tobago, Cuba, Puerto Rico, Brazil, and the southern regions of the United States. In addition, the Oku (or Aku) people of Sierra Leone, whose presence dates to the era following Britain's formal abolition of the slave trade in 1808, have strong links to the Yoruba. Finally, there are the more recent Yoruba-speaking migrant communities who left Yorubaland in the 1960s, 1970s, and 1980s, in pursuit of the "greener pastures" of global capital worldwide. These communities are most densely represented in the United Kingdom, Europe, and North America. For the purposes of this chapter, I will focus on the Yoruba-speaking migrant communities in North America and, more specifically, Canada.

According to the 2016 census, Canada is home to 9,585 individuals who self-identify as Yoruba (up from 5,340 in 2011), roughly 42 percent of whom (4,055) reside in Ontario. Of the Ontario residents, nearly three-quarters live in the metropolitan Toronto area, 1,105 of them within the City of Toronto itself.[1] This is not surprising, given that migrant communities tend to be concentrated in large urban centres, owing to better job prospects and the multicultural appeal of cities with diverse demographics.

Yoruba Cosmology: The Fusion of Matter and Spirit

Yoruba culture reflects a distinctive worldsense, that is, a particular way of mapping out and experiencing the world. As Yoruba feminist scholar Oyèrónké Oyěwùmí (1997, 2–3) explains, in Indigenous contexts, the term *worldsense* is more appropriate than *world view:*

> The term "worldview," which is used in the West to sum up the cultural logic of a society, captures the West's privileging of the visual. It is Eurocentric to use it to describe cultures that may privilege other senses. The term "world-sense" is a more inclusive way of describing the conception of the world by different cultural groups.

Overemphasis on the visual is problematic from a Yoruba standpoint because spirituality and/or spiritual forces are inaccessible to the human eye. The word *view* also implies a looking outward, on something external to the self, rather than an inner experience. Hence, the term *world view* does not fully reflect the complexity of Indigenous Yoruba culture and how life is understood from a multisensory position.

Fundamental to a people's worldsense is cosmology, on which Indigenous knowledge systems are founded. Yoruba cosmology rests on the principles of relatedness, complementarity (Olajubu 2003, 2; ; Soyinka 1976, 121) and interconnectedness, in that Orun (the world of spirit), Aiye (the physical world of living beings), and Ile (the earthworld) are all interdependent: they cannot exist on their own. Orun is inhabited by the Supreme Being, Olodumare, who is also known as Eleda (the Creator) and Olorun (literally, the owner of Orun), and more than four hundred divinities known as *orișa*—many of whom once walked the earth as human beings with mystical

---

1 Figures for 2016 can be accessed at "Census Profile, 2016 Census," *Statistics Canada,* https://www12.statcan.gc.ca/census-recensement/2016/dp-pd/prof/index. cfm?Lang=E (last modified 17 May 2018), by entering "Canada," "Ontario," or "Toronto" in the "Place name" search window. For the 2011 figure, see "NHS Profile, 2011, *Statistics Canada,* https://www12.statcan.gc.ca/nhs-enm/2011/dp-pd/prof/ index.cfm?Lang=E (last modified 24 May 2018).

powers and were then deified after death. The lives of the *orisa* are continued through the supernatural powers of various forces of nature such as water, wind, fire, thunder and lightning, as well as powers that reside in the earth and in trees. The Yoruba universe is also inhabited by a variety of spirits such as *egungun* (ancestors), *egbe* (our mirror selves or spiritual twins), *ebora*, *iwin* (supernatural beings with magical powers), and *ara orun* (beings of the otherworld, including the unborn).

The Yoruba understand human life to be a journey from the world of spirit to the physical world—to the "marketplace" that we call Earth, the place where matter is infused with spirit to create the various life forms that exist in Aiye. The forces of Orun are always influencing and in communion with the people who inhabit Aiye, who will one day die and become one with *ile* (the soil or earth), which is our last resting place as we move back into the spirit world. The earth, with its connection to the dead, is so sacred to Yoruba people that relatives of recently buried loved ones take small portions of soil from their grave and use it for swearing oaths (Abimbola 1997, 68), a practice that illustrates the interconnection between the living and the dead through the power of the earth. As John Mbiti (1990, 74) reminds us, among African peoples, the spiritual world and the physical world operate in concert: the two "intermingle and dovetail into each other so much that it is not easy, or even necessary, to draw the distinction or separate them."

Central to Yoruba cosmology is the concept of *ori*. The Yoruba believe that every human being was born with a destiny or purpose (*ori*) and was called to Earth to discover and fulfill that purpose. The term *ori* literally means "head," that is, the physical human head, which, as Oyeronke Olajubu (2003, 33) explains, "is conceived by the Yoruba as a representation of the inner essence in humans; it symbolizes the individual's essential nature"— the person's *ori-inu*, or "inner head," as distinct from the physical, or outer, head. Understood in this inner sense, *ori* is "intractably connected with human destiny": it is "the essence of human personality which rules, controls and guides the life and activities of the person" (Balogun 2007, 118). Before our birth, while we are still in the realm of spirit, we choose our "head" and, with it, the course of our worldly existence.

Consider the following verses from the *Ogunda meji*, a collection of oral verses that forms part of the Odu-Ifa—the corpus of texts holding thousands of chapters, commonly referred to as "Odu," which are sacred to the Ifa system of divination. Ifa texts contain complex and multifaceted teachings within each Odu and are designed to develop the self and facilitate the learning of key lessons that help one remember one's calling on earth. The *Ogunda meji* tells the tale of three friends and how they chose their *ori* (destiny) before journeying to Aiye. The tale demonstrates how *ori* becomes the common denominator that joins the spiritual realm to the physical world. In the verses below, the lesson involves patience. Two of the friends, Oriseeku and Orileemere, lack patience and are rash in their choice of a "head" (*ori*). In their haste, when they arrive at the home of the sculptor, Ajala, they choose faulty heads, which results in an unhappy life on earth:

> They then took them to Àjàlá's store-house of heads.
> When Orísèékú entered,
> He picked a newly made head
> Which Àjàlá had not baked at all.
> When Orílèémèré also entered,
> He picked one very big head,
> Not knowing that it was broken.
> The two of them put on their clay heads,
> And they hurried off
> On their way to earth.
> . . .
> They worked and worked,
> But they had no gain.
> If they traded with one half-penny,
> It led them
> To a loss of one and one-half pennies.

Concerned, the two decide to seek advice from Ifà elders who specialize in divination. And so they come to understand the problem:

> The wise men told them that
> The fault was in the bad heads they had chosen.

In contrast, the third friend, Afuwape, takes the time to select a good *ori*, rather than letting himself be seduced by the shiny exterior of the many flawed heads in Ajala's storehouse. And so his destiny is very different:

When Afùwàpẹ́ arrived on earth,
He started to trade.
And he made plenty of profit. (Abimbola 1976, 128–29, 132)[2]

The teaching here lies in the importance of developing one's interior character and spirit, rather than focusing on physical exteriors. While the passage might seem to endorse an ethic of materialism, if that success is symbolized by monetary gain, this would be a gross misreading of the lesson, one that reflects a Western preoccupation with external circumstances. When these verses are understood within the context of a Yoruba worldsense, the focus shifts inward, with the emphasis falling on character and on understanding the importance of developing a good character as a human being on Earth. Similarly, for the Yoruba, good character, or *iwa pele,* is regarded as the essence of a beautiful person: beauty is not a matter of physical appearance.

In Yoruba cosmology, spiritual forces are known to be fluid and in constant flux, which makes it possible to alter one's destiny. Balogun (2007) argues that the Yoruba embrace a "soft" form of determinism, pointing out that, whereas a fatalist "easily resigns himself to fate with respect to future situations, the Yoruba as soft-determinists are hopefully gratified of being able to help future situations" (127). Thus, despite their choice of flawed heads, Oriseeku's and Orileemere's fate is not forever sealed: the opportunity always exists to modify a bad destiny so that it becomes a more positive one. This opportunity resides primarily in consulting a *babalawo* or *iyalawo* (a spiritual elder who specializes in divination) and seeking his or her guidance in shifting negative or malevolent spiritual energies to ones that are benevolent, empowering, and positive. Such efforts often involve ritual, ceremony, and sacrifice from the individual seeking this spiritual transformation to a more affirming destiny.

In Yoruba cosmology, spirit is eternal and transcendent. A human being is created by the infusion of matter with spirit, and, when the person dies, that individual self moves back into the spiritual field, merging into the universal "self." The Yoruba understanding of cosmology thus involves a continuous fusion of the physical with the metaphysical, and human life is

---

2 See also the discussion of this story in Oyěwùmí (1997, 38–39).

understood as part of the eternal existence of spirit. In this sense, the Yoruba approach to cosmology is circular, based on a philosophy of continuity, community, reciprocity, and balance among ancestors, the living, and the unborn (John 2003, 12). The individual self is relational, in the African sense that "there is no I without the we": no entity can exist without the others. All are threads of equal importance that come together to form the whole circle. In essence, there is no beginning or end; there is only a powerful continuity of life through eternal transmutation.

The importance of the circle is evident in Yoruba ritual, as indicated by Bolaji Idowu (1996, 142) in *Olódùmarè: God in Yoruba Belief*: "The Yoruba worshipper makes a circle of ashes or white chalk; within the circle, which is a symbol of eternity, he pours a libation of cold water, and in the centre he places his kola-nut on cotton wool." The circle reflects how the individual exists within the context of the larger community of living human beings and how the living self is intertwined with the worlds of the ancestors and the unborn. The circle is, in its continuousness, a symbol of eternity. Said differently, each individual self extends throughout the cosmos rather than simply being restricted to the world of human beings here on earth.

Yoruba Worldsense and Decolonization: The Principle of Connectedness

Embedded in the philosophy of continuity, community, reciprocity and unity is the foundational principle of connection: connection between the self and one's larger community, between the physical and metaphysical, and between humanity and all other species with which humans share the Earth. This principle of connectedness is especially important where questions of the relationship between diasporic Africans and the Indigenous peoples of Turtle Island are concerned, because it means understanding that our struggles as peoples colonized by Europeans are connected, despite differences in how colonization has played out historically and continues in the present day, especially in terms of the forced movement of bodies and the impact this has on our lands. We may differ in how we relate to our Indigenous lands and how we struggle for control over those lands, but we are similar in our struggles to decolonize—to achieve liberation, empowerment, and self-determination.

Given that, for the Yoruba, reliance on one another—the foundation of continuity, community, reciprocity, and unity—is essential to survival, I would argue that the principle of connectedness demands that we engage with and support the decolonizing struggles and realities of Indigenous peoples of North America. Doing so signifies our understanding that the liberation of Indigenous peoples in North American is integral to liberation as a whole. As is common in many Indigenous cultures, the Yoruba hold the natural world to be sacred, as is reflected in our belief in ancestors, the *oriṣa,* and in spirits that are associated with natural phenomena such as mountains, hills, the earth, rivers, lakes, the ocean, trees, and wind (Awolalu 1979, 45). Our connection to these phenomena signifies a connection to land, which has traditionally meant our Indigenous lands in Yorubaland. However, I would argue that another critical element of decolonization involves acknowledgement of the connection to lands in the African diaspora—in this case, Turtle Island, or what is hegemonically known as Canada and the United States. In connecting to these lands ourselves, we recognize that they are the lands of the Indigenous peoples of Turtle Island, and, through this shared connection, we are encouraged to declare solidarity with the Indigenous peoples of Turtle Island as allies. In this declaration, the Yoruba worldsense assists us in understanding that we are all connected and therefore interdependent.

However, the principle of connectedness that stands at the nexus of the Yoruba worldsense is antithetical to the Western construction of the individual as an independent entity, as well as to the prevailing Cartesian dualism according to which our minds are separate from our bodies—a binary that, as we have seen, also effectively denies the existence of spirit. As Devi Mucina illustrates in his chapter in this collection, colonial frameworks have fragmented African subjects as individuals, families, and communities. The ideological hegemony of the Cartesian approach to the self continues the colonial process of our spiritual, emotional, physical, and intellectual fragmentation and dissonance, making the goal of a harmonious, integrated self seem beyond reach.

In her chapter in this volume, Candace Brunette-Debassige similarly discusses the destructive impact of colonization on Indigenous peoples, an experience that fractured the self and taught us to disassociate from our bodies by restricting our breath and suppressing our words. I argue that such moments of disembodiment—moments when our hearts may be racing with thoughts, excitement, and fear—are an inescapable constant in the classroom, where the knowledges, cultures, and contributions of racialized and otherwise minoritized students are neither reflected nor taught, For this reason, and because the formal education system is a primary agent of socialization, Western colonial education and its accompanying Cartesian constructions of the self need to be decentred, deconstructed, and ultimately decolonized.

For my understanding of decolonization, I draw on Linda Tuhiwai Smith's (1999, 39) observation that, for Indigenous peoples, the decolonizing of research methodologies involves deliberately "centering our concerns and world views and then coming to know and understand theory and research from our own perspectives and for our own purposes." In Smith's conception, decolonization also involves developing "a more critical understanding of the underlying assumptions, motivations and values which inform research practices" (20). Given that theory and research are the foundations of pedagogical practice, I understand her comments to apply to teaching and learning as well.

In this connection, Yoruba understandings of the self offer an important critical challenge to the Cartesian self because they allow for an integrated identity, both individually and collectively—individually in the sense that one's body, mind, and spirit are integrated and collectively in that one's integrated being is connected to and anchored in one's community and cosmology. In other words, decolonization also means becoming conscious of the spiritual dimension of our physical existence, and this requires particular attention in a Euro-dominant world that equates progress and education with the intellect, with written knowledge, and with the visual. It is from within this integrated framework of mind, body, and spirit that I approach Eve Tuck and Wayne Yang's (2012) understanding of decolonization as an un-settling. Because "settler sovereignty imposes sexuality, legality, raciality, language, religion and property in specific ways," they write, "decolonization likewise must be thought through in these particularities," and not as a metaphor but as a material process that "specifically requires the repatriation of Indigenous land and life" (21). Decolonization in the context of education means decolonization in all areas of life. Much like my insistence that educators understand and teach students as *whole* beings, decolonization cannot be confined within the walls of the classroom.

Understanding Embodiment from an Indigenous Worldsense

Grounded within a Yoruba worldsense, I have come to understand embodiment in a number of interrelated ways. First, embodiment is the confluence of the body, mind, and spirit, all of which are interdependent, with no one of them greater than the others. As I noted earlier, embodiment implies the integration, within our material human bodies, of multiple forms of consciousness—physical, emotional, intuitive, and spiritual, as well as intellectual. In an oft-quoted comment, Lorde (1984, 38) states: "The white fathers told us: I think, therefore I am. The Black mother within each of us—the poet—whispers in our dreams: I feel, therefore I can be free." Lorde's emphasis on feeling stands in direct opposition to Cartesian mind-centric (and Platonic sight-centric) ways of knowing, which colonize the subjugated self by variously dismissing, inferiorizing, and absenting the body and spirit. Self-integration thus requires a critical revisiting of the dominant hegemonic meanings assigned to the head-mind-intellect. For one cannot *feel* without the body; one cannot *sense* without the spirit; one cannot *see* without the eyes. All are codependent and interreliant; this is the essence of our humanity.

This leads me to the second way in which I understand embodiment, which is as the self-awareness that comes to us through *all* our senses. As Oyěwùmí (1997) suggests in her critique of the term *world view,* the Yoruba worldsense values the multiple senses of the body, which together give rise to experiences beyond those that we perceive as thoughts or ideas. This sensory-based approach to embodiment can be found in the work of other feminist scholars who ground their work in Indigenous knowledge frameworks. For example, Batacharya (2010, 6) argues that "embodiment is experienced through sentient perceptions that may be discerned in part, and not exclusively, as mental, physical, emotional, and spiritual." For her, embodied learning involves "a deepening of one's awareness of sentient-social lived experience."

The notion of embodiment as "sentient-social" lived experience brings me to the third strand in my understanding of embodiment, namely, that our embodiment is at once both material and social. As Batacharya (2010, 6) points out, our awareness of our bodies is not entirely a matter of sentient perceptions: embodiment is also "a socially constructed experience produced through material and discursive effects of 'social relations of power.'" Here, Batacharya references Dorothy Smith's (1987, 1990) work, reminding us that our experience of our bodies is influenced by social hierarchies of race and ethnicity, gender, social class, and so on—or by what Lorde (1984) terms "externally imposed definition." As Batacharya (2010, 6) goes on to observe, the "sentient and social components of embodiment are inextricably co-constituted and 'intra-acting.'"[3] Our socially constructed identities—in my case, as a heterosexual, able-bodied Black woman of Yoruba ethnicity—are constantly being reconfigured and remapped onto our bodies, a process that influences not only our experience of our physical embodiment but also our perceptions and interpretation of the world in which we are embedded (and by which we are, in some sense, created). Our bodies are, in other words, a dynamic product of our material form and our social, spiritual, and cultural world. I might say that we are our bodies, but we are also more.

To build on this last statement, I offer my final insight into embodiment, which draws on the Yoruba understanding of the body as the dwelling place of spirit. As Jacqui Alexander (2005, 297) puts it, "To know the body is to know it as a medium for the Divine. . . . It is to understand spiritual work as a type of body praxis, as a form of embodiment." More specifically, embodiment means knowing the body as the vehicle to one's *ori*. Cynthia Dillard (2006, 42) argues that "as human beings"—that is, as creations of the Creator—"we are meant to continue being creative, as the divine Creator's force extends through us, manifesting the dreams of the universe through the work that we do." Embodiment is what enables that work, allowing us to search for and respond to our *ori*, as it plays out over the course of the journey of human life in what the Yoruba call the "marketplace" of the physical Earth.

---

3 On the concept of "intra-acting," Batacharya cites Karen Barad's "Posthumanist Performativity: Toward an Understanding of How Matter Comes to Matter," in *Material Feminisms*, edited by Stacy Alaimo and Susan Hekman, 120–54 (Bloomington: Indiana University Press, 2008).

The Counterhegemonic Potential of *Ori*

Indigenous knowledges have been aptly described as "a way to recover from the artificial split between mind and body brought on by the theorizing of the western European Enlightenment, and a challenge to the ways in which Western knowledges have become hegemonic" (Dei, Hall, and Rosenberg 2000, 155). Revealing the split among body, intellect, and spirit as artificial disrupts the colonial framing of the self as fragmented, offering instead a framing that is holistic and integrated. In this way, the dominance of Cartesian understandings of the self is resisted and subverted. It was while I was engaged in research for my dissertation (Adefarakan 2011) that the Yoruba concept of *ori* emerged as a counterhegemonic entry point for decolonizing conventional pedagogy and ways of knowing that fragment the body and mind, primarily because it encourages the conceptualization of the self as the embodied fusion of body, mind, and spirit. Of the sixteen research participants I interviewed, more than half mentioned *ori,* prompting me to pay careful attention to this concept.

In my research, I sought to engage in an in-depth exploration of Yoruba lived experiences and understandings of Yoruba cosmology from within the larger context of Euro-dominant culture. My goal was to open up a space where Yoruba ways of knowing could be affirmed, especially in settings that have rendered these knowledges invisible or hopelessly overlaid with racist colonial constructions. I also wanted to centre Indigenous ways of knowing as decolonizing frameworks that respect and honour the communities from which these knowledges come. I thus chose to employ anticolonial and African/Black feminist methodologies. By placing the emphasis on both process and outcome, these methodologies validate the experiences, voices, and agency of colonized and marginalized people, including my research participants.

In the course of the interviews I conducted, I came to recognize that cosmology and worldsense are foundational to the politics of knowing—especially among Indigenous peoples who have been marked by a history of colonialism. Even though my research participants were inclined to bring an internalized Eurocentric world view to bear on their perception of Yoruba knowledges and spirituality, embedded in their understandings and discussion of these topics was resistance. They spoke of the self in a way that was not complicit in a Euro-Christian world view but was noticeably aligned with protest against the very same hegemonic discourses in which my participants were entangled. The themes that emerged—resistance to hegemonic perspectives, Indigenous agency, the self as a fusion of body, mind, and spirit, the need for healing and decolonization—all pointed to the power of *ori* to support both the discourse and practice of decolonization. As I came to appreciate, *ori* is not merely a concept or idea but a state of being with which Yoruba consciously engage on a daily basis.

In particular, research participants repeatedly invoked *ori* as a concept salient to their understanding of themselves as spiritual beings. One research participant, whom I have called Mr. Awoniyi—a father of four who had been living in Canada for more than twenty-five years and who described himself as Nigerian and Canadian—emphasized the multilayered nature of *ori*. As he pointed out, *ori* is "not just the physical head":

> It's like an aura that surrounds you as a being, and it's not just a one-layer aura: it is in stages, in levels. . . . Now all those are referred to as *ori*. [But] *ori* could also mean "crown." Because it depends on how you see it, how you describe it. *Ori* is also your destiny, and we believe that it is something you bring with you from Orun.[4]

As Mr. Awoniyi suggests, our *ori* envelops us and surrounds us, like an aura, so that we cannot separate ourselves from it. But our *ori* is not revealed from the beginning, as a whole; rather, it unfolds in stages, over the course of time. Mr. Awoniyi went on to describe the role of ritual in safeguarding a child's destiny. As he explained, children are born with "a certain type of thing that comes with them," a distinctive feature with which their destiny is bound up. For example, some children are born with the umbilical cord wrapped around their neck, in which case they are called "Ojo." Similarly,

> Dada come with locks in their hair, you understand? Dada [are] a group of people that may not be connected physically, but spiritually, unknowing, they are connected, you understand? [. . .] And you don't cut it—you just leave it. It grows, and all you do is just keep it clean. [. . .] Then it gets to a certain age when you want to really cut the hair. For some of them, if as soon as you see the locks, you cut it, they

---

4 All research participants were given pseudonyms. The interview with Mr. Awoniyi took place on 21 April 2007 in Toronto.

might react to it—get ill, create fever, or they become feverish. You have to really consult some oracle or do some things, you know, to avert anything happening to that child.

The first time the child's hair is cut is thus a ritual occasion, designed to ensure that the child's destiny will not be harmed by this action and that he or she will be welcomed into the community:

We call it *saara,* which is just a type of sacrifice and calling all little children in your whole area and providing them with lots of goodies, you understand? [. . .] And it will be in the memory of that child forever that, you know what? "The day my hair was cut, oh boy, did I have a very big party!" You understand? But, mind you, it's not just a big party, because you do not know what *ori* each of these child[ren] have been called. So now you are appealing, you are giving them gifts that, you know, accept my child into this clan of children, you understand? [. . .] I will say it in a very shrewd or crude way: it's like buying your way into the community.

Mr. Awoniyi's discussion of *saara* reminds us of the centrality of community in Yoruba culture for ushering in important life events such as birth. For the Yoruba, birth is a journey of travel from pure spirit to earthly existence. When we are born, we bring certain aspects of our being with us that not only make us unique but also provide the community with some clues about our destiny. Yoruba often refer to *ori to gbe wa,* that is, the destiny that a person brought along.

With regard to a child's *ori,* one of the most important rituals within Yoruba communities is *isomoloruko,* or a baby's naming ceremony. Commonly held on the seventh or eighth day of life, this ceremony introduces the child to the community and the world through the revelation of the child's name. Before a child is named, the forces of Orun are consulted by elders, with the help of a *babalawo* or *iyalawo* (diviner), so as to determine a suitable name, one that reflects the child's destiny or purpose here on earth. The Yoruba have a saying, *Ile la man wo ka to somoloruko,* meaning that we look at the family history and the events surrounding a child's birth before we name the child. In this sense, context, history, and especially communication with the forces of the otherworld are interwoven with a Yoruba child's identity and *ori,* as formally introduced to the larger community through the *isomoloruko* ceremony.

Twenty-one-year-old Dele, who was completing an undergraduate degree in the arts and who described himself as both "Yoruba" and "Black," associated the physical head (*ori*) with luck, which, like destiny, can be bad or good.[5] In this view, one's destiny (*ori*) is susceptible to human influence through its embodied representative, the head:

> For Yorubas, there's something about knocking on your head [that] is [a] bad luck kind of thing. Like, if a stranger knocks you on the head or something, it's bad luck or something—or that it's not good to get knocked on the head. Or, you know, when parents threaten you when you're behaving bad, they say, "*ma fun e nko*" [I'll give you a knock on the head]. Another thing is, when I was coming to Canada, my grandma, she did something to my head . . . she called some man that did something on my head as if [for] some kind of protection.

Dele's comments remind us that integral to the Yoruba worldsense is a constant awareness of various spiritual forces that can assist or hinder a person. His understanding of luck also raises interesting questions about the extent to which the *ori* with which we are born can subsequently be modified through the manipulation of spiritual energies—an issue that his mother, Sade, took up more explicitly.

Sade (a pseudonym) is well known in the African Canadian community as an artist, storyteller, comedian, dancer, and actor. In our interview, she identified herself as Yoruba first, Nigerian second, and Canadian third and was quite vocal about the importance of education, cultural knowledge, and "respect for elders," which she viewed as essential elements of Yoruba culture that must be passed on to future generations.[6] She also discussed *ori:*

> When we talk of destiny, the belief is that before you come into the world, you have chosen whatever you are going to be. That's our own belief—I don't know that of the Western world. But then even sometimes in the olden days, they used to go and consult the oracle and find out the type of destiny that that child brought into the world. So

---

5 The interview with Dele was conducted on 11 March 2007 in Toronto.

6 Sade was also interviewed on 11 March 2007 in Toronto.

they try to guide, to continue with that . . . and if there is anything that is not too good [that] they see, they ask, what can they do in order to help him move a better way, get a better destiny, right? Yeah, they used to do that. So destiny can never be changed, they say, but then, if it's bad destiny, they still have to appease God or do something in order for that bad destiny to change.

Here, Sade points to a tension between the belief that *ori* is immutable ("destiny can never be changed") and efforts to determine a child's *ori* so as to eliminate its negative aspects. Implicit in this discussion is the idea that these negative aspects reflect a misalignment of the child with his or her intended destiny, which in turn implies an imbalance or lack of integration among body, mind, and spirit. The *isomoloruko*, or naming ceremony, is crucial in this regard, as the choice of name helps to ensure the proper alignment with *ori*. It is important that children be given a name that reflects their *ori-inu* (the "inner-head," or essential being) and their guiding spirit, or *orisa*. As a spiritual force, these *orisa* protect the child's *ori-inu*, which, in turn, is linked to the child's name so that every time that name is spoken or brought to mind, the child's destiny is reconfirmed and continuously charged with *ase* (dynamic life-force). The spiritual energy embedded in the *isomoloruko* ceremony vibrates with every breath in which a child's name is uttered, announcing the child's *ori* to the universe.

Dele's experience offers an example of the power of *ori*. Entering university, he had originally enrolled in a pre-med program, but he had a keen interest in music and entertainment and was particularly intrigued by Nigeria's film industry, Nollywood, which he saw as a means of teaching Yoruba culture to younger generations. So he decided to switch into an arts program—a decision that, rather ironically, displeased his artist-mother, Sade, who encouraged him to return to the pre-med program. I would argue that Dele's passion for the arts was a calling, and in choosing to forgo a career in medicine, he was answering the call of his *ori*. From the perspective of Yoruba worldsense, Dele's naming ceremony, as well as the ritual of protection arranged by his grandmother, allowed Dele to remain aligned, to gravitate toward and explore his interests, despite his mother's disapproval. While uncertain and probably anxious about his choice, Dele felt a pull toward the arts, and he followed the promptings of his *ori*.

At first glance, the insights into *ori* offered by my research participants may not seem relevant to pedagogy. I return to Tuck and Yang's (2012) argument that decolonization must be material rather than metaphoric—that it cannot be contained within the classroom but "requires the repatriation of Indigenous land and life" (21). Indigenous "life" is inextricable from Indigenous worldsense, and the understandings of *ori* presented above reflect the Indigenous self as the union of body, mind, and spirit. Decolonization means that when this integrated Indigenous self enters the classroom; it is not forced to disintegrate—to leave body and spirit at the door.

Knowing one's self as an integrated and embodied being is fundamental to finding one's purpose and to holding onto the knowledge that despite all obstacles—racism, classism, sexism, homophobia, and so on—there is a reason for one's presence on Earth. The challenge for us, both as individuals and as a collective, is to discover, remember, and honour that purpose as we simultaneously navigate the complex terrain of marginalization and oppression. Responding to that challenge requires recognizing that one of the spaces of oppression is the education system and that this space nonetheless holds the possibility of unlearning and relearning in ways that will counter disembodiment, oppression, and amnesia.

As a state of being that is essential to the Yoruba understanding of the self as an integrated, embodied being, *ori* holds immense pedagogical possibilities for decolonization, especially in the setting of formal education. It is here that Yoruba and other Indigenous knowledges can be ethically and respectfully utilized to engage in multilayered, self-reflexive learning and discussion within the context of Euro-dominant culture. Through this process, the colonial construction of Indigenous knowledges as silent, invisible, and subjugated will be displaced by one in which such knowledges are affirmed not only as legitimate but as inherently valuable.

Pedagogical Implications of the Concept of *Ori*

My many years as an educator have made me astutely aware that it is not simply young "minds" that teachers shape; rather, it is a whole person, a human being whose material body and immaterial spirit, heart, and soul are also part and parcel of formal schooling, as well as educational experiences more broadly. While *ori* is a specifically Yoruba concept and way of understanding the self, the lessons and knowledge encapsulated in the idea of *ori* apply to all human beings and therefore to all students and teachers. Put another way, the Yoruba concept of *ori* as a state of being can be expanded and adapted to the classroom.

While by no means the only Indigenous system of knowledge that is holistic and integrative, Yoruba ways of knowing and understanding the world can have a transformative impact on formal schooling by encouraging and enabling educators to work with students as whole people, as connected people—that is, as spiritually embodied social beings, not simply academic bodies, whose lives extend beyond the classroom. The classroom then becomes a space in which educators recognize the dangers of replicating Cartesian models of pedagogy that depoliticize, de-emphasize, or simply erase students' physical bodies, along with the dominant social and political meanings ascribed to them. In other words, with this effacement of bodies comes a denial of the social and political implications of our racialized identities and the hegemonic Eurocentric inequities that shape them, as well as a rejection of the spiritual basis of human existence.

In *Teaching to Transgress: Education as the Practice of Freedom*, bell hooks (1994, 16) discusses the Cartesian-informed basis of the Western academy and her realization that she needed to "make a distinction between the practice of being an intellectual/teacher and one's role as a member of the academic profession":

> It was difficult to maintain fidelity to the idea of the intellectual as someone who sought to be whole—well-grounded in a context where there was little emphasis on spiritual well-being, on care of the soul. Indeed, the objectification of the teacher within bourgeois educational structures seemed to denigrate notions of wholeness and uphold the idea of a mind/body split, one that promotes and supports compartmentalization.

In contrast to narrow Cartesian models of pedagogy, this chapter asks educators to ethically and respectfully consider using Indigenous knowledges to inform their pedagogical practice. Incorporating the Yoruba concept of *ori* into one's pedagogical practice, for example, involves shifting to a philosophical, cosmological, and cognitive understanding of the self as integrated whole. It means understanding that *ori* is not an endpoint but a state of being—that, as human beings, we are here on Earth to answer a call, which requires us to figure out what we came here to do. It also means recognizing that discovering our purpose, our destiny, demands an inner awareness and a willingness to explore new things despite whatever fears may have hindered us in the past—to summon the courage to try something that we've always wanted to try or to pursue something in which we already have an interest or to which we are passionately drawn. In other words, the teaching that is embedded in *ori* respects the requirement of process, which in turn necessitates some form of practice.

As Batacharya (2010, 15) points out, the issue of practicing embodiment in education is not merely important but tends to be neglected, in that "few embodiment scholars speak to practices and pedagogies that counter dichotomous thinking in ways that involve more than just thinking." Roxana Ng speaks of "embodied learning" or a "pedagogy of embodiment," a practice in which the means to knowledge construction does not negate the materiality of our being and that allows us to "interrogate how our consciousness is developed and changed" (Ng 2000, 186). It is in this context that I offer an example of how *ori* can be integrated into teaching, embodiment, and decolonization for Yoruba and non-Yoruba teachers and students alike at either the post-secondary or secondary level.

In encouraging teachers to introduce the concept of *ori,* I am in no way advocating the cultural appropriation of Yoruba knowledge systems—or any other Indigenous knowledges, which must always be taught ethically and respectfully. To this end, I suggest that non-Yoruba teachers invite a Yoruba elder or someone from the Ifa community to coteach the first three weeks of a unit to provide important background and foundational knowledge about the Yoruba people, and the cosmology and culture. I also strongly recommend that teachers develop lesson plans for at least a four- to six-week unit, with titles such as "Destiny, Purpose, and Calling from an African Worldsense" or "Exploring Destiny from an African Indigenous Perspective." The goal is to allow students plenty of time to absorb and understand the lessons in the unit as a process and to apply ideas and practice activities in a gradual and unhurried manner. I also suggest that the unit include lessons about the philosophies and the fundamental principles of connectedness and interdependence that underpin Yoruba worldsense. Also recommended is a discussion of the complexities of theorizing embodiment and the decolonization of education while using Indigenous knowledges on land to which one is not Indigenous. Students can be encouraged to think about their own relationship with the Indigenous peoples of North America within the context of their education to date.

More specifically, here are some suggested ways to integrate *ori*—acknowledged as a concept inextricably enmeshed in the broader Yoruba worldsense—into an embodied and decolonizing pedagogical practice:

- Students are first taught background and contextual knowledge about *ori* as an Indigenous concept from the Yoruba ethnic group.

- Students are taught the multilayered meaning of *ori,* with particular stress on the spiritual and embodied components of the concept and on the idea that, in order to understand *ori* from a Yoruba perspective, they will be exploring what their own calling may be.

- To aid them in experiencing *ori* as both a process and a state of being, students are encouraged to incorporate some form of embodied practice beyond their cognitive or thinking self as part of their exploration—practices such as dance, drumming, theatre, sculpture, and singing.

- Students are encouraged to research a figure in their community of choice (i.e. a community they identify with in some way) who is (or was) professionally engaged in an embodied practice, whether as a full-time or part-time, profession, they sometimes use (or used) as a vehicle for addressing social justice or equity issues.

- To assist in their exploration of what their *ori* may be, students are encouraged to try something that they have always wanted to do, or that they feel passionate or curious about.

- Students are asked to keep a journal, in which they record their feelings, thoughts, dreams, fears, and to pay attention to what happens to and around them when they recording these things.

In students' exploration of their *ori,* the emphasis is on the process and on becoming alert to information and messages that emerge. In other words, the objective of this approach is to allow students to gain an embodied sense of awareness, creativity, and critical self-reflexivity:

Awareness includes an awareness of the journey toward awakening and/or remembering one's *ori,* as well as an awareness (and conscious embrace) of one's whole self, and especially of the inseparability of the body and spirit from the mind. Awareness also includes an affirmation of Indigenous knowledges as important sources of holistic and embodied knowledge and of one's self as part of a larger human community in which we are all connected.

Creativity entails the active involvement of one's body and spirit in creating new ways of knowing that give rise to new knowledges. Creativity means understanding the empowering possibilities of knowing the self through an awareness of one's material body and creating a grounded consciousness of one's embodied state of being.

Critical self-reflexivity involves learning how one's self and one's *ori* are both embedded in one's social location. In other words, it means beginning to explore and understand that rolled into the answer to the question, What did I come here to do? are the social and political identities inscribed on our bodies and variously privileged or minoritized by the ideological constructions of a patriarchal, heteronormative, white, Christian, Euro-centric and deeply capitalist culture.

Conclusion

The Yoruba concept of *ori* can be a powerful tool in a decolonizing pedagogy, primarily because it offers the potentially transformative teaching that *all* of our being is important, thereby subverting hegemonic Cartesian-based models of knowing, teaching, and learning. Understanding *ori* from a Yoruba worldsense allows us to remember and reclaim the integration of matter and spirit that lies at the source of our individual and collective existence. That is, it allows us to know ourselves as embodied spiritual beings, whose minds cannot be divorced from our bodies or from our hearts and souls. From this integrated awareness comes the "fullest concentration of energy" of which Lorde speaks.

Decolonization cannot occur within the classroom: it is a far larger project. However, the success of that project rests on our ability to reconnect with our inner essence, our integrated body-mind-spirit, and let the power of that integration flow through us. As long as we remain fragmented, we remain oppressed. The classroom can, I would argue, be a site of renewal and reinvigoration, a space within which we can experience integration, learn to value our whole selves, and begin to discover what we are being called to do, our purpose—our *ori*.

References

Abimbola, Wande. 1976. *Ifá: An Exposition of the Ifá Literary Corpus*. Ibadan, Nigeria: Oxford University Press.

———. 1997. *Ifá Will Mend Our Broken World: Thoughts on Yoruba Religion and Culture in Africa and the Diaspora*. Roxbury, MA: Aim Books.

Abiodun, Rowland. 1994. "Understanding Yoruba Art and Aesthetics: The Concept of *Ase*." *African Arts* 27(3): 68–78, 102–3.

Adefarakan, Temitope E. 2011. "Yoruba Indigenous Knowledges in the African Diaspora: Knowledge, Power, and the Politics of Indigenous Spirituality." PhD diss., Ontario Institute for Studies in Education, University of Toronto.

———. 2015. *The Souls of Yoruba Folk: Indigeneity, Race, and Critical Spiritual Literacy in the African Diaspora*. New York: Peter Lang.

Alexander, M. Jacqui. 2005. *Pedagogies of Crossing: Meditations on Feminism, Sexual Politics, Memory, and the Sacred*. Durham, NC: Duke University Press.

Awolalu, J. Omosade. 1979. *Yoruba Beliefs and Sacrificial Rites*. London: Longman.

Balogun, Oladele Abiodun. "The Concepts of Ori and Human Destiny in Traditional Yoruba Thought: A Soft-Deterministic Interpretation." *Nordic Journal of African Studies* 16(1): 116–30.

Batacharya, Janet Sheila. 2010. "Life in a Body: Counter Hegemonic Understandings of Violence, Oppression, Healing, and Embodiment Among Young South Asian Women." PhD diss., Ontario Institute for Studies in Education, University of Toronto.

Dei, George J. Sefa, Budd L. Hall, and Dorothy Goldin Rosenberg, eds. 2000. *Indigenous Knowledges in Global Contexts: Multiple Readings of Our World*. Toronto: University of Toronto Press.

Dillard, Cynthia B. 2006. *On Spiritual Strivings: Transforming an African-American Woman's Academic Life*. Albany: State University of New York Press.

Drewal, Henry John, and John Pemberton III. 1989. *Yoruba: Nine Centuries of African Art and Thought*. With Rowland Abiodun. Edited by Allen Wardell. New York: Center for African Art, in association with Harry N. Abrams.

hooks, bell. 1994. *Teaching to Transgress: Education as the Practice of Freedom*. New York: Routledge.

Idowu, E. Bolaji. 1996. *Olódùmarè: God in Yoruba Belief.* 2nd ed. Ikeja, Nigeria: Longman Nigeria.

John, Catherine. 2003. *Clear Word and Third Sight: Folk Groundings and Diasporic Consciousness in African Caribbean Writing.* Durham, NC: Duke University Press.

Lorde, Audre. 1984. *Sister Outsider: Essays and Speeches by Audre Lorde.* Freedom, CA: Crossing Press.

Mbiti, John S. 1990. *African Religions and Philosophy.* 2nd ed. Oxford: Heinemann Educational.

Ng, Roxana. 2000. "Revisioning the Body/Mind from an Eastern Perspective: Comments on Experience, Embodiment, and Pedagogy." In *Women's Bodies, Women's Lives: Health, Well-Being, and Body Image,* edited by Baukje Miedema, Janet M. Stoppard, and Vivienne Anderson, 175–93. Toronto: Sumach Press.

Olajubu, Oyeronke. 2003. *Women in the Yoruba Religious Sphere.* New York: State University of New York Press.

Oyěwùmí, Oyèrónké. 1997. *The Invention of Women: Making an African Sense of Western Gender Discourses.* Minneapolis: University of Minnesota Press.

Smith, Dorothy E. 1987. *The Everyday World as Problematic: A Feminist Sociology.* Toronto: University of Toronto Press.

Smith, Linda Tuhiwai. 1999. *Decolonizing Methodologies: Research and Indigenous Peoples.* London: Zed Books.

Soyinka, Wole. 1976. *Myth, Literature, and the African World.* Cambridge: Cambridge University Press.

Tuck, Eve, and K. Wayne Yang. 2012. "Decolonization Is Not a Metaphor." In *Decolonization: Indigeneity, Education, and Society* 1(1): 1–40.

Warner-Lewis, Maureen. 1997. *Trinidad Yoruba: From Mother Tongue to Memory.* Repr. Kingston, Jamaica: Press University of the West Indies.

9 "Please Call Me by My True Names"

A Decolonizing Pedagogy of Mindfulness and Interbeing in Critical Social Work Education

Yuk-Lin Renita Wong

In writing this chapter on an embodied and decolonizing pedagogy of mindfulness, I begin with my bodily experience in this moment: the sensations of each in-breath and out-breath as the air enters and leaves the nostrils, the chest, the abdomen; of the fingertips touching the keyboard as I type these words; of the contact between the body and the chair and between the feet and the floor; of the sensations and the energetic field in the body as the mind is searching for words to express the thoughts and experience in this moment.

But let us pause for a moment. Notice any bodily sensations you might be experiencing and any feelings or thoughts that are passing through your mind in this moment as you are reading this paragraph. What is your breathing like? Is it long or short, deep or shallow? Is your mind leaping to control the breath? Let it be. Simply let the breath come to you, just as it is. How does your body feel in this moment? Is there tension in the body? Do you wish I could move on quickly to talk about the "real" stuff, instead of "wasting" time to be with the bodily experience in this moment?

What do you notice in this pausing?

Originating in the teachings of Siddhārtha Gautama (or Gautama Buddha; c. 563 BCE/480 BCE–c. 483 BCE/400 BCE), mindfulness is about being fully aware of what is going on in the moment with equanimity. In Pali, the language in which early Buddhist texts were recorded, the word for mindfulness is *sati* (Sanskrit: *smṛti*), meaning "recollecting" or "remembering." As Thich Nhat Hanh (1999, 64) says, "Mindfulness is remembering to come back to the present moment," Bhikkhu Bodhi (2011, 25) asserts that in the Buddha's teaching *sati* has acquired a new application based on the older meanings. Bodhi argues that mindfulness is best characterized as "lucid awareness," which includes recognition of objects pertaining to the past and awareness of present happenings. The English translation for mindfulness is misleading since it explicitly points us to the mind, but we can be present only when we are grounded in the body. The body anchors us in the here and now, while the mind often takes us into the past or the future (Chödrön 1997, 2; Nhat Hanh 2006, 34). The Chinese character for mindfulness is 念, also meaning "remembering." The upper part of this character (今) means now and the lower part (心) means heart-mind: that is, the heart-mind in the now. It is not uncommon to hear Chinese people say: "My heart thinks"; or ask "What is your heart thinking?" This reflects the conception of a nonseparate heart-mind. In *Discourse on the Establishments of Mindfulness* (the *Satipaṭṭhāna Sutta*), one of the Buddhist texts on mindfulness, mindfulness of "the body in the body" (*kāya-sati*) is the first of the four "establishments" of mindfulness, followed by mindfulness of "the feelings in the feelings" (*vedanā-sati*), "the mind in the mind" (*citta-sati*), and "the objects of mind in the objects of mind" (*dhammā-sati*) (Nhat Hanh 2006, 13–14). It is important to note that the third establishment, mindfulness of the mind in the mind, is awareness of "mental formations" (Nhat Hanh 1999, 73), which include both emotions and cognition. In Buddhist psychology, emotions and cognition are all part of the *citta*. Thus, mindfulness is about being present with the unity of body, heart, and mind to the full range of experience and the fullness of life in the moment. It is an open and direct awareness of the fluidity of the experience of the present moment. It disrupts the habit of the mind to react, categorize, and control our experience of the world and of life (Wong 2004).

When we are present to what is going on, without our habitual reaction of judgment or preference, we are able to see more clearly. And the more clarity we have in our awareness of what is within us, the clearer we can be about what is outside of and around us. As we develop this awareness, we also begin to see that what is inside and what is outside are not separate, just as the air coming in and out of the body when we breathe is not separate from the air around us. As Thich Nhat Hanh (2000, 40) explains, the forests are our lungs. If they do not breathe, there will be no oxygen for us to breathe. Similarly, I would add that the cars which produce pollution in the air around us are also our lungs. Thus, the forests, the cars, and the air around us are constitutive of and interconnected with each other; that is, we, "inter-are" (Nhat Hanh 1991, 95–96).

In this chapter, I discuss a graduate course I taught using a mindfulness-based pedagogy to engage students in embodied critical reflection for social work practice and social justice work. A number of students in this course experienced, through mindfulness, a process of decolonization from the Eurocentric consciousness that separates and elevates the mind above the body, heart, and spirit, as well as from the essentialist, dualistic, and individualistic construction of self as separate from others and from all things. Feedback from these students illustrated how mindfulness promotes the healing of body, heart, and spirit—healing that many Indigenous and anticolonial scholars and educators have increasingly been calling for in recent years in our efforts toward decolonization. As they transformed from within, these students experienced the restoration and burgeoning of the creative inner life force that goes beyond the binaries and categories of identities. They then extended this creativity outward in their participation and action in the world. In the following pages, I discuss my journey to a mindfulness-based pedagogy and then focus on the decolonizing effects of mindfulness on three students in the graduate course, effects that they experienced not only in their professional lives as social workers but also in their efforts to support healing among their people.

Who Am "I"? A Decolonizing Journey to a Mindfulness-Based Pedagogy

In "Critical Perspectives in Social Work," a graduate course that I taught for nine years, from 1999 to 2008, I asked students, in the second class, to bring an object that they felt best represented and introduced them to their peers. The objective of this class was to increase students' awareness of how our personal experiences within social, cultural, and structural contexts and the deep-seated assumptions we have about ourselves, others, and the world are embedded in histories of power relations (Fook and Askeland 2007), histories that inevitably implicates us in the reproduction and/or subversion of power as we work towards social justice.

I, too, participated in this exercise with the students. What follows is my self-introduction in those years:

> Water can best represent me, fluid and ever-changing. Water makes up 75 percent of my body. I am the water I drink, manifesting in many different forms—vapour, cloud, rain, snow, ice, dew, river, lake, ocean, and many more. I am the cloud that becomes rain watering the vegetables, rice, and wheat that I eat. I am the farmer who grows the rice, wheat, and vegetables. I am the truck driver who transports this produce to the market. I am both the family corner store owner and the entrepreneur who owns superstore chains where I do my grocery shopping. I am the cheap labour on the farms and in the supermarkets in this country and many parts of the world.
>
> I am my parents who were from poor peasant families in southern China and who later became low-income manual labourers in garment factories, the British navy, hotels, and hospitals in Hong Kong. The name my parents gave me, Yuk-Lin (玉蓮 'jade lotus'), represents the Chinese and Buddhist symbol of purification and awakening through and from the mud of life. I am the British colonizer who established the Hong Kong colonial education system, in which I grew up and thrived. The name Renita speaks of this colonial history, as I was required to pick an English name on my first day at the missionary school where I completed my secondary school education (the equivalent of junior high and high school in North America). I am all of my cultural and spiritual ancestors, from whom I have inherited the teaching of my/our "interbeing" with the Earth and all sentient beings.
>
> I am more than what you see and think. As water, I manifest in different forms and cannot be contained in any one form, such as the form of a woman, a Chinese person, a person of colour, or a teacher. When you see (or read) me in one or all of these forms, they may elicit assumptions and some of your past experiences with people who seemed to share my 'traits.' I invite you to become aware of these assumptions and ask yourself: How did you come to know these concepts, assumptions, or knowledge? Where did they come from?
>
> Seeing (or reading) me in the form of a person of colour, some of you may feel uncomfortable when I talk about race. If discomfort

arises in you, I invite you to allow yourself some quiet moments to greet your discomfort with a friendly smile, say hello, and ask: "My dear friend discomfort, can you tell me where you came from? Is there something you want to teach me that I have yet to learn?" In my experience, discomfort has been my best friend, offering me many rich learning moments. It pushes me to reflect and grow. I have been made uncomfortable around issues of ableism, heterosexism, and even racism. And I am grateful for these learning moments because they have made me confront my implication in power and privilege and renew my commitment to inclusivity and social justice.

Inspired by Thich Nhat Hanh's (1991, 74–75) poem "Please Call Me by My True Names," this self-introduction has evolved over the years, based on mindful contemplation of who "I" really am. When I turn inward and bring mindfulness to the everchanging internal process of the mind and body, I see directly the coming and going of thoughts, feelings, and somatic experiences that make up "me" or "my" experience. I see how they affect each other and the conditions that produce them. Mindfulness calls for an open and humble heart and a fierce commitment and willingness to be present to what shows up in the moment, even when it is not pleasant. With mindfulness of the flow and fluidity of moment-to-moment experience, I can see no fixed or solid identity that I can call "me": Chinese, woman, or person of colour. Nor can I draw a clean line between the colonized and colonizer, consumer and capitalist, oppressed and oppressor, human and nonhuman, or good and bad, and simply place myself in the first group within each of these dualistic constructions.

This direct seeing is a critical moment of decolonization. It ruptures the Eurocentric colonial knowledge and essentialist construction of a self separate from the other, and it disrupts separation of the mind from the body, human from nonhuman. Rather, it reflects an ontology of "interbeing" (Nhat Hanh 1991, 95–96), the interbeing of my life with all lives and all things, and it highlights my ethical responsibilities in all my relations. According to De Lissovoy (2010, 280), "decolonial theory" confronts, challenges, and undoes "the dominative and assimilative force of colonialism as a historical and contemporary process, and the cultural and epistemological Eurocentrism that underwrites it." In Memmi's words (1991, 152), the colonized "must cease defining himself [sic] through the categories of colonizers."

It is important to note Tuck and Yang's (2012) assertion that "decolonization is not a metaphor" and that it must address repatriation of land; it does not stop at developing a critical consciousness or at freeing the mind from colonization. For people of former colonies who have been displaced and/or have migrated to North America, the legacy of colonization is entrenched in the entire fabric of life as well as in the psyche and the mind. Many have become permanently "unhomed" (Bhabha 1994, 9), whether they have stayed in the territories that have been returned to them or are living in their new host country. The impact of colonization continues after the repatriation of land and return of sovereignty and the departure of colonizers from occupied territories. To decolonize, therefore, we, the colonized, need to unsettle the Eurocentric ontological and epistemological positions that have governed how we see and experience who we are in the world, while also recognizing the Indigenous Peoples of Turtle Island and our own implication in white settler colonialism. Drawing on the work of Anzaldúa (1987), Bhabha (1994), and Trinh (1989), Nina Asher (2010, 398) argues that "the self, implicated as it is in the colonizer-colonized relationship, is split." It is thus "by acknowledging one's implicatedness and recognizing that one is 'at the interstices' that one can engage in both the intellectual and the psychic/emotional work of decolonization."

My self-introduction above was also a response to my students' perceptions, assumptions, and expectations of me as an Asian female professor. Not only did I interrupt the assumptions they would normally attach to the constructed identities of "Asian woman"; I also hoped to prepare them for the challenge and discomfort they would experience when their own self-identities and implications in power imbalances were deconstructed in the course. Indeed, this was what first brought me to a mindfulness-based pedagogy: I needed to sustain my spiritual, emotional, and mental well-being if I were to continue teaching critical social work (Wong 2004). Instead of promising students a "safe space" in which to explore issues of identities and power, I felt that it was more important to support them in staying with and learning from their discomfort, with openness and kindness, just as a mindfulness practitioner would do in the face of difficult experiences.

Furthermore, in my years of teaching critical social work, I have found the emphasis on the discursive-conceptual mind in conventional critical pedagogical methods limiting. As well, its binary framing of oppression and anti-oppression implies the moral categories of "bad" and "good." Such erroneous dualistic conceptions of oppression and anti-oppression allow those who self-identify as anti-oppressive (and morally "good") or as the oppressed to claim innocence and to avoid examining their own implication in oppression along the multiple axes of power (Wong 2004). It can also result in those who are deemed privileged becoming defensive, frozen, or guilt-stricken. At worst, students may become further separated from each other in their constructed identities instead of coming together to work toward an inclusive and socially just world.

Moreover, in the early years of teaching this course, when I used conventional critical pedagogical methods, I commonly found that students gradually deflated into despair or paralysis, since they felt trapped in the pervasive power relations in their personal and professional lives. When I asked students what they aspired to for a "better world," many could only envision it in negative terms, such as "a world without oppression" or "without injustice." While critical analysis helped them deconstruct power, the dominance of the discursive-analytical mind had stifled their inner life force of hope, creativity, and imagination. It offered little support for healing from territorial, cultural, or epistemic colonization and injustice; restoring their humanity (of both the "oppressed" and the "oppressor"); reconnecting them to the spirit that sustained or elevated them and their communities to see what gives life (Longboat 2009); or imagining and creating what is possible (Shahjahan, Wagner, and Wane 2009, 70–71).

Over the years, it has thus become increasingly crucial for me to support students in learning ways to engage with their emotional reactions to power or holding with gentleness their rage or their wounds from colonization and social injustice, which might be reopened in class discussion. As Asher (2010, 399) writes, "We need to think and *feel* our way out of oppression and colonization" (emphasis in original). When allowed the space to connect to their hearts, which had been closed off in the conventional academic analytical classroom, students were often eager to express their yearning for healing and the restoration of spirit. This is the "decolonizing learning space" that George Dei (2010, 8) advocated for in the classroom after reading Frantz Fanon's work on decolonization and education. Fanon (1967) showed us that the violence of colonization lies not only in the occupation of geopolitical space but also in the colonization of the psychic space. Thus a "decolonizing learning space" needs to address "the spiritual and emotional harm" of colonization (Dei 2010, 9). Decolonizing, then, also involves "a process of healing" from "the spiritual, cultural and mental alienation of the self that creates a sense of hopelessness and despair" and a regaining of "our lost humanity" (Dei 2010, 3). Many Indigenous and anticolonial educators and scholars have also emphasized healing and the restoration of spirit as integral to their personal, intellectual, and collective journeys of decolonization (e.g., Asher 2003, 2010; Graveline 1998; hooks 2003; Longboat 2009; Shahjahan, Wagner, and Wane 2009; Smith 1999).

Shauna Butterwick and Jan Selman (2012), Randee Lawrence (2012), and Roxana Ng (2000) further argue that the body is a critical site of decolonization and healing. According to Butterwick and Selman, "processes of colonization separate mind and body" (64). To decolonize, we therefore need to return and reconnect to the body (Ng 2011) to release and heal the psychic colonization housed in the body and to liberate and revive our inner life force. Many studies have shown evidence for the presence of an ongoing body-mind dialogue that creates emotional maps in our consciousness, as well as for the interconnectedness of mind, body, and personal transformation (Damascio 1999; Forester 2007; Pagis 2009; Siegel 2010). Candace Brunette-Debassige's chapter in this collection speaks powerfully of this process, as does the chapter by Alannah Young Leon and Denise Nadeau.

In recent years, as I began to bring students' attention closer to their sensory experience through mindfulness exercises, some students came to an awareness of their bodily existence in relation to all beings and all things and awakened to their interconnectedness and ethical responsibilities in the world, processes that did not occur to the same degree and depth through conventional critical pedagogy (Wong 2013, 2014). Other educators who have attempted to go "beyond the educated mind" (Bai 2001) through contemplative or mindfulness-based pedagogies in their teaching of environmental and global justice have had similar results (see also Kahane 2009).

Spirituality and Critical Social Work

In May and June 2010, I taught a graduate elective course titled "Spirituality and Critical Social Work." The course provided a space for both contemplation and action and for an integrated bodily-emotive-mental-spiritual knowing for critical reflection in social justice work and critical social work practice. Core to critical social work is the deconstruction of power in practitioners' relationships with clients along relations of race, class, gender, sexual orientation, religion/spirituality, age, and dis/ability. Critical social work addresses the discursive construction and systemic conditions of social and individual problems.

Class Format and Learning Activities

Students sat in a circle in all the classes. The first hour of the class normally began with a ten- to fifteen-minute mindfulness exercise, such as mindful breathing, mindful eating, mindful walking, or loving-kindness meditation. Going around the circle, students then shared their experiences of the exercise. They could pass if they wished. In one class, students spent thirty minutes in solitude, listening to trees.

The fifth session was a six-hour silent retreat on a Saturday. Both the retreat and its preparatory assignment were adapted and expanded from a similar learning activity developed by Teresa Macias, who had taught the course two years before. Students submitted a two-page plan prior to the retreat to identify one area of their spiritual journey on which they would like to reflect or a question they would like to explore on their spiritual journey. In the retreat plan, they specified contemplative practices or texts they would use to guide their reflection. Three readings were recommended to help students plan their retreat (hooks 1996; Kabat-Zinn 2005; Nouwen 1975). On the day of the retreat, students first met in class for a twenty-minute mindfulness meditation to allow the body-heart-mind to settle. They were then encouraged to allow the flow of the day and the moment to guide them, even if that meant not sticking to their retreat plan. Students then found a spot on campus to conduct their contemplative practice in solitude. They came together at midday to share a silent meal together. At the end of the retreat, they shared briefly their experience of the day.

Every week, students wrote two to three pages in their ungraded reflective journals on their daily centring practice and class readings. Students were asked to engage in a ten- to twenty-minute daily centring practice of their choice, such as a mindfulness exercise introduced in class or a contemplative practice that helped them stay centred and grounded. While mindfulness was the foundational practice shared in class, it was important to honour the diversity of spiritual traditions that students brought to the classroom. Many students chose mindful breathing, walking, and/or eating, along with other contemplative practices such as prayer, Bible reading, quiet time in nature, gardening, poetry, calligraphy, painting, yoga, mountain biking, and music. Students reflected on what they noticed during the practice and how it helped them relate to themselves, others, and the world differently. For their weekly journal writing, students were also asked to reflect on a sentence or a longer excerpt from two or three of the weekly assigned readings, excerpts that opened their heart or inspired their spirit, raised a question of significance for contemplation, or invited them to practice critical social work differently. These readings included authors from various cultural and spiritual traditions and topics on ecology and social justice, Indigenous knowledges and decolonizing social work practice, spirituality, and social activism.

Interviews

In February 2011, almost one year after the completion of the course, I invited all of the twenty-one students who had taken the course to participate in an individual, semi-structured, in-depth interview of approximately an hour to talk about their experience of the course's contemplative pedagogy and its impact on their personal life and critical social work practice. I was not teaching any of the students at the time. Some of them had graduated the previous year, while some expected to graduate in June 2011. Two students could not be reached, since their email contact information was no longer valid. Ten of the remaining nineteen students volunteered to participate in the interviews, which took place from March to July 2011. It was a time when graduating students were preoccupied and overwhelmed with the completion of their practicums, course work, and Major Practice Research Paper, and many were involved in job searches.

I make no attempt to present a comprehensive analysis of all ten interviews in this chapter, choosing instead to focus on the experiences of three students—Juana, Daphne, and Wanda (pseudonyms)—all of whom experienced a decolonizing process in their personal and professional lives through the mindfulness-based pedagogy.

Grounded in the Body, Rooted in Interconnectedness

When asked in the interview what parts of the course had stayed with her, Juana was very quick in her response: "The word interconnectedness really stays with me." It was like a "flashlight" in every class for her. More specifically, it helped her see the "bigger picture" of the "webs of relationships" in the different contexts of her life. Not only did she begin to ask how she was interconnected with her surroundings, her relations, her work, and her passion, but she also wanted to learn more about the histories and stories of the clients with whom she worked and to understand their interconnections. Most importantly, the course took her back to certain questions: Who am I? What is my history? How am I connected to my roots? How am I connected to the bigger picture of those roots?

Listening to my self-introduction in class, especially with regard to my names, Juana was struck by the realization of how her name represented the colonial history and the associated Catholicism forced upon her people. Her Spanish surname was the colonial name "pressed upon" her ancestors. Since completing the course, she had tried to learn more about the history of her family, her people, and their community in Canada. "That has been very challenging," Juana said, "I have this longing to find out where my ancestry is . . . but I can only know so much, because after a certain point, my history has been erased, has been changed." Although Juana yearned to connect to her roots, her lineage, her ancestry, and the history of her people "amidst the Spaniards, the Americans," she struggled to express her desire: "There are so many layers I have to uncover, not to find the truth, cause I don't think there is a truth to it; trying to find where my people, um, not started, cause I don't think we started." Her articulation of what she is *not* trying to find speaks poignantly of the violence of colonization. There is no beginning or "truth" of her ancestry to be found, since it has been erased or altered, and has "always been a question mark." Who she is can now only be located among the multiple constructed identities of the colonial past and present.

Not being able to trace her ancestry, Juana turned to rooting herself in "the interconnectedness of all my relations." It was very important for Juana to be rooted and grounded; she pictured a tree that could "easily be swayed" or "easily fall down" if not rooted. "If you are not rooted," she asked, "how do you regenerate, how do you grow?" Being able to anchor herself in the interconnectedness of her relations helped Juana develop a wider perspective of her origins, of "what's important" and what her passion and mission is. It helped her believe that her "life has had meaning."

I asked Juana what it was in the course that had led her to anchor herself in interconnectedness. She talked about "the silent time" in the mindful eating exercise, which helped her "declutter, taking away the noise or the systemic chatter" that kept her from being grounded or understanding her interconnectedness. The term *systemic chatter* was introduced in the course by Jana Vinsky, a guest speaker in one of the sessions. It refers to "the dominant narratives, which are both informed by and support the structures found within our society. Systemic Chatter shows up within our internal and external dialogue reflecting inherited power relations within historical and contemporary conversations" (Prevatt-Hyles and Vinsky 2005).

In the mindful eating exercise, students were asked to take the time to bring their full presence and all their senses to the experience of eating a tangerine and several grapes: to see the different shapes and colours of each piece of fruit, to smell the subtle scents, to feel its weight and texture through the sensation of touch in their fingers and hands, to hear the sound of the fruits, and to chew them slowly, one by one, at least ten times to fully taste them. At the time of the interview, Juana continued to maintain this mindful and silent eating practice in her daily life, especially at breakfast:

> When I'm eating, I will remember to just stop myself . . . to have that silent time, and that grounding. Before, I would be, like, what's the next thing to say, or we can do something more productive with our time than just being silent. But now . . . that exercise allows me to slow down and centre and ground myself, and [be] a lot more aware of my physicality.

This grounding and awareness of her physicality was pivotal to bringing Juana back to herself and the wholeness of her being—physical, emotional, intellectual, and spiritual. To Juana, her wholeness is her interconnectedness. The mindful eating exercise quiets the Enlightenment discourse that elevates the mind above the body. While she found that all the other courses in the program challenged her intellectually, they pushed her "to the limit" of "mental and physical exhaustion" from "staying up at night drinking coffee" in order to complete the coursework and then going to placement the next day. She said, "Your course brought me back to myself, to listen to myself again, and not just listen to all those intellectual voices." This listening to herself included attending to her bodily needs rather than letting the intellect take over her life. She would tell herself, "Hold on, Juana, you need to eat; Juana, you need to rest. . . . If I was tired, I'm not going to push myself. If I was hungry, I'm not going to continue, pressing on, be unkind to myself. I'm kinder to myself now."

The neglect of the body that Juana mentioned was not uncommon among the students in the course—and, I would also add, among academics and professionals in our increasingly competitive and fast-paced world. Daphne, a student of Asian descent, also reconnected to her wholeness—all the elements, people, and histories that made her who she was—through the slow sensory experience of the mindful eating exercise:

> The meditative eating, eating slowly, tasting everything, feeling everything; thinking back about where the tangerine came from, all the people involved. . . . So I am aware of these particular things that have helped me become who I am. That's my wholeness. . . . Yes, all these things help to develop who I am today, all the experiences, the history, events.

This wholeness is bigger than her individual self.

Quieting the Mind, Listening to the Heart

Slowing down was instrumental for Daphne to turn inward and become aware of who she was in her wholeness. Along with the mindful eating exercise, Daphne also talked about what the silent retreat in the course brought her: "just finding myself again, who I am and what completes me." When I asked her to describe her image of wholeness, she immediately said, "My heart, my heart, just the image of my whole physical body coming into view as if my heart [was] pumping in blood to all extremities. . . . I start at my heart and become more who I am when I see my blood rushing everywhere in my veins; that creates the whole picture of me." And she added, "Wholeness in my heart, when I experience it in my heart, it's like love. At first, I wanted to say a lack of pain, but that's not totally true, because sometimes love includes pain. I think to be able to express myself in emotions and feelings—that is what I feel makes me whole."

So the body, the heart, and the mind are inseparable to Daphne. Her image of wholeness starting at her heart—like love that sometimes includes pain—reflects bell hooks's vision of spiritual self-recovery in relationship to the political self-recovery of oppressed and colonized peoples. hooks (1999, 117) asks: "What is the place of love in this recovery?" To hooks (1996, 289), love is a foundation that "takes us more deeply into practice as action in the world." It defies the dualistic identity construction of good or bad, right or wrong in "a culture of domination" and colonization. hooks urges us to dissolve these dualities and "to identify anchors to hold on to in the midst of fragmentation, in the midst of a loss of grounding" (289). She identifies her anchor as "love," which calls for a capacious seeing. "It is life-sustaining," she says, "to understand that things are always more complex than they seem. . . . Such understanding is more useful and more difficult than the idea that there is a right and wrong, or a good or bad, and you only have to decide what side you're on" (289).

For Daphne, the silent retreat helped her rediscover what invigorated her body, mind, and spirit, which reconnected her to her heart: "I feel like my heart was shining. You couldn't see the heart. I just see bright light. . . . I felt connected." Inside this heart was herself, or a "little lady" who "illuminates in my heart" and "speaks softly." Daphne had to be quiet in order to listen. She explained, "I guess the metaphor is listen to your heart; listen to your inner teacher; listen to that wholeness that is there." This listening is a quieting of the dominant academic and colonial chatters that exclude the body and the heart and that promote self-alienation and disavowal among colonized and marginalized bodies (Dei and Simmons 2010).

This quiet listening connected Daphne to the life force and the love within her—her heart and blood, she said, "rushing everywhere in my veins that creates the whole picture of me." This "whole picture" is fluid: "I can only see my whole body as the blood comes out, and it doesn't come out, like, solid; it goes in and out." This sense of fluidity and ongoing movement and nonseparation came from Daphne's own history of having gone through many phases in her life, including her teenage raving phase with drugs, and of recognizing all the big and small things and people that had impacted her and made her who she is today.

While Daphne did not talk about colonization and oppression or identify herself with these terms, she spoke passionately about her teenage clients who were confined within the professional and medical labels of "operational defiance" or "mentally ill" and were not allowed a voice. She felt connected to them, saw them beyond their labels, listened nonjudgmentally to their stories and wholeness, and supported them in finding their voice. "The course helped me realize that everything is connected, fluid, and ever-changing," Daphne said, "and everything makes an impact on something else, whether big or small." Extending her quiet inward listening outward, she recognized the ever-changing nature of people and trusted that a small act of nonjudgmental listening could go a long way. She said, "Even the small positivities can be impactful because things are connected." This listening with acceptance, to self and others, is love. It requires one to see the interconnectedness of all things and all lives within a person's being, and it breaks down an essentialist and fragmented construction of people.

Juana experienced a similar process of reconnecting to her heart, or what she called her "aura" and "inner guide," as she attended to her body and grounded herself in her physicality. This "aura" and "inner guide" represents to her a deeper meaning of life that is rooted in her community and her interconnectedness with all things. This reconnection took her beyond "the ego" based in individual accomplishments that she had worked hard to build up and took pride in for some time; she realized that her ego was "not rooted in anything" when life fell apart. Juana had been an improviser and had written with much "heart and emotion." Academic study had separated her from this heart connection, and her writing had become intellectual and cold. The "aura" that had emerged in the course was still "shy," Juana said, but it was getting stronger. During the course, she added, "the silent time really helped."

Her "inner guide" prompted Juana to ask how she could move outward to the life around her and to her community, now that she had begun to experience her interconnectedness with all things and all lives. "If I am connected to you, and you are suffering," she asked, "what can I do in this life, in this world, to alleviate that suffering? How can I continue going on and see the suffering and injustice in your life and not do something about it, because I am connected to you?" This is an ontology and an ethic of interbeing, and it contrasts sharply with the Eurocentric and individualist way of being in the world. As De Lissovoy (2010, 283) notes, the hallmark of Eurocentric colonialism is the "partitions and divisions of the world" and the conceptual separation of self and others. Juana's awakening to her interconnectedness with all things and all lives, from the vanity and rootlessness of the life focused on individualist pursuits that she had previously led, is a significant decolonizing shift of consciousness and way of being in the world.

Seeing the discord in her community as a result of the colonial injustice her people had carried, Juana particularly hoped to bring her people together, to inspire that aura of "light, warmth, love, compassion, and togetherness" in her community. Furthermore, she aspired to support the youth in her community to come back to "their centre" and to "nurture that aura"—that is, to "give them a space where they can be who they are" and not live in fear of being excluded. She wanted to "give them that room to just be, whatever they may be . . . to bring up that wholeness in them, and help them to be grounded in something more than themselves, more than this oppression." Early in her life, bell hooks (1999, 116) became "determined to live a life in the spirit." And when we bring this spirit to our discussion about race, gender, and class, we are called not only to name the injustice and oppression but also to "understand that I'm more than that, and understand that I can be more than that with others" (124).

Recognizing Multiplicities, Reclaiming Wholeness

Another student, Wanda, also commented on her name, which she said carried "a huge story." Until she heard the stories behind my names, it had not occurred to her to remember and tell hers when she introduced herself in class. She said, "I don't often associate all the history behind my name [with] what I go by" because "there is a disconnect between that and what my name is." This "disconnect" permeated her family, who "hid and didn't talk about" the Indigenous ancestry in the family history. "It was not the part that we celebrated," Wanda said. For a long time, she was afraid to claim that part of herself; since she had not been raised with a recognition of being Indigenous, she "was afraid of being, like, a faker" and "being rejected as somebody who didn't deserve to have that connection." When she was asked about how the course had impacted her, Wanda said that the contemplative silence, the reflective time in nature, and the mindfulness exercises—breathing, walking, and eating—helped her reconnect to that hidden and uncelebrated part of herself and her heritage.

In the mindful walking exercise, students were invited to go outside the school building, which was surrounded by tall trees and spacious lawns. Mindful walking is meditative practice in motion. Students were asked to bring their attention gently to the sensations of contact between their feet and the ground, the soil, the grass, and to feel the motion of their body as they walked. They were also invited to coordinate their breathing with their steps. Using the instructions about mindful walking often given by Thich Nhat Hanh in his dharma talks, I suggested to the students that they could say silently to themselves: "Breathing in, I take one step. Breathing out, I take another step." Or students could silently say "arriving" as they took one step and "here and now" as they took the next step. In walking meditation, we are not walking in order to go somewhere. We are simply arriving in the here and the now with each step. Most often, when we walk, we walk with projects in our head, with anxieties or worries about the future or regrets about the past. Mindful walking brings us back to the present moment with each step. It helps the mind come back to the body, to quiet down, and to gain clarity of what is here.

At the time of the interview, Wanda continued to practice mindful walking (though not as slowly) while walking home from work, mindful eating during lunch outside the office when the weather was favourable, and mindful breathing when working with clients in difficult situations. These practices all helped Wanda come back to her centre. Since "colonial domination and oppression materialize in the here and now of the processes and practices of our everyday lives" (Tejeda, Espinoza, and Gutierrez 2005, 16), Wanda's consistent mindfulness practice while going about her day is significant in loosening the colonial grip of her being in the world.

Wanda reported that in feeling more "grounded, more present, and more aware" in her body through mindfulness in contemplative silence, she began to recognize "all the pieces of what make me," including her Indigenous heritage. Even though she was not raised in it, she began to see that it was "still a huge part of me." Wanda began to feel more comfortable "honouring" the deep connection she had felt since childhood with Indigenous spirituality and mythology. This internal recognition of who she was did not need any external validation. "I don't need from the government that I qualify to be Indian," she said, adding that she felt no need to prove that her maternal grandmother was Indigenous. She did, however, need to come to terms with the materiality of her inability to connect to the Indigenous community because of her family's denial of and separation from their Indigenous heritage.

I asked Wanda what image came up for her when she recognized all the different pieces of herself. She said, "It is almost like a column of light housing in my body. . . . When the pieces of myself are out there, the light is dim. When they come together and are pulled back into the centre, that light has the space to grow." This column of light grew as she grounded herself in and cared for her body and as she connected with nature, all her relations, and her Indigenous ancestry. When the pieces of herself were back in her centre, fueling the column of light, she felt "calm, grounded, present, strong," and "very powerful and large, in a good sense."

Wanda talked about how this "stronger sense of self" helped her challenge oppression: "When I'm feeling comfortable in my skin, . . . when you have that strong rooted sense [of who you are], I feel I'm in a better position to challenge it, and to find the strength to stand up and advocate for people, and demand people's rights to be honoured." This stronger rooted sense of self, she said, supported her in standing up for a client against pressure from the medical staff to discharge her before a suitable placement could be arranged. This client was experiencing mental health challenges and had no home and no one to return to. Wanda recognized that she needed time to think through the different scenarios and sort things out for the client; she would not have an answer for the medical team on the same day of their discharge decision. In the past, Wanda would have been concerned about how not having an immediate answer would reflect on her as a professional. But after the course, in which she "worked on taking the time, slowing down, really reflecting on things, and being more secured in who I was," she felt more confident in herself and in her own judgment. In that incident, instead of speeding forward with hasty solutions to appease others, she felt the confidence to slow down, to take the time, to be aware of herself and the reasons for the decision she was making. Wanda said, "Awareness is at the root of being whole." Her re-embodiment of her heart, mind, and spirit through the mindfulness exercises and reconnection to nature set in motion a process of self-reclamation (Dei 2010, 18) and freed her to act with strength, for self and others, from her centre.

(Not a) Conclusion

The writing of the first draft of this chapter spanned ten months, during which I had two episodes of acute neuropathic pain running from the base of my neck through the right shoulder, down my arm, and into my fingers. It was debilitating. Both times, I only needed a few more days to complete the first draft, but then I stopped writing to allow the body to heal. This might have been a coincidence, but I could not help wondering whether the body was screaming and releasing the unattended pain of a lifetime of colonization. The surfacing of pain is often necessary for deep healing to take place. It is a cleansing process that calls for mindfulness—awareness with gentleness and loving kindness—in our care of and listening to the integrated wholeness of body, heart, mind, and spirit on our journey of decolonization. The stopping and slowing down of the writing process was a mindful response. Through mindfulness, I stopped negating my body and spirit; the dominant mind could no longer dictate the timeline of this writing project, and the balance of wholeness of my being was restored.

Just as the students reclaimed their wholeness through mindfulness, I was on the same journey with them. It is an ongoing process. Our mind, heart, body, and spirit are inseparable in the wholeness of our existence. There is no body-mind duality and no hierarchy among these foundations of our being in and knowing of the world. And when the students were grounded in the physicality of their being through mindfulness, they also began to recognize their interbeing and interconnectedness with all things and all their relations. This deep inward seeing not only supported them in reclaiming who they were in their history of relations but also invigorated them to extend outward and act in the world from the centre of their being, based in a consciousness of relationship and interbeing.

In integrating the wholeness of their being through mindfulness, these students also recognized the fluidity and multiplicity of their identities. Their "true names" defy the colonial Eurocentric essentialist and dualistic categories of identities that separate and hierarchize. This speaks to part of Frantz Fanon's (1967) decolonization project in *Black Skin, White Masks* to go beyond fixed categories or binaries of being. He writes, "I should constantly remind myself that the real leap consists in introducing invention into existence. In the world through which I travel, I am endlessly creating myself. I am a part of Being to the degree that I go beyond it" (229)—that is, beyond the enslavement of empire, colonization, and nationalism.

The processes of colonization, however, continue today. In recent years, divorced from its Buddhist roots, mindfulness has been popularized in the health and mental health fields, and even in the corporate world, in North America and England. Numerous quantitative measurement scales have been developed to measure mindfulness and the effectiveness of mindfulness in reducing stress or regulating other health or mental health problems (Baer, 2007, 2011; Cardaciotto et al., 2008; Feldman et al., 2017; Lau et al., 2006), even though mindfulness is an internal, fluid process of moment-to-moment consciousness that cannot be fully captured by quantification. Moreover, as a number of my students have informed me, some health and social service agencies push their frontline service staff to teach mindfulness to their clients without providing the staff with any mindfulness training. Mindfulness has been commoditized as a cost-saving technique to be added to the Western toolbox to treat modern ailments such as stress and mental distress (Bunting 2013). This has been done without examining the socioeconomic and sociopolitical conditions that contribute to the production of stress and mental health issues in this global, neoliberal, capitalist era.

A version of mindfulness practice has also been adopted to train soldiers to reduce stress while serving in the US military (Watson 2013), leaving the causes and consequences of war unquestioned. Mindfulness practice, despite benefiting many, has been misused in the West to perpetuate the harm that militarization and capitalist-driven productivity has caused in people's lives. The practice is particularly susceptible to misuse when it is removed from its context as a 2,600-year-old Buddhist practice grounded in ṣīla—a code of ethical conduct based on self-discipline and on a commitment to nonviolence and a refusal to cause harm. As Thich Nhat Hanh (1999, 82) reminds us, these ethical precepts are essential to mindfulness: "If we don't practice the precepts, we aren't practicing mindfulness."

The colonial appropriation of ancient practices from non-Western cultures is not new. Yoga, an Indigenous practice rooted in thousands of years of spiritual tradition in India, has been associated with New Ageism (Batacharya 2010) and commoditized for Western consumption. Reclaiming ancient practices such as yoga and mindfulness practice from such contemptuous and potentially dangerous cultural appropriation and (re)colonization will require the persistent efforts of many in our continuous project of decolonization. Our task is not to decry any Western adoption of yoga or mindfulness practice but rather, as Brunette-Debassige suggests in her chapter in this volume, to call for a more critical engagement of spiritual practices that are not of our own tradition. It is to maintain a critical pedagogy that refuses to allow the colonization of mindfulness into yet another Eurocentric and capitalist commodity. Most importantly, it is to reassert the foundation of *sīlas* in mindfulness practice.

Finally, as Tuck and Yang (2012) remind us, "decolonization is not a metaphor." As the journey of decolonization continues, I have become increasingly aware of the physicality of my here-and-now existence on the continent of Turtle Island and the ethics of my interbeing with the Indigenous peoples in Canada. While reviewing this chapter, I saw how this awareness was obscured at the time I taught the "Spirituality and Critical Social Work" course. The violence of settler colonialism in Canada blocked this awareness until I audited a course taught by Bonita Lawrence on the treaties and the history of Canada from Indigenous perspectives. Decolonization in the context of Canada must be connected to the materiality of this history. The teaching and practice of mindfulness thus requires the grounding of awareness in the presence of the Indigenous peoples, as well as in the incommensurability and yet interconnectedness of settler colonialism in Canada and Western colonization in many parts of the world. This recognition is mindfulness: an ongoing process with an open and humble heart to the unfolding of who "I" am, and who we are, in the ethics of our interbeing.

Now let's come back to our breathing. What is the breathing like right now? Is it long or short; deep or shallow; fast or slow? Where do you feel the breath most strongly in the body? Let the breath come through us. This is not "my" breath, "your" breath, nor "our" breath. This breath comes from all lives and connects us to all lives and all things. It awakens us to our responsibility to each other and to the world, human and nonhuman, animate and inanimate.

References

Anzaldúa, Gloria E. 1987. *Borderlands / La Frontera: The New Mestiza.* San Francisco: Aunt Lute Books.

Asher, Nina. 2003. "Engaging Difference: Toward a Pedagogy of Interbeing." *Teaching Education* 14(3): 235–47.

———. 2010. "Decolonizing Curriculum." In *Curriculum Studies Handbook: The Next Moment,* edited by Erik Malewski, 393–402. New York: Routledge.

Baer, Ruth A. 2007. "Mindfulness, Assessment, and Transdiagnostic Processes." *Psychological Inquiry* 18(4): 238–42.

———. 2011. "Measuring Mindfulness." *Contemporary Buddhism* 12(1): 241–61.

Bai, Heesoon. 2001. "Beyond the Educated Mind: Towards a Pedagogy of Mindfulness." In *Unfolding Bodymind: Exploring Possibility Through Education,* edited by Brent Hocking, Johnna Haskell, and Warren Linds, 86–99. Brandon, VT: Foundation for Educational Renewal.

Batacharya, Janet Sheila. 2010. "Life in a Body: Counter Hegemonic Understandings of Violence, Oppression, Healing, and Embodiment Among Young South Asian Women." PhD diss., Ontario Institute for Studies in Education, University of Toronto.

Bhabha, Homi K. 1994. *The Location of Culture.* New York: Routledge.

Bodhi, Bhikkhu. 2011. "What Does Mindfulness Really Mean? A Canonical Perspective." *Contemporary Buddhism* 12(1): 19–39.

Bunting, Madeleine. 2013. "Zen and the Art of Keeping the NHS Bill Under Control." *The Guardian,* 7 April. http://www.guardian.co.uk/lifeandstyle/2013/apr/07/zen-buddhism-nhs.

Butterwick, Shauna, and Jan Selman. 2012. "Embodied Knowledge and Decolonization: Walking with Theatre's Powerful and Risky Pedagogy." *New Directions for Adult and Continuing Education* 134 (Summer): 61–70.

Cardaciotto, LeeAnn, James D. Herbert, Evan M. Forman, Ethan Moitra, and Victoria Farrow. 2008. "The Assessment of Present-Moment Awareness and Acceptance: The Philadelphia Mindfulness Scale." *Assessment* 15(2):204–23.

Chödrön, Pema. 1997. *When Things Fall Apart: Heart Advice for Difficult Times.* Boston: Shambhala.

Damasio, Antonio. 1999. *The Feeling of What Happens: Body and Emotion in the Making of Consciousness.* San Diego: Harcourt.

Dei, George J. Sefa. 2010. "Rereading Fanon for His Pedagogy and Implications for Schooling and Education." In Dei and Simmons, *Fanon and Education,* 1–27.

Dei, George J. Sefa, and Marlon Simmons, eds. 2010. *Fanon and Education: Thinking Through Pedagogical Possibilities.* New York: Peter Lang.

———. 2010. "The Pedagogy of Fanon: An Introduction." In Dei and Simmons, *Fanon and Education,* xiii–xxv.

De Lissovoy, Noah. 2010. "Decolonial Pedagogy and the Ethics of the Global." *Discourse: Studies in the Cultural Politics of Education* 31(3): 279–93.

Fanon, Frantz. 1967. *Black Skin, White Masks.* Translated by Charles Lam Markmann. New York: Grove Press. Originally published as *Peau noire, masques blancs* (1952).

Feldman, Greg, Adele Hayes, Sameet Kumar, Jeff Greeson, and Jean-Philippe Laurenceau. 2007. "Mindfulness and Emotion Regulation: The Development and Initial Validation of the Cognitive and Affective Mindfulness Scale-Revised (CAMS-R)." *Journal of Psychopathology and Behavioral Assessment* 29(3):177–90.

Fook, Jan, and Gurid Aga Askeland. 2007. "Challenges of Critical Reflection: 'Nothing Ventured, Nothing Gained.'" *Social Work Education* 26(5): 520–33.

Forester, Cressida. 2007. "Your Own Body of Wisdom: Recognizing and Working with Somatic Transference with Dissociative and Traumatised Patients." *Body, Movement, and Dance in Psychotherapy* 2(2): 123–33.

Graveline, Fyre Jean. 1998. *Circle Works: Transforming Eurocentric Consciousness.* Halifax: Fernwood Publishing.

hooks, bell. 1996. "Contemplation and Transformation." In *Buddhist Women on the Edge: Contemporary Perspectives from the Western Frontiers,* edited by Marianne Dresser, 287–92. Berkeley, CA: North Atlantic Books.

———. 1999. "Embracing Freedom: Spirituality and Liberation." In *The Heart of Learning: Spirituality in Education,* edited by Steven Glazer, 113–30. New York: Jeremy P. Tarcher / Penguin.

———. 2003. *Teaching Community: A Pedagogy of Hope.* New York: Routledge.

Kabat-Zinn, Jon. 2005. "Moments of Silence." In *Coming to Our Senses: Healing Ourselves and the World Through Mindfulness,* 573–75. New York: Hyperion.

Kahane, David. 2009. "Learning About Obligation, Compassion, and Global Justice: The Place of Contemplative Pedagogy." *New Directions for Teaching and Learning* 118 (Summer): 49–60.

Lau, Mark A., Scott R. Bishop, Zindel V. Segal, Tom Buis, Nicole D. Anderson, Linda Carlson, Shauna Shapiro, James Carmody, Susan Abbey, and Gerald Devins. 2006. "The Toronto Mindfulness Scale: Development and Validation." *Journal of Clinical Psychology* 62 (12):1445–67.

Lawrence, Randee Lipson. 2012. "Coming Full Circle: Reclaiming the Body." *New Directions for Adult and Continuing Education* 134 (Summer): 71–78.

Longboat, Diane. 2009. *Living Spirit: Awakening the Spiritual Warrior Within.* Workshop, 18–19 April, Toronto, organized by Gitche M'Qua Centre.

Memmi, Albert. 1991. *The Colonizer and the Colonized.* Boston: Beacon Press.

Ng, Roxana. 2000. "Toward an Embodied Pedagogy: Exploring Health and the Body Through Chinese Medicine." In *Indigenous Knowledges in Global Contexts: Multiple Readings of Our World,* edited by George J. Sefa Dei, Budd L. Hall, and Dorothy Goldin Rosenberg, 168–83. Toronto: University of Toronto.

———. 2011. "Decolonizing Teaching and Learning Through Embodied Learning: Toward an Integrated Approach." In *Valences of Interdisciplinarity: Theory, Practice, Pedagogy,* edited by Raphael Foshay, 343–65. Edmonton: Athabasca University Press.

Nhat Hanh, Thich. 1991. *Peace Is Every Step: The Path of Mindfulness in Everyday Life.* New York: Bantam Books.

———. 1999. *The Heart of the Buddha's Teaching: Transforming Suffering into Peace, Joy, and Liberation.* New York: Broadway Books.

———. 2000. *The Path of Emancipation.* Berkeley, CA: Parallax Press.

———. 2006. *Transformation and Healing: Sutra on the Four Establishments of Mindfulness.* Berkeley, CA: Parallax Press.

Nouwen, Henri J. M. 1975. "Creating Space for Strangers." In *Reaching Out: The Three Movements of the Spiritual Life,* 65–77. New York: Doubleday.

Pagis, Michal. 2009. "Embodied Self-Reflexivity." *Social Psychology Quarterly* 72(3): 265–83.

Prevatt-Hyles, Dianne, and Jana Vinksy. 2005. "LPI Approach." *Liberation Practice International.* http://www.liberationeducation.com/LPI_approach.htm

Shahjahan, Riyad Ahmed, Anne Wagner, and Njoki Nathani Wane. 2009. "Rekindling the Sacred: Toward a Decolonizing Pedagogy in Higher Education." *Journal of Thought* 44(1–2): 59–75.

Siegel, Daniel J. 2010. *Mindsight: The New Science of Personal Transformation.* New York: Bantam Books.

Smith, Linda Tuhiwai. 1999. *Decolonizing Methodologies: Research and Indigenous Peoples.* London: Zed Books.

Tejeda, Carlos, Manuel Espinoza, and Kris Gutierrez. 2005. "Toward a Decolonizing Pedagogy: Social Justice Reconsidered." In *Pedagogies of Difference: Rethinking Education for Social Change,* edited by Peter Pericles Trifonas, 9–37. London: RoutledgeFalmer.

Trinh, Minh Ha. 1989. *Woman, Native, Other: Writing Postcoloniality and Feminism.* Bloomington: Indiana University Press.

Tuck, Eve, and K. Wayne Yang. 2012. "Decolonization Is Not a Metaphor." *Decolonization: Indigeneity, Education, and Society* 1(1): 1–40.

Watson, Julie. 2013. "US Marines Studying Mindfulness-based Training." *The Associated Press,* January 20, 2013. https://medicalxpress.com/news/2013-01-marines-mindfulness-based.html

Wong, Yuk-Lin Renita. 2004. "Knowing Through Discomfort: A Mindfulness-Based Critical Social Work Pedagogy." *Critical Social Work* 5(1). http://www1.uwindsor.ca/criticalsocialwork/knowing-through-discomfort-a-mindfulness-based-critical-social-work-pedagogy.

———. 2013. "Returning to Silence, Connecting to Wholeness: Contemplative Pedagogy for Critical Social Work Education." *Journal of Religion and Spirituality in Social Work* 32(3): 269–85.

———. 2014. "Radical Acceptance: Mindfulness and Critical Reflection in Social Work Education." In *Mindfulness and Acceptance in Social Work: Evidence-Based Interventions and Emerging Applications,* edited by Matthew S. Boone, 125–43. Oakland, CA: New Harbinger.

10 Poetry

Learning Through Embodied Language

Sheila Stewart

The way my words yearn to be embodied, visceral, pulled
from the mind's dull corridors to the world's bright flesh.
> Maureen Scott Harris, from "Epistemology:
> The World Speaks," *Slow Curve Out* (2012)

November 11th

In the library basement my yoga teacher
announces a few minutes of remembrance
—the whole building silent. I prefer
yoga's own silence.

My friend beside me leaving a lifetime's
teaching to write poetry—her last
Remembrance Day assembly. Final time
leading a straggle of children

into the auditorium. The principal talks
peace, but fills the students with Flanders Fields.
(I was good at standing still.) My friend tells me
of Nathan who screams in class as if a bayonet

pierces his side. She says to the children,
Have you ever been hurt? I have. She lets
them see her cry. The statue in the park
tells us courage is a man on horseback.

Grandfather returned from the war,
beat Gran. (My uncle told my brother told
me.) For the woman in the far corner
coming to yoga class is an act of courage—

leaving her room, combat. Stillness
on any ordinary day, an act
of remembering and not. *Let*
your spine sink into the ground.

(Stewart 2012, 72)

What does "yoga's own silence" have to do with pedagogy and decolonization? Yoga has everything to do with my own embodied learning, helping me to ground myself and quiet the busy, critical mind that tells me I am *not enough.* It helps create a sense of space and rest, from which I am more open to learning of all kinds. The Saturday yoga class I have been attending for the past fifteen years also creates community and supports the yoga practice I am developing at home, which in turn supports my writing process.

Conscious embodiment might be described as an attempt to decolonize body and spirit. Sheila Batacharya (2010, 6) describes embodied learning as "a deepening of one's awareness of sentient-social lived experience." Her work highlights how our experiences of our own and other people's bodies are shaped by social location, dominant discourses, and material realities. As Batacharya points out, the individualistic New Age ways in which yoga has often been taken up in North America "tend to efface social relations of power" (6), and she challenges us to work with a more complex social understanding of embodiment.

Much occurs in Batacharya's hyphen between "sentient" and "social." The concept of sentient-social embodiment helps me think about what poetry attempts to do through language. Poetry is poised in the moment between the sentient and the social, a moment of dialogue. Many poets try to *be with* and *write from* the senses, bodily awareness, context, as well as from their poetic interests. Poetry also occurs between the psyche and the social, a place of bodily knowing attempting to become words, with both unconscious and conscious aspects of mind engaged. I do not want to make broad claims about poetry and decolonization, and certainly not all poetry is written or read from a decolonizing point of view, but I find the perspectives of embodiment and decolonization helpful as I consider my intentions as a poet.

What do I mean when I talk about decolonizing body and spirit? Eve Tuck and Wayne Yang's "Decolonization Is Not a Metaphor" provides a caution against the "ease with which the language of decolonization has been superficially adopted into education and other social sciences" (Tuck and Yang 2012, 2). They point out that "decolonization" is often used in a way that separates it from the current uncomfortable realities of colonization, including the material reality of settlers living on Indigenous land. They argue that decolonization cannot be subsumed under the causes of social justice, critical methodologies, or antiracism; rather, decolonization is about the "repatriation of Indigenous land and life" (1) and "offers a different perspective to human and civil rights based approaches to justice, an unsettling one, rather than a complementary one" (36).

In *Decolonising the Mind: The Politics of Language in African Literature* (1986), novelist and Kikuya scholar Ngũgĩ wa Thiong'o explains how culture is a key tool of imperialism. Ngũgĩ is well-known for having made the decision to write in Giyuku, his mother tongue, rather than in English. "The effect of a cultural bomb," he writes, "is to annihilate a people's belief in their names, in their languages, in their environment, in their heritage of struggle, in their unity, in their capacities and ultimately in themselves" (Ngũgĩ 1986, 3). I agree with Tuck and Yang that the word *decolonization* has slid into common use among educators, and I appreciate their caution about using it as a metaphor. I find it helpful to think about decolonizing the mind, spirit, and body, and also to think with Tuck and Yang about how "decolonization brings about the repatriation of Indigenous land and life; it is not a metaphor for other things we want to do to improve our societies and schools"(2012, 1). Decolonization is not just a metaphor; the material reality of processes of colonization is deeply entwined with the process of naming and struggle through language.[1]

My work is situated in the expanding field of poetic inquiry (Butler-Kisber 2010; Prendergast, Leggo, and Sameshima 2009a, 2009b; Thomas, Cole, and Stewart 2012). Poetic inquiry developed from arts-informed research (Knowles and Cole 2008) and arts-based research (Finley 2008), which not only challenge us to think about how form and content work together but also attempt to make research accessible beyond the academy. Poetic inquiry asks questions about how poetry can be a mode of knowing, being, and telling. "Poetry helps us confront ourselves in language; poetic inquiry sheds light on this confrontation" (Thomas, Cole, and Stewart 2012, xii). Poetry as inquiry contributes to new kinds of knowledge in such fields as education (Guiney Yallop 2010), health (Galvin and Todres 2012), and social work (Gold 2012). Poetic inquiry can be a means of analysis, presentation, and representation. As inquiry, it invites different kinds of knowing, including the awareness of not knowing.

My poem "November 11th" brings together themes of memory, school-ing, trauma, vulnerability, and the embodiment sought through yoga. In this chapter, I blend poetry and prose in an attempt to disrupt traditional academic language and find ways of writing that are more attuned to my efforts at embodiment. I approach embodiment, pedagogy, and decoloniza-tion as an arts-informed researcher, former literacy practitioner-researcher, and poet, inquiring into shame and the challenges of listening and learning across social differences. I write from the position of a settler, a middle-class Irish Canadian, living on the traditional lands of the Mississaugas of the New Credit First Nation in Toronto. Poetic writing can be a way to *dwell* in the complex space of connections and disconnections among body, word, and place, where learning, integration, and healing are possible. How does this relate to decolonization and the land where I live and write? Tuck and Yang's examination of decolonization prompts me to consider the ways in which embodiment may allow for a greater tolerance of being unsettled, of inhabiting an uncomfortable space of learning.

---

1 Thank you to Sheila Batacharya for her observation that "decolonization is not *just* a metaphor," made in a small discussion group about the Tuck and Yang article at an event at the Ontario Institute for Studies in Education. Held in the spring of 2013, this event gave participants the opportunity to remember Roxanna Ng and her work.

A Body Cloaked in Shame

Understandings and practices of embodiment are used in various social service and alternative educational settings, including adult literacy (Miller and King 2011). In the community-based literacy work I did in the late 1980s and 1990s, the other literacy workers and I drew on understandings of learning as holistic and incorporated body, mind, emotion, and spirit into our work.[2] My work and subsequent literacy research (Stewart 2008a, 2008b, 2009) was influenced by Jenny Horsman's examination of the effects of violence on learning, most notably her book *Too Scared to Learn* (1999). Horsman writes about how her research participants pointed out that "issues of low literacy and violence are both hidden. Neither have a public face, both are unspeakable, and to experience either is seen as shameful" (29).

In literacy classes, students speak of shame, which is shaped by how our society views limited literacy skills as shameful, as an individual lack. Everyday discourses of literacy—which circulate, for example, in government documents, movies, and daily conversation—come from a deficit model in which the person with low literacy skills is lesser than people with stronger literacy skills (Auerbach 1996; Caspe 2003). I recall meeting with a student years ago who spoke of how badly she felt, how much she wanted to get work, how her friends said she could get work if only she could learn to read and write. This particular student had a developmental disability and lived in extreme poverty. Work might be a possibility, but learning to write her name could be a place to begin and a way to value what she did know. In teaching and learning, we often begin with shame, vulnerability, and other intense feelings entwined with coming forward to ask for help and wanting to learn. Who wants to be identified by something they lack?

Similarly, it is uncomfortable to describe oneself as a "victim" of violence. Parker Palmer (2004, 169) defines violence as "*any way we have of violating the identity and integrity of another person.*" To this definition, Judy Murphy (2008, 180n1) adds some examples: "Experiences of violence can include spousal abuse, child abuse, fleeing homelands because of oppression or war, and marginalization through issues of poverty, class, race, lack of

---

2 A number of literacy practitioners write about holistic literacy practices, including Katrina Grieve, Cheryl Reid, and Judy Murphy. Judy Murphy and Cheryl Reid are also yoga teachers who use yoga in their literacy practice and write about this process.

education and/or culture." Shayna Hornstein (2008, 212) defines violence as "inherently an abuse of *power*—whether that power is manifested as physical assault, sexual violation, shaming or humiliation." I was drawn to literacy work in part by a connection with literacy students who had experienced violence of various kinds. Research I conducted with literacy practitioners, on their reasons for being involved with literacy work and their connection with violence, pointed to the complexity of listening. Practitioners talked about the challenges for students and themselves of trust, voice, comfort, hope, and shame (Stewart 2008a).

When we work with students who have experienced multiple kinds of violence, including physical violence, we see trauma in *their* lives but may not wish to see it in our own. Certainly, there are degrees of violence and trauma, but seeing trauma as belonging to others rather than ourselves can be an attempt to a distance ourselves from it. Whether personal, systemic, or vicarious, trauma is endemic in our society, and its experience is multiplied through the media. It helps me to understand my own life when I recognize that violence is more than physical.

Sara Ahmed (2004) writes about the intersubjective, intercorporeal nature of shame. In her chapter "Shame Before Others," she refers to "the phenomenological experience of shame in the intercorporeal encounters between others" (103). The social nature of shame is highlighted by other thinkers as well, such as psychologist Judith Lewis Herman (1992). We feel shame before another person, even when the other has become an internalized voice. According to feminist philosopher Sandra Bartky (1990, 85), "shame is the distressed apprehension of the self as inadequate or diminished." Shame often involves concealment (85), and trauma (Herman 2007). Shame can permeate learning and often arises in a rupture in relationship, making it a potential barrier to learning.

The visceral experience of shame may include blushing and cringing. Maria Mazziotti Gillan (2010) writes about shame and shaming in families in her poem "Betrayals," which begins with the following stanzas:

> At thirteen, I screamed,
> "You're disgusting,"
> drinking your coffee from a saucer.
> Your startled eyes darkened with shame.

You, one dead leg dragging,
counting your night-shift hours,
you, smiling past yellowed, gaping teeth,
you, mixing the eggnog for me yourself
in a fat dime store cup,

how I betrayed you,
over and over, ashamed of your broken tongue,
how I laughed, savage and innocent,
at your mutilations.

I am struck with the words "savage and innocent," words that generally portray a dualism in our thinking-feeling; here, the poet joins them with "and."

Embodied/Disembodied

Embodiment scholars, including Batacharya (2010), discuss embodiment as a way to move beyond the Cartesian duality of mind and body. I use poetry to bring mind and body closer.

Autumn

breath shallow   I flit from articles to books
leaf through dissertations
trying to write

embodiment is not body
pedagogy is not teaching and learning
decolonization not   due in two weeks

today I read, walked in High Park, went to yoga
thought about the chapter I did not write

Tomorrow will be better, tell myself.
I have a start, tell myself.
I don't write in a scholarly enough way.
How much should I reflect on my own experience? I ask.

Beyond getting the reader's attention, what is the purpose
of poetry? I ask the reader.

are the mice in the ceiling really raccoons, how much would
it cost to remove them? has my daughter in Halifax eaten
dinner?   when will the call come?—
Granny or Granddad died, who will go first,   then what?

I sit at the computer   lost
in pace
     check past email

              call the dog
         step into the sentient world
        sidewalk burnt, red and gold

The authority and evaluative nature of academic writing can fill me with fear—of saying something I regret, not saying much at all, being inappropriate, not being smart enough: failure. In scholarly writing, I try to bring tensions to the surface and be clear about what I think. Making a poem is a different process, using words to create a cluster of meanings; an energetic working with words draws in the reader, often evoking sensory experience and memory. I use poems in academic writing to bring in more of the body, the difficult-to-say, other modes of knowing, and the unexpected.

In writing about embodiment, I want to dislodge logic from its pride of place. Poet and essayist Maureen Scott Harris (2004, 74) begins one of her poems with the line "To speak directly would be a new thing." Poetry can be used as a way of hiding, as can academic writing and other kinds of prose. Prose usually pushes me to speak more directly, but in some cases, I can be more direct and clear in a poem. Prose works with the conscious mind trying to become more conscious; poetry's purview is wider, working with the unconscious, fragments and shards of memory, and bodily sensation becoming conscious. Poetry prompts us to ask, What counts as knowledge? Working at the border of poetry and prose, I am aware of the privileging of prose in academic writing, but I also do not want to set up "academic writing" as a straw man. Multiple forms of writing and scholarship are needed, as we struggle to think beyond the binaries.

Beginning doctoral studies in my late forties, I encountered traces of my earlier embodied and disembodied states.

Reading Room

The next generation is taller,
smooth skin, angora sweater,
jeans slim over hips, a bit of belly
exposed.

I look at gowned men in ornately
framed portraits, try to imagine
the past.

My young full-faced self, schooled
in another era, another university's
similar rooms, dark with regal
wood.

I have been buried in the stacks without
a word. Being watched, as if that were
enough.

My essay on Donne,
undone.

Studying philosophy and English at Queen's University in the late 1970s and early 1980s, I felt "buried in the stacks without / a word." I very rarely spoke in class and struggled to write essays. I looked up literary criticism on poems, and the weight of scholars' words and dusty hardcover books, almost all by long-ago European or American men, crushed my words. "Being watched" or feeling I was being watched, I often left my body as I sat in class or walked down the street. My spoken and written voices "failed to thrive," to use the words of Maureen Scott Harris (2004, 52). Having been a child well trained to obey authority, I failed to find my own authority or relationship with texts, except to adore them and be intimidated by them. Harris writes, "I have floated rootless and drowning, held my tongue, denied the flood" (52).

Living in a Girl's Body

My understanding of embodiment is rooted in my experience of being a United Church minister's only daughter growing up in Stratford and Waterloo, in small-town southwestern Ontario. I was born a few years after my parents and brothers emigrated from Northern Ireland in the 1950s. My father served as a Presbyterian minister in a village in Ireland and was excited to join a more open-minded church in Canada. My mother did not want to leave Ireland and her large family. My father's profession meant that my parents and brothers arrived in Brechin, Ontario, to a furnished manse and a respected place in the community.

My Protestant Northern Irish background situated me in the mainstream of the communities I grew up in. In the 1950s and 1960s, the 12th of July Orange Parade was still a major cultural event in many parts of Ontario. Even though my parents had recently arrived in Canada, I was never asked, Where are you from?

"I was good at standing still"—it's a line in parentheses, an aside, in this chapter's opening poem. Comportment, posture, and reserve were important in my family. I watched my mother, other women, and girls for clues as to how to move, how to be, what to say, and what to think. My father was seen as the one who "knew" in our home; my mother's silence and constant support for my father seeped into my bones. Living in the manse, we attended church because we had to. I notice a struggle to include my girl's body in this section, in spite of its presence in the words of the title. An absent body.

My first poetry collection, *A Hat to Stop a Train,* is an examination of my mother's life and my relationship with her (Stewart 2003). I approached my mother through memories of her stories of childhood, her clothes and hats, her illnesses and role as a minister's wife. I lingered with memories, attempting to better know my mother and myself.

When I look back at *A Hat to Stop a Train,* I find my mother's often frail body as well as glimpses of my childhood body.

Service

Mum touches my knee to make me stop swinging my feet beneath
the pew. Her shiny, black purse sits between us. Mum touches my
hand when I fidget and shuffle. She looks at me when I bang the
pew in front by mistake.

She used to bring me a little notebook to draw and write in. Now
I read the bulletin, the little offering envelopes, the welcome card
for visitors, *Alpha* and *Omega* above the organ pipes. I use the
red ribbon attached to the hymnbook to mark the first hymn and
envelopes for the others. I count the men and the women in the
choir, the bald heads, the glasses. When the choir stands to sing, I
watch the orange smudge of lipstick on Mrs. Thrasher's front teeth.

Then we get to stand up and sing. Taking a deep breath, I belt out
the hymn. Mum's tone deaf. When she went to piano lessons, her
teacher taught her how to cover butter boxes instead. Mum mouths
the words. Sometimes, I hear a small thin voice coming from her.
Mum likes to hear me sing. She says it drowns out her mistakes.
(Stewart 2003, 53)

This poem, written around 1999, was part of my early inquiry into the role
of the church in our family, which I continue to this day. My writing practice
is entwined with efforts to understand a disquieted childhood, shaped by
my mother's ill health, my brother's mental health issues, and the church's
notions of God looming over being sexualized as a child. I try to illuminate
my journey to re-engage bodymind and investigate how trauma shapes lives
and learning. Good writing stands at the edges of personal and social transformation, as an invitation. Writers debate about the ways in which writing
may or may not be healing; I believe some art to be profoundly healing for
the artist and, potentially, for the audience/reader. Writing within the form
of a poem contains its own pleasure and ways to work with difficult material.
By healing, I mean something different from seeking individual happiness;
similarly, in writing poetry, my desire is not to escape into the joy of lyric.

As a child, I was trained to use words in tactful, solicitous ways, upholding the sanctity of family and church, institutions that create and re-create

dynamics of authority in multiple ways. Finding new ways to use words is slow and often painful. I have been writing in journals from the age of ten, starting with a three-month visit to Ireland; through my teen years, I wrote to pour out feelings that had few other venues, to feel less alone, and to hold onto threads of self. Writing sometimes felt secretive and I feared my journal would be read.

When I was discussing this chapter with poet Julie Berry, she asked, "Do you remember a time when you didn't feel ashamed of your body?" (Berry, pers. comm., 29 October 2012). I struggle to remember my childhood body and realize that my poetry is an attempt to write my way back to a more embodied sense of self.

The manse was also a privileged and book-filled place to grow up. My family background placed me comfortably in the centre of school discussions about where parents were from and what they did. There were no secrets there. The privilege of being part of dominant culture was invisible to me.

Being a good girl at home and church prepared me to be the same at school, quiet and obedient. What could be said in the halls of the church and the manse? *Be careful what you say. If you say the wrong thing in the wrong place, it may come back to haunt you.* That which is unspoken or unexpressed festers and corrodes.

Poetry as Embodied Learning

In *Knowing Her Place*, poet and qualitative researcher Lorri Neilsen Glenn (1998, 264) describes research as "the attuned mind/body working purposefully to explore, to listen, to support, to transgress, to gather with care, to create, to disrupt, and to offer back, to contribute, sometimes all at once."

My poetic practice is shaped by growing up in the church and is entwined with the process of creating a more embodied self. Poetry, like a church service, sits at the nexus of oral and written language, and my love of poetry is interwoven with reverence for and suspicion of the written word. But poetry needs to be spoken and heard, embodied. It works with oral language's visceral quality. Its performative nature includes attention to cadence, rhythm, sound, voice, and breath. In *Threading Light: Explorations in Loss and Poetry,* Lorri Neilsen Glenn (2008, 63) writes, "Only a fingertip's sensitivity to touch can match the singular sound of a human voice. When I hear a poet speak her words, the poem is transformed."

Poetry also works with the space on the page, making use of form and the space around and between words and lines. Playing with the arrangement of words on the page is a way to work with body, breath, the sense of delight in pattern, and aesthetic pleasure. Rhythm and the aesthetics of the page can be a way to transform painful knowing and partial knowing. Poetry's ability to work with visceral experience and the unconscious *through* language deepens my embodied inquiry.

Walking to the Body's Rhythm

Through practices of walking and yoga, I seek greater internal and external attunement, reclaiming a sense of body as *knowing,* unlearning limiting lessons of church, family, and school. Maureen Scott Harris (2012, 16), in "Epistemology: The World Speaks," writes,

> Back up, begin again. There may be snow,
> but walking is necessary—my longing to move
> through weather as my shoulders unclench
> beneath the visible sky. Walking may empty
> the mind's geometry, unhook its angles
> from their linked confusion, that oxymoronic
> insistence on contained space.

Harris's words, especially "Walking may empty / the mind's geometry, unhook its angles / from their linked confusion," help me think about how my own walking practice is tied to thinking and writing. I am fortunate to live a few blocks from Toronto's High Park. When we moved to Toronto in 1989, we lived in an apartment with a view of the park. A woman had recently been raped in the park, and I did not go there on my own. A few months later, in December 1989, fourteen women were murdered in what became known as the Montreal Massacre. What happens in the body when we hear of local danger and attacks against women? I recall my twenty-nine-year-old self, cycling to my literacy work in Parkdale.

A few years later, when my daughters were born, I began to go to the park with other mothers, our babies in strollers. I came to love the up and down and curves of the roads and paths and the chance to talk with other parents as our children played in the playground. We needed a place to go, and how lucky to have such a park. Later, writing brought me to the park: when I took a year off from adult literacy to work on my writing, I walked in the park most days, watching the goldenrods turn from yellow to white. I was completing *A Hat to Stop a Train* and beginning to think of my next book, wanting some of it to be about High Park, as a physical location and a psychic space.

How are we embodied in certain landscapes and certain buildings, living in relationship to our surroundings? My family moved frequently when I was a child because United Church ministers are expected to stay for not more than about six years with one congregation. The Irish landscapes that shaped my parents were Glen Farm, County Down, where my mother grew up, and Tandragee, County Armagh, where my father grew up. These were the landscapes of my parents' imaginations, and of mine, too. Now, I walk to try to come to *know* a place.

Memories of certain buildings fill me with emptiness and fear: St John's United Church and our home, the manse. I lost my sense of being embodied early in life; experience flattened. Fear. Inhale, exhale. My glasses streaked with salt—what do I see?

How do I inhabit my body when writing an academic chapter? Shoulders up, brow furled. Roll out the yoga mat. This discipline is a different kind of learning.

What Poetry Can Approach

Poetry can help us approach topics that are not safe. Poet Julie Berry (1995, 15) writes about sexual abuse in her long poem, "quiet as walls," the second poem in her collection *worn thresholds*. "quiet as walls" contains six short poems: "sisters going nowhere in particular," "family waking," "queen of shovel," "quiet as walls," "hail storm," and "arrangement." Here I quote the title piece, "quiet as walls," to give you a sense of how Berry's fragmented language conveys trauma:

> **quiet as walls**
>
> of beds full
> and beer too
> many covers
> big sister wakes up

he her cool
fingers he breathing
under hot
under covers

& face
shut & burning red
window up there
door over there

o not
o not
he makes
he her

when she tells
blank mother father
stare the bricks everything
quiet as walls

Berry's simple language captures a child's world. The choppy syntax echoes the dislodgement of experience, conveying a sense of shock and trauma. Poetry can express such experience in powerful ways.

Ronna Bloom, the University of Toronto's Poet in Community and also a therapist, describes what poetry writing can do for university students: "The aim is to make room for people to feel on paper and in the world, to make room for the emotional culture to breathe and shift by including the presence of poetry, to normalize the poetic response and see it as a simple, human one" (Bloom 2012, 424). This approach to poetry invites embodiment, opening space for multilayered learning and supporting possibilities for personal and social transformation.

How Does Poetry Relate to Decolonization?

Poetry can be a means of social intervention, a means of witnessing, a response to colonization and oppression, and possibly a tool for decolonization. Audre Lorde's (1984) famous essay "Poetry Is Not a Luxury" is a call to embrace the vitality and social potential of poetry. Poetry is a tool for social change in such strong political work as that of Dorothy Allison (1983, 1991, 1995), Dionne Brand (1983, 1997, 1998, 2002, 2010), Di Brandt (1995, 2003), Chrystos (1988, 1991, 1993, 1995a, 1995b), Marlene NourbeSe Philip (1993, 1991, 2008), Sina Queyras (2009), and Adrienne Rich (1984, 1986, 1991), to name just a few.[3] People of colour, gay, lesbian, bisexual, two-spirited, trans and gender variant people, disabled people, women, and other socially disadvantaged people have published poetry in increasing numbers over recent decades, their work a resistance to dominant discourses that ignored their stories or represented them in stereotypical and derogatory ways, sometimes portraying them as less than human. In some ways, the publishing done in adult literacy was part of this movement to circulate the stories of working-class and poor people, to bring stories by people with limited literacy skills into print to be read by themselves, their peers, and hopefully a wider audience.[4] As Neilsen Glenn (2011, 87) says, "The philosopher Martha Nussbaum argues that works of arts are not only a primary means for an individual to express her humanity through catharsis, as Aristotle claimed, but, because of the attunement to others and to the world that creation invites, the process can sow the seeds of social justice."

I do not want to romanticize poetry or see it as a cure for an ill society. Adrienne Rich (2007, 21) writes, "I hope never to idealize poetry—it has suffered enough from that. Poetry is not a healing lotion, an emotional massage, a kind of linguistic aromatherapy. Neither is it a blueprint, not an instruction manual, not a billboard. There is no universal Poetry anyway, only poetries and poetics and the streaming, intertwining histories to which they belong."

Rich helps me to notice how I tend to speak of poetry as a universal and to see it as a plural endeavour coming from "streaming, intertwining histories." For one thing, poetry has a multitude of forms and traditions,

---

3 These are a few of the many Canadian and American poets whose work addresses issues of multiple forms of oppression. Traditions of dub poetry and spoken word take up oppression directly; see, for example, the work of Toronto dub poet Lillian Allen (2012).

4 See Scott and Friday-Cockburn, eds. (1992) for an analysis of the history, complexities, and ethical issues surrounding literacy student writing and publishing in Toronto.

including lyric, narrative, language, experimental, dub, and spoken word. Some poetry, like other forms of literature, perpetuates stereotypes and dominant discourses. Some has the potential for helping us see things afresh and for social intervention. Most poetry exists outside of the economic system that turns art into a commodity. Readers do not consume poems; they take them in, in different ways, often lingering with them, drawn into a state of contemplation.

In Dorothy Allison's (1995) memoir *Two or Three Things I Know for Sure,* she uses two refrains: "Let me tell you a story" and "Two or three things I know for sure, and one of them is . . ." This powerful book about being working class, lesbian, and a survivor of sexual abuse was written originally for performance, changed for each production, and revised substantially for publication. Allison's stories of family, lovers, conversations with sisters, abuse, and violence are punctuated with her reflections on the ways stories and storytelling work. Allison writes, "Two or three things I know, two or three things I know for sure, and one of them is that to go on living I have to tell stories, that stories are one sure way I know to touch the heart and change the world" (72). I love the colloquial, plain-spoken quality of the phrase "two or three things I know" and the poetic repetition "two or three things I know for sure." Allison uses this phrase again and again in an understated, lyrical act of knowledge making.

The Menominee poet Chrystos speaks powerfully about lesbian desire and relationships in their five collections, as well as about colonization, racism, and abuse. Like Audre Lorde and Lee Maracle, Allison and Chrystos take up the erotic as a way to talk about embodiment as sentient and social. They write from lesbian, bisexual, and two-spirited lived experience—in a sense, speaking/writing the body. I might have thought of the act of writing these books as a kind of decolonizing the body and the self, but I am bearing in mind Tuck and Yang's (2012) caution about metaphorizing decolonization. Chrystos also speak of metaphor, particularly in their poem "Savage Eloquence," from *Not Vanishing,* where they write, "No metaphors / Mountains ARE our mothers Stars our dead." Ten lines later, they write, "Vanishing is no metaphor" (Chrystos 1988, 40).

But what does poetry specifically have to do with decolonization? In a short essay, "Oka Peace Camp—September 9, 1990," at the beginning of *Bobbie Lee: Indian Rebel,* Lee Maracle (1990, 57) writes, "The language is battered: battered in the interest of sanctioning the scarring of the land in the interest of profit. . . . For us language is sacred. Words represent the accumulated knowledge, the progression of thought of any people." Maracle's assertion about the sacredness of language and her connecting of language as "battered" with the "scarring of the land" speaks to this inquiry into decolonization, pedagogy, and embodiment.

Poet Marilyn Dumont's words make me slow down and listen. She begins her poem "Sky Berry and Water Berry" (Dumont 2013) with delicacy and lushness:

> her sisters, the flowers
> her brothers, the berries
> emerge from her beadwork
> chokecherry red, goldenrod yellow, and juniper berry brown
> sky berry and water berry
> swell from her fingertips
> sprout runners and cleave
> to stems near the scent
> of warm saskatoons
> and sour gooseberries
> petal, berry, stem, and leaf
> sewn down now in seed bead lines
> flourish bright from her hands
> through her fingers stretch fields of strawberries
> their starched white petals
> raised heads above layers of green leaf

Dumont weaves together images of hands working on beadwork with land, sky, water, family relations, and the sensory nature of berries and petals in a kind of praise-song.

Marlene NourbeSe Philip's *Zong!*

Some poetry engages directly with the process of colonization, such as the collection *Zong!* by Toronto author Marlene NourbeSe Philip (2008). Born in Tobago, Philip is trained as a lawyer and is well known for her 1993 poetry collection *She Tries Her Tongue, Her Silence Softly Breaks.* In *Zong!* Philip tells a "story that must be told; that can only be told by not telling" (194). In 1781, the captain of the slave ship *Zong* ordered 150 Africans to be thrown overboard so that the ship owners could collect insurance money for lost "cargo." Philip limits herself to the words of the legal decision involving the ship's owners and the insurance company, using the only record of the ship and the people on board, to write poetry that pulls language apart and wrestles with the meaning-making project that is language itself.

In "Notanda," the essay that accompanies the poetry, Philip writes that she uses the text of the legal decision "to lock myself into this particular and peculiar discursive landscape" (191). Using this limited "word store" raises issues of how "language appears to be a given—we believe we have the freedom to choose any words we want to work with from the universe of words, but so much of what we work with is a given" (191–92). Philip describes how "law and poetry both share an inexorable concern with language—the 'right' use of the 'right' words, phrases, or even marks of punctuation; precision of expression is the goal shared by both" (191). Philip's work looks more like language poetry than lyric: she makes use of the space on the page and breaks up words. The first section, "Os," begins with "Zong! #1" (3):

```
w   w   w       w       a   wa


    w       a       w a       t


er          wa              s
```

Some poems are a mixture of words and sounds sprinkled across the page. "Tearing" and "cutting" the language (193–94), Philip says,

> I fight the desire to impose meaning on the words—it is so instinctive, this need to impose meaning: this is the generating impulse of, and towards, language, isn't it—to make and, therefore, to communicate, meaning? How did they—the Africans on board the *Zong*—make meaning of what was happening to them? What meaning did they make of it and how did they make it mean? (194)

In some poems, Philip uses unusual syntax and spacing to wrestle with meaninglessness. "Zong! #19" (33–34), for example, begins drowned the law

        their thirst &

        the evidence

        obliged the frenzy

in themselves

in the sea

        ground the justify

        in the necessity of

when

who &

which

The poem ends with the words

   against the rest in preservation

        the save in residue

   negroes exist

        for the throwing

Philip examines her writing process, including a trip to the Liverpool docks, where slave ships left for the Caribbean. Poetry can work as witness and testimony, often witnessing an individual life and a specific incident. Philip takes on a major colonial practice, the transport of enslaved Africans, and their genocide.

Language comes up against itself in the endeavour to speak about atrocity. Philip writes,

I deeply distrust this tool I work with—language. It is a distrust rooted in certain historical events that are all of a piece with the events that took place on the *Zong*. The language in which those events took place promulgated the non-being of African peoples, and I distrust its order, which hides disorder; its logic hiding the illogic and its rationality, which is simultaneously irrational. (197)

Philip takes language to its limits, wrestling with words in a way I would describe as embodied. Philip brings us close to an unfathomable experience and, in her essay, repeats "there is no telling this story" like a kind of mantra. She works with deeply traumatic material, approaching this material as a black woman born in Tobago and writing of her ancestors' lives and deaths. She describes her process as a kind of quest that involves pilgrimages to Africa and Liverpool, lighting candles, and other rituals of writing. Her public readings of *Zong!* sometimes feel ceremonial or ritualistic.[5] She begins with the pouring of libations to the ancestors.

Zong! is a witnessing of colonization's horrific abuse of authority and power. Philip's poetry and her accompanying poetic essay give her a way to use language to reflect on the complicity of the English language and the structures of thought that it supports in justifying genocide. Philip allows the pain she writes about to shape her language and writing practice. Dwelling with the materiality of colonization in this way is important. I am interested in how Philip reshapes language, moulding something new, a different kind of vessel that is uniquely shaped for the material at hand.

Where and How to Walk?

I walk from a twelve-storey university tower across Bloor Street down through the Queen Alexandra Gate into Philosopher's Walk. I need to move, get away from the overheated windowless rooms and windows that don't open. I am thinking about a writing workshop I will lead for graduate students struggling with thesis writing; I am struggling to write this piece and want the walking to help me think. I want my relationship to the land to

---

5 NourbeSe Philip's reading from *Zong!* at The Limbo-o: A Night of Poetry at Trane Studio, 16 July 2012, had a ceremonial tone to it. She invited the audience to read with her, not in unison, but voices starting and stopping at various times, creating a cacophony of sounds.

be more than that of a tourist. I am a settler here, unsettled, asking, What kind of settler do I want to be? I want something more than that walking serves my thinking. I plan to talk with the thesis-writing students about how walking and writing can work together, walking and feeling more whole, feeling that they have something to say. Near the university, we can walk just north to Taddle Creek Park, named for one of the many streams under Toronto, or we can walk to Queen's Park, where I head now.

I pause before an oval University of Toronto sign, the U of T crest and name at the top:

> Well before European settlers arrived, the natural ravine now known as Philosopher's Walk was a likely gathering place for Anishinaabe people (Mississauga Ojibway). During the spring, the stream that ran through this site would have been teeming with wildlife and native fishermen would have lined the banks with gill nets and fish weirs to partake of this bounty. For them, the stream would have been a sacred site—a place of powerful and audible spirits.

This sign disturbs me—"the stream would have been a sacred site" and "for them." The sign assumes that its readers are all settlers. It assumes that *at one time* it would have been sacred for Anishinaabe people, but what is it now for Anishinaabe or other First Nations people? The sign seems to assume that these peoples are gone.

I walk on along a winding path, which was once Taddle Creek. I come to Queen's Park to be near the trees. A huge statue of King Edward VII on horseback towers over the centre of the park. A plaque by the Toronto Historical Board tells me that the park was opened in 1860 by the Prince of Wales, later King Edward VII, and "named in honour of his mother Queen Victoria." I read another plaque about the same statue:

> Originally standing in Edward Park, Delhi, India, this statue was erected on the present site through the generous subscriptions of the citizens of this area.
>
> William Dennison, Mayor
May 24, 1969

Colonialism is everywhere, but these vestiges are particularly blatant. It seems that India, no longer a colony, did not want this statue of a British king and that Canada, still a colony, did want it.

Gathering Threads of Inquiry

How can poetic inquiry bring the body's knowing to discussions of pedagogy and decolonization? Can it help us stretch beyond our socially constructed identities, habits of thinking, and ways of approaching teaching and learning? Perhaps poetic attention can help us work with the discomfort and shame entwined with being objectified by others and noticing when we have participated in objectification. It may help us use language in ways that are less grasping, that unsettle some of our dichotomies and desire for certainty.

In this chapter, I have explored how the fragmentary, imagistic nature of poetry allows us to work with material beyond the rational—with the unconscious, the partiality of memory, and the untellable. Poetry attempts to take language *to* and *beyond* its usual limitations. In this way, the process of writing poetry can work with more fluid thinking-feeling states and embrace embodied forms of learning and being.

I began this chapter with the poem "November 11th," which points to state-prescribed commemorative practices. In that poem, public space such as a city park is pedagogical space, attempting to teach us that "courage is a man on horseback." The friend in that poem who reflects on her teaching is Julie Berry, whose poem "quiet as walls" helps me speak about the way in which poetry can approach trauma and dis/embodiment. In the poem, she is a teacher who reveals her vulnerability in an embodied way in the classroom.

This chapter begins to inquire into what poetry has to do with decolonization. It grapples with the metaphorical and pedagogical nature of language in the face of the call not to use *decolonization* as a metaphor. Philip's *Zong!* commemorates what cannot be told of people being forcibly taken from their homelands into slavery and thrown overboard in the effort to redeem money for so-called lost cargo. The spaces between her words and fragments of words speak to what cannot be uttered but is embodied. Her writing is at once about the mechanisms of colonization and about reckoning with how language, loss, and land are entwined. I begin to ask about the relationship of language to embodied and disembodied experiences of land, particularly the land we live on and our relationship to it—in my case, as settler.

Holding this broad sense of decolonization, I ask what the word means in terms of embodied learning and the knowledge of body, mind, emotions, and spirit. How do we teach in a way that opens space for students to understand their dis/embodied experience of land? Digging into our own reflexivity, discomfort, shame, positionality, and multiple kinds of knowing is a place to start. Using words in different ways can help us gather more aspects of our embodied selves. We confront words on plaques and monuments and wrestle with how words are used in poems and classrooms. What have we been taught to remember and to know? How does this relate to land, as we, individually and collectively, seek an embodied sense of self?

References

Ahmed, Sara. 2004. *The Cultural Politics of Emotion*. New York and London: Routledge.

Allen, Lillian. 2012. "What is Dub Poetry?" *Lillian Allen: Video.* http://www.lillianallen.ca/video.

Allison, Dorothy. 1983. *The Women Who Hate Me*. Brooklyn, NY: Longhaul Press.

———. 1991. *The Women Who Hate Me: Poetry 1980–1990*. Ann Arbor, MI: Firebrand Books.

———. 1995. *Two or Three Things I Know for Sure*. London: Dutton.

Anzaldúa, Gloria. 1997. "La Conciencia de la Mestiza: Towards a New Consciousness." In *Chicana Feminist Thought: The Basic Historical Writings*, edited by Alma M. García, 270–74. New York and London: Routledge.

Auerbach, Elsa. 1996. "Toward a Social-Contextual Approach to Family Literacy." *Harvard Educational Review* 59(2): 165–81.

Bartky, Sandra Lee. 1990. *Femininity and Domination: Studies in the Phenomenology of Oppression*. New York and London: Routledge.

Batacharya, Janet Sheila. 2010. "Life in a Body: Counter Hegemonic Understandings of Violence, Oppression, Healing, and Embodiment Among Young South Asian Women." PhD diss., Ontario Institute for Studies in Education, University of Toronto.

Berry, Julie. 1995. *Worn Thresholds*. London, ON: Brick Books.

Bloom, Ronna. 2012. "To Feel on Paper (or Fragments, Blessings, Poems)." In Thomas, Cole, and Stewart, *Art of Poetic Inquiry*, 411–26.

Brand, Dionne. 1983. *Winter Epigrams and Epigrams to Ernesto Cardenal in Defence of Claudia*. Toronto: Williams-Wallace International.

———. 1997. *Land to Light On*. Toronto: McClelland and Stewart.

———. 1998. *No Language Is Neutral*. Toronto: McClelland and Stewart.

———. 2002. *Thirsty*. Toronto: McClelland and Stewart.

———. 2010. *Ossuaries*. Toronto: McClelland and Stewart.

Brandt, Di. 1995. *Jerusalem, Beloved*. Winnipeg: Turnstone Press.

———. 2003. *Now You Care*. Toronto: Coach House Books.

Butler-Kisber, Lynn. 2010. "Poetic Inquiry." In *Qualitative Inquiry: Thematic, Narrative, and Arts-Informed Perspectives*, 82–101. London: Sage.

Caspe, Margaret. 2003. "Family Literacy: A Review of Programs and Critical Perspectives." Harvard Family Research Project. http://www.hfrp.org/publications-resources/browse-our-publications/family-literacy-a-review-of-programs-and-critical-perspectives.

Chrystos. 1988. *Not Vanishing*. Vancouver: Press Gang.

———. 1991. *Dream On*. Vancouver: Press Gang.

———. 1993. *In Her I Am*. Vancouver: Press Gang.

———. 1995a. *Fire Power*. Vancouver: Press Gang.

———. 1995b. *Fugitive Colors*. Cleveland: Cleveland State University Poetry Center.

Dumont, Marilyn. 2015. *The Pemmican Eaters: Poems*. Toronto: ECW Press.

Finley, Sandra. 2008. "Arts-Based Research." In Knowles and Cole, *Handbook of the Arts in Qualitative Research*, 71–81.

Galvin, Kate, and Les Todres. 2012. "Caring for the Experience of Stroke Recovery: Embodied Interpretations of Others' Worlds." In Thomas, Cole, and Stewart, *Art of Poetic Inquiry*, 178–86.

Gillan, Maria Mazziotti. 2010. "Betrayals." *What We Pass On: Collected Poems, 1980–2009*. Toronto: Guernica.

Gold, Karen. 2012. "Poetic Pedagogy: A Reflection on Narrative in Social Work Practice and Education." *Social Work Education* 31(6): 756–63.

Guiney Yallop, John J. 2010. *Of Place and Memory: A Poetic Journey*. Big Tancock Island, NS: Backalong Books.

Harris, Maureen Scott. 2004. *Drowning Lessons*. Toronto: Pedlar Press.

———. 2012. *Slow Curve Out*. Toronto: Pedlar Press.

Herman, Judith Lewis. 1992. *Trauma and Recovery: The Aftermath of Violence—from Domestic Abuse to Political Terror*. New York: Basic Books.

———. 2007. "Shattered Shame States and Their Repair." John Bowlby Memorial Lecture, 10 March. http://www.challiance.org/Resource.ashx?sn=VOVShattered2oShameJHerman.

Hornstein, Shayna. 2008. "Navigating Practitioner Discomfort: Reflections on Power and Self-Care." In Evelyn Battell, Shayna Hornstein, Jenny Horsman, Christianna Jones, Judy Murphy, Ningwakwe / E. Priscilla George, Kate

Nonesuch et al., *Moving Research About Addressing the Impacts of Violence on Learning into Practice*, 207–44.

Horsman, Jenny. 1999. *Too Scared to Learn*. Toronto: McGilligan Press.

Knowles, J. Gary, and Ardra L. Cole, eds. 2008. *Handbook of the Arts in Qualitative Research: Perspectives, Methodologies, Examples, and Issues*. London: Sage.

Lorde, Audre. 1984. *Sister Outsider: Essays and Speeches by Audre Lorde*. Freedom, CA: Crossing Press.

Maracle, Lee. 1990. *Bobbi Lee: Indian Rebel*. Toronto: Women's Press.

Miller, Mev, and Kathleen P. King, eds. 2011. *Our Stories, Ourselves: The EmBODYment of Women's Learning in Literacy*. Charlotte, NC: Information Age.

Murphy, Judy. 2008. "The Body's Song: Can You Listen in the Stillness?" In Evelyn Battell, Shayna Hornstein, Jenny Horsman, Christianna Jones, Judy Murphy, Ningwakwe / E. Priscilla George, Kate Nonesuch et al., *Moving Research About Addressing the Impacts of Violence on Learning into Practice*, 157–84.

Neilsen [Glenn], Lorri. 1998. *Knowing Her Place: Research Literacies and Feminist Occasions*. Great Tancook Island, NS: Backlong Books.

———. 2008. "Lyric Inquiry." In Knowles and Cole, *Handbook of the Arts in Qualitative Research*, 93–102.

———. 2011. *Threading Light: Explorations in Loss and Poetry*. Regina: Hagios Press.

Ng, Roxana. 2011. "Decolonizing Teaching and Learning Through Embodied Learning: Toward an Integrated Approach." In *Valences of Interdisciplinarity: Theory, Practice, Pedagogy*, edited by Raphael Foshay, 343–65. Edmonton: Athabasca University Press.

Ngũgĩ wa Thiong'o. 1986. *Decolonising the Mind: The Politics of Language in African Literature*. Nairobi: East African Educational.

Palmer, Parker J. 2004. *A Hidden Wholeness: The Journey Toward an Undivided Life*. San Francisco, CA: John Wiley.

Philip, Marlene NourbeSe. 1991. *Looking for Livingstone: An Odyssey of Silence*. Toronto: Mercury Press.

———. 1993. *She Tries Her Tongue, Her Silence Softly Breaks*. Charlottetown, PEI: Ragweed Press. Originally published Havana, Cuba: Casa de las Américas, 1988.

———. 2008. *Zong!* Middletown, CT: Wesleyan University Press.

Prendergast, Monica, Carl Leggo, and Pauline Sameshima, eds. 2009a. *Poetic Inquiry: Vibrant Voices in the Social Sciences*. Rotterdam, Netherlands: Sense.

———, eds. 2009b. Special Issue: "Poetic Inquiry." *Educational Insights* 13(3). http://www.ccfi.educ.ubc.ca/publication/insights/v13n03/toc.html.

Queyras, Sina. 2009. *Expressway*. Toronto: Coach House Books.

Rich, Adrienne. 1984. *The Fact of a Doorframe: Poems Selected and New, 1950–1984*. New York: W. W. Norton.

———. 1986. *Your Native Land, Your Life*. New York: W. W. Norton.

———. 1991. *An Atlas of the Difficult World: Poems, 1988–1991*. New York: W. W. Norton.

———. 2007. *Poetry and Commitment*. New York: W. W. Norton.

Scott, Jude, and Nancy Friday-Cockburn, eds. 1992. *As Our History Unfolds: Publishing Learner Writing in Metro Toronto*. Toronto, ON: Metro Toronto Movement for Literacy.

Stewart, Sheila. 2003. *A Hat to Stop a Train*. Toronto: Wolsak and Wynn.

———. 2008a. "Stories That Breathe: Opening Windows and Doors on Learning and Violence." In Evelyn Battell, Shayna Hornstein, Jenny Horsman, Christianna Jones, Judy Murphy, Ningwakwe / E. Priscilla George, Kate Nonesuch et al., *Moving Research About Addressing the Impacts of Violence on Learning into Practice*, 83–108.

———. 2008b. "Laughter Breaking Out of Brackets: A Reflective Practitioner Research Project about Story and Diversity." *Literacies: Researching Practice, Practicing Research* 9: 17–20.

———. 2009. "How I Want to Keep Saying It." *Educational Insights* 13(3). http://einsights.ogpr.educ.ubc.ca/v13n03/articles/stewart/index.html.

———. 2012. *The Shape of a Throat*. Winnipeg: Signature Editions.

Thomas, Suzanne, Ardra L. Cole, and Sheila Stewart, eds. 2012. *The Art of Poetic Inquiry*. Arts-Informed Inquiry Series, vol. 5. Big Tancock Island, NS: Backalong Books.

Tuck, Eve, and K. Wayne Yang. 2012. "Decolonization Is Not a Metaphor." *Decolonization: Indigeneity, Education, and Society* 1(1): 1–40.

11   Patient Stories

Renarrating Illness and Valuing the Rejected Body

Wendy Peters

When we were at the bar together, you asked me, "What is embodied knowledge anyway?" I quickly shrugged my shoulders, shook my head, and replied, "I don't know. It's a lot of things." If you had asked me, "What is semiotics?" I would have said, "It is the science of signs." To the question of what embodied knowledge is, I cannot respond so easily. I want to understand embodiment better and I have a growing sense of why embodied knowledge is so difficult to comprehend within Western-colonial archives of knowledge. To acknowledge the glimmers of understanding that I have found, I offer a reflection on the past. To do so, I return to the only journal that I have ever kept in my adult life—one that documents the period between learning that I had a pituitary tumour in early 1997 up until my postsurgery recovery much later that year.

To begin, I situate my illness journal and this chapter as examples of embodied knowledge. I trace the profound and mundane effects that these benign cells had, and still have, on my writing, knowledge, and life. I return to my illness narrative, examining how Western-colonial constructions of the body—previously beyond question in my mind—informed my understanding, experience, and narration of illness. I employ Susan Wendell's (1996) conceptualizations of "bodily normalcy" and the "rejected body" in order to interrogate how these normative discourses and their attendant identities—as related to health and illness—have affective, social, and material consequences. Specifically, I foreground how the expectation of perpetual good health operates in relation to identity, friendship, social interactions, and social relations within a neoliberal political economy. In revealing my complicity and internalized dominance in relation to the ideal of bodily normalcy, I elucidate some of the ways in which privileged subjectivities operate, interact with each other, and are bound together with rejected bodies. As my journal reveals, my identity is implicitly constituted within and through the marginalization of those who are rejected and devalued in relation to bodily normalcy, neoliberalism, and Western medicine.

This work was inspired by a graduate-level seminar titled "Embodied Learning and Qi Gong," created and taught by Roxana Ng, which I had the pleasure of taking in 2001. Through assigned readings on Western and Traditional Chinese Medicine and through the practice of qigong, Ng created a classroom encounter that challenged colonial hierarchical thinking, specifically in relation to embodiment, mindfulness, health, and illness. In addition to teaching breathing techniques, focused intention, and the internally focused martial art of qigong, she offered tools that enabled and urged students "to be open to critical analysis of their own social location and what these obscure from their view, what remains unarticulated in their language, and what has been absent from their thoughts" (Nakata et al. 2012, 135). Ng's course offered "an entry point for understanding the presence of other ways of viewing the world and one's position in it" (132), a place where "students can be led to develop awareness of the limits of various positions, the persistent pervasiveness of 'all-knowing,' 'taken-for-granted' Western frames" (133). Ng urged her students toward "thinking about thinking" (133) and gaining "knowledge about knowledge" (126). She also challenged Western norms of classroom space and university content as students actively moved about the room, using our bodies and focusing on our breath. In keeping with Ng's pedagogical aims, this chapter, which is based on a paper I wrote for the seminar, demonstrates my attempts to recognize and comprehend the positioning effects of Western knowledge and claims to know, as well as the social relations that ground these discourses in bodies and everyday lives.

While drawing examples from my own journal makes such evidence inherently anecdotal, I make every effort to contextualize the excerpts and highlight how my beliefs, experiences, and emotional responses are not solely the result of individual consciousness or intention but are formed within Western discourses in popular circulation. As Rubén Gaztambide-Fernández (2012, 42) writes, "The characteristics of this particular moment are neither spontaneous nor natural. . . . White supremacy and hetero-patriarchal order violently enforce colonial modes of human relationality, fabricating subject positions through intersecting and interlocking discursive regimes of gender, race, class, sexuality, and ability, among others." For the purposes of this chapter, I focus specifically on privileged subject positions and social relations produced within dominant Western discourses of health and illness. It is my hope that the following examples will begin to answer the question that I answered so poorly when we spoke at the bar that night.

Illness Life-Writing: Context, Content, and Embodied Learning

In 1997, I was diagnosed with a tumour on my pituitary gland. (You don't know this about me.) I was sick for at least two years before my surgery; I stopped menstruating, my breasts lactated, and I experienced severe headaches. After my surgery to remove the tumour, I began writing about my experience of becoming ill. I felt powerfully compelled to document my experience for myself and for others. I was afraid that I would forget this experience that had changed my life. Nancy Mairs (1997, x–xi) observes that illness and disability life-writers tend to write the book that they themselves would most like to read, a book that would inform them about this uncharted terrain and allow them to guide and support an imagined reader in similar distress during this isolating and frightening time. Wilfrid Sheed, for example, "recounts his surviving polio, addiction-depression, and cancer of the tongue" in his 1995 memoir, *In Love with Daylight* (quoted in Mairs 1997, x):

> I would have sold my soul cheerfully (if I could have done anything cheerfully) just to hear from someone else who had passed this way and could tell me what was actually happening to me and what to expect next. But among all the thousands of inspirational and pseudoscientific words I could find . . . not one came close either to describing what I was going through, or suggesting anything useful to do about it. . . . So I've had to write it myself, scene for scene—all the things I would like to have read back then.

As Thomas Couser (1997, 15) notes, "Generally, illness narratives reflect mixed motives: an urge for self-exploration and a desire to serve those with the same condition." My desire to write my own illness narrative was strongly tied to each of these reasons: to chart the territory for others in similar situations, to understand and explore what happened to me, and to remember the experiences for myself.

I wrote in my journal about being given the diagnosis of having a pituitary tumour (casually, over the phone, while at work), going through CT scans (with their mysterious and disconcerting warning that "you may feel a powerful urge to void during the test"), exhaustive blood tests (and getting rear-ended en route back to work with one arm severely emaciated following the onerous triple bolus test), and then waiting seven months for surgery. I wrote about my anxieties, relationships with friends and family, the experience of learning that I would probably not be able to have children, and reconceptualizing my body from a healthy one that required (seemingly) no thought on my part to a sick body that I hardly knew how to relate to. I wrote about the support that I received from my partner, the difficulties of getting time off from my job and still maintaining some privacy around my illness, the many interactions with doctors, the medical tests, and the science behind my illness. I wrote a veritable novel about my experience, and it is a piece of writing that I hold very dearly. My story of illness seemed to pour onto the pages, where the words are still almost too hot, bloody, and salty to read. During my postsurgery recovery, I became obsessed with writing this story and I remember sitting at my desk throughout the night, writing and crying.

A concealed mind-body connection underpins my illness journal: I wrote ecstatically, fuelled by daily doses of the steroid prednisone. This drug, ingested and digested by my body, produced the predicted side effects of insomnia and euphoria. The steroid inspired what felt like boundless creativity, and I wrote by hand for hours and hours, even as I could barely walk from one end of my small apartment block to the other. The content of the journal is also implicitly embodied, since "rogue" pituitary cells produced these thoughts, words, and reflections. In fact, abnormal cell division led not only to these very specific insights but also to broader changes that I made in my life. While illness is typically and, at times, understandably regarded as an inherently negative event, my tumour awoke in me (at least temporarily) the ability to perceive a wider range of options for my life. As Yuk-Lin Renita Wong notes in her contribution to this collection, the mind shifts perpetually between past, present, and future, but the body is always in the present. It is not surprising, then, that being diagnosed with a tumour directed my attention toward my body and the present, ultimately revealing dissatisfaction with my life as it existed. These cells contributed to my decision to leave my partner, immediate and extended family, friends, job, and life in Winnipeg to undertake graduate school in Toronto, where I took Ng's course. I believe that these cells inspired my life as it exists today in the most dramatic and mundane ways. I sit at my desk in North Bay overlooking Lake Nipissing because of these cells; I would not have left Winnipeg otherwise. I have a PhD because of these cells; my life was on a very different path prior to my diagnosis. The phone rings as I write and it is the ophthalmologist's assistant reminding me of my appointment tomorrow, a yearly follow-up because of the tumour. During the writing of this chapter, I receive an email informing me that Ng has passed away. I mourn now, but with a sense of gratitude, because of the path these cells set me on. These "disordered" and "abnormal" cells shaped my life and learning in profound and ordinary ways, just as their absence gave form to my existence previously.

I regard my journal and this chapter as embodied texts, learning, and knowledge. The journal narrates a new awareness of my body, a shift away from a physically normative and healthy body that I did not have prior cause to think about. I grapple with my identity, since it is premised on a normative body that is simultaneously foundational to how I understand myself and—through the sleight of hand available to normative, privileged, universalized identities and discourses—completely invisible to me. My journal reveals how bodies appear and disappear in relation to Western medical discourse. In writing from the perspective of a primarily normative and "healthy" person—then and now—I interrogate the troubling implications and effects of such identifications and discourses as they appear in my journal.

Constructing Experience and Affect

To focus on the material existence of these cells and their lasting impact on my life is to overlook how Western-colonial knowledge implicitly shaped my response to having a pituitary tumour. For example, at the time of my diagnosis, my doctor pointed to the centre of her forehead to give me a sense of the location of the pituitary gland and the tumour. Yet later that day, when my friend Michelle located information online about pituitary tumours under the heading "brain tumours," I was utterly shocked and far more terrified. I wrote in my journal,

> The word brain had not been mentioned. Why was the information in that section? Was it an error? Was the pituitary part of the brain? Oh my God! And there were many tears shed to the mantra in my head of "brain tumour." *That*—I could not believe. It sickened me. (9 November 1997)

I had a brain tumour and would be having brain surgery. There was something distinctly and, to my mind, self-evidently ominous about these word combinations.

In 2001, Ng explained to me that within Traditional Chinese Medicine, the brain is conceived of as "a gelatinous mass" that is of no greater importance than any other organ. Shortly thereafter, I encountered Linda Tuhiwai Smith's ([1999] 2006, 48) characterizations of the brain and mind: "Whilst the workings of the mind may be associated in Western thinking primarily with the human brain, the mind itself is a concept or an idea. In Maori world views, for example, the closest equivalent to the idea of a 'mind' or intellect is associated with the entrails and other parts of the body." It was only through learning about non-Western understandings of the brain that I could reread my fear as steeped in Western conceptions that consider the brain to be the seat of personality and cognition while simultaneously elevating these faculties above other abilities. Encountering differing conceptions of the brain and the mind—their meanings and consequences—highlighted how Western knowledge imbued my experience with certain affective and experiential effects while ruling out other outcomes.

In Foucauldian notions of discourse, power operates through and produces the Western medical discourse of the brain while placing this knowledge beyond question. My response to having a brain tumour is characteristic of Foucault's understanding of power as productive; I learned and internalized the common-sense Western discourse about the brain, and this belief, in turn, produced fears and emotions that were particular to the discourse. While fears and emotions are often understood as natural—even primal and beyond question—they can also be understood as discursively constructed effects of power. In another discourse, a brain tumour might evoke entirely different responses and emotions. Learning about non-Western paradigms enabled me to understand my original illness narrative, as well as my embodied and emotional experience of having a pituitary tumour, as constructed, relational, and produced within Western discourses concerning the brain and the mind.

Licence to Be Ill: Handing Bodies Over to Science

Western medicine structured my illness experience in other ways as I gave it absolute primacy over all other forms of knowledge. Extremely painful headaches and the cessation of my period became fake or dubious without a doctor to validate these signs and symptoms. For example, when I reflected on the moment that I first saw the results of my CT scan, I wrote,

> It was a relief now to finally know all of the facts, after almost three months of waiting. Yes, I had a tumour, it was big, and it was coming out. And I felt vindicated. I had not been malingering. [My partner] and I had both seen the tumour, and it existed. (11 November 1997)

Foucault's theory of power enables the observation that in my choice of words like "the facts" and "malingering," Western medical discourse can be seen here to have the "effects of truth" (Foucault 1980, 118). Western medicine offers diagnoses that make bodily symptoms and signs appear real and legitimate. I desired vindication through a medical diagnosis in order to be proven right and reasonable and, perhaps more troubling, to be cleared of blame or suspicion. The implication of such a commentary is that people who experience bodily signs and symptoms but lack a Western medical diagnosis are unreliable and pathological. Within this logic, embodied knowledge alone lacks the credibility to produce the effects of truth.

Furthermore, in an era of neoliberalism, an ideology whereby responsibility is assigned to individuals rather than institutions, my suggestion that not having a diagnosis is equal to malingering presumes that the failure to receive a diagnosis is not a systemic failure of medical science but an individual failure of an ostensibly manipulative and deceitful person. Such a perspective may appear anecdotal in this context, but it certainly reflects the experiences of people with recently disputed illnesses, such as myalgic encephalomyelitis, chronic fatigue syndrome (Brown 1995), and fibromyalgia (Jutel 2011). Their bodily signs and symptoms have been negatively structured in terms of medical validation. Handing over bodily authority and credibility to Western medical systems also has material consequences, including the allocation of government benefits for disability assistance or worker's compensation (Walsh, Stephens, and Moore 2000, 159). Power operates through Western medical diagnoses to organize patients' experiences of their bodies and their credibility as "legitimately" sick or malingering subjects. My journal entry illustrates how the authority ascribed to Western medical diagnoses and the lack of credibility accorded to bodily knowledge are taken up and lived by individuals in the culture. The cultivated Western practice of handing over bodies and their reality to medical science makes it especially challenging to understand and interpret embodied knowledge.

Bodily Normalcy and the Rejected Body

Conceptualizing my experience as both materially driven (for example, by abnormal cell division) and discursively constructed by Western discourses enables a further analysis of how my narration of having a pituitary tumour reflects and privileges the Western ideal of a perpetually healthy body. My journal highlights a fissure between having "the 'normal' body . . . a young, energetic, pain-free body with all parts present and a maximum range of graceful movement" and having a "rejected body" when "our ability to meet the standards is threatened in some way" (Wendell 1996, 91, 88). Susan Wendell explains:

> Implied in any idealization of the body is the rejection of some kinds
> of bodies or some aspects of bodily life. I use the terms "rejected
> body" and "negative body" to refer to those aspects of bodily life (such
> as illness, disability, weakness, and dying), bodily appearance (usually
> deviations from the cultural ideals of the body), and bodily experience
> (including most forms of bodily suffering) that are feared, ignored,
> despised, and/or rejected in a society and its culture. (85)

Similarly, my journal reveals fear, ignorance, and a rejection of having a "sick" body, as well as the attendant identity of "sick people." Reflecting on the day of my CT scan, I wrote:

I can't believe that this machine is around me. Aren't these for sick people? Whenever I have seen them on TV I always assumed that these people in my place were fighting off death. I'm not sick, what am I doing here? (12 November 1997)

My writing reflects an unwillingness to view my body as a changing and organic form and demonstrates an explicit rejection of illness, death, and sick people.

While my crisis of identity and fearful denial appear unique and personal, they are predictable enactments of dominant Western discourses. Wendell (1996, 91) explains:

It is not just from fear of being or becoming abnormal that the rejected body is shunned. It is also shunned from fear of pain, illness, limitation, suffering, and dying. Yet the cultural banishment of the rejected body contributes to fear of those experiences by fostering ignorance of them. . . . They belong to those with disabilities and illnesses, who are marginalized, not "ordinary" people, not "us."

My illness narrative mirrors this powerful discourse as I recoil from having been diagnosed as having a rejected body and am evidently horrified at the prospect of being sick. I fear and deny the illness that I embody, while rejecting all other sick people who might similarly call attention to the impossibility of lifelong bodily normalcy. I enact what Foucault ([1978] 1990, 55) characterizes as "a stubborn will to nonknowledge" when I deny and ignore the realities of illness and death, particularly as they affect me.

Importantly, Wendell (1996, 88) highlights how the discourse of bodily normalcy produces an attendant and often taken-for-granted identity in those who conform closely to this privileged Western discourse and, I would add, have no cause to identify strongly with those who do not:

For many of us, our proximity to the standards of normality is an important aspect of our identity and our sense of social acceptability, an aspect of our self-respect. We are unlikely to notice this until our ability to meet the standards is threatened in some way. An injury or a prolonged illness often draws the attention of non-disabled people to this previously unnoticed facet of their self-images.

Predictably, prior to being diagnosed with a pituitary tumour, I did not notice how my subjectivity was implicitly a "healthy" self forged in opposition to sick people. This invisibility is in keeping with all privileged identities in which the position of dominance is favoured, unmarked, universalized, unexamined, and therefore often indiscernible to those who embody it. Those who conform closely to the dominant position are not readily encouraged to be aware of their own subject position or the unearned privileges accrued as a result. In contrast, those with less or no access to the privileged subject position are often in a better position to recognize its existence. For example, an individual with a chronic illness or one who is near death is, in theory, in a better position to recognize the ubiquity of the discourse of perpetual good health and the pain-free body, as well as the social avoidance of those who cannot conform to this ideal. True to form, it is only in the fissure between health and illness that my universalized and privileged "healthy" subjectivity became visible to me. My proximity to bodily normalcy allowed me to rely on the discourse as an integral part of my self-image—as I demonstrate when I insist that I am not like sick people—yet remain uncritical of its impossible expectations and harmful implications.

Disclosure, Discomfort, Disruption

I was in the privileged position of being able to pass as healthy during the time leading up to my surgery, and disclosures concerning my illness became a frequent focal point in my journal. Disclosures to close friends, acquaintances, and work colleagues each revealed unique issues in relation to the discourse of bodily normalcy and its effects. Internalized and externalized forms of discipline were revealed through my anxieties prior to and following disclosures, others' reactions to my disclosures, and (perceived) material consequences for making my illness known in the workplace. My focus here is on "'governmentality' or, as Foucault puts it, the conduct of conduct, which governs our governing of our selves" (Titchkosky 2007, 83). In engaging with the journal excerpts below, I assert that discomfort and anxieties leading up to and surrounding disclosures of illness serve to discipline the speaker, implicitly urging them to remain silent in order to actively preserve and protect the discourse of bodily normalcy. Not disclosing illness, for example, implicitly sustains the myth that bodily normalcy—with its impossible expectation of perpetual good health—is real and attainable.

As the following examples suggest, those who fail to live up to the ideal are often positioned as awkward and challenging.

In recollecting the process of diagnosis and waiting for surgery, I wrote,

> I remember that largely, it was difficult for me to tell my friends. It's a difficult topic to bring up in a relationship built on common assumptions of mutually good health. I felt daunted by the shock that I would inflict and have to deal with. (10 November 1997)

In my own words, the social relations between friends who conform closely to the expectations of bodily normalcy manifest in the everyday as "common assumptions of mutually good health." These expectations operated as unarticulated presumptions and premises within my existing friendships and were only detectable to me when I was placed in the position of having to shatter the shared and unacknowledged assumption that we would all be healthy forever. In my journal, I regard my disclosure as causing a disturbance, and in many ways such disclosures do disturb. They expose the unspoken discourse of bodily normalcy and reveal the social relations that ground it in reality.

Another Western discourse that shaped my experience is the relegation of illness to the private realm. In positioning sickness as a private matter, it becomes improper to discuss this topic in "polite" conversation. To introduce such a taboo topic is to risk making others uncomfortable. Furthermore, positioning illness as private favours independence over interdependence. As Thomas Couser (1997, 177) articulates in relation to discourses pertaining to physical disability, "Society commonly considers disabled people the embodiment of trauma, personal disaster, or failure; ignoring the profound ways in which we are all interdependent, Western culture's individualism stigmatizes or blames those who fail to be 'self-sufficient.'" While physical disability and illness are not interchangeable, the neoliberal injunction to be independent—financially, physically, and emotionally—resonates with my own illness narrative and can be seen obliquely in the next two journal excerpts regarding disclosures of illness to acquaintances and at work. Furthermore, the imperative to keep such matters private serves the purposes of a culture that fears, ignores, and rejects those who cannot conform to bodily normalcy.

The following passage from my journal illustrates some of these tensions:

I recall one instance where I ran into an awkward situation, when I met up with [an acquaintance] at the folk festival and she said that she had heard that I was "unwell." Yes, I had a tumour I told her, but I was going to be okay. "Where?" she asked. "Brain," I said, a little too abruptly. [The woman], with her children seemed rather shaken and tried to tell me about a yoga group for women with cancer. I was not at all interested, but I let her bumble along as she could not remember where it was or the name of the woman who put it on. This was an unsettling exchange and I left feeling sorry that it had to be that way. My friend said "I feel sorry for that poor woman," as we walked away. It had been an odd moment for all involved. Sometimes I wished that my personal life could stay completely private, but in the end, the support of others helped me immensely. (10 November 1997)

As Susan Wendell (1996, 91) points out, rejected bodies suffer from "cultural banishment," and this is revealed, arguably, in this very awkward casual conversation concerning my brain tumour. Even though I was clearly asked to provide the private information that transgressed the norms of casual conversation, it is notable that my friend and I were left feeling sorry for the person who received the information that I had a brain tumour; she appeared to be taken aback, disconcerted, and anxious. Disrupting the discourse of bodily normalcy may create a personal crisis for the sick person, but it also creates a social crisis for those around them.

Furthermore, the last line of the journal excerpt signals a tension between wanting and needing the support of others (interdependence) and feeling bad about disclosing my illness because these are ostensibly private matters (independence). Conforming to the neoliberal expectation that individuals should take care of themselves or extend their support group narrowly to their immediate family, such encounters exerted an often not-so-subtle social pressure to keep silent and endure my illness alone rather than seek extended community or collective support. These social norms around "polite" conversation marginalize the realities of sickness and sick people while upholding the discourse of bodily normalcy. Returning to neoliberalism and the practice of assigning responsibility to individuals, the "problem" of illness is not configured in my interaction with this woman as a systemic issue of normalizing a discourse of bodily normalcy that all will fail to attain in the long term; rather, the sick individual is held accountable for embodying and failing to conceal the knowledge that the culture wants to forget. In these uncomfortable interactions, the problem is not usually figured or experienced as the unreasonable expectations of the listener but is attributed to the disclosure.

A disclosure that reveals further dimensions of the social relations of bodily normalcy relates to my employment as a counsellor at that time. About trying to decide whether to tell my boss about my illness, I wrote the following:

> I decided not to tell my boss, although I liked her a lot. I wanted her to know [that I was sick] because I was often upset and emotional, but I knew too well that my term was up in April and as a sick employee, I might lose the credibility that I had worked hard for. I did not want to be terminated over this. (9 November 1997)

In this passage, I am most struck by the word *credibility* and the notion that I had worked hard for it. There are numerous slippages and conflations here, and in retrospect, I identify the credibility that is (ostensibly) at risk as simultaneously discursive and material. Discursively, I see this excerpt as reflecting a dominant Western notion that a "good employee" conforms to rationality and bodily normalcy. My credibility as a counsellor and an employee was implicitly predicated on a silent body, perfect health, normative abilities, restrained emotions, and "appropriate" behaviours: in other words, on a privileged body that acts as a vessel for the rational mind. The credibility that I feared losing was premised, at least in large part, on my proximity to the favoured discourse of bodily normalcy and therefore was actually credibility that I had *not* worked for. My narration favours a liberal notion of power that obscures social inequalities while conflating privilege with hard-earned success. Such thinking "masks the fact that some benefit more than others from the present situation (and also exonerates from guilt those who benefit)" (Gaztambide-Fernández 2012, 58). Correspondingly, I characterize my successes in individualistic and self-flattering terms rather than as someone jeopardizing a systemically *unearned* privilege that in turn has produced material privileges. This notion allows me to establish myself as hard-working, deserving, and credible in opposition to those whose bodies are rejected and marked as other; their credibility as employees is implicitly questioned in my narrative.

Materially, I feared losing my contract renewal if I disclosed that I would be going on sick leave only a few months into my new contract. If employers privilege profits or fiscal financial restraint over responsibility to their employees, it is in one's best interest to conceal information regarding illness if one is in the privileged position of being able to do so. My narrative points to the (perceived) necessity of maintaining bodily normalcy in some workplaces, especially in a neoliberal economic context with growing dependence on a contractual and "flexible" workforce; it also reveals the ways in which the "good employee" implicitly conforms to the discourse of bodily normalcy. Those who cannot conform are figured as lacking in credibility and perhaps even failing to work hard enough. As Susan Wendell (1989, 113) writes, "When you listen to this culture in a disabled body, you hear how often health and physical vigour are talked about as if they were moral virtues. People constantly praise others for their 'energy,' their stamina, their ability to work long hours." This health, stamina, and credibility stands in opposition to those who cannot conform to these expectations, expectations that may eventually undermine one's own health. The demand to work harder in "flexible" and contractual contexts creates circumstances of high stress and high labour turnover, making it increasingly difficult for employees to maintain a healthy body and mind. Furthermore, the material and discursive pressures to exhibit boundless physical vigour and energy in the workplace while keeping silent about illness serve to privilege and normalize the discourse of the normative and "universal" healthy body while rejecting those who cannot embody the standards of bodily normalcy. Such workplace expectations perpetuate an imagined norm in relation to which we are all bound to fall short, and even those who conform closely are still only close enough. In some sense, revealing and critically understanding the discourse of bodily normalcy dissolves the self-other binary that this discourse produces, since no self can ever meet its expectations.

While the excerpts from my journal appear particular to me, they are not original or unique. They are Western discourses played out at the level of the individual and their interactions, the social relations that give life and currency to the discourses of bodily normalcy and rejected bodies. These discourses can be seen to animate identities, relationships, actions, experiences, emotions, and knowledge for those who are marginalized *and* for those who are privileged within them.

Postscript

In choosing to (belatedly) share my experience of having a brain tumour, I worried that you would expect a story of tragedy. I hope we can now agree that it is more of a mystery. How is it that the myth of bodily normalcy remains so tenacious in the face of everyday and inevitable illness, bodily suffering, disability, aging, and death? In banishing rejected bodies—culturally, conversationally, visually—we cannot actually avoid the vicissitudes of life. In analyzing my illness narrative, it seems to me that the rejections, investments, and justifications that I enacted largely served to protect and naturalize the privileges accorded to those whose bodies (temporarily) fall closely in line with the myth of bodily normalcy. These everyday social relations simultaneously reinforce and obfuscate social inequalities that marginalize and blame all who (inevitably) cannot conform. My journal elucidates how privileged subjects' sense of self and other are constituted within a neoliberal symbolic order that frames unearned privileges as invisible, earned, and well deserved while holding marginalized individuals responsible for failing to live up to its untenable terms.

As Randelle Nixon and Katie MacDonald suggest in their contribution to this collection, privileged subjects are often hailed as benevolent rather than as implicated and complicit in the oppression of others. In analyzing my illness narrative, I seek to contest and reveal aspects of Western-colonial knowledge, including privilege, complicity, and internalized dominance in the realm of health and illness. I do so with the recognition that the discursive questions that I employ largely sidestep embodiment and the physical body, even as bodily normalcy is the focus of the analysis. Such a slippage is analogous to Eve Tuck and Wayne Yang's (2012) observation that anti-oppression educators have readily taken up notions of decolonizing knowledge and minds while avoiding discussion of the decolonization of land. As this collection aims to redress, the material world of social justice is too often overlooked. While Ng always foregrounded the importance of materiality in her work, she also taught her students that a commitment to social justice requires understanding how privilege operates, actively resisting disembodiment, and transforming discursive and material inequities embedded within Western medicine, epistemologies, and knowledge. In critically reflecting on the construction and enactment of the privileged "I" within Western medical discourse, the myth of bodily normalcy, and neoliberalism, I offer this chapter as a starting point toward material and symbolic transformations rather than as a conclusion.

References

Brown, Phil. 1995. "Naming and Framing: The Social Construction of Diagnosis and Illness." Extra Issue: *Forty Years of Medical Sociology—The State of the Art and Directions for the future. Journal of Health and Social Behavior* 35: 34–52.

Couser, G. Thomas. 1997. *Recovering Bodies: Illness, Disability, and Life Writing.* Madison: University of Wisconsin Press.

Foucault, Michel. 1980. *Power/Knowledge: Selected Interviews and Other Writings, 1972–1977.* Edited by Colin Gordon. Translated by Colin Gordon, Leo Marshall, John Mepham, and Kate Soper. New York: Pantheon Books.

———. (1978) 1990. *The History of Sexuality.* Vol. 1: *An Introduction.* Translated by Robert Hurley. Reprint, New York: Vintage Books. Originally published as *Histoire de la sexualité, 1: La volonté de savoir* (1976).

Gaztambide-Fernández, Rubén A. 2012. "Decolonization and the Pedagogy of Solidarity." *Decolonization: Indigeneity, Education, and Society* 1(1): 41–67.

Jutel, Annemarie Goldstein. 2011. *Putting a Name to It: Diagnosis in Contemporary Society.* Baltimore: Johns Hopkins University Press.

Mairs, Nancy. 1997. Foreword to Couser, *Recovering Bodies*, ix–xiii.

Nakata, N. Martin, Victoria Nakata, Sarah Keech, and Reuben Bolt. 2012. "Decolonial Goals and Pedagogies for Indigenous Studies." *Decolonization: Indigeneity, Education, and Society* 1(1): 120–40.

Smith, Linda Tuhiwai. (1999) 2006. *Decolonizing Methodologies: Research and Indigenous Peoples.* 2nd ed. London: Zed Books.

Titchkosky, Tanya. 2007. *Reading and Writing Disability Differently: The Textured Life of Embodiment.* Toronto: University of Toronto Press.

Tuck, Eve, and K. Wayne Yang. 2012. "Decolonization Is Not a Metaphor." *Decolonization: Indigeneity, Education, and Society* 1(1): 1–40.

Walsh, Mark, Paul Stephens, and Stephen Moore. 2000. *Social Policy and Welfare.* Cheltenham, UK: Stanley Thornes.

Wendell, Susan. 1989. "Toward a Feminist Theory of Disability." *Hypatia* 4(2): 104–24.

———. 1996. *The Rejected Body: Feminist Philosophical Reflections on Disability.* New York and London: Routledge.

12 Embodied Writing and the Social Production of Pain

Susan Ferguson

*Writing is a deep practice. Even before we begin writing, during
whatever we are doing—gardening or sweeping the floor—our
book or essay is being written deep in our consciousness. To write
a book, we must write with our whole life, not just during the
moments we are sitting at our desks.*
                    Thich Nhat Hanh (1998, 91)

There is a story in every line of theory.
                    Lee Maracle (1990, 7)

Let me begin with a story.

During my first semester of graduate school, I took a course on embodied learning with Roxana Ng. One of the course requirements was that we keep a journal, comprising both responses to the course readings and reflections upon our experience of qigong, a traditional Chinese practice that was central to the course curriculum. In one of my final journal entries, I wrote that I would have liked a more explicit antiracist theoretical framework through which to engage with course content. While my comment was intended to highlight the importance of politicizing knowledge production when learning about Indigenous health and healing systems, it also betrays the limitations of my perspective at the time—that is, the extent to which my understanding of antiracism and critical pedagogy was located within the realm of an activist-academic approach that privileges the mind and intellect, often at the expense (or erasure) of our bodies and of bodily knowledge.

In her response, Ng acknowledged my critique but made a political assertion of her own. In the margins of my course paper, she wrote, "I believe that profound shifts must come from self-reflection and interrogation, not just from intellectual understanding." While I agreed with her about the importance of self-reflection and interrogation, at the time I understood these as primarily intellectual activities, and I recall insisting (to myself) that we need theory and analysis if we are to do our politics properly. I later came to realize that Ng was suggesting a different kind of reflection and interrogation, however—one that calls into question the very foundations of Western academic knowledge production.

It took several years of engagement with mindfulness meditation and a variety of other bodywork practices—which share among them an attentiveness to the different dimensions of bodily life—for me to fully appreciate the significance of Ng's assertion that personal and social transformation are intertwined processes that cannot be accomplished through analysis alone. Through working with a chronic pain condition and holding this embodied process in conversation with the work of writing and theorizing the body in knowledge production, I came to a deep awareness of how body and culture are fully imbricated; how history in its many manifestations lodges itself in the body. As I learned to attend to my body and expand the frameworks I was using to understand the nature of pain, and bodily life in general, I also discovered that our epistemological locations matter a great deal.

This notion of location, coupled with a concern with how we orient ourselves toward bodily knowledge and experience, and to what effect, became a key theme in my work. In particular, I became interested in how our epistemological locations—that is, those theoretical, discursive, and methodological frameworks through which we approach our practices of knowledge making—shape, and often delimit, the very possibilities of critique. Given my broader commitment to decolonizing methodologies, I also took my interest in embodiment and social theory as an occasion to explore the boundaries of critique and, conversely, the opportunities opened up by working through and across those boundaries. By tracing dominant Western, medicalized understandings of the body across social theories of pain and embodiment, I was able to appreciate both the social and historical specificity of these theories and their relationship to wider histories of colonial knowledge production, and in so doing, to establish their contingency. In order to disrupt these dominant, taken-for-granted ways of knowing about pain and embodiment, however, I ultimately needed to reach outside common Western research methods and cultivate an approach that could help me to "suspend inherited habits of knowing," as feminist scholar Jacqui Alexander (2005, 310) puts it, and centre the body within my writing and research.

It was through mindfulness practice that I was able to cultivate a different way of knowing about the body, through the body, which allowed me to read and write the body differently than I had before. I came to understand my approach as a form of embodied writing practice, and I began to read widely, across different disciplines and literatures, in search of other examples of embodied writing practices. Embodied writing, as I have come to conceptualize it, refers to the complex interplay between those discursive and material practices of reading, writing, and research that reach beyond Western objectivist and normalizing representations of the body and that instead seek to animate the body, and bodily diversity, such that representations of embodiment emerge through bodily subjectivity itself. Embodied writing, then, is writing that embraces open-ended, intertextual, and intersubjective representations of embodiment and that acknowledges both differently located bodies and diverse conceptual frameworks for understanding embodiment.

The remainder of this chapter explores the possibilities of embodied writing for social research and its implications for decolonizing knowledge production about and of the body. Beginning with the understanding that writing is a key, but contested, site of knowledge production in Western society (Richardson 2004; Smith 1999), I treat writing as a social and bodily practice. Using an examination of the social production of bodily pain to exemplify my approach, I describe how feminist autobiography, mindfulness meditation, and phenomenologically informed interpretive sociology can be brought together to foster an embodied writing practice.

After mapping my methodological approach, I turn to Lata Mani's (2001) memoir of pain and disability, *Interleaves*, to illustrate what I mean by embodied writing and to explore its potential to shape bodily knowledge production that treats the experience of pain as a social activity mediated by discursive and material processes that move among and across various disciplinary, historical, temporal, and corporeal boundaries. I suggest that through her use of mindfulness meditation, embodied narrative strategies, and textual practices that disrupt dominant Western academic writing conventions, Lata Mani's work represents the possibility of writing through pain and disability toward a space of decolonizing and liberatory praxis. In closing, I return to my argument that by attending to our epistemological locations, which are themselves always deeply political, we might open up opportunities to generate differently imagined relations to embodiment and, in turn, develop creative methodological and pedagogical practices that seek to engage, rather than negate, embodied difference.

Throughout the chapter, I also reflexively engage my own narrative of living with and writing through pain and disability, revealing that an embodied writing practice is also a pedagogical practice. Here I am taking a broad understanding of pedagogy, recognizing that any practice of knowledge production also involves teaching ourselves (Alexander 2005). If writing is a process of coming to know, as I believe it is, then surely there is a pedagogical imperative within all scholarly writing, and especially within writing that seeks to engage one's own narrative and experience, as mine does. As Chandra Mohanty (2003) notes, it is in fact experience that makes critical theory possible—we turn to theory to make meaning of our experience, connect this experience to wider social and political histories, and, in turn, shape new theories and understandings. Furthermore, Mohanty (2003) argues, we must understand these emergent knowledges "pedagogically" and take them up as a form of practice if we are to genuinely intervene in dominant structures of knowing. This is, then, to also recognize that our scholarly and pedagogical practices inform one another. And while I would argue that methodology is always to some degree pedagogical, this is especially true for those of us involved in education insofar as we teach from our experience, our research, our theoretical and political commitments—and, conversely, we research, write, and learn from how and what we teach. This is consistent with Indigenous research and educational practices, which do not impose rigid distinctions between narrative, experience, knowledge production, and pedagogy (Smith 1999).

In this chapter, my approach mobilizes and makes explicit the reciprocal relationship between methodology and pedagogy through my use of feminist autobiography and autoethnography: I trace my own narrative throughout this work as it anticipated, informed, engaged, and intersected with my scholarly inquiries. In particular, I make my writing process visible throughout the work as a way to ground my argument in practice. In so doing, I hope to intervene in normative bodily relations to text as they are typically manifested through academic writing conventions such that I might exemplify to readers not just what I mean to say but how it might be accomplished. Embodied writing, then, necessarily resists the closure and coherence that much traditional academic writing seeks to achieve. One way to decolonize knowledge production through our writing practices, I argue in this chapter, is to highlight the provisional nature of writing and the very (embodied) process of coming to know. I begin with the body and social theory.

Writing the Body

Writing is central to Western education, knowledge production, and social research methodologies. Writing is also a political activity. As Maori scholar Linda Tuhiwai Smith (1999, 36) reminds us, academic writing and its role in the generation of theory is never "innocent" (see also Maracle 1990). However, at the same time as it carries with it a legitimacy reflective of wider social histories of Western knowledge production, imperialism, and domination (Smith 1999), writing can also represent a politicizing space through which to contest, reflect upon, and rewrite hegemonic narratives (Mohanty 2003). Sheila Stewart's essay in this collection provides an example of embodied writing that resists the closure typical of academic language, argumentation, and structure.

While the significance of writing to social inquiry and the possibilities offered by nontraditional forms of writing have been well-documented (see, for example, Clifford 1983; Richardson 2004), the relationship between the body and our writing practices has been given less attention. Although feminist scholarship, in particular, has moved to redress the mind-body split characteristic of social science research through an acknowledgement of the researcher as an experiencing subject, an examination of the ways in which writing is both a social and a bodily activity remains curiously absent.

As Thomas Csordas (1994, 4) noted some twenty-five years ago, social theories of embodiment have likewise taken up their subject matter "without much sense of 'bodiliness.'" This often remains the case. Although the body has come to occupy considerable space within disciplines such as women's studies, sociology, and education, theories of embodiment often reproduce dominant bodily relations to knowledge production through their emphasis on the body as a site of representation and their reliance upon normative notions of embodiment: rarely, for example, does the ill body, the body in pain, the disabled body appear, and when it does, it is most often as an anomaly or negation (Garland-Thomson 1997). As Csordas (1994, 4) argues, the lack of "bodiliness" in theories of embodiment has consequences for knowledge production about and of the body:

> This tendency carries the dual dangers of dissipating the force of using the body as a methodological starting point, and of objectifying bodies as things devoid of intentionality and intersubjectivity. It thus misses the opportunity to add sentience and sensibility to our notions of self and person, and to insert an added dimension of materiality to our notions of culture and history.

And so while I have found social theories of the body, and particularly feminist accounts, indispensable to my understandings of embodiment, pain, and disability as always already in story, I am also cautious about the limitations, both political and epistemological, of approaches which employ those scholarly conventions that reproduce a disembodied relation to knowledge production.

Phenomenologically informed interpretive sociology is helpful here because it both highlights that writing is always already a social and bodily practice and can help to reveal the effects, scholarly and otherwise, of normative bodily relations to text. Maurice Merleau-Ponty's (2004) phenomenological work tells us, for example, that it is through our embodied perception of the world that our understandings take shape. It follows, then, that if writing is not merely a method of knowledge transmission but a process of knowing more deeply, then our writing practices are also mediated by our embodiment. There is a tension here, however, for within the normative orders of Western academic knowledge production, we can also say that the inverse is true: our textual practices simultaneously mediate our understandings of bodily life. This is to say that when we write, we write something into being; the form this writing takes thus writes, and indeed rewrites, an embodied relation to the world as it is represented in the text. This complex interplay points to a dynamic relation between body and form, which can be traced through the embodied and narrative strategies we put to work in our writing and theorizing.

By reflexively attending to the practices of reading and writing that shape knowledge production about the body, it becomes possible to destabilize objectified representations of the body and begin to write diversity, complexity, and intersubjectivity into our theories of embodiment and the knowledge that flows from them. Tanya Titchkosky (2007, 210–11) describes the relationship between embodiment and textual knowledge production in this way:

> To know that the body is made manifest through our word-filled relations to embodiment actualized through our reading and writing of the body, is to know that any manifestation of language is an embodied activity that might open us to something other than what appears on the page. Reading and writing are socially oriented activities of embodied actors situated in the same world they are busy making. Attending not only to the sense in which texts give us versions of embodiment, but also to the ways in which we apperceive these versions, can teach us much about the ordering of relations to the bodies of ourselves and others through the medium of everyday texts.

This suggests that experiences of embodiment such as pain and disability are firmly located within those cultural contexts that give meaning to those experiences; in reading and writing any bodily experience we necessarily engage in interpretive work that involves the use of wider social narratives through which many different versions of embodiment are constructed. Embodiment is thus an intersubjective phenomenon, accomplished through social interactions and practices which reveal, as Gail Weiss (1999, 5–6) tells us, that "the experience of being embodied is never a private affair." I am interested, then, in what bearing this interpretive approach has on the ways we read and write the body in pain, particularly given that bodily pain is most typically characterized as intensely private, subjective, and individual by nature (see, for example, Bonica 1990, 18; Scarry 1985, 4).

Reading and Writing the Body in Pain: Or, the Discursive Limits of Critique

Pain is an extraordinarily common yet varied human experience. It is one way in which our bodies communicate with us and is present in our language, appearing often in daily life and conversation as a metaphor for that which is difficult or undesirable. Pain is the object of medical knowledge and practice and is a commodity of the medical-pharmaceutical-industrial complex. Pain is also an emotional experience and is used often as a narrative device in the stories we tell about the world. Pain appears in film, media, and advertising; in books ranging from fiction and memoir to medical texts and popular health books; in doctor's offices and clinic waiting rooms; and in medical charts, questionnaires, and test reports. If we are attentive, we will notice pain all around us.

And yet pain is also nowhere. We feel it but we often do not talk about it, and we generally wish it would go away. It cannot be objectively seen or measured, and it regularly evades explanation and resolution by medicine, which subsequently seeks to suppress it. Pain often evades language, and thus, while pain is often evoked metaphorically, it is much less often described. We avoid pain, have difficulty acknowledging pain, and often retreat in the face of the pain of others.

And so pain is both here and not here. An integral part of our daily lives as embodied beings yet also a space of silence and absence. Despite the very common experience of pain, it is most often narrated as a sign of anomaly, concern, even crisis—requiring and yet defying explanation. This interplay between the presence and absence of pain is revealing, because it suggests that pain is a socially produced phenomenon, always already in story, part of an ongoing and incomplete relation to embodiment. Brian Pronger (2002, 80) writes of absence and the work it does: "Absence lies before presence, in anticipation. Just as absence lies in the foreground of presence, so too presence lies in the anticipation of absence. . . . Absence must receive presence, or there will be no making present." Pain is thus made and unmade through the conditions and locations of its appearance; the absence of pain grounds, indeed constitutes, its presence, while the presence of pain desires its absence. The commonsensical understanding of pain as troublesome and undesirable needs, then, to be understood through an analysis of the conditions of possibility enabling its appearance in order to reveal both how it works as a socially produced phenomenon and the work it is doing. Let us now examine the language of pain and its dominant discursive representation in Western society—that of medical discourse.

The word *pain* can be traced to the Greek and Latin words meaning punishment—*poinē* and *poena,* respectively (Bonica 1990, 18). The representation of pain through language is thus underwritten by the notion that it is an undesirable response to a transgression of some kind. The International Association for the Study of Pain (IASP) similarly defines pain as "an unpleasant sensory and emotional experience associated with actual or potential tissue damage or described in terms of such damage." As a note following this definition indicates, pain is "always subjective," and while "it is unquestionably a sensation in a part or parts of the body," pain is "always unpleasant and therefore also an emotional experience."[1]

This common medical definition of *pain* reflects both the etymology of the word and dominant social understandings of bodily pain as troublesome and undesirable. While the reference to the emotional dimensions of the pain experience (assuming that the physical and emotional body can be held in separation) acknowledges that pain is more than just a physical sensation, pain ultimately derives its explanatory power through its biological facticity, as evidenced by the reference to tissue damage in the above medical definition. Interestingly, at the same time as medicine claims authority over pain—and even over its very existence—this definition also provides a kind of escape clause in suggesting that pain might only be "*described* in terms of such damage" (my emphasis) but still be diagnosed as pain.

The tenuousness of the diagnostic process in determining and treating pain, and particularly chronic pain, is well documented (for example, Good et al. 1992; Wainwright et al. 2006). Scientific theories of pain within Western medicine have undergone a number of changes (Kugelmann 1997, 45), pointing to the indeterminacy of medicine's explanatory models for

---

1 See IASP Taxonomy Working Group, *Classification of Chronic Pain,* 2nd edition (revised), part 3, "Pain Terms: A Current List with Definitions and Notes on Usage," http://www.iasp-pain.org/files/Content/ContentFolders/Publications2/Classificationofchronicpain/Part_III-PainTerms.pdf, 3. The second edition of this standard reference work was published in 1994; the revised, online edition incorporates updates dating to 2011 and 2012. The full text is available on the IASP website at http://www.iasp-pain.org/PublicationsNews/Content.aspx?ItemNumber=1673&navItemNumber=677.

understanding pain. In modern times, a major shift occurred when pain ceased to be treated as a sensation, the dominant approach until around 1950, and instead came to be understood primarily through Melzack and Wall's "gate control theory" (Kugelmann 1997). Mirroring the shift from biomedical to biopsychosocial approaches to health—which recognize individual health not as solely biological but as a complex of interactions between the biological, psychological, and social aspects of human life— the gate control theory shifted dominant Western medical conceptions of pain from understanding it as a *signal* to understanding it as a *process* within the human body (54). While the former model understood pain as a physiological reaction to injury mediated by specific nerves (55), Melzack and Wall's gate control theory of pain emerged in response to the "puzzle" of pain and the apparently inconsistent relationship between the existence of pain and (verifiable) injury (Melzack and Wall 1988, 3). This is a pain that attempts to acknowledge variety, cultural context, the role of language in describing pain, and the impact of personal history on the experience of pain; for Melzack and Wall, all these subjective dimensions to pain refuted any direct relation between injury and sensation and demanded a new definition and approach to understanding pain itself (12–14). This new definition ultimately signalled a key shift away from treating pain as a symptom toward treating pain as an illness unto itself (Baszanger 1998, 122).

Medical theories and definitions of pain do not simply reside in medical textbooks, however. Rather, they circulate and make their way into daily life through both medical practices that seek to treat the illness of pain and the many ways in which medical discourse permeates different arenas of Western social life. The practice of clinical medicine strongly shaped Melzack and Wall's theory of pain, and a major contribution of the gate control model was the measurement tool they developed to improve the treatment of pain—the McGill Pain Questionnaire, which asks the patient to rate the intensity and qualities of the pain they are experiencing. This questionnaire is widely used as a way of assessing what type of pain a person may be experiencing and is regarded as a way of bridging the very personal, subjective nature of pain with the objective needs of Western medical treatment regimes (Melzack and Wall 1988, 41). In shifting pain from a sensation with a singular source within the body to a process with multiple pathways throughout the body, the possibilities for pain treatment were also expanded. In this model, there are two different pathways through which pain may be treated: intervening in organic structures of the body and intervening in mental processes. A wide variety of treatment modalities, including alternative or complementary treatments, were thus legitimated for use in the medical treatment of pain (Baszanger 1998).

This overview of the dominant Western biomedical understanding of pain is by no means comprehensive. What I hope it demonstrates, though, is that pain is a contested space. And yet, despite the indeterminacy of knowledge about pain in Western society, pain tends to remain within the objectivist authority of medical science. By attending to the language of pain in the definition above, however, and the theories of pain and embodiment that it reflects, we can better understand how pain gains its sensibility and secures its facticity as a medicalized phenomenon.

Pain, the accepted medical definition above tells us, needs language to enter medicine; pain needs to be described. As Emma Whelan (2003, 477) argues, "There is no medical way into pain except via patient subjectivity, however much some medical experts may want to minimize the role of subjectivity in medical claimsmaking processes." This is especially true if pain is to be treated. The act of describing pain, however, facilitates a slippage between the subjective description of sensory experience that is labelled as pain and the diagnosis of damage that is said to produce the pain. Even when there is no observable evidence of injury, as is often the case, pain is understood by medicine as a transgression of the body; something has *happened* to the body. (Indeed, the demand of pain's absence is often the very thing that makes it present.) And so while pain is acknowledged to be experiential, emotional, and subjective, requiring language to gain its sensibility, the epistemological move that links pain with medical treatment has the effect of securing the body as the body-object—that is, the body known objectively by science—thereby foreclosing other ways of understanding the body and the body in pain. This is one way in which medicine works to position itself as science despite its reliance on interpretive practices (Good and Good 1993).

The continuities and paradoxes among different conceptualizations of pain also reveal it to be an interpreted phenomenon, achieved through complex, interactive, and often conflicting processes of knowledge production.

Notably, the interactions that produce pain as a medical scientific phenomenon are profoundly social—they occur between bodies. Despite the dominant characterization of pain as deeply individual, it is only through engagement with another, and with the social, that pain is given its meaning as pain. By this, I do not simply mean to say that our experiences of pain, like illness, have meaning in our own lives, as some scholars have suggested in an attempt to intervene in medical discourse (Kleinman 1988); rather, I mean that the very conditions of pain's appearance precede and inflect the experience of pain itself. In this sense, pain is only pain—only *becomes* pain, perhaps—in the midst of others.

By highlighting the social production of pain, I am not seeking to deny or dismiss the painful experience that most often is pain. Indeed, my work on this subject was, for a long time, shaped by my desire to *not* be in pain. Rather, I want to trouble those Western epistemological practices that produce pain as only ever one possible sensation or experience. This is important because not only does Western medical discourse delineate the boundaries of knowledge production about pain and the body, but these discursive boundaries also limit the possibilities of critique if we take these boundaries for granted and perform our scholarly work within them. To deny that we are always already engaged in meaning-making about pain and the body is thus to deny that meaning-making is always political. This is especially problematic when meaning masquerades as an objective truth, or that which "just is." And so, by treating pain as a socially produced phenomenon, I am concerned not only with intervening in those dominant medicalized understandings of pain that circumscribe the discursive boundaries of pain but also with the epistemological implications of taking Western medicalized discourses of pain and embodiment as self-evident. Indeed, as Judith Butler (2004, 4) reminds us, critique often emerges from those tenuous spaces between the dominant discourses and practices through which we know ourselves and the ways in which our experience exceeds the structures of knowing available to us. Our embodied experiences and perceptions are one such example. For critique to be transformative, however, it must reach beyond those structures of "settled knowledge" (27) towards the possibility of different ways of being in the world.

Writing and Rewriting the Body in Pain: Toward an Embodied Writing Practice

As I described earlier in this chapter, my interest in developing an embodied writing practice was motivated by a desire to animate the body within my writing and research and disrupt normative bodily relations to knowledge production—a desire that acquired a kind of critical urgency when I developed a physical impairment that profoundly affected my ability to produce written text and thus to participate in academic knowledge production. As Roxana Ng (2004) notes, our bodies are an integral but taken-for-granted aspect of our intellectual work; for me, the reciprocal relationship between my body and my scholarly work only became clear to me when I suddenly found that I could not write and was unable to participate in the intellectual work of the university (Ferguson and Titchkosky 2008). Disability and its intervention into my experience of typical bodily relations to writing thus shaped my interest in exploring how an embodied writing practice can intervene in those dominant epistemological practices that serve to secure the authority of particular bodies of knowledge and recognize only particular bodies as knowledgeable.

My commitment to embodied writing—particularly when it involved myself—initially remained quite intellectual insofar as I did not know how to know through any other means. Mindfulness practice helped me cultivate a different way of knowing about the body, through the body. My body. (And this was very important, because it allowed me to reach outside an objectified relation to embodiment and write the body's subjectivity.) I began to experience my body, and in particular the pain I lived with, quite differently. My sensory experience became more nuanced and the boundaries of my perception of my embodiment more expansive. I became at once more conscious of my sensory experience and, because I was more aware of the variety and changeability of this experience, less invested in it and its (possible) meaning or significance. Pain became part of a much broader set of sensory experiences than it had been for me in the past.

Knowing that I could experience my body differently was a profound confirmation that the body is indeed socially produced (Butler 1993). While I had previously been committed to this perspective, I came to understand this at the level of bodily experience (itself an interpretive process) and not solely as an intellectual interest in social theories of embodiment. During this time, I also began to explore the potential for embodied writing to support a project of decolonizing knowledge production. Colonial histories continue to shape the social organization of knowledge; colonialism is not just a political and economic project that occurred in the past but is part of ongoing social and geopolitical formations that structure discourse in the present. Decolonization, then, does not only require a radical reconceptualization of human relationships to land and each other, including the return of land to Indigenous peoples (though this, too, is essential; see Tuck and Yang 2012); it also demands that we interrogate those knowledge systems founded upon colonial ideologies and the practices of exclusion that flow from them. Indeed, the discursive practices of colonialism have profoundly material effects, and it is critical that we recognize the ways in which the material and discursive are mutually constitutive. Within this context, I became interested in how various forms of dualistic thinking that rest upon colonial ideologies prohibit more integrative approaches to knowledge production and, more specifically, in tracing how this inflects writing as a site of epistemological practice.

Recalling my opening narrative, I returned to Ng's assertion that if critical reflection is to be put to the service of social transformation, it must be an embodied activity. In her work on embodied pedagogy, or embodied learning (2000a, 2000b, 2004, 2011), Ng argues that oppressive social relations are upheld by the division between the mind/intellect and body/spirit that is foundational to Western education and knowledge production. This leads to a disjuncture between analysis and practice, or "way of being in the world" (2004, 3). Even (or perhaps especially) critical education, with its explicit social justice agenda, tends to reproduce this disjuncture through its emphasis on critical thinking at the expense of embodied or spiritual understanding. Ng's (2004) model of embodied pedagogy seeks to redress this disjuncture through an integrative praxis that highlights Eastern health and meditation practices in the classroom as a way of disrupting the mind-body split and facilitating students' capacity for embodied (self-) reflection and critical insight. (For an example of how mindfulness-based pedagogy can foster critical reflection in social work education, see Yuk-Lin Renita Wong's essay in this collection.) Jacqui Alexander (2005) similarly charts a relationship between colonization and systems of dualistic thinking, arguing that the work of decolonization requires a critically engaged, integrative approach that bridges the secular and the spiritual and is premised on a dynamic relation between radical self-determination and collective interdependence. Alexander's insistence upon recognizing the spiritual in our practices of knowledge production is echoed in Temitope Adefarakan's chapter in this volume, where she argues that we must recognize that students are not solely academic bodies but also spiritual bodies, as a strategy for resisting Eurocentric teaching practices that rest upon the bifurcation of mind/intellect and body/spirit.

Central to the work of decolonization, then, is the notion of practice and the possibility offered by integrative work that disrupts those hierarchical dualisms that are foundational to Western social thought (mind/body, male/female, reason/affect, nature/culture, for example). This is to say that without pedagogical, methodological, and other practices to accompany the work of knowledge production, our theorizing cannot support a project of decolonization. Epistemologically, Ng's (2004) approach is instructive because it allows for knowledge production about the body to take place through the body, thereby displacing the primacy of objectivist, scientific ways of knowing. Importantly, however, it also acts as a critical intervention into Western philosophies of the body by providing a set of alternative theories and practices of the body. In doing so, this approach not only demonstrates that the body is always already a space of interpretation (Butler 1993) but also locates our social and cultural understandings of the body, and relationships to our bodies, within wider histories of colonial knowledge production. (See Wendy Peters's chapter in this collection for a powerful example of an embodied narrative that similarly contests the dominance of Western medical knowledge.)

Philosopher Annemarie Mol (2002) suggests that we critically reflect upon how bodies are *done* through an analysis of those material practices that shape the experience and interpretation of bodily life. Mol warns of the risk involved in treating bodies as solely a space of interpretation and meaning-making, suggesting that "the body's physical reality is still left out; it is yet again an unmarked category" (11). Methodologically, this insistence upon the intersections between those material and discursive boundaries shaping bodily life is important when theorizing embodied experiences such as pain because it thoroughly denaturalizes any embodied relation while at the same time allowing for the recognition that theorizing has consequences that must be lived with.

Furthermore, as Mol (2002, vii) asserts, "Attending to enactment rather than knowledge has an important effect: what we think of as a single object may appear to be more than one." It is this kind of multiplicity and complexity that I sought to uncover regarding pain and the body, as a strategy for opening up the ways in which we experience and narrate our sensory experiences of pain and contesting dominant medical frameworks that discipline pain as an embodied phenomenon. I want now to take up Mol's methodological proposal to explore the possibilities of embodied writing practices that reveal the multiplicity, intersubjectivity, and sociality of bodily pain and bodily life. In particular, I argue that mindfulness meditation offers one way of "doing" the body such that knowledge can be produced *through* the body and through bodily diversity.

Mindfulness Meditative Practice as Method

Mindfulness meditation is a central practice within Buddhism. While the term *meditation* actually refers to a variety of techniques developed over centuries, including different forms of yoga and sitting meditation, these practices share the aim of cultivating embodied awareness in the present moment (Orr 2002, 488). Most simply put, mindfulness meditation is about "paying attention" (Kabat-Zinn 2005, 21) without judgment. The most common means of mindfulness meditation practice involves using a stable and relaxed seated posture and breath work to ground us in our bodies such that we can be more aware of what we are feeling and experiencing (Rosenberg 1998). In this way, the practice of mindfulness creates a relationship of "witnessing" oneself and one's body such that it fosters greater reflective awareness (Zhao 2006, 91). While this practice of paying attention can be developed through dedicated meditation time, mindfulness can also be taken into daily life through the cultivation of attentiveness to common activities such as walking, talking with others, and writing.

Mindfulness fosters a kind of attentiveness that aims to interrupt those cognitive thought patterns that lead us to narrate our experiences as we experience them. These "storylines," as they are often called, are forms of received knowledge, acquired through our individual and social histories; mindfulness practice asks that we suspend what we think we know such that we can experience our bodies and our selves more fully and deeply. Through heightened awareness of our feelings and sensations, mindfulness also helps to highlight the notion of impermanence—the idea that no particular state is permanent because the world is constantly changing. With this heightened awareness, we can clearly perceive the fluidity and variability of embodied experiences. This is particularly helpful when working with feelings or sensations that are generally understood to be troublesome or undesirable, such as pain.

I have found the practice of mindfulness meditation to be consistent with phenomenology through the shared emphasis on reflection, embodied awareness, and openness between self and other. (In fact, I began to appreciate the methodological potential of mindfulness practice when the body work I was doing in my conscious movement classes began to resonate with the phenomenology I was reading at the time.) Methodologically, phenomenology involves sustained reflexive engagement with research material through an "attentive awareness" to the subject matter and to the world as it is lived rather than as it is theorized (van Manen 2006, 713). Marianne Paget (1993, 8) describes it in this way:

> Phenomenological work involves both the subject's experience and the phenomenologist's experience. Experience means that which is lived through, *Erlebnis*. The subject or subject matter is not an object in the sense of a thing. The subject or subject matter is explored through the subjectivity of the phenomenologist who perceives the subject matter, the phenomena, as a dialectical relation between self-understanding and understanding the other. Work in this tradition is reflexive and tacks back and forth between the subject matter and observing the subject matter reflexively.

Meaning is thus co-created, and while it inevitably draws upon multiple histories and subjectivities, it also fosters a kind of reflective present/presence.

Larry Rosenberg (1998, 16), a Buddhist scholar and teacher based in the United States, describes mindfulness as a way of being intimate with the world as we experience our world. When we are mindful, he suggests, the distinctions we tend to create between self and other can dissolve. Similarly, reflection in the phenomenological tradition is a way of "bringing into nearness that which tends to be obscure, that which tends to evade the intelligibility of our natural attitude of everyday life" (van Manen 1990, 32). Mindfulness and phenomenology also share a commitment to openness of both the body and thought processes; they are not concerned with reflection as a form of truth-telling but rather with the cultivation of a reflexive practice that allows for sustained embodied engagement with and through the world. In this sense, mindfulness can help to achieve phenomenology's hope for cultivating understanding through the recognition of the inseparability between subject and object, self and other.

Embodied Writing and the Social Production of Pain in Lata Mani's *Interleaves*

Lata Mani's (2001) autobiographical text, *Interleaves,* offers a good illustration of how mindfulness meditation can shape an embodied writing practice and thus act as an intervention into those normative writing conventions that position the body as subordinate to (and, in the case of disabled bodies, interfering with) the privileged work of the intellect. Lata Mani is a scholar, poet, and cultural critic. Formerly a professor at the University of California, Davis, Mani sustained a head injury as a result of a major car accident. In the author's (2001, 73) own words, *Interleaves*

> is about an individual's journey through the social landscapes of our time, through the ways in which society constructs wellness, illness, success, failure, worth, worthlessness, as these are experienced by one woman attempting to live consciously through the trials and tribulations of brain injury. The social construction of illness meant that the rupture brought about by a physical disability and a medical emergency became also an existential crisis, one in which the broader questions of life and death, pain and suffering, belonging and outsider- ness had to be confronted every day and, at times, with every breath.

The book is divided into two parts. Part 1, titled "The Journey," consists of a series of ruminations, as the author calls them, on living with disability and chronic illness. Part 2, "Contemplations," is a series of reflections on seven spiritual principles that the author developed as she learned to live through disability, pain, and suffering. The book blends narrative, critical reflection and poetry and makes use of a variety of different narrative and stylistic devices throughout.

Interleaves is also available as an audio CD, reflecting the medium through which the book was written: the spoken word. Mani initially tape-recorded the text and then had it transcribed—a writing practice that was necessitated by her embodied relationship to knowledge production. Following her car accident, Mani's cognition occurred through hearing; she shared in media interviews that she was no longer able to read or engage in sustained, continuous narrative (Rao 2001). As a result, the narrative structure of the book is quite fluid, comprising relatively short and often overlapping chapters that, when taken together, explore many different aspects of the social location of disability but do not build a comprehensive argument. Instead of offering traceable analytic trajectories or conclusions to anchor the various chapters, Mani shares with readers what she has learned from her experience of disability. However, these pedagogical reflections are themselves provisional because they are grounded in another embodied practice of knowledge production—meditation and breath work.

I want now to examine how the body in pain is being *done* (Mol 2002, 31–32) in *Interleaves* and how this is accomplished through an embodied relationship to knowledge production as it is revealed within the text. The body as something we *do* is highlighted through the emphasis on reflections that have emerged through the embodied practice of meditation; in this sense, key meditation practices such as conscious breath work, observation without evaluation and attachment, and being present in the moment can also be understood methodologically. The text moves between description and discussion, but significantly, Mani returns the reader again and again to the present, to the embodied moment of reflection and the open possibilities of that reflexive space. This represents quite a different intention and temporality than the progressive movement of modernist Western practices of knowledge production that gain authority through coherent, forward-facing narrative and theorizing. In contrast, this text uses a kind of reflective, intersubjective present as a space to consider the workings and sociality of the body, pain, and disability. So while Mani writes of the body, and of *her* body, throughout the text, she consistently writes this body knowledge through her embodied relationship to that knowledge, achieved through meditation practice, and with the reflexive sense that it could also be otherwise. This is exemplified in the following excerpt from Mani (2001, 26–27), drawn from a chapter titled "Pain":

Pain throbs. Pain shreds. Pain darts. Pain weaves sly patterns across the length and breadth of the body. Pain stabs. Pain pulses. Pain plummets the body into a vortex unknown and at times fearful. Pain nags. Chronic pain drones repetitiously, monotonously, ad nauseam. Pain flays the surface of the skin, turning it almost translucent with frailty. Pain makes one so weak that the whole world is experienced through its omnipresent filter. Pain drains everything into its core. Pain can be as focused as the point of a pinhead or as dispersed as one's consciousness and, if suffered long enough, the pinpoint can seem to grow and swallow one's entire physical being. Pain can be as hard as steel or as soft as a ripe pear. Pain shudders. Pain shivers.

Yet, to speak of pain like this is to suggest that it is an entity, a thing, when it is in fact something very difficult to grasp and hold. For when one does not resist pain so it pools, swirls, finds a crevice in the body in which to stay put, pain is revealed as a diaphanous energy permeable, dissolvable, transformable by breath. Pain, it turns out, is not an ice floe that must be hacked away, but a little pocket of stuck energy that can be released by softening, loosening, relaxing, by conscious breathing.

In this passage, knowledge about the body is certainly being produced. But this knowledge, much like embodied life itself, is represented as active, contradictory, and suggestive of other possibilities and experiences. This contingency is most clearly revealed through the break in the narrative, and narrative positioning, of pain's description. Whereas the section begins with a direct rendering of pain as an embodied phenomenon, with the paragraph break, the narrative perspective shifts to a reflexive space, mirroring the process of mindfully working with pain as an embodied experience. While the dominant approach to pain understands it as negation and something to manage, suppress, and eliminate—something to be "hacked away"—Mani's description suggests that through meditation, or "conscious breathing," pain can also be something else.

Pain is thus represented as a relationship between people and their bodies, and as such, it is an intersubjective phenomenon—a social activity mediated by the discourses, practices, and other meaning-making devices available to us. (This is one way in which bodies are *done*.) Mani (2001) also offers us her own body work with breath and meditation and, in so doing, contests medical discourses that seek to categorize, measure, and manage pain. (These are two more ways in which bodies are *done*.) Mani thereby writes the complexity, vulnerability, and social locatedness of embodied life into her narrative and her narrative practice, thus suggesting that one way of contesting those epistemological boundaries that represent bodily pain as somehow outside the social is to shift the very grounds of our theoretical and methodological approaches. (And here are many more ways in which bodies can be done.)

To feel pain, to live with pain, to be in pain is almost certainly accompanied by the desire to not be in pain, in this world. I do not wish to question or negate that desire, even while I would like to unsettle it. What I do desire is that we pay attention to how the body in pain is being accomplished and what this can tell us about bodily norms and difference and the boundaries of knowledge production about and of the body. While this relation to pain as a desired and potential absence is present in Mani's narrative above, I read this as a present-absent dialectic that exists among several different relations to bodily pain. In the text, pain is felt; pain is narrated; pain is written; pain is worded; pain is worked with; pain is held and pain is released; pain is theorized and pain is imagined. Perhaps most significantly, pain is both of the body and beyond it. Pain, when attended to with mindfulness, is a space of shifting, relational encounters with oneself and others. Pain will always exceed its narration.

Mani's narrative also reveals the contingency and indeterminacy of knowledge production about pain and the body. Just as there are multiple relations to pain in the narrative above, so too are there multiple bodies— her body writing, her body doing a mindfulness exercise, her body telling a story, to name a few. In attending to how the body is accomplished through different narrative practices, interpretive devices, and approaches to language, we can clearly appreciate both the multiplicity of the body and embodiment as a social phenomenon. In grounding her narrative in an embodied practice that reaches beyond dominant Western relations to both embodiment and writing, Lata Mani's narrative disrupts the singular authority of medicalized Western knowledge production about pain and the body. In so doing, her embodied narrative practice opens up the possibility of cultivating bodily knowledge that is also resistant knowledge. Indeed, as Mani herself has commented, bringing a sense of spacious attentiveness to our practices of investigation can foster understanding of both self and other that is "explicitly open to perceptual frames being liquefied or recast by the observational and experiential process" (Gunawardena 2011, 24).

Conclusion

In reorienting ourselves to our bodily knowledge, mindfulness meditation offers the possibility of generating not simply new knowledge or critique but, importantly, new ways of being in the world (Ng 2011). This was certainly my experience. What began as an academic interest in the most typical sense became an immersive inquiry into the very grounds of that interest. While this was precipitated by my own experience of pain and disability as it shaped my ability to write and participate in academic knowledge production, it was also informed by a deep commitment to decolonizing research and educational practices. Only by grounding my inquiry firmly within my embodied experience of (re)reading and (re)writing through pain and disability, however, as that experience was enabled by a mindfulness meditation practice, was I able to understand the depth of my investment in normative bodily relations to knowledge production such that I could begin to work at their edges and, at times, to reach beyond them.

As Butler (1999, 17) reminds us, dualistic thinking has important social effects—it is not merely an issue of philosophy in the abstract—for it "invariably supports relations of political and psychic subordination and hierarchy." Bringing together mindfulness meditative practice and phenomenological approaches to knowledge production to foster an embodied writing practice can help to decolonize the tendency toward dualistic thinking that is characteristic of Western social thought and shift the very grounds of our critiques such that the meanings and experiences of embodied phenomena like pain, disability, and embodied difference can be reimagined. To open ourselves up to different ways of understanding and experiencing bodily life thus constitutes an important intervention into those dominant Western practices of knowledge production that reproduce hierarchies of social difference through their reliance upon understandings of embodiment and subjectivity that are underwritten by the mind-body split and other forms of dualistic thinking.

When taken up in the service of social transformation, embodied writing can support a project of decolonization when it intervenes in those academic conventions that discipline our scholarly practices such that colonial discourses of Western modernity retain their grip on our imaginations and our theorizing. Bringing mindfulness together with writing as an embodied practice is suggestive of liberatory possibility, then, insofar as it summons marginalized knowledge and experience (Alexander 2005) and opens up our writing, and the stories we tell, to allow for the presence of embodied and textual difference.

References

Alexander, M. Jacqui. 2005. *Pedagogies of Crossing: Meditations on Feminism, Sexual Politics, Memory, and the Sacred.* Durham, NC: Duke University Press.

Baszanger, Isabel. 1998. "Pain Physicians: All Alike, All Different." In *Differences in Medicine: Unraveling Practices, Techniques, and Bodies,* edited by Marc Berg and Annemarie Mol, 117–43. Durham, NC: Duke University Press.

Bonica, John J., ed. 1990. *The Management of Pain.* 2nd ed. 2 vols. Philadelphia: Lea and Febiger.

Butler, Judith. 1993. *Bodies That Matter: On the Discursive Limits of "Sex."* New York and London: Routledge.

———. 1999. *Gender Trouble.* New York and London: Routledge.

———. 2004. *Undoing Gender.* New York and London: Routledge.

Clifford, James. 1983. "On Ethnographic Authority." *Representations* 1(2): 118–46.

Csordas, Thomas J. 1994. *Embodiment and Experience: The Existential Ground of Culture and Self.* Cambridge: Cambridge University Press.

Ferguson, Susan, and Tanya Titchkosky. 2008. "The Contested Space of the Body in the Academy." In *Whose University Is It, Anyway? Power and Privilege on Gendered Terrain,* edited by Anne E. Wagner, Sandra Acker, and Kimine Mayuzumi, 61–76. Toronto: Sumach Press.

Good, Byron J., and Mary-Jo DelVecchio Good. 1993. "Learning Medicine." In *Knowledge, Power, and Practice: The Anthropology of Medicine and Everyday Life,* edited by Shirley Lindenbaum and Margaret Lock, 81–107. Berkeley: University of California Press.

Good, Mary-Jo DelVecchio, Paul Brodwin, Byron J. Good, and Arthur Kleinman, eds. 1992. *Pain as Human Experience: An Anthropological Perspective.* Berkeley: University of California Press.

Gunawardena, Devaka. 2011. "In Conversation with Lata Mani." *CSW Update Newsletter.* 3 January.

Kabat-Zinn, Jon. 2005. *Full Catastrophe Living: Using the Wisdom of Your Body and Mind to Face Stress, Pain, and Illness.* Rev. ed. New York: Delacorte Press.

Kleinman, Arthur. 1988. *The Illness Narratives: Suffering, Healing, and the Human Condition*. New York: Basic Books.

Kugelmann, Robert. 1997. "The Psychology and Management of Pain: Gate Control as Theory and Symbol." *Theory and Psychology* 7(1): 43–65.

Mani, Lata. 2001. *Interleaves*. Koramangala, India: Lata Mani.

Maracle, Lee. 1990. *Oratory: Coming to Theory*. North Vancouver: Gallerie.

Melzack, Ron, and Patrick D. Wall. 1988. *The Challenge of Pain*. 2nd ed. Markham, ON: Penguin Books.

Merleau-Ponty, Maurice. 2004. "Preface." In *Phenomenology of Perception*. Translated by Colin Smith. New York: Routledge. Originally published as *Phénoménologie de la perception* (1945).

Mohanty, Chandra Talpade. 2003. *Feminism Without Borders: Decolonizing Theory, Practicing Solidarity*. Durham, NC: Duke University Press.

Mol, Annemarie. 2002. *The Body Multiple: Ontology in Medical Practice*. Durham, NC: Duke University Press.

Ng, Roxana. 2000a. "Revisioning the Body/Mind from an Eastern Perspective: Comments on Experience, Embodiment, and Pedagogy." In *Women's Bodies, Women's Lives: Health, Well-Being and Body Image*, edited by Baukje Miedema, Janet M. Stoppard, and Vivienne Anderson, 175–93. Toronto: Sumach Press.

———. 2000b. "Toward an Embodied Pedagogy: Exploring Health and the Body Through Chinese Medicine." In *Indigenous Knowledges in Global Contexts: Multiple Readings of Our World*, edited by George J. Sefa Dei, Budd L. Hall, and Dorothy Goldin Rosenberg, 168–83. Toronto: University of Toronto Press.

———. 2004. "Embodied Pedagogy: New Forms of Learning." Workshop given in the Department of Sociology, Umea University, Umea, Sweden, 5 May, and presentation at Gavle University College, Gavle, Sweden, 10 May.

———. 2011. "Decolonizing Teaching and Learning Through Embodied Learning: Toward an Integrated Approach." In *Valences of Interdisciplinarity: Theory, Practice, Pedagogy*, edited by Raphael Foshay, 343–65. Edmonton: Athabasca University Press.

Nhat Hanh, Thich. 1998. *The Heart of the Buddha's Teaching: Transforming Suffering into Peace, Joy, and Liberation—The Four Noble Truths, The Noble Eightfold Path, and Other Basic Buddhist Teachings*. Berkeley: Parallax Press.

Orr, Deborah. 2002. "The Uses of Mindfulness in Anti-oppressive Pedagogies: Philosophy and Praxis." *Canadian Journal of Education* 27(4): 477–90.

Paget, Marianne. A. 1993. *A Complex Sorrow: Reflections on Cancer and an Abbreviated Life*. Philadelphia: Temple University Press.

Pronger, Brian. 2002. *Body Fascism: Salvation in the Technology of Physical Fitness*. Toronto: University of Toronto Press.

Rao, Sandhya. 2001. "Looking Inward, Growing Outward." *The Hindu*, 24 June. http://www.hinduonnet.com/2001/06/24/stories/1324017d.htm.

Richardson, Laurel. 2004. "Writing: A Method of Inquiry." In *Approaches to Qualitative Research: A Reader on Theory and Practice,* edited by Sharlene Nagy Hesse-Biber and Patricia Leavy, 473–95. New York: Oxford University Press.

Rosenberg, Larry. 1998. *Breath by Breath: The Liberating Practice of Insight Meditation.* Boston: Shambhala.

Scarry, Elaine. 1985. *The Body in Pain: The Making and Unmaking of the World.* New York: Oxford University Press.

Sen, Asha. 2013. *Postcolonial Yearning: Reshaping Spiritual and Secular Discourses in Contemporary Literature.* New York: Palgrave Macmillan.

Smith, Linda Tuhiwai. 1999. *Decolonizing Methodologies: Research and Indigenous Peoples.* London: Zed Books.

Garland-Thomson, Rosemarie. 1997. *Extraordinary Bodies: Figuring Physical Disability in American Culture and Literature.* New York: Columbia University Press.

Titchkosky, Tanya. 2007. *Reading and Writing Disability Differently: The Textured Life of Embodiment.* Toronto: University of Toronto Press.

Tuck, Eve, and K. Wayne Yang. 2012. "Decolonization Is Not a Metaphor." *Decolonization: Indigeneity, Education, and Society* 1(1): 1–40.

van Manen, Max. 1990. *Researching Lived Experience: Human Science for an Action Sensitive Pedagogy.* Ann Arbor, MI: Althouse Press.

———. 2006. "Writing Qualitatively, or the Demands of Writing." *Qualitative Health Research* 16(5): 713–22.

Wainwright, David, Michael W. Calnan, Claire O'Neil, Anna Winterbottom, and Christopher S. Watkins. 2006. "When Pain in the Arm Is 'All in the Head': The Management of Medically Unexplained Suffering in Primary Care." *Health, Risk, and Society* 8(1): 71–88.

Weiss, Gail. 1999. *Body Images: Embodiment as Intercorporeality.* New York and London: Routledge.

Whelan, Emma. 2003. "Putting Pain to Paper: Endometriosis and the Documentation of Suffering." *Health* 7(4): 463–82.

Zhao, Xiaolan. 2006. *Reflections of the Moon on Water: Healing Women's Bodies and Minds Through Traditional Chinese Wisdom.* Toronto: Random House Canada.

13 Class and Embodiment

Making Space for Complex Capacity

Stephanie Moynagh

> *Like washing on a line, these theories flap in a contradictory*
> *wind, creating sound and limited insight constrained by the pegs*
> *that hold them.*
>
> Tanya Lewis (1999)

The ways in which our feelings and intuition can and do guide our move-ments through life is an intriguing area for exploration, one that is gaining space within discourses of embodiment and pedagogy. While settler-colonial institutions are far from valuing any knowledge that does not fall within the dominant paradigm, which privileges rational thought, nondominant ways of being and knowing have always existed and persisted. In this chapter, I discuss the value of emotional and spiritual ways of knowing and delve into some of the complex roots that condition and strengthen these forms of intelligence. More specifically, I focus on how social class experience relates to somatic knowledge. Emotional and spiritual intelligence are clearly woven into our daily lives, but the societal structures within which we live often repress and devalue these competencies. Later in this chapter, I exam-ine how nondominant forms of knowledge can be specifically valued within formal learning environments.

My discussion of emotional and spiritual capacity and experience is rooted in frameworks of embodied knowledge, especially those informed by feminism and critical race theory, and is influenced by theoretical traditions concerned with intersectionality, decolonization, and phenomenology. As will become clear, I am indebted to the scholarship and activism of many Indigenous and Black women, including bell hooks, Leanne Simpson, and Jacqui Alexander, who have helped me reflect on social class and understand my position as a white settler. Joe Kadi's *Thinking Class: Sketches from a Cultural Worker* (1996) has also had an immense impact on my thinking about the connections between class and knowledge.

My exploration of class, embodiment, and ways of knowing includes the profound impact of structural violence inherent to living under colonial, white supremacist, ableist, capitalist, heteropatriarchal systems. Though an in-depth exploration of how systemic, social, and interpersonal forces shape embodied knowledge is beyond the scope of this chapter, the complex and intersectional nature of social experience underpins its entire conversation. In sum, this discussion focuses on exploring the impacts of the privileging of mind-intellect; the embodied knowledges rooted in poverty-class cultures, whether they are related to the impacts of violence and trauma or are simply nondominant ways of being; and the emotional and spiritual intelligences that are often cultivated within poverty-class communities.

Throughout this exploration, I attempt the complex and difficult task of honouring survival while at the same time calling for transformative structural change. My lived experiences as a white, working-class, queer, currently able-bodied woman from poverty-class roots and French Acadian and Irish Catholic settler ancestry frame the doorway through which I enter this conversation. I strive continually to understand that my ideas and lived experiences occur within the contexts of settler colonialism and white supremacy, to recognize the grave importance of situating class oppression within the ongoing processes of colonialism and white supremacy, and to acknowledge the particularity of my experience and perspective. As a white settler, I am profoundly limited in my ability to develop a felt understanding of such processes since I do not experience the daily violence of racism or colonialism in the ways in which racialized and Indigenous people do. Certainly, experiences of poverty are vastly different for different people because of intersecting identities related to race, Indigeneity, and many other aspects of social identity. Beyond the limitations in my understanding, I am also implicated in the reproduction of the colonial nation and of white supremacy; thus, I carry the lifelong responsibility of acknowledging this history and ongoing reality and of working toward dismantling oppressive forces and building alternatives.

My understanding of class oppression across the settler-colonial state of Canada begins with its direct relation to colonialism, since the production of poverty through capitalism would not survive without the theft and exploitation of Indigenous lands. Maile Arvin, Eve Tuck, and Angie Morrill (2013, 12) describe settler colonialism as a "persistent social and political formation in which newcomers/colonizers/settlers come to a place, claim it as their own, and do whatever it takes to disappear the Indigenous peoples that are there. Within settler colonialism it is the exploitation of land that yields supreme value." The appropriation of Indigenous land was especially crucial to the development of capitalism in Canada, a country whose economy continues to be founded on resource extraction and export. Respect for life and the relationships between living beings and the rest of the natural world is not important to the capitalist Canadian settler-colonial state (Woroniak and Camfield 2013). In 2013, Leanne Simpson, a Mississauga Nishnaabeg writer and spoken-word artist, discussed the close ties between colonialism and capitalism with Naomi Klein:

> Colonialism and capitalism are based on extracting and assimilating. My land is seen as a resource. My relatives in the plant and animal worlds are seen as resources. My culture and knowledge is a resource. My body is a resource and my children are a resource because they are the potential to grow, maintain, and uphold the extraction-assimilation system. The act of extraction removes all of the relationships that give whatever is being extracted meaning. Extracting is taking. Actually, extracting is stealing—it is taking without consent, without thought, care or even knowledge of the impacts that extraction has on the other living things in that environment. That's always been a part of colonialism and conquest. (Simpson, quoted in Klein 2013)

Writer and activist Harsha Walia emphasizes the need for social justice movements to recognize the structural relationship between systems of oppression and settler colonialism:

Indigenous communities face deliberate impoverishment. It's not a coincidence that Indigenous communities and predominantly communities of colour face mass impoverishment.

Patriarchy within settler colonialism is organized around the destruction of Indigenous nationhood, Indigenous families and the deliberate targeting of Indigenous women. Obviously land destruction and environmental degradation are also part and parcel of settler colonialism. (Quoted in Hadley 2014)

Understanding the connections among colonialism, white supremacy, capitalism, and class oppression has helped me to understand what decolonization means to me as a white settler invested in transformative change. Decolonization can (and does) mean many things, and I believe that it is the right of Indigenous peoples to define and direct its meaning. As a white settler, I aim to be accountable to the reality that my ancestors and I have been complicit in colonial violence from our arrival on this land to this day. Though I am still learning what it means to be accountable to ongoing colonialism, to me this work includes supporting Indigenous sovereignty and self-determination and actively working toward dismantling and building alternatives to the systems in place that prevent living sustainably with the land. First and foremost, in understanding my role and responsibilities as a white settler, I strive to continue listening to Indigenous people and actively supporting Indigenous-led movements.

My experiences of growing up on social assistance, being raised by a single mother who was excluded from the wage-labour system because of her disability, moving every year in search of safer housing, and facing other poverty-related challenges have informed my drive to understand how oppressive systems are connected and how we can build coalitions to work toward transformative structural change. My early understandings of the world included an embodied awareness of injustice through multiple and varied experiences related to being a girl and being poor. Though the colonial and white privileges that I and my family members experience have, in many ways, shaped our lives beyond measure, my class-based experiences have also impacted my world view and informed my relative lack of investment in dominant systems, institutions, and ideologies since childhood.

The embodied knowledges I bring to this discussion are in constant flux as I continue learning how to recognize and honour different forms of knowledge. My perceptions also continue to evolve as I move through a lifelong process of understanding all the ways in which my experiences and perceptions have been informed by the oppressive systems from which I benefit. These evolving perceptions also inform my ultimate limitations in speaking to the connections as well as the vast differences that exist within the intersectional experience of poverty as it relates to emotional and spiritual capacity. As such, the embodied knowledges that I discuss in this chapter are rooted in my particular experiences of class culture and trauma survivorhood.

Mind-Intellect Privileging and Embodied Experience

Though embodiment studies, with its wide scope, has significantly reformulated how we understand bodies and their engagement with the external world, an enormous gap remains between the validation afforded to many by such critical work and the assumptions that continue to inform dominant practice within state institutions. Much literature exists outlining the harmful impact of the Cartesian paradigm that dominates Eurocentric ideologies of the body and that privileges mind-intellect over any other form of knowledge. Such work is compelling in its call to recognize the disembodying consequences of the dominant paradigm and the far-reaching practices that continue to be built on its premises.

Heesoon Bai (2001, 86) identifies two such consequences in making clear that she reproves the "intellectualist bias and resulting disembodiment in our educational practice." Bai contends that this bias has resulted in both "lack of intrinsic valuing of the world and inability to translate knowledge into action." She explains that our linguistic-conceptual mind is "inherently disembodying in that it replaces percepts by concepts; when this happens, our ability to experience reality directly as a perceiving and feeling being is severely limited by the excessive (and obsessive) engagement with concepts" (87–89).

I have drawn heavily from theorists such as Bai in their interrogation of dominant knowledge-producing paradigms and this work has led me to explore the idea that "our" linguistic-conceptual mind, as referenced by Bai, may manifest differently depending on one's social experiences. Though everyone educated within settler-colonial state institutions is influenced by the dominant Cartesian paradigm, nuanced distinctions remain in how we are socialized outside of such institutions, particularly as influenced by pervasive power systems that shape constructions of race, gender, and social class. One's social experience outside of formal learning environments can contribute significantly to the complex interaction with systems that promote what Bai describes as the pervading "emotional alienation" from material reality as a result of "the hyperactivity of the linguistic-conceptual mind" (Bai 2001, 91). Later in this chapter, I come back to the impact of social class on one's relationship to the notion of having a sensing and perceiving body; I simply note here that institutionalized mind-intellect privileging is not the only force at play.

The privileging of intellectual forms of knowledge ingrained in the state education system and much of the public arena at large has very real, detrimental, and multifaceted impacts on people across social locations, and in very different ways. Since all state institutions were built on colonialism and white supremacy, it is not surprising that the education system continues to maintain oppressive class structures, racial hierarchies, and a multitude of other forms of violence. In Peter McLaren's widely cited book, *Life in Schools*, he describes how students are shaped by the "hidden curriculum," which he defines as "the unintended outcomes of the schooling process." McLaren explains that the hidden curriculum of a traditional education system "favors certain forms of knowledge over others and affirms the dreams, desires, and values of select groups of students over others, often discriminatorily on the basis of race, class, and gender" in order to "prepare students for dominant or subordinate positions in the existing society" (1989, 183). Deborah Orr (2002, 479) echoes many others in her description of how the hidden curriculum continues to persist in schools (479). Orr further details how sexism, racism, classism, and homophobia produce privileged groups that are identified with "the mind and intellectual activities of cultural production, while subordinated groups are affiliated with the body, emotion, and physical and reproductive labour" (479).

The failure of education systems to respect and value the intelligence of what is often perceived as the "mindless" body includes emotional and spiritual knowledge. Marjorie O'Loughlin (2006, 145) argues that "what needs to be given greater emphasis is the recognition of the role of the body as agent within a world of bodies which continually transform themselves and their world." As she goes on to point out, "Knowledge is not simply that

which must be understood; it is always felt and responded to *somatically*"
(my emphasis).

One's relationship to somatic experience and somatic ways of knowing can be greatly influenced by the socialization embedded in social class
structures. A number of academics have written about the connections
among class, embodiment, lived experience, and ways of knowing. Emily
Martin's (2001) research regarding different forms of resistance to dominant
discourses involving women's bodies speaks to these connections. Martin's
research reveals that working-class women are less inclined to adopt medical understandings about women's bodies, preferring instead to emphasize
how their own body *feels, looks, or smells*. It is reasonable to assume that the
somatic responses given by women in Martin's research stemmed largely
from their direct lived experience of social class. Of course, given the intersectional nature of class-based lived realities, the somatic experience of
poverty is vastly different for different people and communities. My childhood experience of (white) poverty, for example, which resulted from a
single mother's exclusion from the ableist wage-labour system, is in many
ways incomparable to the added somatic and psychic experiences of poverty
related to colonial violence and racism.

Although many aspects of social experience contribute to somatic knowledge, Martin's research suggests that lived experience of marginalization,
including exclusion from certain levels of formal education, fosters particular kinds of nondominant knowledge. In the American context of Martin's
research, poverty-based barriers to health care provision force reliance on
one's own knowledge and that of one's community, combined always with
knowledge fostered within cultures rooted in other social identities and
collective experiences related to race, ethnicity, ability, sexuality, and more.
Martin's research asserts that this everyday resistance to dominant ideology acts as an example of a phenomenological perspective, in contrast to
perspectives informed by the Western medical model, which are divorced
from accounts of women's direct experience (2001). Her work illustrates the
distinct quality of somatic experiences and expressions of working-class
women, who could very well contribute to knowledge discourse if they were
more widely recognized as worthy of such.

Along the same lines, Kathy Davis (2007) speaks of Paula M. L. Moya's
(1997) criticism of the poststructuralist rejection of experience from the

perspective of marginalized women of colour. Davis discusses the ways in which the bodily experiences of socially marginalized groups have been excluded from dominant medical *and* postmodern feminist discourses alike. She references Dorothy Smith (1990) in calling for space to be made for discursive agency in exploring "how women knowledgeably, competently, and flexibly draw upon, interpret, and re-articulate cultural discourses as they negotiate their life circumstances" in ways that include somatic experience (Davis 2007, 59). This affirmation speaks to the need to recognize that experience, including emotional experience, is always mediated by cultural discourse and institutional practice, yet it can and should be given genuine credence for the information and knowledge it contributes to discourse and theory formulation itself. Along the same vein, Kadi (1996) writes of how middle- and upper-middle-class academics have traditionally sought out the experiences and stories of working-class and poor people for use in shaping theory. The drive behind my desire to write about class culture and knowledge is informed and inspired by Joe Kadi, Dorothy Allison, and others who have written about their own class-based identities and who have insisted on valuing the many knowledges that arose from the materiality of their lives.

Embodied Trauma: Coexisting Winds

The attachment of meaning to our embodied experiences is not a simple process. Embodied experience varies widely, always shaped by the pervasive impacts of power structures that affect different bodies in different ways. Making sense of our somatic experience is also influenced by cultural discourse and by the limitations of cognitive processes of understanding. The research cited above relating to working-class lives, sentient experience, and knowledge needs to be grounded in ever-deepening understandings of the impacts of an extremely harmful economic world order, intersecting forms of oppression, and the complex experiential effects bred by the material realities of so many people's lives. Membership in identity categories such as working-class, working-poor, poverty-class, low-income, or cash-poor is also confusing because class-based experience and identity can shift dramatically over time.

My understanding of class as culture aligns with Rita Mae Brown's description of class in her essay "The Last Straw" (as quoted in hooks 2000,

103): "Class is much more than Marx's definition of relationship to the means of production. Class involves your behavior, your basic assumptions, how you are taught to behave, what you expect from yourself and from others, your concept of a future, how you understand problems and solve them, how you think, feel, act." Brown's comment speaks to the expansive ground that forging links between class experience and sentient knowledge attempts to cover. The exchange of labour for low wages and/or the systemic exclusion from the wage-labour system and making ends meet with very limited resources is conducive to engendering an array of embodied knowledges, some of which we may wish to celebrate and honour, but we must never lose sight of the violent structures that produce poverty and continue to cause great harm. The intersecting oppressions rooted in colonialism and white supremacy (and the concomitant patriarchal, ableist, and heteronormative forces) shape one's embodied experience of poverty in distinct and immeasurable ways.

Dorothy Allison, an American writer with lived experience of intergenerational poverty, has explored themes of class struggle and childhood trauma and has spoken to the multifaceted nature of knowledge carried by white, southern US-based poverty-class communities. Through her novels and essays, Allison points to the need to discuss openly and honestly both the pride and the shame that many people experience around poverty and class culture. "I have loved my family so stubbornly," she writes, "that every impulse to hold them in contempt has sparked in me a counter-surge of pride—complicated and undercut by an urge to fit us into the acceptable myths and theories of both mainstream society and a lesbian-feminist reinterprctation" (Allison 1994, 15).

The systemic and interpersonal violence stemming from colonialism, racism, poverty, and other oppressive structures can result in both embodying and disembodying experiences. Carla Rice and Vanessa Russell (1995) discuss the impacts of systems of oppression on the body in terms of the daily experiences of dehumanization in people's lives, including the effects of poverty and classism, which are often compounded by other intersecting forms of violence. They acknowledge the ways in which many girls and women disconnect from their feelings and bodies and distrust their knowledge of the world because of experiences related to abuse and oppression (23). Rice and Russell name this survival strategy "female disembodiment."

Disembodiment is a defining effect of traumatic experience, and systemic oppression is increasingly being recognized as a fundamental source of trauma—trauma being the lasting effects of violence in the body-mind-spirit. Yolo Akili (2011) discusses this idea in his article "The Immediate Need for Emotional Justice":

> Oppression is trauma. Every form of inequity has a traumatic impact on the psychology, emotionality and spirituality of the oppressed. The impact of oppressive trauma creates cultural and individual wounding. This wounding produces what many have called a "pain body," a psychic energy that is not tangible but can be sensed, that becomes an impediment to the individual and collective's ability to transform and negotiate their conditions. (Akili 2000, para. 1)

Akili's message here is pointed and powerful. I believe that the embodied energy, the "pain body," that he speaks of can be the source of enormous and valuable capacity. This takes nothing away from the critical need to recognize the injustice and violence that is the source of this pain, nor does it negate calls for dismantling hegemonic systems. It is simply another conversation from a different angle, one that recognizes the capacities that can be generated through traumatic experience and pain—not for the purpose of minimizing the violence of oppression but to honour survival modes and skills and to validate the knowledge that is built through them.

The remainder of Akili's article and his notion of emotional justice speaks precisely to this idea of cultivating a deep respect for emotional-sentient experience. Though he does not use the word *knowledge,* he speaks of taking emotional pain seriously and drawing from our embodied injuries to push forward our struggles for justice and change: "Emotional justice is about working with this wounding. It is about inviting us into our feelings and our bodies, and finding ways to transform our collective and individual pains into power" (Akili 2011).

Vanissar Tarakali (2010) contributes to this discussion through her psycho-educational work on trauma and oppression. She views the effects of trauma on embodied beings through a lens that gives space and value to survival skills. She acknowledges that interpersonal violence and trauma, as well as repeated experiences of social oppression (racism, sexism, classism, ableism, transphobia, homophobia, antisemitism, ageism, and other forms of systemic oppression), result in individuals and communities practicing whichever strategies have helped them survive in the past. She names these strategies—caretaking, appeasing, hypervigilance, spacing out, avoidance, withdrawal, isolating, and many other behaviours. I believe that Tarakali's framing of survival strategies is valuable and important, especially in the context of raising awareness about trauma and healing. However, I also think it is valuable and important to examine the embodied effects of trauma that contribute to ways of knowing and being that can grow our capacities, serve us and those around us, without legitimizing or glorifying the violent nature of oppression.

I have found it confusing at times to separate capacity born out of traumatic experience from the aspects of poverty and working-class culture and existence that simply give rise to nondominant ways of being. Coexisting identities and experiences related to Indigeneity, racialization, gender identity, ability, sexuality, and citizenship (and many more) are often entwined with our experiences of class and shape our vast capacity for embodied knowledge. In navigating these intersecting pathways, I endeavour in this discussion to forge connections between class culture and sentient knowledge while recognizing the ways in which power structures affect bodies differently, producing variant somatic experiences. I also aim to create space for uncomplicated pride, for the pain, grief, rage, and limits imposed by systemic oppression and trauma, and for valuing the capacities and heightened senses that grow out of the combination of these elements.

Emotional and Spiritual Knowledge

As I sit in a nondescript coffee franchise writing this paper, as the ideas I am mulling over stimulate the cerebral areas of my brain, I am simultaneously holding in awareness (and at times am overcome by) the young employee working alone behind the counter, contending with the constant and impatient stream of early holiday shoppers wanting coffee. He has acknowledged that he is new to the job; he is visibly stressed and overwhelmed by the never-ending line. I am permeable to the emotional energy emitting from where he stands. Empathy provokes me to feel the tension of everyone's demands on his newly trained skills, his spectrum of emotion, his possible resentment for being made to work a solo shift on a Saturday afternoon in December. I can physically feel some of the tension induced by silent frowns, tapping feet, and pointed glares shot his way when the full cash tray accidentally slips from his hands to the floor. Before conscious thought, I send empathetic glances toward him. I make a joke in an attempt to loosen the anxiety, vocalize at some point that it must be hard to single-handedly run the cafe on a day like today. Until the line finally clears, I attempt to hold the space with him while simultaneously doing my own work, and he seems to feel it (though I can never be sure).

I am aware that we project our own emotional experiences onto others to some extent in all encounters and that social location impacts our projections as well. Even with the enmeshed element of projection, though, the dynamic in this particular encounter remains clear: emotional engagement, an embodied interaction, is taking place alongside my exercise in intellectualizing the experience on this page, and at times, it takes precedence. This inclination has not always served me well. It can require intense personal reflection and careful attention to emotional boundaries. However, I believe that an act like this could be considered a form of intelligence, insofar as it lends itself to faculties of understanding, to connection and the ability to shift dynamics in the social world. Marjorie O'Loughlin (2006) describes this phenomenon as "fellow-feeling" and emphasizes the importance of developing and sustaining the capacity to empathize, coupled with a willingness to engage, all of which contrasts with dominant rational, objective, and detached ways of knowing and being. O'Loughlin asserts that she sees "the root of all emotions as lying in prior events in the lives of individuals and social groups which, over time, build a certain reservoir of reactions and response" (125). Her affirmation supports the notion that class identity and experience make significant contributions to the development of one's emotional being and emotional capacity.

Kadi (1996, 147) speaks frankly and directly to the existence of such capacities for emotional response within working-class cultures:

> Working-class people express feelings more than rich people, know
> how to laugh, cry, and love with abandon, find happiness in every-
> day life. And not because of anything innate, biological or essential.
> These tendencies clearly illustrate the workings of the class system. As
> working-class people, we haven't been socialized into grim, restrictive
> sets of manners, social codes and behaviours. We don't have to act
> politely or formally, don't have to dole out emotions and feelings

carefully and precisely, little bits at a time. . . . This doesn't mean we're all emotionally healthy and vibrant, able to express and feel deep, authentic emotion. But there's more possibility for any of this to arise.

It is notable that Kadi, a self-identified feminist, does not acknowledge the profound influence of gender conditioning on emotionality. I do not believe that Kadi would negate or minimize the impact of such social forces; rather, through his omission, Kadi speaks to the weight that class culture, in all its complexity, places on emotional capacity.

While I believe that being socialized as female greatly influenced my emotional inclinations, certain aspects of my disposition and willingness to engage often feel markedly different from many of the women I walk alongside who come from more class-privileged backgrounds. My experiences with a poverty-induced unstable home life during childhood also contributed much to the emotional intelligence that I gained and carry with me today. Being immediately attuned to the emotional energy in a room and relieving tension if possible was probably paramount to my survival during my developmentally formative years. As a result, emotional attunement and perceptiveness are among the qualities that I relate most directly to my early life experiences, which were deeply shaped by the poverty-class conditions of the homes and communities I grew up in.

Stress, instability, and shame resulting from systemic discrimination and the weight of living with limited resources have profound effects on all aspects of health and family systems. Again, I can only speak to my own particular experience of poverty as a white, cis-gendered child of settler ancestry in urban maritime and southwestern Ontarian contexts. One's experience of poverty at a different social intersection would look and feel very different. In my experience and observation, conditions of poverty and the instability that ensues can pose severe limits on one's ability to cope and navigate social mores, while also serving to sharpen certain skills that guide survival and produce particular ways of moving around with more ease. The ability to be emotionally attuned to those around, to be highly perceptive and empathetic, to be able to summon scanning searchlights to suss out danger, to carefully consider all possible eventualities, to be incredibly resourceful—these are only some of the competencies that are shaped by experiences associated with poverty and working-class backgrounds.

In addition to focusing on class structure, feminist theorists have written extensively regarding discourse on sexism and racism, emotional conditioning, and knowledge production. O'Loughlin (2006, 126) details the historical "characterization of emotion as irrational because of its supposedly compulsive and disruptive nature, but also because of its historic association with women and 'the feminine,'" as well as "its depiction as threat to the functioning of cognition and rationality." This history, informed by profoundly racist and classist colonial ideologies and discourse, produces the systemic devaluing of emotional ways of knowing. Sara Ahmed's critique of how emotions are perceived and discussed, in *The Cultural Politics of Emotion* (2004), also contributes much to this discourse. Ahmed argues for the importance of examining how emotions are *produced* and cautions against thinking about emotionality as a characteristic of individual or collective bodies. She states that emotions become "qualities" that seem to reside in objects only through an erasure of the history of their production and circulation; that it is the objects of emotion that circulate, not the emotion itself (11). This notion is relevant to the conversation about how class conditions emotional capacity in that it is important to be clear that this conditioning is rooted in social and cultural forces and that one's emotional response is subject to such forces at all times.

In exploring the sociality of emotions, cultural theorists have pointed to the sociohistorical contexts that produce systemic exclusionary practices around nondominant forms of intelligence. Kadi (1996), for example, speaks of "intelligence" as being similar to social constructions such as "race" in that it is defined in a limited and narrow way by the ruling class. Kadi asserts that despite the privileging of mind-intellect in the West, many different kinds of intelligence exist:

> Equally valid types of intelligence enable a child to design and build a bird house, a mother to balance a budget with no money, an "uneducated" man to enthrall listeners with stories, . . . three young women to invent scathing responses to catcalls and whistles. These types of intelligence require creativity, humor, ability to ask questions, care, a good memory, compassion, belief in solidarity, ability to project an image of something that doesn't physically exist. (51)

Emotional and spiritual capacities are closely entwined. People connect with spirit and embodied knowledge in a myriad of ways. My sister and I have always discussed the spiritual connections we feel despite not having been raised with religion or taught any spiritual practices. As we have worked on building containers for understanding our experiences, I've reflected on the factors in our lives that may have contributed to the openness we have had to recognizing moments where we sense the spirit world, listening to dreams and intuition and experiencing sensations that seem distinctively unphysical. In my own experience, I believe that growing up around the nonnormativity of poverty-class culture—which includes more emphasis on interdependence, less investment in "rational" ways of being, less faith in dominant institutions and the "truths" they espouse, and the out-loud-ness of different ways of being and experiencing the world that are characteristic of many poverty-class communities—informed my receptiveness to instances that I can't immediately understand or classify, such as the sensing of spirit.

Jacqui Alexander's (2005) compelling personal account of her own spiritual life and critical call for meaningful validation of spiritual knowledge has contributed immensely to discourse relating to social location and forms of knowledge that continue to be marginalized within dominant institutions. Her sentient expressions of sacred accompaniment—of guidance, identity, and the importance of "knowing who walks with you"—illustrate just one aspect of the deep wealth of knowledge possessed by many who live with strong spiritual connections. Alexander's words are powerful in their frank assertion of truths and their critique of dominant values around knowledge production, including those within postmodern feminist discourse:

> Those who would characterize this world of the post-modern and
> the identities of its inhabitants as absent of this essence or core would
> seem to be at odds with the thought systems of a great number of
> people in the world who live the belief that their lives are intimately
> and tangibly paired to the world of the invisible. (327)

Alexander goes on to assert that "taking the Sacred seriously would propel us to take the lives of primarily working-class women and men seriously, and it would move us away from theorizing primarily from the point of marginalization" (328). Though the extent to which a spiritual world view is seen by many to be vital to human well-being is beyond the scope of this chapter, spirituality is often cited as a source of personal and collective power. David Este and Wanda Thomas Bernard (2006) focus on the spiritual lives within a community of African Nova Scotians. They discuss the lived experience of people who speak of their spiritual health as an important aspect of physical health and overall well-being. That the material realities inherent to intergenerational poverty and working-class culture can be conducive to spiritual knowledge is widely accepted. It's the devaluing and marginalization of such knowledges that closet what Alexander (2005, 301) calls "the strengthening of intimacy between personhood and sacred accompaniment."

In my own family experience, my maternal grandmother spoke out loud to invisible worlds alongside connections with those physically present. Several different, coexisting narratives accumulated around her life and other family members' experiences over time—including the presence of the invisible, internal stimuli, wisdom, spiritual devotion, mental health, psychiatrization, and intergenerational trauma. I use this example to reiterate the existence of simultaneous realities and to touch on the many different forms of spiritual connection. Reflecting on my own family also calls me to recognize the ways in which social location mediates our experience. It is undeniable that various members of my family would probably have faced very different consequences if they had not benefited from colonial and white privilege. Though forced psychiatrization and incarceration due to nonnormative behaviour are a part of my family's experience, I know that if my grandmother had been Indigenous, she may not have had the privilege of keeping her six children, nor would she have been spared from residential schooling, displacement, loss of language, and cultural and spiritual genocide. Such experiences engender an array of psychic and spiritual knowledges that I could not personally speak to, but which many have written about.

Alongside the harm that my grandmother did bear as a result of the way she experienced life and expressed herself, it was also clear that her understanding of the world, largely informed by her relationship with an invisible realm, contributed to her capacity to communicate, intuit, and offer comfort and guidance to others.

I return here to Jacqui Alexander's (2005, 326) question: "What would taking the Sacred seriously mean for transnational feminism and related radical projects, beyond an institutionalized use value of theorizing marginalization?" As Rice and Russell (1995) and Alexander (2005) suggest, there is a great need to move embodiment discourse beyond theorizing marginalization and toward making real space for the lives and experiences of those whose knowledges have been devalued and whose contributions should be integral to the development of theory itself. I aim to add to the many voices calling for the recognition of nondominant knowledge—including the capacity for genuine empathy, perceptiveness, and interconnection between embodied beings and the spirit world.

Implications for Pedagogy

All learning environments, both formal and informal, need to make meaningful space for nondominant ways of knowing and relating to the world: Indigenous knowledges, emotional and spiritual ways of knowing, trauma-induced forms of knowledge, and the widely varying learning styles that are born from widely varying experiences, to name a few. Orr (2002, 480) asserts that even the most radical pedagogies remain largely cognitive, thus functioning primarily on the intellectual level and inherently limiting the potential to effectively create the necessary conditions to achieve deep levels of transformation in students' lives. Until such a time when the way we organize ourselves socially is dramatically different from the oppressive structures currently in place, formalized education systems would better serve students by integrating embodied approaches to teaching and learning. If a strong sense of humour, spiritual attunement, skills based in social and emotional communication, cooperative efforts, perceptiveness, intuition, camaraderie, storytelling, creativity, innovation, and materially resourceful inclinations were genuinely valued as intelligences equal to those perceived as "intellectual" competencies, more people living poverty-class lives may feel a sense of meaning, validation, and mobility within educational walls. Other examples are offered by Jenny Horsman in her work on women, violence, and literacy, where she argues that a society that values one form of reading—the reading of print—discounts all other forms. Horsman (1999, 31) makes reference to Indigenous educator Priscilla George, who talks about "stressing the value of the traditional 'reading' of the environment—the weather, tracks and so on—skills that many Indigenous people know well which are often discounted [in dominant institutions]."

As many educators have noted, current modes of teaching do not treat the learner as an embodied subject, and critical calls have been made for more holistic pedagogies that proactively acknowledge the interconnectedness of our mind, body, emotion, and spirit in the construction and pursuit of knowledge (Ng 2011, 1). As teachers and learners, we need to develop the language needed to express how we embody our emotional and spiritual struggles within learning environments, to recognize the capacity to feel strongly and to think, and to be supported in this process. We need to recognize ourselves and each other as whole people—mind, body, and spirit. We need to value our lived experiences and the intelligences that are cultivated through struggle and survival as much as we value more conventional notions of achievement.

Conclusion

In this chapter, I have aimed to highlight connections among colonialism, white supremacy, and class oppression as a starting point to a full discussion on how class-based experiences can give rise to particular knowledges and capacities. I discussed the notion that the historical entrenchment of rationality, foundational to Western-colonial social thought, takes a stronger hold among people who have benefited most from white supremacy, heteropatriarchy, and capitalism and among those whose bodies reflect most closely the privileged norm. Valuable and varying forms of knowledge exist among people living outside of dominant norms in a multitude of ways, including people living within poverty and working-class cultures.

In delving into some of the complex roots that condition and strengthen nondominant knowledge, I explored how systemic and interpersonal violence and trauma stemming from conditions of poverty can result in both embodying and disembodying experiences. I have attempted to place this reality in conversation with the notion of honouring survival, valuing the existing array of poverty-class knowledges and competencies, and, at the same time, calling for counterhegemonic change. In the vein of holding complex realities, the aforementioned ideas stand to show that injury and resiliency can and generally do coexist—that one need not cancel out the other and that our education systems in particular need to make more space for forms of knowledge that reflect the full spectrum of lived realities. Finally, beyond reform to current structures, a massive dismantling of these structures is required in order for transformative change to take root. The success of this effort depends on broad-based connection building among people whose lived experiences inform our shared investment in nondominant ways of knowing, being, healing, teaching, and learning.

References

Ahmed, Sara. 2004. *The Cultural Politics of Emotion*. New York and London: Routledge.

Akili, Yolo. 2011. "The Immediate Need for Emotional Justice." *The Crunk Feminist Collective*, 16 November. http://crunkfeministcollective.wordpress. com/2011/11/16/the-immediate-need-for-emotional-justice/.

Alexander, M. Jacqui. 2005. *Pedagogies of Crossing: Meditations on Feminism, Sexual Politics, Memory, and the Sacred*. Durham, NC: Duke University Press.

Allison, Dorothy. 1994. *Skin: Sex, Class, and Literature*. New York: Firebrand Books.

Arvin, Maile, Eve Tuck, and Angie Morrill. 2013. "Decolonizing Feminism: Challenging Connections Between Settler Colonialism and Heteropatriarchy." *Feminist Formations* 25(1): 8–34.

Bai, Heesoon. 2001. "Beyond the Educated Mind: Towards a Pedagogy of Mindfulness." In *Unfolding Bodymind: Exploring Possibility Through Education*, edited by Brent Hocking, Johnna Haskell, and Warren Linds, 86–99. Brandon, VT: Foundation for Educational Renewal.

Davis, Kathy. 2007. "Reclaiming Women's Bodies: Colonialist Trope or Critical Epistemology?" In *Embodying Sociology: Retrospect, Progress, and Prospects*, edited by Chris Shilling, 50–64. Malden, MA: Blackwell.

Este, David, and Wanda Thomas Bernard. 2006. "Spirituality Among African Nova Scotians: A Key to Survival in Canadian Society." *Critical Social Work* 7(1). http://www.uwindsor.ca/criticalsocialwork/spirituality-among-african-nova-scotians-a-key-to-survival-in-canadian-society.

Hadley, Candida. 2014. "In Canada Every System of Oppression Is Organized Around Settler-Colonialism: An Interview with Harsha Walia." *Halifax Media Co-op*, 22 February. http://halifax.mediacoop.ca/story/canada-every-system-oppression-organized-around-se/21813.

hooks, bell. 2000. *Where We Stand: Class Matters*. New York and London: Routledge.

Horsman, Jenny. 1999. *Too Scared to Learn: Women, Violence, and Education*. Toronto: McGilligan Books.

Kadi, Joe. 1996. *Thinking Class: Sketches from a Cultural Worker.* Cambridge, MA: South End Press.

Klein, Naomi. 2013. "Dancing the World into Being: A Conversation with Idle No More's Leanne Simpson." *Yes Magazine,* 5 March. http://www.yesmagazine. org/peace-justice/dancing-the-world-into-being-a-conversation-with-idle-no-more-leanne-simpson.

Lewis, Tanya. 1999. *Living Beside: Performing Normal After Incest Memories Return.* Toronto: McGilligan Books.

Martin, Emily. 2001. *The Woman in the Body: A Cultural Analysis of Reproduction.* Boston: Beacon Press.

McLaren, Peter. 1989. *Life in Schools: An Introduction to Critical Pedagogy in the Foundations of Education.* Toronto: Irwin Publishing.

Moya, Paula M. L. 1997. "Postmodernism, 'Realism,' and the Politics of Identity: Cherríe Moraga and Chicana Feminism." In *Feminist Genealogies, Colonial Legacies, Democratic Futures,* edited by M. Jacqui Alexander and Chandra Talpade Mohanty, 125–50. London and New York: Routledge.

Ng, Roxana. 2011. "Decolonizing Teaching and Learning Through Embodied Learning: Toward an Integrated Approach." In *Valences of Interdisciplinarity: Theory, Practice, Pedagogy,* edited by Raphael Foshay, 343–65. Edmonton: Athabasca University Press.

O'Loughlin, Marjorie. 2006. *Embodiment and Education: Exploring Creatural Existence.* Dordrecht: Springer.

Orr, Deborah. 2002. "The Uses of Mindfulness in Anti-oppressive Pedagogies: Philosophy and Praxis." *Canadian Journal of Education* 27(4): 477–90.

Rice, Carla, and Vanessa Russell. 1995. "Embodying Equity: Putting Body and Soul into Equity Education—Part 1: How Oppression Is Embodied." *Our Schools / Our Selves* 7(2): 14–36.

Smith, Dorothy E. 1990. *The Conceptual Practices of Power: A Feminist Sociology of Knowledge.* Boston: Northeastern University Press.

Tarakali, Vanissar. 2010. "Surviving Oppression; Healing Oppression." *Vanissar Tarakali's Blog,* 1 May. http://www.vanissar.com/blog/tag/healing/.

Woroniak, Monique, and David Camfield. 2013. "Choosing Not to Look Away: Confronting Colonialism in Canada." *New Socialist,* 27 January. http://www. newsocialist.org/676-choosing-not-to-look-away-confronting-colonialism-in-canada.

14   Fighting Out

Fractious Bodies and Rebel Streets

Jamie Magnusson

Fighting Out began in downtown Toronto as an Adult Education and Community Development program offering qigong and civil self-defence to the LGBT2Q community. In this chapter, I explain how the collective practice of civil self-defence can be an effective way to build social movements and transform social relations organizing political violence. From practicing civil self-defence in a community space, LGBT2Q collectives can go on to organize events that hook into social movements and work toward solidarity building. In contrast to traditional self-defence curricula, the Fighting Out pedagogy encourages collective grassroots action against state violence—a frequently experienced form of violence for Indigenous, racialized, queer, and trans women. Soon after Fighting Out was initiated, it became inte grated into a program for sex workers operating out of the All Saints Church and Community Centre in downtown Toronto. In this context, qigong and self-defence became an extension of a harm-reduction philosophy of community engagement and adult education.

Fighting Out is examined as an example of embodied social movement learning in the tradition of Marxist feminist grassroots community organizing. Fighting Out, I argue, is organized in the context of a project of reclaiming urban spaces from global financialized imaginaries which are characterized by gentrification and state violence against poor women via criminalization, incarceration, and expulsions from public housing that are slated for closure, and then redeveloped as privatized condos. Fighting

Out fits into efforts to reclaim and decolonize urban spaces and engage in feminist community development.

Some Background

My own interest in bringing together civil self-defence practice with political organizing began many years ago. Through practicing a particular Okinawan martial art, goju ryu, I came into contact with women from various martial arts styles who shared a vision of connecting what they had learned within traditional masculinist and often militarized martial arts spaces with feminist, queer, antiracist grassroots organizing. Many of these women had been politicized during the second-wave feminist movement and had been very active in the student movements of the time. Living within a zeitgeist of social movements sweeping the globe, they participated in the civil rights, peace, LGBT, labour, socialist, Red Power, and prison abolition movements, among others. Many are dykes who, in the 1950s and 1960s, were some of the first women in North America to become highly trained in various martial arts.

Fighting Out was fashioned after the feminist-inspired community programs developed by many of these women over the years. I was able to study these programs initially through discussions with Wendi Dragonfire, an early innovator in this area, who then introduced me to other women practitioners and training collectives. Although many excellent programs emerged and continue to emerge, in developing Fighting Out, I borrowed extensively from Brooklyn Women's Martial Arts (BWMA), founded by Annie Ellman and Nadia Telsely in 1974 and later renamed the Center for Anti-violence Education (CAE). The CAE continues to run programs and remains very active in political organizing, thereby providing a space wherein women, youth, and LGBT2Q folk can build community and become involved in anti-violence activism. For example, in the 1970s, the BWMA became involved in supporting black women in the United States who were prosecuted for defending themselves in domestic assault situations. More recently, CAE has been active in the Occupy Movement and in post-9/11 anti-imperialism activism, as well as supporting Muslim women through self-defence training when they became targets of street-based Islamophobic violence. CAE activism has thus kept pace with the political times, offering opportunities for meaningful civic engagement in and through civic self-defence training.

Fighting Out was initiated specifically for LGBT2Q folks in Toronto, but it has since been extended to include sex workers. For the LGBT2Q community, I offer workshops on the goju ryu form known as tensho—which involves deep breathing and continuous, flowing movement—and on the self-defence practice associated with tensho movement. These are usually offered in spaces I am able to access because of my connections within the martial arts community and the Centre for Women's Studies in Education (CWSE) within the Faculty of Education at the University of Toronto. For sex workers, I generally enter into their women's-only trans-positive space at Friday morning drop-ins at a community centre. In this boisterous and warm space, I simply demonstrate some helpful counters against common attacks and then move into the auditorium and do the tensho movement series, or "form," and self-defence practice with whoever cares to join me. Over the past couple of years of doing this work, women have often consulted with me privately about incidents that occurred in their work, and I have offered some possibilities for self-defence. I have also been drawn into much more outreach work with street-based sex workers, including participatory action research with youth who have been trafficked in the domestic sex industry.

Through a wonderful development of working across these community sites, one of the women from the LGBT2Q workshops now joins me on Friday mornings to help with the drop-in for sex workers. Janice Clanfield is a lesbian trans woman who transitioned later in life and did not have the opportunities earlier in her life to work in women's-only spaces and participate in feminist collectives. She has enthusiastically embraced opportunities to develop as a feminist activist later in life. Since we have been working together in the LGBT2Q and sex work context, we have often discussed feminist anticapitalist politics, and I have had an opportunity to learn more about trans politics. We have also "taken to the streets" with sex workers and allies, many of whom are trans.

One such event was a Reclaim the Streets march bringing together sex workers and allies, street-involved youth, Indigenous activists from the Missing and Murdered Indigenous Women movement, antiracist and trans activists, the Toronto Anti-Poverty Coalition, and the general community. This particular event raised awareness of a profound increase in violence against women in the area, including rapes, murders, domestic sex-trafficking, police violence, and transphobia. The action also continued an ongoing mobilization effort to advocate for a twenty-four-hour women's shelter in the area. Two weeks after the event, Toronto City Council passed a motion to establish such a shelter. The primary shelter in that particular locale has operated for years as a men's shelter, and so the historical redress is significant.

The Fighting Out initiative, then, offers an opportunity to build community and participate in local grassroots organizing and global social movements that offer possibilities to dismantle multiple and integrated hierarchies that organize violence. It offers an alternative to trauma-centred interventions that have had their own institutional histories and have spawned an industry of institutionally based trauma professionals who focus on post-trauma stress disorder and psychological healing. Many of the concepts from these trauma-centred approaches came from work with military veterans and were later extended as a medicalized-psychiatric model to women who have experienced sexual and domestic violence.

Many women-centred martial arts and self-defence programs and interventions also work within this framework. For some Indigenous and racialized women, however, this could be viewed as a colonial model, especially because it individualizes the systemic problems of racism and colonialism as a personal psychiatric problem. Fighting Out, in contrast, honours personal histories of resilience and offers a means of community building and a collective framework for addressing historically shaped violence. It works from a materialist framework flowing from Marxist feminist activism. As such, it problematizes psychologically based approaches that privilege individualizing ontologies that Marxist feminists recognize as forms of alienated consciousness located in capitalist histories. That is, this framework always refers back to the social relations organizing violence, rather than pathologizing individual women as victims and assigning them "psychological diagnoses". As discussed in the chapter in this volume by Alannah Young Leon and Denise Nadeau as well as that by Candace Brunette-Debassige, trauma healing work must address historically shaped violence as part of a decolonizing and antiracist framework for Indigenous women. In the sections that follow, I explain some of these concepts and approaches by outlining and unpacking some of the guiding concepts used in the Fighting Out initiative.

Feminist Civil Self-Defence Collectives Versus Martial Arts Regimes

Following Patrick McCarthy (1995), I distinguish between "civil self-defence arts" and "martial arts." Whereas martial arts are located in ruling regimes and are part of militarized apparatuses of ruling, civil self-defence arts belong to *the people*. Unlike militarized martial arts, arts of civil self-defence are not regimented, standardized, or practiced in hierarchized, enclosed spaces. Rather, they come together as a multiplicity of shared genres and practices that intersect and fuse and are practiced in popular spaces. In contrast to a standardized curriculum that can be institutionalized or commodified, practicing civil self-defence arts, like street-based breakdancing, encourages sharing, blending, creolization, experimentation, and innovation.

I see myself more as a busker than as a "head teacher." The busker inhabits popular spaces rather than the enclosed hierarchized spaces through which the term "martial arts master" is typically articulated. I have a repertoire of skills acquired over two decades of diligent practice, but I share these skills with my peers in community drop-in spaces and parks, much like how breakdancers practice together, showing one another new moves and polishing tried and true moves. When I hold classes in a space that is donated to us by a nonprofit community club, I leave my hat by the door. After class, if people have a toonie or two to spare, and if they are so inclined, they drop a donation into the hat. Generally, folks drop enough into the hat so that nonprofits get a little extra for the kindness of hosting us. When I show up to the drop-in for sex workers, I get coffee and the best breakfast in Toronto.

However, feminist civil self-defence collectives are more than breakdancers. They are more like "war machines" as described by Gilles Deleuze and Félix Guattari in their treatise on "nomadology" (Deleuze and Guattari 1987). Deleuze and Guattari used the term "nomadology" to describe noninstitutionalized epistemology that evolves when those participating in the knowledge process are connected to the creative process of life and survival in ways that are not "territorializing"—that is, not formed through hierarchies of control characterizing "the state apparatus"—but rather are "de-territorializing." For the purpose of this chapter, we can think of the state apparatus as constructed through the accumulation of interests of the ruling class and as consisting of regimes of imperialism and colonialism that are part and parcel of the racist, heteronormative nation-building project. The state war machine is characterized by hierarchical arrangements through which territorial control is achieved and a war is carried out against those who have been exteriorized by the state. For example, "the university" is a part of the systems of knowledge constructed through the territorializing agenda of the state apparatus and is characterized by epistemologies woven through social relations that are hierarchical and subjectifying. To concretize this idea, think of the STEM fields (science, technology, engineering, and math) and how relationships to nature are constructed through reductionist positivism. STEM academics are taught that prediction and control are the most valued standards against which to validate truth claims. Prediction and control are critical to territorializing projects.

Deleuze and Guattari (1987) argue that those who are exteriorized by the state do not have a "territory" that is "home" and are therefore nomadic (queers, sex workers, diasporic people, Indigenous people, and agricultural peasants, for example, as well as many other folks). They are necessarily "on the move" because the state seeks to eradicate them in its territorializing project. The material relations of nomadic existence emerge in and through territorialization, the exteriorization that results, and the survivalist imperative to fight back against eradication. Fighting back against eradication requires "warring" tactics that are not institutionalized, not regimented, and that are oriented to deterritorializing imperatives. The cumulation of knowledges, technologies, and so on, and indeed the entirety of knowledge-making connected to the material social relations of nomadic war machines, is referred to as "nomadology." Whereas state apparatuses have "epistemologies" (woven through subjectifying relations of imperialist territorializing), nomadic groups have "nomadologies" (woven through tactical survival, the will to thrive, and the material social relations of deterritorialization by which state heirarchies are dismantled). In contrast to state war machines (i.e., the military apparatus), feminist self-defence collectives are nomadic war machines.

The Production of Fractious Bodies in the City

Whereas Deleuze and Guattari talk about war machines as pre-existing, as well as being defined by their exteriority to the state, I am emphasizing how the enclosures connected with the primary accumulation of capital (as described by Marx) *produce* exteriorization and hence the fractious body.

That is, class dialectics is very much a part of the analysis I am developing, in distinction from the (anti-Hegelian) nondialectical approach developed by Deleuze and Guattari. The argument is laid out as follows.

If martial arts are located in the territorialized state ruling apparatus, then fractious bodies emerge from their expulsion from the territorialized state. Queers and sex workers are produced as outlawed rebel collectives, ontologically defined through exteriority. Fractious bodies emerge in antagonistic relation to the territorializing state and are in constant motion and change relative to state strategies of containment, control, and extinction.

Silvia Federici (2004) explains how historical enclosures of common land for the purpose of primitive accumulation were productive of exteriorized bodies and gendered migrations to cities. These expulsions were part of the historical process by which "prostitution" (I am using the term that came to be used to denigrate women) became massified and poor women became criminalized. She further explains that this process of accumulation through enclosures and dispossession—what Marx referred to as "primitive, originary, or primary accumulation"—was productive not only of a concentration of landless workers, who now had to sell their labour for subsistence and reproduction, but also of an accumulation of differences and divisions within the working class. Hierarchies built on gender, race, and sexuality became constitutive of class rule and the historical formation of the proletariat. However, these hierarchies also became the basis for exteriorizing processes and the production of the fractious body.

In *Red Skin, White Masks,* Indigenous scholar Glen Coulthard (2014, 7) takes up the issue of violent dispossession of lands in connection with First Nations people:

> In thinking about colonialism as a form of structured dispossession, I have found it useful to return to a cluster of insights developed by Karl Marx in chapters 26 through 32 of his first volume of *Capital.* This section of *Capital* is crucial because it is there that Marx most thoroughly links the totalizing power of *capital* with that of *colonialism* by way of his theory of "primitive accumulation."

Coulthard applies this to Canada:

> In this respect, Canada is no different from most other settler-colonial powers: in the Canadian context, colonial domination continues to

be structurally committed to maintain—through force, fraud, and more recently, so-called "negotiations"—ongoing state access to the land and resources that contradictorily provide the material and spiritual sustenance of Indigenous societies on the one hand, and the foundation of the colonial state-formation, settlement, and capitalist development on the other. (6–7)

In the contemporary version of this analysis, expulsions continue to occur as imperialist and neocolonial land-grabbing takes place for territorial control over natural resources, leading to a global intensification of gendered and racialized migrations to megacities. Coulthard therefore suggests a conceptual shift that "takes as its analytical frame the subject position of the colonized vis-à-vis the effects of *colonial dispossession,* rather than from the primary position of 'the waged male proletariat [in] the process of commodity production,' to borrow from Sylvia Federici's useful formulation" (11; emphasis in the original). The mass migrations to cities have now produced the urban landscape as a site of accumulation through programs of austerity. That is, within cities, austerity programs are forcing the poor from what has become prime real estate for speculative developers, resulting in housing insecurity. As Federici (2012, 103) puts it:

Where "austerity" programs and land grabbing could not reach, war has completed the task, opening new grounds for oil drilling and the harvesting of diamonds or coltan [an ore]. As for the targets of these clearances, they have become the subjects of the new diaspora, siphoning millions of people from the land to the towns, which more and more resemble encampments. Mike Davis has used the phrase "Planet of Slums" in referring to this situation, but a more correct and vivid description would speak of a planet of ghettos and a regime of global apartheid.

As I have written recently in a chapter on the financialized economy, the transformation of cities as described above is proceeding rapidly as global accumulation becomes increasingly financialized and cities become a site of accumulation via ongoing acts of dispossession facilitated through austerity politics (Magnusson 2015). Raymond Lotta (2013) points out that by the year 2000 more than half of humanity lived in cities. Mike Davis (2006) provides evidence that slum growth throughout the Global South is surpassing urbanization. Productive stagnation has become a stable characteristic of our current economy (often referred to as monopoly-finance capitalism), normalizing underemployment and low wages globally (Magdoff and Foster 2014). The most accessible employment opportunities, particularly for women, are in the informal and illegal economies within cities.

Migration to cities is also productive of a queer diaspora characterized by LGBT2Q folks seeking community within sprawling megacities undergoing fractionalization and erosion of stable infrastructures under neoliberal and austerity policies. Cities such as Toronto, where homosexuality has been decriminalized, are simultaneously desired destinations for the queer diaspora and spaces where racialized LGBT2Q folk continue to be exteriorized through laws that threaten to revoke citizenship of racialized peoples who can be labelled as "terrorists" for challenging the racist heteropatriarchal state (Bain 2014).

The pandemic of missing and murdered Indigenous women reveals how the violence of dispossession and migration to cities is gendered and is an aspect of the racialized project of genocide that is embedded within colonialism (see Arvin, Tuck, and Morill 2013; Simpson 2014; Smith 2005). Martin Cannon (2012) extends this analysis to the regulation of sexualities through historically specific policies such as the Indian Act, showing how Euro-Christian values around gender, sex, and reproduction entered into the colonial nation-building project, institutionalizing rigid forms of gender binaries and social relations of Euro-patriarchy. Similarly, in a postcolonial setting, Jacqui Alexander (1991) explores the reconceptualization of sexual behaviour in terms of morality, offering a decolonizing reading of Trinidad and Tobago's 1986 Sexual Offences Bill, which outlawed homosexuality and sodomy.

The contemporary urban landscape provides the context for programs such as Fighting Out. The Reclaim the Streets action described above would have occurred without Fighting Out. However, the Fighting Out initiative contributes an embodied learning dimension to these politics, as well as access to the means by which a safer life can be secured for members of the queer diaspora and for increasing numbers of racialized women and homeless youth involved in street-based sex work. It functions as a queer, feminist, antiracist commons constructed against the enclosures and privatization of safe spaces to inhabit. Speculative real estate in the urban context requires the production of unsafe spaces within the city in order to accumulate through the enclosure and commodification of safe gentrified spaces. Initiatives such as Fighting Out can contribute to a revolutionary project along the lines of Henri Lefebvre's (2003) "urban revolution"—a vision that has been revived by contemporary urban activists and writers. To rephrase David Harvey (2012), when exteriorized fractious bodies come to constitute a critical mass for whom the struggle over the city as a whole frames the struggles of many groups, including the queers and sex workers. The Fighting Out initiative provides a forum for embodying politics of anticapitalist social movements that may have possibilities to intervene in the neoliberal fragmentation, homogenization, and hierarchization that is part and parcel of urban gentrification under monopoly-finance capitalism.

An intriguing possibility raised by Glen Coulthard (2014) and Leanne Simpson (2014) in connection with the Idle No More movement is that interventions into such neoliberal and financialized urban design can be infused with resurgent Indigeneity, which, as Simpson argues, can be a queer resurgence. We can imagine urban landscapes being restored to communities that lend each other interregional and international solidarity. Similarly, the recent tent-city set up by Black Lives Matter Toronto exemplifies the kind of social movement building and pedagogies of solidarity by which urban space is reclaimed. The communities would be able to draw from life genres informed by historical land-based and contemporary urban community practices. Transnational connectedness could be the basis of a kind of grassroots "globalization," as a counter practice to global financialized imaginaries. As Coulthard (2014, 172) explains,

> We also have to acknowledge that the significant political leverage required to simultaneously block economic exploitation of our people and homelands while constructing alternatives to capitalism will not be generated through our direct actions and resurgent economies alone. Settler colonization has rendered our populations too small to affect this magnitude of change. This reality demands that we continue to remain open to, if not actively seek out and establish, relations of solidarity and networks of trade and mutual aid with national and transnational communities and organizations that are also struggling against the imposed effects of globalized capital, including other Indigenous nations and national confederacies; urban Indigenous people and organizations; the labor, women's, GBLTQ2S (gay,

bisexual, lesbian, trans, queer, and two-spirit), and environmental movements; and of course, those racial and ethnic communities that find themselves subject to their own distinct forms of economic, social, and cultural marginalization.

The Fighting Out initiative is very small in scale compared to these visionary challenges to urban space shaped through apartheid capitalism. However, the initiative affords a pedagogy of community and solidarity building that challenges the various forms of violence—including state/colonial/capitalist violence—that shape the lives of LGBT2Q people. It works at the intersections of movements such as Missing and Murdered Indigenous Women, Black Lives Matter, and Trans Pride for example. In the next section, I review some aspects of Fighting Out as a community praxis.

Qigong, Self-Defence, and Embodied Politics

In this section, I describe Fighting Out as a praxis, detailing what happens in a typical Fighting Out class session, how community is formed through the initiative, and how the activities of a Fighting Out class come to be linked to activism and social movements. I show how a collective civil defence qigong practice can be theorized through an ontology of "the social," in distinction from the idea of individual empowerment.

There are countless examples of women's self-defence programs, usually set up as a workshop series, that offer a collection of de-escalation skills, boundary-setting exercises, and physical self-defence techniques. Some of these programs are characterized by trauma-centred approaches, as explained in the previous section, and there are surprisingly few examples of programs such as the Center for Anti-violence Education in Brooklyn, which coordinates the activities of civil self-defence learning such that they hook into relevant social movements for radical change. Moreover, while self-defence workshops are wonderful, the physical self-defence techniques are typically not presented as an integrated art form but as a disconnected series of moves such as groin kicks, release from grabs, and strikes. The practices that are a part of the discipline of meditation and breath work are seldom, if ever, a part of women's self-defence training packages.

The Fighting Out curriculum is grounded in the Okinawan goju ryu art form and flows from a particular kata ("form") known as tensho ("rotating palms"). Kata are sets of movements that, when practiced on one's own, embody self-defence applications against various kinds of attacks. The form is also an Okinawan self-defence qigong exercise learned from families of Chinese merchants and modified within a context of Okinawan fighting arts. That is, it is already a cultural fusion of material practices rather than a static, essentialized spiritual methodology, as it is sometimes represented. The Fighting Out practice sessions begin with tensho as a qigong exercise that involves a moving breath meditation. From a movement and body memory perspective, the tensho form is simple and is easily learned over the course of about four to six sessions. After that, this beautiful moving meditation can be practiced every day for a lifetime to promote health and mindfulness.[1]

Incorporating mindfulness into qigong practice is explained by Andy James (2004)—who is my shifu (someone who is adept at and teaches the practice) and also my vipassana meditation teacher. In his text *The Spiritual Legacy of Shaolin Temple,* he examines the complex historical and philosophical interconnections represented by Buddhism, Daoism, and the energetic arts:

> Within the qigong and internal martial arts stream, it is important to remember that the ultimate goal of "mind regulation" is enlightenment and "return to the Dao." For this, surrender is unavoidable and an enlightenment practice necessary. In this book, I have suggested vipassana as an enlightenment practice that would fit seamlessly with qigong and the internal martial arts and at the same time recall the urgency for enlightenment for which Chan is famous. Prajna, or insightful wisdom, is an important element in both Chan and vipassana. (171)

Hence, James advocates vipassana meditation for his students, to be practiced separately but as part of a daily practice that includes qigong: "I am not of the opinion that other meditation practices including concentration, samatha, visualizing, and qigong detract from vipassana, as long as these are not done during vipassana meditation to make the sitting more interesting or to obtain 'higher' states" (167).

---

1 For an in-depth discussion of mindfulness as embodied practice, see Yuk-Lin Renita Wong's chapter in this volume.

In this respect, certain qigong practices such as goju ryu tensho, like practices such as vipassana meditation, orient the practitioner to the present moment via the breath and attention to the subtle sensations emanating from the body in movement. As James (2004, 167) suggests, "A less intense form of body mindfulness, suitable for everyday activities, is noting your body's every change in posture: sitting, standing, walking, running, reclining, kneeling, and lying."

With this in mind, when teaching tensho, I encourage participants to practice tensho mindfully. This is an important practice for some of the women who are involved in sex work and who experience almost daily violence, including forced confinement, rape, and brutal beatings. Some of the youth with whom I have been involved talk about being on constant alert after running away from their pimps and being in constant fear of being spotted and kidnapped to be brought back into trafficking. The women who have been street involved for years seldom "stay in the moment" because their survival depends on continually thinking through every possible future scenario and making moment-to-moment decisions based on what could go wrong in the future.

Tensho is a "fighting art" breath form that orients participants to their breath and their body in the present moment. It is a moving meditation. When practiced mindfully on a regular basis, tensho may lead to other forms of mindfulness practice, including sitting meditation with breath (such as vipassana). Today, a great deal of research is available about the plasticity of the brain and the possibility for these kinds of practices to mitigate the kind of emotional-physical reactivity that develops through unrelenting exposure to stress (see Schmidt and Walach, 2014). Moreover, practicing as a collective teaches about creating and living in social relationships that are woven through an ethic of antiviolence and mutual nourishment.

Because the tensho series of movements only takes about five minutes, we are able to practice it a few times per session; each time, I offer feedback to improve the breath and bodywork dimensions. After practicing the set, each class session focuses on one to two self-defence applications and on partner practice. As we wind down the class session, there is opportunity for discussion and relationship building.

Discussions can take the form of political pedagogy. These can include organizing for upcoming political actions, such as a trans march during

Pride Week or talking through the politics of state violence, colonialism, or family violence. Discussions can also include productive solidarity building and moving toward appropriate action. For example, as mentioned earlier, one Take Back the Streets action at a local LGBT2Q community centre was organized as an antiviolence event extending solidarity "From Turtle Island to Palestine," thereby connecting the international dots of colonialism, imperialism, and the violence of white heteropatriarchal capitalism.

The self-defence applications are interesting for me as teacher/busker, because I have always practiced tensho in the way it was taught to me by my goju ryu teacher, Bill Hind, with a soft breath and soft body. Tensho is just as likely to be practiced as a "hard" form by other practitioners, with a loud, hard, long breath and muscle tension. However, my teacher emphasized the importance of tensho as a soft, slow practice that allows the body to experience mindful breath work as a circulating flow, to contrast with breath work as "*kime* practice," or projecting energy into a singular focal point, as is practiced with the other foundational breath kata in goju ryu, namely sanchin. Sanchin—performed with hard breath, muscle tension, and energy focused into a single point of intentionality—is referred to as "external practice." Tensho is often practiced this way as well, but in my own practice, I perform tensho as an internal art, with soft breath, soft body, and continuously moving, circulating energy. As Shifu James suggests, the internal martial arts are not based on opposing force with force, as one might evidence in external martial arts, but rather on a flowing combination of yin (yielding) and yang (opposing) energy. There is circularity and flow rather than the staccato, start/stop of, say blocking and punching.

I found early on that class sessions flowed much better when qigong was introduced through a soft breath form such as tensho rather than a hard breath form such as sanchin or even a combination of sanchin and tensho. Hard breath forms appear to be difficult for the absolute beginner and can detract from learning a qigong set within the space of four to six workshops. Currently, our practice sessions follow a predictable pattern: a warm-up much like that used in tai chi, tensho instruction and practice, self-defence and partner practice, a cool-down, and discussion. The irony is that tensho practiced with soft breath and soft body is generally considered a sophisticated beginning point for learning the goju ryu art form. The self-defence applications require meeting an attack with a relaxed yet ready-to-spring-into-action mind-body, and the counters require learning how to flow with the attacker's energy and redirecting through spiralling. Even after twenty-plus years of practice, I am still learning how to greet hard energy with alert softness. Nevertheless, I have been able to offer many kinds of self-defence applications that make street sense while at the same time helping participants develop a "fighting art" moving meditation practice with breath work.

I think of the qigong practice in terms of materially framed, embodied breath concepts through which mindfulness practice can extend to political activism. In terms of political activism, mindfulness practice can encourage "right action" and "right speech." For example, right action and speech in an activist context can take the form of social activism through a consciousness that mindfully avoids reproducing violence in the process of dismantling hierarchies through which relations of subjectification are produced.

This praxis of building collectives—practicing moving meditation that incorporates learning self-defence, talking through politics that structure violence, building capacity for political engagement, and so on—works through the dialectics of deep personal transformation and social change. The pedagogy flows from materialist praxis that connects qigong to civil self-defence, social movements, transformative political processes, and historical consciousness. We practice the tensho set as moving meditation with breath work but not as an essentialized spiritual practice and not as a sacred methodology alienated from our historical locations. From breath flows to body throws, from deterritorializing the body to reclaiming the city streets, the practice works through the dialectics of politically organized violence to dismantle relations of subjugation that organize the day-to-day actualities of racialized queers and sex workers in the city.

Dialectics of the Mind-Body

Queers and sex workers may encounter insurmountable difficulties trying to train in a traditional martial arts school. Not only do tuition fees and trans/homophobia pose significant barriers, but the martial arts are often, at best, mostly irrelevant to the daily encounters of violence negotiated by fractious bodies and, at worst, a reinscription of that very violence. Civil self-defence collectives of the sort described here interrupt exclusionary enclosures of practice space and provide a space for wellness practices that resignify dominant cultural scripts and practices of "the desired body," "the disposable body," "the hateable body."

The city streets can be unforgiving for homeless LGBT2Q youth, street-based sex workers, trans folk facing housing and food insecurity, and the queer diaspora struggling to negotiate a new urban landscape. Substance abuse, partner abuse, and so on can come to form part of the daily struggle. Qigong is a practice that has been used successfully in substance abuse contexts; Jan Parker, an artist and tai chi practitioner on Bowen Island, British Columbia, is an early innovator in this respect. Qigong can also be used in connection with other kinds of healing and wellness practices. I am currently learning medical qigong, which, as my teacher Shifu Donna Oliver suggests, "strengthens the whole unit consisting of body, mind, breath and spirit" (pers. comm., 2015). The "fight" can be in the form of, say, yiquan practice, which is loosely translated as "mind boxing." As Donna Oliver puts it, "This to me implies a perhaps different form of fight. The battle of the conditioned, acquired mind and the spiritual conscious mind, which through constant practice of yiquan qigong triumphs." Life as, say, a racialized LBT woman can be rife with microsociologies of violence that are experienced as body-damaging stress. At the same time, qigong practice can promote resilience. Through regular practice, queers and sex workers can write their own scripts of what is beautiful and desirable: big beautiful women, muscular bois, elegant elderly women, feminine men, beautifully multiracial, gracefully differently bodied, and so on. As bodies are engaged as "social bodies," the social politics of "the city" also transforms: that is, the struggle over cities cannot be separated from the struggle over the social body or from a democratic project involving enfolding fractious social bodies into a politics of rightful belonging.

Cultural Expansion of Civil Self-Defence Collectives

Last year, I had the opportunity to develop a series of Fighting Out workshops for the first ever Pan-Caribbean Women and Sexual Diversity Conference, strategically held in conjunction with Curacao's first ever Pride Week. The purpose of the workshops was to introduce the idea of qigong and civil self-defence collectives to women activists working in diverse Caribbean contexts of women's health, rape crisis centres, sexual diversity initiatives, and so on. The series began with an introduction to a theoretical framework useful in organizing this kind of work and then, each morning, qigong and self-defence practice. By the final day of the conference, women were able to do the qigong set from beginning to end as a group and to confidently execute a number of key self-defence moves. More importantly, the participants discussed how this kind of work could be set up in their own communities as a viable political project linked to building a social movement focused on antiviolence and decriminalization of homosexuality within a decolonizing, anti-imperialist, anticapitalist, and antiracist framework. For example, building self-defence collectives in order to work through the politics by which patriarchal colonialism shapes and regulates sexualities can build capacity that is both personally and politically transformative.

My hope in writing this chapter is that similar collectives will be created in other urban contexts globally. David Harvey (2012, 5) writes that "to claim the right to the city" means "to claim some kind of shaping power over the processes of urbanization, over the ways in which our cities are made and re-made and to do so in a fundamental and radical way." A civil self-defence collective can be more than a four-day women's workshop on de-escalation techniques and defending against strikes. The models generated by early innovators beginning in the 1970s can be re-examined in the contemporary context of slum expansion, the ongoing production of fractious bodies, and our collective process of reclaiming urban spaces from global financialized imaginaries in order to build transnationally networked communities informed by resurgent Indigeneity and economies.

Acknowledgements

I would like to express my sincere gratitude to the following martial arts teachers who have inspired me and guided me: Shifu Andy James and Shifu Donna Oliver, from the Tai Chi and Meditation Centre in Toronto; Bill Hind, Sensei, the most senior practitioner of goju ryu in Canada; Fran Turner, Sensei, my aikido teacher, who also taught me the lovingkindness meditation when I accompanied her to the Elizabeth Fry Society to do outreach work; the many students of all my teachers who have helped me along my learning path; Wendi Dragonfire, Sensei; Nadia Telsey and Annie Ellman. The memory of my friendship with Roxana Ng was a particular inspiration for me as I was writing this chapter. I dedicate the piece to her memory.

References

Alexander, M. Jacqui. 1991. "Redrafting Morality: The Postcolonial State and the Sexual Offences Bill of Trinidad and Tobago." In *Third World Women and the Politics of Feminism,* edited by Chandra Mohanty, Ann Russo, and Lourdes Torres, 133–52. Bloomington: Indiana University Press.

Arvin, Maile, Eve Tuck, and Angie Morrill. 2013. "Decolonizing Feminism: Challenging Connections Between Settler Colonialism and Heteropatriarchy." *Feminist Formations* 25(1): 8–34.

Bain, Beverly. 2014. *Unsettling Sexual Citizenship: Immigration, Nationalism, Homonationalism, and Violence.* Paper presented at the Caribbean Studies Association Conference, April, Merida, Mexico.

Cannon, Martin. 2012. "The Regulation of First Nations Sexuality." In *Queerly Canadian: An Introductory Reader in Sexuality Studies,* edited by Maureen FitzGerald and Scott Rayter, 51–63. Toronto: Canadian Scholars' Press.

Coulthard, Glen S. 2014. *Red Skin, White Masks: Rejecting the Colonial Politics of Recognition.* Minneapolis: University of Minnesota Press.

Davis, Mike. 2006. *Planet of Slums.* London: Verso.

Deleuze, Gilles, and Félix Guattari. 1987. *A Thousand Plateaus: Capitalism and Schizophrenia.* Translation and foreword by Brian Massumi. Minneapolis: University of Minnesota Press. Originally published as *Capitalisme et schizophrénie,* vol. 2, *Mille plateaux* (1987).

Federici, Silvia. 2004. *Caliban and the Witch: The Body and Primitive Accumulation.* New York: Autonomedia.

———. 2012. *Revolution at Point Zero: Housework, Reproduction, and Feminist Struggle.* Oakland, CA: PM Press.

Harvey, David. 2012. *Rebel Cities.* London: Verso.

James, Andy. 2004. *The Spiritual Legacy of Shaolin Temple: Buddhism, Daoism, and the Energetic Arts.* Boston: Wisdom.

Lefebvre, Henri. 2003. *The Urban Revolution.* Translated by Robert Bononno. Minneapolis: University of Minnesota Press. Originally published as *La révolution urbaine* (1970).

Lotta, Raymond. 2013. "On the 'Driving Force of Anarchy' and the Dynamics of Change—A Sharp Debate and an Urgent Polemic: The Struggle for a Radically Different World and the Struggle for a Scientific Approach to Reality." *Revolution,* 4 November. http://revcom.us/a/322/on-the-driving-force-of-anarchy-and-the-dynamics-of-change-en.html.

Magdoff, Fred, and John Bellamy Foster. 2014. "Stagnation and Financialization: The Nature of the Contradiction." *Monthly Review* 66(1): 1–24.

Magnusson, Jamie. 2015. "Financialization." In *Marxism and Feminism,* edited by Shahrzad Mojab, 142–162. London: Zed Books.

McCarthy, Patrick. 1995. *The Bible of Karate: Bubishi*. Boston: Tuttle.

Simpson, Leanne B. 2014. "Not Murdered, Not Missing: Rebelling Against Colonial Gender Violence." *Leanne Betasamosake Simpson*. https://www.leannesimpson.ca/writings/not-murdered-not-missing-rebelling-against-colonial-gender-violence.

Schmidt, Stefan, and Harald Walach. 2014. *Meditation: Neuroscientific Approaches and Philosophical Implications*. Cham, Switzerland: Springer International Publishing.

Smith, Andrea. 2005. *Conquest: Sexual Violence and American Indian Genocide*. Cambridge, MA: South End Press.

Afterword

Sheila Batacharya and Yuk-Lin Renita Wong

The contributors to this collection explore the sentient-social experience of embodiment in relation to pedagogical practices and to processes of decolonization. Writing both from within and beyond academic settings, the authors consider ways of knowing that contest the hegemony of Eurocentric knowledge production, variously seeking to develop embodied ways of teaching and learning that provide scope for additional sources of knowledge. In so doing, they offer a series of possible responses to an overarching question: If we seek to unsettle approaches to education that rest on Western epistemological frameworks and serve to perpetuate colonial relations of power, then how might attention to embodied experience help us to develop more equitable and inclusive models of learning, ones that contribute to, rather than hinder, the work of decolonization? In approaching this question, each author moves with conviction and purpose, but their collective goal is not prescriptive. They deliberately resist Western expectations of closure, visible in the assumption that questions will be given definitive answers. Rather, their essays mark a point along a continuum of challenges and investigations, one that remains, and should remain, open-ended.

Apart from its consideration of integrative approaches to embodiment, pedagogy, and decolonization, what sets this collection apart from the bulk of scholarship on embodied learning is its understanding of embodiment as a process of becoming critically attuned to sentient-social experience. From this perspective, the development of alternative pedagogical models demands attention to the symbiotic relationship between the discursive and the material aspects of embodiment. Our experience of our material bodies, as the site of knowledge, physical sensations, and of emotion and intuition, is inevitably conditioned by the ways in which our bodies are inscribed with meaning through discursive processes of racialization, gendering, and queering, as well as through differences in socioeconomic class and in physical and mental ability. In considering embodied learning and its relationship to decolonization, the contributors to this volume refuse to draw a line between the discursive and the material. More broadly, they resist the imposition of oppositional binaries and instead uphold integrated, holistic ways of knowing that are more relational than dichotomous.

In emphasizing the material foundations of human experience, the essays in this collection push both educators and scholars of embodiment to engage with decolonization not as an abstract concept, the meaning of which can too easily be expanded to encompass other socially transformative projects, but instead in terms of material relations of power. In Canada, these relations of power are evident in the juxtaposition of discursive expressions of concern, on the one hand, and, on the other, the continued refusal of the state to fully honour treaty obligations, the willingness to accept poverty and ill health as facts of Indigenous life, and the denial of the rights of Indigenous peoples to cultural, political, and economic self-determination. Integral to altering material relations of power is the reclamation of Indigenous knowledges, methodologies, and practices, which serve to reconnect the individual to the relational collective and to the land and, in so doing, promote the resurgence of an inner life force of wholeness.

Understood in this way, as a process of healing and renewal, decolonization is not simply a negation or an undoing, the antithesis of colonization. At the same time, in contrast to New Age appropriations of Indigenous spirituality and healing traditions, decolonization in no way denies the violence and oppression generated by and perpetuated through colonialism, racism, imperialism, and capitalism. Indeed, the issue of cultural appropriation comes up in several of the chapters in this volume. Especially from the standpoint of counterhegemonic knowledge production, incorporating Indigenous knowledges into contexts other than those in which they originated can be productive, provided that ethical and political considerations are fully engaged. Indigenous knowledges have value: they benefit people in ways both tangible and intangible. In drawing on them, one must therefore honour not only the integrity of the knowledges themselves but also those who created them and are willing to share them. One must ask how traditional knowledges can be shared and used in a way that contributes to equity and that respects the dignity and the right to self-determination of the communities to whom these knowledges belong.

The practice of embodied writing, on which a number of the authors in this collection focus, contributes to the decolonizing of knowledge production by exposing the weaknesses of hegemonic cognitive frameworks and the dichotomies that these construct between mind and body, intellect and spirit, self and other, and discourse and matter. These authors also call into question the idea of writing as solely a cognition-based activity. Exploring the limitations of Western knowledge production undermines the taken-for-granted supremacy of Eurocentric thinking, including the ways that definitions of rationality and objectivity have been used to marginalize and posit Indigenous knowledges as not scientific and coherent in their own right. Another theme in the collection—the need to unsettle privileged subjectivities and interrogate the intertwined relations of colonialism and capitalism—similarly highlights the degree to which hegemonic discourses and ways of organizing societies are unsustainable, exploitative, and destructive of life and spirit.

We are certainly not the first to critically examine the legacies of colonialism, nor are we the first to point to the shortcomings of conceptual frameworks grounded in Western liberal thought. However, it can, in fact, be difficult to escape the influence of dominant ways of thinking and being. Over the course of her career, Roxana Ng examined historical materialist research and activism, on the one hand, and the mechanisms of internalized oppression and embodied strategies for resisting it, on the other—only to circle back and critique the ways in which those embodied strategies are themselves bound up with socially constructed and organized relations of power. Her approach was not linear, and such ongoing self-reflexive critical scrutiny is arguably a means to avoid inadvertently capitulating to hegemonic frameworks that reinforce dichotomies and attempt to discipline the parameters of thinking—and thus to limit resistance. The need for critical vigilance also suggests one of the fruits of collaboration, as others may see what we do not.

Indeed, for us, the process of editing this collection has demonstrated that academic activity can be enhanced by a focus on relationship building.

Roxana Ng's research and teaching certainly provided a model to emulate. Over many years, she collaborated in both academic and community contexts in order to learn and teach qigong and integrate this knowledge and practice with her eclectic activist involvements and interdisciplinary scholarship. We thus decided early on that our editorial process required a face-to-face meeting of the authors. Our first thought was simply that such a meeting would help to encourage collaboration—although, as it turned out, the meeting accomplished far more than that: it deepened the authors' appreciation of each other's work, as well as their collective commitment to the book and their trust in the editorial process. At the end of the day, one of the contributors told Renita, "I now know you, sister." We understood this comment to mean, "I will engage in this work in a spirit of relationship and trust." This is the spirit in which we pursued this project, and, looking back, we understand why it was important to proceed as we did. Being physically present and in relationship is sustaining. An embodied approach to scholarly activity—one that is anchored in human presence and that values the ethical aspects of relationship building—produces effects that extend far beyond a single book or project.

We think of this book as an extended conversation around the themes of embodiment, pedagogy, and decolonization, with the themes themselves interlacing and sometimes coalescing, while at other times remaining distinct. And, like many conversations, this one is far from finished. We hope that this book will spark additional exchanges and debates among a wider audience, and we look forward to critical responses and engagement from our readers.

Contributors

Temitope Adefarakan holds a PhD in sociology and equity studies from the Ontario Institute for Studies in Education, at the University of Toronto, with a specialization in feminist studies offered by the university's Women and Gender Studies Institute. Her interests lie in the areas of anti-Black racism, antiracist and anti-oppressive pedagogies, and African Indigenous studies. The author of *The Souls of Yoruba Folk: Indigeneity, Race, and Critical Spiritual Literacy in the African Diaspora* (2015), she is a sociology lecturer in the University of Toronto's Transitional Year Program. She has taught for over fifteen years in a variety of settings, with a focus on equity, women's rights, and anti-colonial thought in the African diaspora. She has also conducted workshops on equity, diversity, and social justice. A proud mother, Adefarakan especially enjoys exploring the world with her little one.

Sheila Batacharya completed her doctoral studies at the Ontario Institute for Studies in Education, at the University of Toronto, under the supervision of Roxana Ng. Her dissertation explored counterhegemonic understandings of violence and oppression, embodiment, and healing among young South Asian women. Her research interests are interdisciplinary, spanning gender studies, sociology, and education, while her work on embodiment and decolonization is also informed by her teaching and practice of yoga. She is the co-editor (with Mythili Rajiva) of *Reena Virk: Critical Perspectives on a Canadian Murder* (2010).

Candace Brunette-Debassige is a Mushkego woman from the Fort Albany First Nation, in northeastern Ontario (Treaty 9 territory). She has been working in Indigenous education for more than fifteen years. She is an educator and storyteller with a background in Indigenous theatre and embodied and story-based approaches to teaching and learning. Running like a thread throughout Brunette-Debassige's work is a commitment to furthering the liberatory struggles of Indigenous peoples in the context of education. She is a PhD candidate in the Faculty of Education at Western University, where she is investigating the storied experiences of Indigenous women who are leading efforts to Indigenize universities in Canada.

Susan Ferguson is director of the Writing and Learning Centre at OCAD University, where she oversees a diverse portfolio that includes student academic support, English language learning programs, and a university-wide Writing Across the Curriculum initiative. Her research interests include the pedagogy of writing, feminist autobiography, embodiment, and pain studies, and her work is informed by interpretive social inquiry, disability studies, and transnational feminist theory. She holds a master's degree in sociology and equity studies from the Ontario Institute for Studies in Education, at the University of Toronto, and has published in the areas of disability history, gender and equity in higher education, and writing in art and design education. Her commitment to decolonizing methodologies is grounded in her former work with Aboriginal youth living with intergenerational trauma, violence, and addictions in inner-city Vancouver.

Katie MacDonald recently joined Capital Region Housing in Edmonton as their Education Lead. Her research interests include transformative pedagogy, learning for social justice, and encounters with difference. She loves knitting, spending time with her dog Rita, and drinking coffee in the sunshine.

Jamie Magnusson is a faculty member in the Department of Leadership, Higher and Adult Education at the Ontario Institute for Studies in Education, at the University of Toronto. She does harm reduction outreach through a program for street-involved sex workers and has been involved in participatory action research with youth who have been exploited in the domestic sex industry. Her work with LGBTQ+ communities includes the Fighting Out program described in her chapter. In her writing, she uses a Queer Marxist feminist lens to examine how urban poverty is organized through interconnected strategies such as real estate speculation, gentrification, and the racist police state. In her teaching, she explores community organizing from the standpoint of topics such as pedagogies of solidarity and social movement learning. She is also an instructor with Toronto's Tai Chi and Meditation Centre.

Stephanie Moynagh is an active community member based in Toronto. She has over fifteen years' experience working alongside low-income people in both nonprofit and community-based settings, with the goal of effecting transformative social change. Her interests include the roots and impacts of trauma, confronting and healing from interpersonal and systemic violence, and transformative justice practices. A firm believer in the power of relationship and in spiritual evolution, she continues to struggle toward a more complete understanding of her role in movement building as a person of white-settler ancestry and identity. She holds an MEd in adult education from the Ontario Institute for Studies in Education, at the University of Toronto.

Devi Dee Mucina is an assistant professor at the University of Victoria in the Indigenous Governance program. Through his father's lineage, he is Maseko Ngoni from Lizulu, which lies on the border between Malawi and Mozambique. Through his mother's lineage, he is Shona from Zimbabwe. In his current research, which is international in scope, he employs an Indigenous intersectional framework, with an emphasis on dialogue and collaborative partnerships, to explore the decolonization of Indigenous masculinities, in part through the renewal of traditional holistic and relational understandings of wellness. In addition to decolonization and Indigenous governance, his interests include Ubuntu philosophy, Indigenous fathering, the impact of incarceration, and the politics of social memory.

Denise Nadeau is an educator of mixed European heritage. She currently is a visitor in the traditional homelands of the Lekwungen Nation on Vancouver Island. Born in Québec, she still spends time in Gespe'gewa'gi and in Montréal, where she is an affiliate assistant professor in the Department of Religions and Cultures at Concordia University. She teaches and writes in the areas of Indigenous-settler relations, the decolonization of the body, and the deconstruction of whiteness and colonialism in Christianity. Her recent publications include "Decolonizing Religious Encounter? Teaching Indigenous Traditions and Colonialism," in *Mixed Blessings: Indigenous Encounters with Christianity in Canada*, edited by Tolly Bradford and Chelsea Horton (2016).

Randelle Nixon is a sessional instructor in the Sociology and Women's and Gender Studies departments at the University of Alberta. She received her PhD in sociology at the University of Alberta, where she explored the relationship between feelings of pride and various manifestations of pride politics. Her research interests include feminist and queer theory, affect theory, body politics, and social justice strategies.

Wendy Peters is an associate professor in the Department of Gender Equality and Social Justice at Nipissing University, in the "near North" of Ontario. She received a PhD in sociology and equity studies from the Ontario Institute for Studies in Education, at the University of Toronto. Her research and teaching interests include representations of privileged and marginalized groups in popular culture, with an emphasis on queer representation on television. She has published in *Canadian Woman Studies / Les cahiers de la femme, Critical Studies in Media Communication, Flow, Journal of Lesbian Studies, Sexuality and Culture*, and *Queer Studies in Media and Popular Culture*.

Carla Rice specializes in embodiment and subjectivity studies and in arts-based and research creation methodologies. She is professor and Canada Research Chair at the University of Guelph, in Ontario, where, in 2012, she founded Re•Vision: The Centre for Art and Social Justice, with a mandate to interrogate systemic injustices and use arts-informed methods to foster inclusive communities and promote equity. She has published three books, *Becoming Women: The Embodied Self in Image Culture* (2014), *Gender and Women's Studies in Canada: Critical Terrain* (2013), and *Gender and Women's Studies: Critical Terrain* (2018), and has received numerous awards for advocacy, research, and mentorship. In 2016, she received the Social Sciences and Humanities Research Council of Canada's Partnership Grant for her project Bodies in Translation: Activist Art, Technology, and

Access to Life. Prior to entering academia, she worked to advance women's health and well-being in Canada and was a founder and director of Canada's National Eating Disorder Information Centre and the Body Image Project at Toronto's Women's College Hospital.

Sheila Stewart is the author of two poetry collections, *The Shape of a Throat* (2012) and *A Hat to Stop a Train* (2003) and is the editor, with Suzanne Thomas and Ardra Cole, of *The Art of Poetic Inquiry* (2012). Her poetry has been widely published, in journals such as *Contemporary Verse 2*, *Grain*, the *Literary Review of Canada*, and the *Malahat Review*, and has been recognized by the gritLIT Contest, the Pottersfield Portfolio Short Poem Contest, and the Scarborough Arts Council Windows on Words Award. Her writing on poetic inquiry has appeared in *Creative Approaches to Research* and in *LEARNing Landscapes*, as well as in numerous edited collections. Formerly a community-based adult literacy worker, she teaches at the University of Toronto in the New College Writing Centre and in the Women and Gender Studies Institute.

Yuk-Lin Renita Wong is a professor in the School of Social Work at York University. In her research and teaching, she seeks to deconstruct the power relations embedded in the knowledge production and discursive practices of social work, as well as to recentre marginalized ways of knowing and being. She brings contemplative pedagogy into critical social work education and, with respect to social justice work, explores mindfulness as a pedagogy of decolonization and a critical reflective practice that nurtures embodied awareness and engages with the integrated whole of body-mind-heart-spirit. Wong has practiced mindfulness meditation since 1998 and has led meditation and mindfulness training since 2007 in the tradition of Thich Nhat Hanh.

Alannah Young Leon is a member of the Opaskwayak Cree Nation (Treaty 5) and a visitor to unceded xʷməθkʷəy̓əm (Musqueam) Coast Salish territories. She develops cross-cultural land-based pedagogies for sustainable ecologies. Her publications include "Weaving Indigenous Women's Leadership," in *Women, Adult Education, and Leadership in Canada* (2016). She teaches courses on Indigenous research epistemologies and methodologies in the Faculty of Education at the University of British Columbia, where she also works with the Faculty of Land and Food Systems, Indigenous Research Partnerships and the Centre for Sustainable Food Systems. In collaboration with Denise Nadeau, she developed the staff and faculty Aboriginal cultural training curriculum for the University of Victoria's LE,NONET Research Project.